Ralph Waldo Emerson

COMPLETE WORKS. *Centenary Edition.* 12 vols. With Portraits, and copious notes by EDWARD WALDO EMERSON.
  1. Nature, Addresses, and Lectures. 2. Essays: First Series. 3. Essays: Second Series. 4. Representative Men. 5. English Traits. 6. Conduct of Life. 7. Society and Solitude. 8. Letters and Social Aims. 9. Poems. 10. Lectures and Biographical Sketches. 11. Miscellanies. 12. Natural History of Intellect, and other Papers. With a General Index to Emerson's Collected Works.
  Little Classic Edition. 12 vols., in arrangement and contents identical with *Centenary Edition*, except that vol. 12 is without index.

EMERSON'S JOURNALS. Edited by EDWARD W. EMERSON and WALDO EMERSON FORBES. Illustrated. 10 vols.

POEMS. *Household Edition.* With Portrait.

ESSAYS. First and Second Series. In Cambridge Classics

NATURE, LECTURES, AND ADDRESSES, together with **REPRESENTATIVE MEN.** In Cambridge Classics.

PARNASSUS. A collection of Poetry edited by Mr. Emerson. Introductory Essay. *Household Edition.*
THE SAME. *Holiday Edition.*

EMERSON BIRTHDAY BOOK. With Portrait and Illustrations.

EMERSON CALENDAR BOOK.

CORRESPONDENCE OF CARLYLE AND EMERSON, 1834-1872 Edited by CHARLES ELIOT NORTON. 2 vols.
THE SAME. *Library Edition.* 2 vols

CORRESPONDENCE OF JOHN STERLING AND EMERSON. Edited, with a sketch of Sterling's life, by EDWARD WALDO EMERSON.

LETTERS FROM RALPH WALDO EMERSON TO A FRIEND. 1838-1853. Edited by CHARLES ELIOT NORTON.

For various other editions of Emerson's works and Emerson Memoirs, see catalogue.

HOUGHTON MIFFLIN COMPANY
BOSTON AND NEW YORK

JOURNALS
OF
RALPH WALDO EMERSON
1820–1876

VOL. X

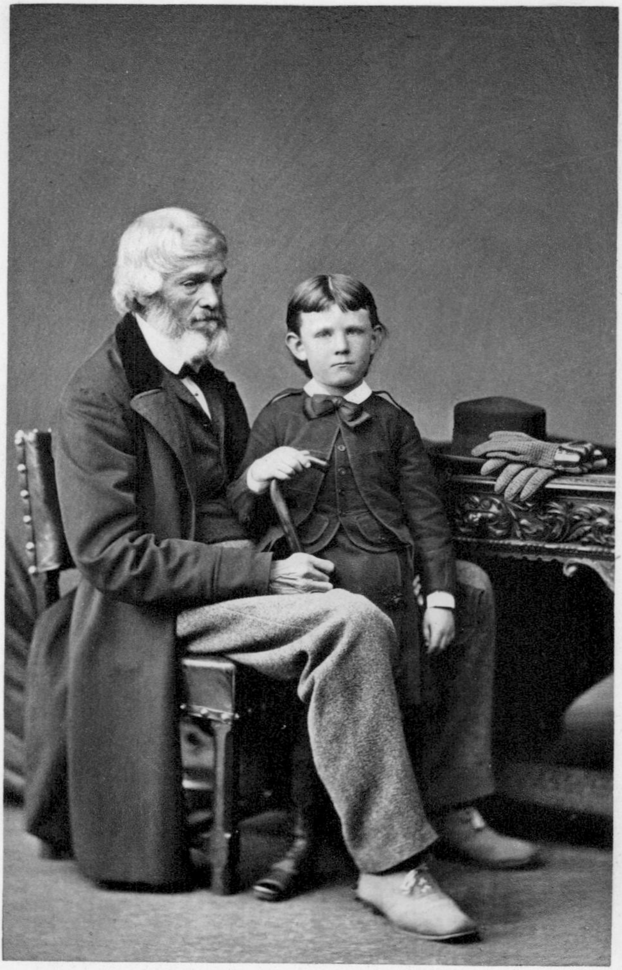

Thomas Carlyle and Ralph Emerson Forbes

JOURNALS
OF
RALPH WALDO EMERSON

WITH ANNOTATIONS

EDITED BY
EDWARD WALDO EMERSON
AND
WALDO EMERSON FORBES

1864–1876

BOSTON AND NEW YORK
HOUGHTON MIFFLIN COMPANY
The Riverside Press Cambridge

COPYRIGHT, 1914, BY EDWARD WALDO EMERSON

ALL RIGHTS RESERVED

Published March 1914

CONTENTS

JOURNAL LV

1864

(From Journals FOR, WAR, DL and KL)

Beecher on mobs. Dinner to General Burnside; Mr. Storey's question. Chapin as a lecturer. Magnificent Florence. Obstacles to philanthropy. Dr. Jackson on gold mines. Saturday Club dinner. Obituaries of Thackeray. Captain O. W. Holmes. France's improvisations. Berthollet's courage. Talk with Alcott; English and American genius. Our clergy's weakening hold on tradition; a new religion of Virtue and Beauty; great sentiment; The Spirit; Enthusiasm. Barriers. Agassiz's success in Chicago; Club meeting; plan for Shakspeare's birthday. Mr. Emerson's plea for Concord schools. *Bons-mots*. Thoreau's letter to a lady. Parents and children. Aerial navigation coming. The hostile English press; infatuated aristocracy. New blood disease. Unmindful nations; selfish leaders. Congenial men. Must read Renan. Conceit and humility; power of individuals. Scholar's method. Bandmann reads Hamlet. Thoreau on a book. Invitations for Shakspeare Tercentenary Festival. School committee notes. Bias. Letter to Matthew Arnold. Blake on Wordsworth.

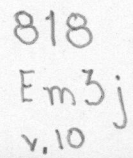

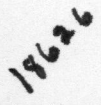

Shakspeare; his felicities; does not speak of tobacco. The Festival, the company; Agassiz's speech. Shakspeare's magic; the wonder at him grows; his courage and competence. Conservative and Reformer. Pascal. Shakspeare again; the sonnets; his language and direct power. A Shakspeare professorship. In the plays the story distracts from the poetry 3–31

Physiology of taste; country life. No age in intellect. Alcott on sons and daughters. Translation of Michel Angelo's sonnet. College mathematics, their overemphasis and abuse; crowd out other studies. Hawthorne's funeral, his friends; James Freeman Clarke's address; the tragic element; Emerson's disappointment in not having reached companionship. The child on the clergyman. The genius of a race. Health the helper. Music's omniscience. Opposition's value. Lesson of the spider. A hotel helps the writer; other helpful circumstances. Occidental respect for human life. The French on English art. Atmospheric influences. The Master of Eton on its influence. Renan on Paris. Advancing years. Helplessness in new conditions. Moral of latent disease. The joy of insight. Raffaele. American reserves; the new inventions. Solitary inspirations. Kings. Manners a castle. Consolations of old age. Every age winnows. Talk with Alcott; Americans have silently passed Debatable Lands. Writers' besetting puerilities. Germany excels in culture; we lack repose. The good Indian. Excellent conveniences of European cities. American independent Thought. Niebuhr on Oracles and on Christ's rank. Family events. Effect of Alcott. England's dis-

CONTENTS

creditable attitude and lost opportunity. The High School. Orchard rule. The "cheating fund" for travel. Affirmative. Visitors at Concord. Agassiz's excellence in counsel; his theory 32–60

September walk with Channing; Nature's speed. "Sacrifice," a verse. America fighting for humanity; Napoleon's prophecy. Plea to Carlyle. Visits. Beauty as a reward. Harness of city conventionality; unspoiled men. We lack enthusiasm. Nature gives wealth; blessings of obscure youth; Aunt Mary on old-time Christians. The war appoints the generals. Talent in reading. Thoughts' retrospective value. Faithful Wordsworth comes to his fame. Drawings in *Punch*. Holmes on lectures. Nature's prodigality; cost of experience, of love; we have more material than we can work up. Meeting with Fowler, a Tennessee Union-man. Historic expressions. Visit at Naushon; John Murray Forbes, his admirable qualities; his talk with Goldwin Smith on danger to England of her marine policy. The dire, τὸ δεινόν, in eloquence; Otis. Lafayette's return to the Assembly. The Age, and Hour. Nature in Bryant's poems. Talk with Henry James; revolutionary force. Skies. The tardy change of England's tone. Adam Smith's clothes and books. Club meeting. The war has made patriotism. Verse, *The Sea-gods*. Miss Hosmer, the teacher. Club again. Cows' merit. Praise of Bryant. Introduction to lecture "Education"; omen of the hour; the Union is triumphing; what America means. Napoleon III's *Life of Cæsar*. Lord Ravensworth on the soil. Victor Cousin on The Pope. Reading . . 61–88

CONTENTS

JOURNAL LVI
1865
(From Journals KL, DL, ML, XO and IT)

Chicago; the lecturer wins his bet. Miss Edith Emerson marries Colonel Forbes. Wilkinson's writing. Hooker's fine general order. Parisian literary men. The peace of victory; the Reconstruction problem. Church as an amusement. Thunderbolt. Samuel Hoar's strength. Reed on Locke. Playground as police. Illusion of words. Mystery of immortality. President Lincoln's equality to his task. Marcus Antoninus. Delmonico's. Lafayette's nobility. The Scribes' doom. Talk with Alcott on Religion; America's coming religion; atheism of scientific men; there must be faith as well as works. Elizabeth Hoar's fair mind. Tactics of argument. The Bible's claimed authority arouses resistance as the pagan scriptures do not. Affirm the Moral Sentiment with dazzling courage. Limited American reading; select books; events that were eras; curious books. Carlyle's demoniac fun. Ethics. Our young soldiers; war *moralizes* as well as demoralizes. America, what it means to the immigrant. The Praise of Intellect. A good cause supplies argument, illustrations, poetry. Drugs and temperance. Being. Jones Very's saying on Shakspeare. Children of the people. The pear blight. Forms *versus* powers. Writings on Immortality do not satisfy. Forceythe Willson. Wendell Phillips's commanding talent. Manners. Scotus Erigena. A resemblance to Lincoln; Nature's

CONTENTS

cunning repetition; the Winthrops. Lingering pro-slavery symptoms. Webster's wrath at young men who forsook him. Potential force. Fitness outranks fashion. Beware the minor key. Stirling's *Secret of Hegel*. Carlyle's intolerances. Collapse following victory. Williamstown; constellations from the observatory. Dr. Jackson's conversation at Thanksgiving. The story of Cass and Albert H. Tracy. College days; Unitarianism as a cure-all. Carlyle's astonishing style. Virtues of Reaction. Illusion of surfaces. Moral sentiment our protection. The old papyrus, Memory; the Past works. Reading 91–126

JOURNAL LVII
1866
(From Journals DL, LN, and ML)

Lecturing. The Task and the Muse. The paid mourner. Common Sense; Mansfield, Brummel. Love's imputation. All-powerful manners. Song of the brook. Home-critics. Education. Criticism from Europe. Caution to the University. Charles XII on Mathematics. Sentences from the Koran. Napoleon and his genius. Hesper. Course on "Philosophy of the People." Laws of the mind. Dr. Johnson's sayings. Intellect. The Celestial Mind. Aunt Mary on Immortality; Van Helmont. The Vikings' code. Uses of an Academy; "Chaldaic Oracles"; Zoroaster on death. Identity. Polarity. Memory is Man's lost Pleiad; Life's allurements to the Mind. War clarifies,

CONTENTS

opens new doors that never shut. Letter to a friend in Europe; advance of old age; Newcomb; Holmes. What Hegel says. Hafiz plays greatly; fears nothing. America's political duty ethical. Goethe. Beauty a miniature of the world; hence concerns all men. Deity and "God." The field and the seven men. Taliessin; Whitman. Poets of a single utterance. Aunt Mary's manuscripts, their attraction and elevation. Visit to the young people's camp on Monadnoc; the storm, the glories. Harvard gives degree of Doctor of Laws. Wither and Lovelace compared. Drinking and tobacco. Charles Lamb. Our debt to Milton. Humanity's nobility through the ages. Calvinism and Greek myths. We want heat. Man and the Muse. The new Atlantic cable. Old light better than new. Political fanaticism. Alcott in New York 129–158

Maya (Illusion) of Hindoos. William Forbes. Gifts, Flowers. Visit to Agassiz; Brazil. Biography. Hindoo theology important; teaches nobility. Self-respect in a family. Anquetil Duperron. Atlantic cable succeeds. Books as doors. Egypt. Hafiz plays with magnitudes; the manly positive degree. Caprice of Fame; degrees of Greatness. Masters. Dr. Charles T. Jackson tells of wild music at Lake Superior; Analyzed sound. Home allows privacy. The Two Facts. The Preacher. Men and Women. Woman's help to cause of Freedom. Necessity. Railroads make republics. Wealth meets the unexpected. To writers. In dreams we play both parts. Success. Kindness. Names. Brag. Useful Theresa. The Negro. Reading 159–177

CONTENTS

JOURNAL LVIII
1867
(From Journals ML, LN, and NY)

Western lecturing. Pleasure in Minnesota; Wisconsin railroads; Long sleigh-rides. Taylor's and Winckelmann's paganism. Eloquence; Landor. Christ's preaching and ours. The mind is true. Natural aristocracy. Intellectual power the presence of God. The guiding whisper. Men of talent, and those who delight in the Eternal Laws. The goading Spirit hides, but is Heaven. Embodied Thoughts. Swedenborg's vision not clear; Milton's vision. The writer's testimony on higher things. Religion is vision enacted; the Soul and the inward law. Good universal, the Law justifies itself. The questions of the Age. American Melioration; this country's office. The human race immortal. Lessing on astronomy. Coming era in Universities. Fathers and sons. Nantasket Beach. Culture partial. The real, daily miracle. Funeral of George L. Stearns. Treatment of Negroes and Jews. Desired tutors. The stately Hudson River. Justice Maule's rebuke. *May-Day* published. Collins's musical quality. Aunt Mary's reading of Tasso, Homer and Milton. Immortality. Dr. Holmes. The old Boston town-crier. Stout hearts of Pindar and Kepler. The lost passage in a book. Mrs. Barbauld. Emerson appointed Overseer at Harvard. Nature's symbols; eyes that can see Identity and Centrality. Death of Mrs. Ripley; her gifts and charm. Charles Newcomb's writing. Parsons's translation of the *Inferno*. Dante's abnormal mind. Quotation or Originality. Johnson on death; a representative Englishman. Elusive dream. Strong preachers and outgrown forms. Identity. The *Natural*. Light. Things incomprehensible yet practical. Zymosis. The grandchild. Peace even-handed. Matthew Arnold on Style. Carlyle's perverse attitude. Holmes on Dr. James Jackson. The deluge. Consul Grattan's wit. The tempting classics. The Quoter gives his past: Kean's admirable *Richard II*. Architecture of thought. Nature's charming repetitions; what is quotation? The joy of reading others' works. English guests. More Western lectures, and peril of the freezing Mississippi. Reading 181–224

JOURNAL LIX
1868
(From Journals LN and NY)

Sickness of William Emerson. Quarrel of boys. Praise of Harriet Martineau's *Eastern Life*. Free trade. Unequal shares of beauty. Charles Norton's lecture. The gods of Egypt. The banker's prophecy of fortunes in Railroads. Knowledge dies with its possessors. America's poets should be patriots. Herodotus on the Egyptians. Aunt Mary's attitude in Heaven. Colonel Theodore Lyman. Dr. Jackson on balloons. President Johnson. "The eye altering alters all." Present day obstructives. Horatio Greenough. Oneness

CONTENTS

of Religion. Richard Owen's request from Turner. Sunday School. The wished-for tower. Alexander and the Brahmin. Poetic results of Science; Unity. The World a school for Heaven. Revolutions wrought by time; great men. Epigrams. Goethe. Books. Aristophanes judged. Education. Tennyson's "Holy Grail"; a later opinion. Leisure. Calvinism, its three legs; Buddhism its opposite. The *Atlantic* authors. The Opposition. Inspirations of fit company. Gurney and others. John Weiss. Scott. Absurd honorary degrees. Fox on versifying. Disraeli. William Morris's *Earthly Paradise*. Beauty a moral effect. Duties done; a daughter. A friend may tell your fortune. Metaphysicians, Berkeley, Hegel; the next step? Enchantments; Shakspeare's poems. The temple builders. The seashore. Visit to Miss Clarke at Newport 226–250

The sea not seen from the wharves; the ocean's surprise. Mrs. Helen Hunt; George Eliot's poems; Wordsworth. Vermont, Middlebury. Mount Mansfield, George Bradford, George Bartlett. Banquet to Chinese Embassy. The University question, faults and shortcomings. Nature's bounty. Evarts and Williams. France's scientific achievement. Joy in woods; in books of reference. Boston course of lectures. Memorable single poems or sentences. George E. Tufts's line. Mediocre books; blessing of libraries. *Zymosis*, ferment of Science. Surprises from within. French tact in writing. John Hunter; his Museum; "arrested development." William R. Ware, his Berkeley St. Church and Harvard Memorial Hall.

xiv CONTENTS

Lowell's poems; tone in poetry. Wordsworth and Tennyson. Michel Angelo; Thomas Gray. English manners. Strong New England families. Culture. Farming. Intellect and physical laws. Reading 251–272

JOURNAL LX
1869
(From Journals NY and ML)

Plan for Readings in Boston; the Bardic poetry, the *Morte d'Arthur*; Byron, Scott, Tennyson. Homer's impartiality. Arab and Greek hospitality. Tone; French poetry, Victor Hugo. Religion, the point of view. Cheering men; the Forbeses, Judge Hoar, Agassiz. Immortality. Political managers. Shakspeare the man. Montaigne on Socrates. Richard Hunt. Readings to class; poetry and prose planned or actually read. The Mountain, verse. Pervading Deity. Imcompatibles. Memory. Talk to Alcott on the Current of Thought. Bunsen. God's dealing with Time. College Committee on Merit and Discipline at Harvard; marks, the Antioch method. Judge Hoar at Commencement dinner. Charles Sumner's character, learning, services; his detractors. Landor compares Austria with Florence alone. Hesiod's sayings. Periodicity on Nature and in Fable. Speech at Humboldt Centenary Celebration. Powers of Intellect enumerated. Command. Experimental poetry. Problem of dreams. General Wayne's foresight. Aunt

CONTENTS

Mary and society. Prune your writing. Plutarch's immortality. The Indian and Eliot. Blessing of warmth. Latent Harmony. Threat of Calvinism. Elect persons. Agassiz's illness. Reading . . 275–306

JOURNAL LXI

1870

(From Journals NY and ST)

Goodwin's *Plutarch's Morals. Society and Solitude.* Charles Ware's dream; Commemoration Day at Harvard; Lowell's Ode. Bettine Brentano and Aunt Mary. Saturday Club. Lowell misprizes Thoreau. The new book sells. Vicious protection in trade. Gentlemen rare. *Musagetes;* a Yankee Muse helps. Alvah Crocker; his Fitchburg Railroad and Hoosac Tunnel; Baldwin. Jealousy of Dream-spirits. Montesquieu. Use of Clubs to hermits. Arago. Carlyle's bequest of books to Harvard University. Varnhagen on impressions. The exclusive Englishman. Goethe's *Musagetes* again. University Lectures established at Harvard; Mr. Emerson asked to give course on Philosophy. Identity; Bias; Schelling and his pupils; Hegel on sensibility? Dog and dress. Fichte. Autograph letters. Plutarch on reacting courtesy; Montesquieu on Age. Philip Physick Randolph. Alexander's weeping rightly told. "Apophthegms of Great Commanders." Philosophies grow old. Socrates's accusers. *Nouvelle Biographie Générale.* Nantasket Beach; its riches and glories. Can I have books hereafter?

xvi   CONTENTS

Mrs. Howe's "Battle Hymn" and "The Flag."
Home. Aunt Mary's moral inspirations; the ancient ethics; the omnipotent *Yea*. Christianity and man react on each other. The September trip to Waterford and Mount Washington. France's fate. Saturday Club. Chivalry a good theme, Imagination unextinguishable. The range of a thought, religion promotes this, in the great writers. Memory. The Master's Degree made real at Harvard. Corner-stone of Memorial Hall laid; admirable services. Freedom given by the private Class. Importance of foreign literature. Couture's important rule applied to writing; Holmes and Hood as examples. Education of familiar intercourse; heredity in culture. Greatness. Greek. Objection to metaphysics. Americans fortunate in individual freedom. Plutarch's *Symposiacs*. History shows that lapses beget protest and reform. Voltaire's *Spinoza*. Classics over-esteemed; Science asserts itself. Plato on Time. The Rememberers. Public speaking. Oliver's *Puritan Commonwealth* underestimates force of conditions. Stories of Rhode Island; holy ancestors. Delight in men who can do things. The mystical double printing. Reading . . 309–344

JOURNAL LXII

1871

(From Journal ST)

Lectures. Organizing the Boston Museum of Fine Arts. Course on Philosophy at Harvard. Age, Taliessin.

CONTENTS xvii

The Spirit has no fear of Science; Identity. Carlyle and Mill. Pusey sends an inscribed book. Müller's gift. Coleridge on Greek women. Chateaubriand and Washington. John M. Forbes carries Mr. Emerson off to California for a rest; the party. Notes of the journey, the Big Tree, California boys. Good comes of evil in the population. Newton on gifts. Coincidences suggest guardian angel. Return home. The fountain inscription. Beauty of woman's hair. Nature's ground plan. "My Men." Historical Society; Scott Centennial; picturesque superstition. Correlation of forces, sciences, men. Splendors of this Age. Poetry must be fresh, avoid emphasis; the man and his visiting angel. The 50th year after graduation. Rhetoric. The Whig poetry of Charles I's time did not live. Thought may expel Memory. Ellery Channing's poems. Alcott's words on Memory. Bret Harte's visit. Ruskin's *Two Paths*. Names. Those facts that Nature teaches; their relation. Poetic necessity of Mind; beautiful revelations of science. Thoughts fugitive. Hero meets his enchanter. Bacon's saying on testimony. Tibullus, on Venus; Epicharmus on the Mind. Geoffroy Saint-Hilaire's heroism, his contest with Cuvier. Culture increasing; more writers and lovers of verse; *vers de Société*. Blessed cheerfulness. Poets have unlucky physique. The father fails to control child; the sympathetic man can. America at disadvantage in literary culture, but has many men of varied power and wit; fine women also. Burnt Chicago; the last Western lecturing journey. Reading 347–373

JOURNAL LXIII

1872

(From Journal ST)

Lectures at Baltimore and Washington. Speech to Freedmen at Howard University; praise of George Herbert; its result. James T. Fields arranges Saturday Afternoon Readings for Mr. Emerson; their success. Notes on Religion. Lecture for Concord on generosity in books and pictures. Memories of childish delights and wonders. Old Age. The good writer will influence, independent of date. Shakspeare a fixed star. The sixty-ninth birthday near childhood's home in Boston; memories. Beauty of girls in Boston streets. Sarah Clarke's visit. Address at Amherst College, guest of President Stearns. The great office of Poetry. The burning of the Concord home. The town family to the rescue; hospitality at the Old Manse. The munificence of the many friends; Dr. LeBaron Russell and Judge Hoar. Provisional arrangements. Mr. Emerson's illness and anxieties. Visit to Maine. Naushon and its restoring hospitalities; its beauty. Mr. Emerson sent to Europe by his friends. London; Colonel Lee and Charles Norton, William Henry Channing and Moncure D. Conway; their attentions. Good effect of rest. Carlyle; Dean Stanley. Canterbury. At Paris with Lowell and John Holmes. Rome; the good Von Hoffmans. Sailing for Egypt; Christmas at Alexandria. Reading . . . 377–401

JOURNAL LXIV

1873

(From Journal ST)

The dismal Delta. Cairo. Meeting friends. Courtesy of General Stone (Pasha). Sailing up the Nile in a dahabeah; the party. Humiliation of ignorance; the sphinxes' scorn. The stately people. Summer in midwinter. Thebes, Assuan, Philæ. The magnet's mystery. Pleasant English visitors. Return to Cairo. Crete. Rome; friends. Florence; John Bigelow, Herman Grimm and his wife. Latter March in Paris with Lowell and John Holmes. J. C. Morison. Meeting with Renan, Taine, Elie de Beaumont. Enjoyment of Paris, its privileges and freedom. Returning strength and spirits. April in London. Happy meetings with Carlyle. Gladstone, Mill, Huxley, Tyndall, Dean Stanley, Thomas Hughes, Helps and others. Visit to the Amberleys. Cyfarthra Castle. Oxford, guest of Max Müller; Jewett, Ruskin, Prince Leopold. Visit to Mr. Flower, Stratford on Avon. The voyage home. Birthday at sea; Mr. Norton's poem. Concord's joyful welcome. Wonder of the restored home. Mrs. Bell's *mot*. Max Müller's tribute. September, Address at opening of Munroe gift of Free Public Library to Concord. Stallo forestalls Darwin. Theologic mysteries. Overseer of College again. Hegel on life. *Boston Tea-Party* anniversary; reading of poem "Boston." Reading . . 405–425

JOURNAL LXV

1874

(From Journal ST)

Quiet life at home, reviewing the manuscripts. Charles Sumner's death; Judge Hoar's letter. Death of two old and valued friends: Abel Adams; Francis Cabot Lowell, obituary notice. The secret of Poetry. Candidacy for Lord Rectorship of Glasgow University; Disraeli wins. Collection of poetry "Parnassus" published; its history. Reading 429–438

JOURNAL LXVI

1875

(From Journal ST)

Mr. Emerson unequal to arranging the promised volume. Mr. Cabot willingly gives the needed aid. *Letters and Social Aims* published. Lecture in Philadelphia: the three old playfellows meet. Centennial celebration of Concord Fight. Emerson unveils French's Minute Man and speaks. Human life and Nature's teaching. Children utter unconscious oracles. Schleiermacher's impatience of university routine. Emerson appointed on committee on Philosophy at Harvard College. Carlyle's 80th birthday. Reading . 441–445

CONTENTS

JOURNAL LXVII
1876

(From Journal ST; also passages from Ledgers of uncertain date)

The Carlyle medal. Address at the University of Virginia in June. Reminiscences at Boston Latin School Celebration in November. William Allingham's poem 449–451

THE LEDGERS
(From Ledger PH)

Idealism, our need of ascent. The miracle of powers combined. Sensibility, joy of human relation. Abnormal minds, Blake, Swedenborg, Behmen; oracular men, Persian, Hindoo. Wonder. Divination by sympathy; Hegel and Kant. The grand masters of thought; instinct to write in verse. No age to Intellect. Inspiration, its periods of sleep; its majesty. Man's witness to the Law. Style. Transition our privilege and power. Your spirit should rank your talent, character must command; heroes win us. Nature leads us. Nature and Mind.

(From Ledger TO)

Hegel faltered, but his teaching did its work. Skepticism useful. Sieze on a man's sanity, ignore the rest. Respect the exempts, they justify themselves. The ascending effort. Hegel's dogma helped on Science. Melioration as well as transition. Genius unsettles everything. Writing must be like Nature's works.

Fame convenient. Mankind's verdict good; Jesus stands at the head of history. Thought wins against Fate; its harmony, its dawn; it is man's distinction. Language proves your thought not new. Divine genius; the sculptor's feeling imbues the marble. Truth vanishes with contradiction; Thoreau's word. The people prefer thoughts to truth. Subjectiveness is dangerously great; Bonaparte's genius dazzled him. Automatic action of thought. Religion is power. Fancy and Imagination; examples from Thoreau's journals; wind, golden-rod, the eagle, the bluebird's song. The scholar's creed.

(From Ledger EO)

Fate; inherited opinions. May and Must, shown in races; souls' varying ration of light; doctrine of Fate hard to state; unity inspires all, yet passes understanding. Hafiz on Fate; love is the safeguard.

(From Ledger PY)

Man's Eastern Horizon. The unseen treasure in uninteresting people, the gleams. Psychology made up of many small contributions. We see what we make.

Mr. Emerson's last years. A few lectures read near home. He reads again his own forgotten works . 452–476

INDEX 479

ILLUSTRATIONS

THOMAS CARLYLE AND RALPH EMERSON FORBES.   *Frontispiece*
Photogravure from a photograph in 1872.

COLONEL WILLIAM HATHAWAY FORBES 160
From a photograph in 1885.

MRS. SARAH ALDEN (BRADFORD) RIPLEY 208
From a painting in the possession of Mrs. James B. Thayer.

GEORGE PARTRIDGE BRADFORD 254
From a painting by Miss Sarah G. Putnam.

JOURNAL

BEECHER. CHAPIN

AMERICAN WRITERS

CONCORD PUBLIC SCHOOLS

ENGLAND'S ATTITUDE

SATURDAY CLUB

SHAKSPEARE'S BIRTHDAY
CELEBRATION

COLLEGE CURRICULUM
MATHEMATICS

HAWTHORNE'S DEATH AND
BURIAL

INSPIRATION. OLD AGE.

AGASSIZ. FORBES. BRYANT

JOURNAL LV

1864.

(From FOR, WAR, DL and KL)

[All page references to passages from the Journals used by Mr. Emerson in his published works are to the Centenary Edition, 1903–05.]

To the Front!

[IT does not appear that the Western lecturing trip was so far or so long this year as often. Mr. Emerson seems to have given lectures in Erie and Pittsburgh, Pennsylvania, and Cleveland, Ohio, and probably other places, but reached home in the third week in January.]

Τέχνη τύχην ἔστερξε καὶ τύχη τέχνην [1]
Agatho.

(From FOR)

January 13, 1864.

Beecher, at breakfast, illustrated the difference between the impulsive mob in New York Cooper Institute and the organized mob in Liverpool

[1] Art (or skill) and luck are on good terms with one another.

meeting. "In one you go by a corner where the wind sucks in, and blows your hat off, but, when you get by it, you go along comfortably to the next corner. In the other, you are on the prairie, with no escape from the irresistible northwester."

(From WAR)

February 8.

At the dinner given the other night, February 4, at the Union Club to General Burnside, after much talk of the accounts of our several battles given by the reporters of the press, in which accounts the General plainly had no confidence, and so of the ignorance on the part of all subaltern officers, who could not know any more than they saw;—in despair Mr. Charles Storey looked up, and said, "Well, General, do you then think we have true history, in Cæsar's *Commentaries?*" There was a sudden laugh which went round the whole table, gradually increasing in volume and cheer.

February 19.

Last night heard Chapin lecture, for the first time. He has a powerful, popular voice which agreeably stimulates the house, and, rarely, he drops the orotund, which is like an infantry company firing one at a time, and uses a quieter tone which penetrates all ears, and deepens the silence. But I thought it is not a question whether we shall be a nation, or only a multitude of people; no, but whether we shall be the new nation, the leading guides and lawgivers of the world, as having clearly chosen and firmly held the simplest and best rule of political society.

What a town was Florence with Dante, Ghiberti, Giotto, Brunelleschi, Da Vinci, Michael Angelo, Raffaelli, Cellini, Guicciardini, Machiavelli, Savonarola, Alfieri, Galileo!

The obstacle the philanthropic movements meet is in the invincible depravity of the virtuous classes. The excellent women who have made an asylum for young offenders, boys of 10 to [18?] years, and who wish, after putting them through their school, to put them out to board in good farmers' or mechanics' families, find the boys do well enough, but the farmer and the farmer's wife, and the mechanic's wife, behave brutally. What then? One thinks of Luttrell's speech about the soldiers fraternizing with the mob, "Egad, it's awkward when the extinguisher catches fire." And I remember that Charles Barnard had not made up his mind whether

Dr. Tuckerman, his chief, relieved or made more pauperism.

Dr. Charles T. Jackson will have nothing to do with the survey of gold mines, because he has no confidence that they can be profitably worked by any stock company: the workmen in such mines will carry off all the gold. In California and Oregon, every miner for himself: and on such terms only can they be wrought.

February 28.

Yesterday at the Club with Cabot, Ward, Holmes, Lowell, Judge Hoar, Appleton, Howe, Woodman, Forbes, Whipple, with General Barlow,[1] and Mr. Howe, of Nova Scotia, for guests; but cramped for time by late dinner and early hour of the return train, — a cramp which spoils a club. For you shall not, if you wish good fortune, even take pains to secure your right and left hand men. The least design instantly makes an obligation to make their time agreeable, which I can never assume. Holmes was gay

[1] Francis C. Barlow, whose brilliant military talent and utter courage raised him from a private volunteer soldier to a Major-General's command, lived in Concord with his mother in his boyhood and attended the Academy.

with his "preadamite mentioned in the Scriptures,— Chap. First," and Appleton with "that invariable love of hypocrisy which delights the Saxon race," etc.

The *Spectator* says of the three obituary notices of Thackeray by Dickens, Trollope, and Kingsley, that only Dickens's is equal to the subject; the others strain to write up, and fail.[1]

Captain O. W. Holmes[2] tells me that the Army of the Potomac is acquiring a professional feeling, and that they have neither panics nor excitements, but more self-reliance.

France, in 1789, improvised war, and in 1803, improvised civilization. (See in Sainte-Beuve, *Nouveaux Causeries*, article "Biot.")

Berthollet's report on the poisoned brandy

---

[1] What follows is printed in "Greatness" (*Letters and Social Aims*, pp. 317, 318).

[2] Captain Holmes, of the Twentieth Regiment, Massachusetts Volunteers, bore a gallant part in the fighting of the Army of the Potomac and had been severely wounded at the battle of *Antietam*. (See "My Hunt after 'the Captain'" in the *Atlantic Monthly*, Dec. 1862, by his father, the Doctor.)

to the Committee of Public Safety. He put the brandy through a filter and then drank it. "How dared you drink it?" said Robespierre. "I did a bolder thing," replied Berthollet, "when I put my name to that Report,"—as having resisted the panic of suspicion which made the tyranny of the Committee of Public Safety.

March 13.

Last night talked with Alcott, who returns much lately to the comparison between English and American genius. I gratified him by saying that our intellectual performance, taken with our sentiment, is perhaps better worth than their performance, taken with their limitation or downward tendency. For certainly we cannot count or weigh living writers with theirs. But how to meet the demand for a religion? A few clergymen here, like Hedge and Clarke, retain the traditions, but they never mention them to me, and, if they travelled in France, England, or Italy, would leave them locked up in the same closet with their sermons at home, and, if they did not return, would never think to send for them. Beecher, Manning, Bushnell hold a little firmer and more easily to theirs, as Calvinism has a more tenacious vitality;—but that is doomed also, and will only die last; for Calvinism rushes to be Unitarianism as Unitarianism rushes to be Naturalism.[1]

How, then, is the new generation to be edified? How should it not? The life of these once omnipotent traditions was really not in the legend, but in the moral sentiment and the metaphysical fact which the legends enclosed; — and these survive. A new Socrates, or Zeno, or Swedenborg, or Pascal, or a new crop of geniuses, like those of the Elizabethan age, may be born in this age, and, with happy heat and a bias for theism, bring asceticism and duty and magnanimity into vogue again.

In the most vulgar times, in the bronze as in the oaken age, a certain number of men of organic virtue are born — men and women of native integrity, and indifferently in high and low families. But there will always be a class of imaginative men, whom poetry, whom the love of Beauty leads to the adoration of the moral sentiment.[2] . . . At any time, it only needs the contemporaneous appearance of a few superior and

[1] The last two sentences, without the names, are printed in "Character" (*Lectures and Biographical Sketches*, p. 116).

[2] The rest of the paragraph is found in "Character" (*Lectures and Biographical Sketches*, pp. 117, 118).

attractive men to give a new and noble turn to the public mind.

I said to Alcott that we old fellows occupy ourselves with the history or literature of the Sentiment, and not, as once, with the essence itself. I remember in my life happy weeks when I said to myself, "I will no longer respect Success, or the finishing and exhibition of my work; but every stroke on the work, every step taken in the dark toward it, every defeat, even, shall be sacred and luminous also. Am I not always in the Great Presence? I will not postpone my existence, but be always great and serene with that inspiration."

Alcott thought that successful men were liable to such fall, but that unsuccessful men had nothing else but the sentiment to return to. And that is just, and the sentiment may, by such habitude, come to steep and meliorate the man, — come to be character instead of a rhetoric.

The resources, I say, remain, or renew, day by day. The old Eternal Ghost, the Jove, refuses to be known, but refuses to depart: then, the sporadic probity I spoke of, capriciously scattered, is yet always present to keep society sweet. Then Enthusiasm — from pure Vision down to its most clouded form of Fanaticism —

is the miraculous leaping lightning, not to be measured by the horse-power of the Understanding.[1] And the unanimous approbation of Society and of Governments is secured, as a rule, to godliness, because of its usefulness.

Barriers of man impassable. They who should be friends cannot pass into each other. Friends are fictions founded on some single momentary experience. . . .

But what we want is consecutiveness.[2] . . .

March 26.

At the Club, where was Agassiz just returned from his lecturing tour, having created a Natural History Society in Chicago, where four thousand five hundred dollars were subscribed as its foundation by nineteen persons.[3] And to which he recommended the appointment of Mr. Kinnicott as the superintendent.

---

[1] This sentence occurs in "Progress of Culture" (*Letters and Social Aims*, p. 228).

[2] The rest of the paragraph is found in "Inspiration" (*Letter and Social Aims*, pp. 272, 273).

[3] *Footnote by R. W. E.* When I visited the "Chicago Natural History Museum" in 1865, the fund had become $50,000.

Dr. Holmes had received a demand from Geneva, New York, for fifty-one dollars as cost of preparing for his failed lecture. Governor Andrew was the only guest.[1] Hedge, Hoar, both the Doctors Howe, Holmes, Lowell, Norton, Woodman, Whipple, were present. It was agreed that the April election should be put off till May, and that the next meeting should be on April 23, intead of 30th, and that we should, on that day, have an open club, allowing gentlemen whom we should designate to join us in honour of Shakspeare's birthday. The committee of the Club might invite certain gentlemen also, as the guests of the Club, Emerson, Lowell, and Holmes being the committee.

(From DL)

[Mr. Emerson was at this time on the School Committee, and the " March Meeting " of the voters was at hand, when it might fall to him to urge the town to liberality in the annual appropriation for the schools.]

School. First, see that the expense be for teaching, or that school be kept the greatest

[1] He was chosen a member shortly after, as were also Martin Brimmer, James T. Fields and Samuel W. Rowse.

number of days and for the greatest number of scholars. Then that the best teachers and the best apparatus, namely, building, furniture, books, etc., be provided. *School*, because it is the *cultus* of our time and place, fit for the Republic, fit for the times, which no longer can be reached and commanded by the Church. What an education in the public spirit of Massachusetts has been the war-songs, speeches, and readings of the schools! Every district school has been an anti-slavery convention for two or three years last past. This town has no seaport, no cotton, no shoe-trade, no water-power, no gold, lead, coal, or rock oil, nor marble; nothing but wood and grass, not even ice and granite, our New England staples; for the granite is better in Fitchburg, and our ice, Mr. Tudor said, had bubbles in it. We are reduced, then, to manufacture school-teachers, which we do, for the Southern and Western market. I advise the town to stick to that staple, and make it the best in the world. It is your lot in the urn. And it is one of the commanding lots. Get the best apparatus, the best overseer; and turn out the best possible article. Mr. Agassiz says, "I mean to make the Harvard Museum such that no European naturalist can afford to stay away from it." Let the Town of Concord say as much for its school. We will make our schools such that no family which has a new home to choose can fail to be attracted hither, as to the one town in which the best education can be secured. This is one of those long prospective economies which are sure and remunerative.

Bons-mots. I am always struck with the speed with which every new interest, party, or way of thinking gets its *bon-mot* and name and so adds a new word to language. Thus Higginson, and Livermore, Hosmer, and the fighting chaplains give necessity and vogue to "muscular Christianity." The language of the day readily suggested to some theological wit to call hell "a military necessity."

Thoreau's Letter.[1] "Do you read any noble verses? For my part, they have been the only things I remembered, or that which occasioned

[1] The letter was written to Mrs. Lucy Cotton (Jackson) Brown, Mrs. Emerson's elder sister, an invalid lady whose experiences had not been fortunate, and whom Thoreau always tried to cheer up, besides being helpful to her in many practical ways.

them, when all things else were blurred and defaced. All things have put on mourning but they; for the elegy itself is some victorious melody in you escaping from the wreck. It is relief to read some true books, wherein all are equally dead, equally alive. I think the best parts of Shakspeare would only be enhanced by the most thrilling and affecting events. I have found it so. And so much the more as they are not intended for consolation."

Old Age. I told Richard Fuller that he would soon come to a more perfect obedience to his children than he had ever been able to obtain from them.

M. Babinet informs us that the problem of aerial navigation is on the point of being solved. I am looking, therefore, for an arrival of the remainder of the prisoners of war from the Libby and Atlanta prisons, by the balloon, descending at some point in Pennsylvania by a night voyage from the South.

The English journals are flippant and spiteful in their notices of American politics and society, but mean abuse cannot be answered.

If the writers were responsible, and could be held to the interrogatory, it would be easy to refresh their short memories with the history of English politics and society. The private memoirs of any age of England are full of scandal. Read Lord Hervey to know how just king, ministers, lords, bishops, and commons were in George I's time. Read Wraxall for George III's. Were the interiors of the court and the behaviour of the great lords in any age great and disinterested? Ask Pepys, ask Swift, Barnet, Bacon. The illusion under which the aristocracy live amounts to insanity. Lord Bristol plainly believes that it is very good of him to exist and the Government owes him unceasing thanks. He does nothing for them. Well, that is the humour of them all in Lord Hervey's pictures. That immensity of condescension in a fat old lubber does not appear at Washington except in men very long distinguished.

It was curious, that, in the first volume of Hervey, the mere mention of Lord Bristol's love for Ickworth, and Walpole's building of his grand seat at Houghton, and Lord Townsend's Raynham, more tickled my fancy, the vision of parks and gardens, than all the history.

April.

Diplomatic. Lord Hervey affirms that, "However incredible, it is literally true, that, when Queen Caroline (of George II) was dying, she advised the king to marry again; whereupon the tears and sobs of the King were renewed, and he exclaimed, '*Non, j'aurai des maitresses*'; to which the Queen made no other reply than, '*Ah! mon Dieu! Cela n'empêche pas.*'"

Old Age. The *Tribune* reports that a New Zealand physician, lecturing on the ignorance in people of their own complaints, was asked by a lady, "What was the subject of his next lecture?" "The circulation of the blood," he replied. She said she should certainly attend, for she had been troubled with that complaint for a long time.

Nations have no memories. They are all such unlicked cubs as we see; great mobs of young men, full of conceit and all manner of emptiness. Lord Hervey, Pepys, Clarendon, Lord Chesterfield, Commines, Wraxall, show up the aristocracy; that it is a gang of rich thieves, instead of a gang of poor thieves.

Garrison. Round him legislatures revolve. "Father of his country more than Washington," said Alcott.

What unexpected revivals we have seen! Maryland and Kentucky are converted. Then Concord may be.

If to the clubhouse people came; if, better, to some town of cheap living we could call twenty deep men to spend a month and take our chance of meeting each in turn alone, that were worth while. When a man meets his accurate mate, then life is delicious.

Alcott said of preachers, the "people want some one who has been where they are now."

I suppose I must read Renan, *Vie de Jésus*, which I fancied was Frenchy. It is a pregnant text, and a key to the moral and intellectual pauses and inactivity of men, "The creature is subject to vanity." There is none almost who has not this misleading egotism. The efficient men are efficient by means of this Flanders horse. But it destroys them for grandeur of aim, and for highest conversation. They all gravitate to cities. God, the inward life, is not enough for them; they must have the million mirrors of other minds, must measure wit with others for mastery, and must have the crowns and rewards of wit that cities give. Yet up and down in every nation, are scattered individual souls with the grace of humility. George Fox, Behmen, Scougal, the Mahometan Saint Rabia, and the Hindoos, have the art to cheapen the world thereby. So Ossian's "Cathmore dwelt in the wood to avoid the voice of praise." Jesus was grand where he stood, and let Rome and London dance after Nazareth. But the thinkers or *littérateurs* of humility are not humble. Thus Alcott, Thoreau, and I know the use and superiority of it, but I cannot praise our practice.

Every saint as every man comes one day to be superfluous.

Who can doubt the potences of an individual mind, who sees the shock given to torpid races, torpid for ages, by Mahomet, a vibration propagated over Asia and Africa, and not yet exhausted? What then of Menu? What of Buddh?

The single word *Madame* in French poetry, makes it instantly prose.

Scholar. Montaigne had rather take Europe into his confidence than to tell so much to a French lord; as one may move awkwardly in a parlour, who walks well enough in a crowd. I heard Bandmann read Hamlet's soliloquy, the other day, at Bartol's. In conversation he was polite and expansive enough, but plainly enjoyed the new expansion that the reading gave him. He stood up, and by musing distanced himself, then silences all the company, and gets out of doors, as it were, by a cheerful cry of a verse or two, and acquires a right to be the hero, and abounds in his own sense, and puts it despotically upon us, in look, manner, and elocution. He brought out the broad meaning of the soliloquy truly enough, but, as all actors will, with an *overmuch*, with emphasis and mouthing. They cannot let well alone, but must have the merit of all the refinements and second senses they have found or devised, and so drive it too finely. It is essential to reach this freedom, or gay self-possession, but temperance is essential, too.

Henry Thoreau wrote in 1840, "A good book will not be dropped by its author, but thrown up. It will be so long a promise that he will not overtake it soon. He will have slipped the leash of a fleet hound."

[It would appear that the celebration of the three hundredth anniversary of Shakspeare's birth had its origin in the Saturday Club, and that Mr. Emerson had been appointed one of a committee of invitations and arrangements. Evidently changes were made in the plan, for these lists and a later one do not quite agree.]

Address Dr. Frothingham, G. C. Verplanck, J. G. Whittier, Dr. Asa Gray, R. H. Dana. April 6, wrote to Everett, Bryant, Bancroft, Quincy, Jr., Ward; April 7, wrote to Sanborn, John M. Forbes, Ticknor, Governor Andrew, Richard Grant White, Cabot, Lowell, Appleton, Holmes, Gould, Frothingham, Whittier.

(Invitation to our centennial celebration of Shakspeare's birthday :)

Club — Agassiz, Appleton, Cabot, Dana, Dwight, Emerson, Forbes, Hawthorne, Hedge, Hoar, Howe, Holmes, Longfellow, Lowell, (Motley), Norton, Peirce, ? Sumner, ? Ward, Whipple, Woodman.

Outsiders — Andrew, Bryant, Bancroft, Verplanck, Curtis, Frothingham, Dana, Whittier,

Everett, Child, Gray, White, Clarke, Hunt, Fields, Phillips, Weiss, Hill, Rowse, Conway, Bigelow, Hillard, Brimmer, Booth.

April 8.

School Committee. Examined Miss E. Skinner, Miss Laura Dutton, Miss Tidd, Miss E. Brown, Miss Abby Brown.

Elected Miss Eliza Hosmer to the Preparatory School; Miss Holden to the Intermediate; Miss E. Brown to the North Quarter School, District No. 7; Miss Skinner to the North Primary School; Miss Jeannie Farmer, East Quarter School, District No. 2; Miss Mary Wood, Bateman's Pond School, District No. 6.

My charge is chairman of the High School and of the East Primary,[1] and I am to provide wood for my school, two and one half cords oak, one half cord pine. Next school committee meeting is first Saturday of May.

The schools to begin again after the summer vacation on August 1.

Bias. How grateful to discover in man or woman a new emphasis, which they put on somewhat, to which you did not know they

[1] Opposite Mr. Emerson's house.

attached value; quite out of themselves; and which they never learned of you or of any other! How respectable they become!

I wrote to Arnold, and should have said: I have heard that the engineers in the locomotives grow nervously vigilant with every year on the road, until the employment is intolerable to them; and, I think, writing is more and more a terror to old scribes.

Of Wordsworth, Blake writes: "This is all in the highest degree imaginative, and equal to any poet, but not superior. I cannot think that real poets have any competition. None are greatest in the kingdom of heaven. It is so in poetry."

Shakspeare the only modern writer who has the honor of a Concordance; the only painter who flatters Nature. Is pulverized into proverbs.

All criticism is only a making of rules out of his beauties.

"Somnambulic security which makes the poet a poet." — MOMMSEN.

[There are] great arts now, but no equal poetry celebrates them.

The surprise in his choice of words so delights us: "foreign levy" —

The trick of making verbs of nouns: —

"Skarf up the tender eye of pitiful day."

Macbeth.

"He lurched all swords o' the garland."

Coriolanus.

"Shunless destiny."

Coriolanus.

"struck
Corioli like a planet."

Coriolanus.

"Were I crowned the most imperial monarch,
Thereof most worthy; were I the fairest youth
That ever made eye swerve; had force and knowledge
More than was ever man's; I would not prize them
Without her love; for her employ them all,
Commend them, and condemn them, to her service,
Or to their own perdition."

Winter's Tale, IV, iii.

I find no mention of tobacco in Shakspeare, — neither pipes nor snuff, — which one would have said the dates permitted. 'T is a remarkable case, like Goethe's chronologic relation to steam locomotives.

April 24.

Yesterday the Saturday Club met to keep the birthnight of Shakspeare, at the end of the third century. We met at the Revere House, at 4 o'clock P.M. Members of the Club present were seventeen: Agassiz, Appleton, Cabot, Dwight, Emerson, Forbes, Hedge, Hoar, Holmes, S. G. Howe, Estes Howe, Longfellow, Lowell, Norton, Peirce, Whipple, Woodman.

Guests: Governor Andrew, Rev. Dr. Frothingham, R. H. Dana, Jr., Esq., Dr. J. G. Palfrey, Richard Grant White, Esq., Robert C. Winthrop, George S. Hillard, George William Curtis, James Freeman Clarke, Francis J. Child, Dr. Asa Gray, James T. Fields, John Weiss, Martin Brimmer, George T. Davis.

We regretted much the absence of Mr. Bryant, and Whittier, Edward Everett, and William Hunt, who had at first accepted our invitations, but were prevented at last; — and of Hawthorne, Dana, Sumner, Motley, and Ward, of the Club, necessarily absent; also of Charles Sprague, and Wendell Phillips, and T. W. Parsons, and George Ticknor, who had declined our invitations. William Hunt graced our hall by sending us his full-length picture of Hamlet, a noble sketch. It was a quiet and happy evening filled with many good speeches, from Agassiz who presided (with Longfellow as *Croupier*, but silent), Dr. Frothingham, Winthrop, Palfrey, White, Curtis, Hedge, Lowell, Hillard, Clarke, Governor Andrew, Hoar, Weiss, and a fine poem by Holmes, read so admirably well that I could not tell whether in itself it were one of his best or not. The company broke up at 11.30.

One of Agassiz's introductory speeches was, "Many years ago, when I was a young man, I was introduced to a very estimable lady in Paris, who in the conversation said to me that she wondered how a man of sense could spend his days in dissecting a fish. I replied, 'Madam, if I could live by a brook which had plenty of gudgeons, I should ask nothing better than to spend all my life there.' But since I have been in this country, I have become acquainted with a Club, in which I meet men of various talents; one man of profound scholarship in the languages; one of elegant literature, or a high mystic poet; or one man of large experience in the conduct of affairs; one who teaches the blind to see, and, I confess, that I have enlarged my views of life; and I think that besides a brook full of gudgeons, I should wish to meet once a month such a society of friends."

And Shakspeare.[1] How to say it, I know not, but I know that the point of praise of Shakspeare is, the pure poetic power: he is the chosen closet companion, who can, at any moment, by incessant surprises, work the miracle of mythologising every fact of the common life; as snow, or moonlight, or the level rays of sunrise — lend a momentary glory to every pump and woodpile.

[1] In the following pages are many paragraphs on Shakspeare, showing that Mr. Emerson was expected to speak. The address, much condensed, is printed in *Miscellanies*. Of the celebration Mr. Cabot, who was present, writes in his *Memoir of Emerson* (vol. II, p. 261): "I remember his getting up, . . . looking about him tranquilly for a minute or two, and then sitting down; serene and unabashed, but unable to say a word [i. e. *impromptu*] on a subject so familiar to his thoughts from his boyhood." Yet on the manuscript of his address Mr. Emerson noted that it was read at the Club's celebration on that occasion, and at the Revere House. The handwriting of this note looks like that when he was much older, and it may very likely have been written in his later years; so it is possible that Mr. Cabot was right. Mr. Emerson may have chanced to leave his notes at home, and without them would unwillingly have ventured to speak.

When I read Shakspeare, as lately, I think the criticism and study of him to be in their infancy. The wonder grows of his long obscurity; how could you hide the only man that ever wrote from all men who delight in reading? Then, the courage with which, in each play, he accosts the main issue, the highest problem, never dodging the difficult or impossible, but addressing himself instantly to that, — so conscious of his secret competence; and, at once, like an aeronaut fills his balloon with a whole atmosphere of hydrogen that will carry him over Andes, if Andes be in his path.

The conservative sends for the doctor, when his child falls sick, though yesterday he affirmed, in the conversation, that the doctors did not know anything. In to-day's exigency he reinforces his faith. So, in politics, he votes new subsidies to the King, and when the reform agitation rages, he votes larger supplies to the Government, — going it blind, so boys say. The Reformer believes that there is no evil coming from Change which a deeper thought cannot correct.

We said that ours was the recuperative age;

Pascal is one of its recoveries; not only the Essay on Love, but the pure text of the *Pensées*.

Shakspeare puts us all out. No theory will account for him. He neglected his works. Perchance he did not know their value? Aye, but he did; witness the Sonnets. He went into company as a listener, hiding himself, Ὃδ' ᾔει νυκτὶ ἐοικώς.¹ Was only remembered by all as a delightful companion. Alcott thinks "he was rhetorician, but did not propound new thoughts." Aye, he was rhetorician, as was never one before, but also had more thoughts than ever any had.

Say first, the greatest master of language, who could say the thing finer, nearer to the purity of thought itself than any other; and with the security of children playing, who talk without knowing it. (And to this point, what can Carlyle mean by saying what he does of Voltaire's superiority to all men in speech? *Life of Frederic*, iv, p. 382.) I admire his wealth. I watch him, when he begins a play, to see what simple and directest means he uses; never consulting his ease, never, in the way of common

1 He moved like Night.

artists, putting us off with ceremonies or declamations, but at once addressing himself to the noblest solution of the problem, having the gods and the course of human life in view. The wonder of his obscurity in his lifetime is to be explained by the egotism of literary men. To me the obscurity of Alcott is a like wonder.

Shakspeare should be the study of the University. In Florence, Boccaccio was appointed to lecture on Dante. But in English Oxford, or in Harvard College, I have never heard of a Shakspeare Professorship. Yet the students should be educated, not only in the intelligence of, but in the sympathy with, the thought of great poets.

The Sonnets intimate the old Aristotelian Culture, and a poetic Culture that we do not easily understand whence it came, — smacks of the Middle Ages and parliaments of love and poesy (and I should say, that a string of poems prefixed to Ben Jonson's or Beaumont and Fletcher's plays, by their friends, are more seriously thought than the pieces which would now in England or America be contributed to any call of literary friendship). And yet, if Whittier, Holmes, Lowell, Channing, Thoreau, Bryant, Sanborn, Wasson, Julia Howe, had each made their thoughtful contribution, there might be good reading.

I must say that in reading the plays, I am a little shy where I begin; for the interest of the story is sadly in the way of poetry. It is safer, therefore, to read the play backwards. To know the beauty of Shakspeare's level tone, one should read a few passages of what passes for good tragedy in other writers, and then try the opening of *Merchant of Venice*, Antonio's first speech.

I am inquisitive of all possible knowledge concerning Shakspeare, and of all opinions. Yet how few valuable criticisms, how few opinions I treasure! How few besides my own! And each thoughtful reader, doubtless, has the like experience.

Sainte-Beuve speaks wisely of the morals of Homer, in *Portraits Contemporains*, Volume iii, p. 434.

Physiology of Taste were a good subject for a lecture.[1] My epicure should sow marjoram in

[1] Mr. Emerson had been reading Brillat-Savarin's *Physiologie du Gout*.

his beds, if it were only to see with eyes the buds; and his windows should look into great gardens.

My physiology, too, would in every point put the real against the showy; as, to live in the country, and not in town; to wear shoddy and old shoes; to have not a fine horse, but an old Dobbin with only life enough to drag a Jersey wagon to Conantum, or Estabrook, and there stand contented for half a day at a tree, whilst I forget him in the woods and pastures (as, in England the point is not to make strong beer, but beer weak enough to permit a great deal to be drunk in hot weather; as Mr. Flower explained to me at Stratford).

The intellect is alike old in the father and in the child. We old fellows affect a great deal of reticence with the young people, but their wit cannot wait for us. Mrs. G—— explained to me that her children (one was fourteen years old) did not know what beef was — she had never allowed them to know that sheep and oxen were killed for our food. But my children knew that her children knew as much as they. Plutarch would use great precautions in young people's reading of the poets; and Plato also.

But when young and old see *Faust* on the stage, or *Midsummer Night's Dream*, or read them in the closet, they come silently to the same conclusions.

No age to intellect.

The cannon will not suffer any other sound to be heard for miles and for years around it. Our chronology has lost all old distinctions in one date, — *Before the War*, and since.

It is hard to remember in glancing over our sumptuous library edition and excellent pocket editions of Chaucer, that for one hundred years these works existed only in manuscripts, accumulating errors and false readings in every individual copy of every new transcriber. 'T is alarming to reckon the risks, and judge of the damage done.

A journalist in London or in New York acquires a facility and *élan* which throws the slow elaborators for the *Edinburgh* and the *North American* into the shade. Thus this lively article "Schopenhauer," in the New York *Commercial Advertiser* of May 31, eclipses Hedge's learned paper in the *Examiner*. Schopenhauer said of chaste persons, "they are thorns which produce roses." He said, "An impersonal God is a word void of sense, invented by professors of philosophy to satisfy fools and hack-drivers. . . . My great discovery is to show how, at the bottom of all things, there is only one identical force, always equal, and ever the same, which slumbers in plants, awakens in animals, but finds its consciousness only in man — the Will." "That is (continues the journalist), the world which we all believe we see is only a phenomenal world; above it, but at a tremendous distance, we find the real world, and this real world is the Will. Between these two, he places a kind of plastic mediator, which he calls *ideas*."

But, it seems, Schopenhauer, in his youth, learned Sanscrit, and learned his secret of the Buddhists. "De tribus impostoribus" means Fichte, Schelling, and Hegel.

It is, I own, difficult not to be intemperate in speaking of Shakspeare; and most difficult, I should say, to the best readers. Few, I think none, arrive at any intelligence of his methods. His intellect does not emit jets of light at intervals, but is incessant, always equal to the occasion, and addressing with equal readiness a comic, an ingenious, or a sublime problem. I find him an exceptional genius. If the world were on trial, it is the perfect success of this one man that might justify such expenditure of geology, chemistry, fauna, and flora, as the world was. And, I suppose, if Intellect perceives and converses "in climes beyond the solar road," they probably call this planet, not Earth, but Shakspeare.

Alcott said, in speaking of children, "I think a son translates the privacy of the family to the public; daughters cannot do it."

Michael Angelo's Third Sonnet

The power of a beautiful face lifts me to Heaven,
Since else in earth is none that delights me,
And I mount living among the elect souls, —
A grace which seldom falls to a mortal.

So well with its Maker the work consents,
That I rise to him through divine conceptions,
And here I shape all thoughts and words,
Burning, loving, through this gentle form:

Whence, if ever from two beautiful eyes
I know not how to turn my look, I know in them
The light which shows me the way which guides me
    to God.

And if, kindled at their light, I burn,
In my noble flame sweetly shines
The eternal joy which smiles in Heaven.

College mathematics.[1] For a fraction of each class, say twenty (though I think that is too many), in a class of more than a hundred, the whole class is oppressed by a course of mathematics, which is a perpetual fatigue, costing frequently, I am told, five or six hours for the learning the daily lesson, and that imperfectly, and thus bereaving the student of his necessary outdoor exercise. Add to this that, at short intervals, occur the mathematical examinations, which are serious, really testing the knowledge which the student has acquired in the foregoing weeks. The Professor is impartial, and resolved to know the proficiency of each pupil. The few good mathematicians easily do their work and leave the room, which remains occupied for five or six hours by the rest, who peform in all that time only a part of the work and retire exhausted and unhappy. The young men are not

[1] It does not appear for what purpose Mr. Emerson wrote out his views on this subject, for he had no official connection with Harvard University until 1867, when he was chosen an Overseer.

thus worked with impunity. They lose flesh, vigour, and spirit. The college, which should be to them a place of delightful labour, where their faculties are invited out to studies useful and agreeable to them, is made odious and unhealthy, and they are tempted to frivolous amusements to rally their jaded spirits. It would be better, no doubt, if they had good teachers. But in the experience of colleges, it is found that, whilst good mathematicians are rare, good teachers of mathematics are much more rare. It has happened that two or three female teachers in our schools have had great success, and that in the college, geometers and analysts of unquestionable ability utterly fail in the power to impart their methods to the willing student. All the aid the student gets is from some chum who has a little more knowledge than he, and knows where the difficulty he has just surmounted lay. I have just seen four of these skeleton sufferers, to whom all the studies in the University are sufficiently attractive, *excepting the mathematics*, and who find this (which they do not wish to acquire) thrust into absurd eminence, absorbing nominally one third of the academic time in the two first years, and, practically, often two thirds, a dead weight on the mind and heart of the pupil, to be utterly renounced and forgotten the moment he is left to the election of his studies, and a painful memory of wasted years and injured constitution, as long as he lives.

Language, Rhetoric, Logic, Ethics, Intellectual Philosophy, Poetry, Natural History, Civil History, Political Economy, Technology, Chemistry, Agriculture, Literary History, as, the genius of Homer, Dante, Shakspeare, and Goethe; Music and Drawing, even, — all these may rightly enter into the curriculum, as well as Mathematics. But it were to hurt the University if any one of these should absorb a disproportionate share of time. The European universities gave a like supreme emphasis to the subtleties of Logic in the days of Ockham, to Theology, when the priesthood controlled education. Until recently, Natural Science was almost excluded, and it is inevitable that a man of genius with a good deal of general power will for a long period give a bias in his direction to a University. And that is a public mischief which the guardians of a college are there to watch and counterpoise. In the election of a President, it is not only the students who are to be controlled, but the Professors, each of which is, in proportion to his talents, a usurper who needs to be resisted.

May 24.

Yesterday, May 23, we buried Hawthorne in Sleepy Hollow, in a pomp of sunshine and verdure, and gentle winds. James Freeman Clarke read the service in the church and at the grave. Longfellow, Lowell, Holmes, Agassiz, Hoar, Dwight, Whipple, Norton, Alcott, Hillard, Fields, Judge Thomas, and I attended the hearse as pallbearers. Franklin Pierce was with the family. The church was copiously decorated with white flowers delicately arranged. The corpse was unwillingly shown,— only a few moments to this company of his friends. But it was noble and serene in its aspect, — nothing amiss, — a calm and powerful head. A large company filled the church and the grounds of the cemetery. All was so bright and quiet that pain or mourning was hardly suggested, and Holmes said to me that it looked like a happy meeting.

Clarke in the church said that Hawthorne had done more justice than any other to the shades of life, shown a sympathy with the crime in our nature, and, like Jesus, was the friend of sinners.

I thought there was a tragic element in the

event, that might be more fully rendered, — in the painful solitude of the man, which, I suppose, could not longer be endured, and he died of it.

I have found in his death a surprise and disappointment. I thought him a greater man than any of his works betray, that there was still a great deal of work in him, and that he might one day show a purer power. Moreover, I have felt sure of him in his neighbourhood, and in his necessities of sympathy and intelligence, — that I could well wait his time, — his unwillingness and caprice, — and might one day conquer a friendship. It would have been a happiness, doubtless to both of us, to have come into habits of unreserved intercourse. It was easy to talk with him, — there were no barriers, — only, he said so little, that I talked too much, and stopped only because, as he gave no indications, I feared to exceed. He showed no egotism or self-assertion, rather a humility, and, at one time, a fear that he had written himself out. One day, when I found him on the top of his hill, in the woods, he paced back the path to his house, and said, "*This path is the only remembrance of me that will remain.*" Now it appears that I waited too long.

Lately he had removed himself the more

by the indignation his perverse politics and unfortunate friendship for that paltry Franklin Pierce awakened, though it rather moved pity for Hawthorne, and the assured belief that he would outlive it, and come right at last.

I have forgotten in what year[1] [Sept. 27, 1842], but it was whilst he lived in the Manse, soon after his marriage, that I said to him, "I shall never see you in this hazardous way; we must take a long walk together. Will you go to Harvard and visit the Shakers?"

He agreed, and we took a June day, and walked the twelve miles, got our dinner from the Brethren, slept at the Harvard Inn, and returned home by another road, the next day. It was a satisfactory tramp, and we had good talk on the way, of which I set down some record in my journal.

Reginald Taylor, a child of six years, was carried to see his mother's kinsman, President Day. On his return home, he said, "Mother, I think that old man loves God too much. You know I say my prayers when I go to bed; well, he talks just so all the time."

---

[1] The paragraph which follows was later added to the above by Mr. Emerson.

(From KL)

June (?)

"Logic the fist, rhetoric the hand." — ZENO.

The genius of a race or family is a stream always equal to itself and if the present tenant fishes it too much, the next tenant, his son, will find the stream poor, and must withhold his nets and seines. Hence we say, A great man has not a great son. But this proverb has marked exceptions: and, it is also observed that intellect runs in races.

I, too, am fighting my campaign.

So many things require the top of health, the flower of the mind; the engraver must not lay stone walls, nor the king's lapidary pave streets. 'Tis fine health that helps itself with lucky expressions and fit images: — all things offer themselves to be words and convey its meaning. But lassitude has nothing but prose.

What omniscience has music! So absolutely impersonal, and yet every sufferer feels his secret sorrow soothed.

Within, I do not find wrinkles and used heart, but unspent youth.

Value of an opposition. Only the heat of party can hatch the egg — can formulate the truth which your party overlooks, and which is, and will hereafter be admitted to be, the needed check on your statement.

'T is bad when believers and unbelievers live in the same manner; — I distrust the religion.

La carrière ouverte aux talens. A good stand. I notice that the spider finds it a good stand wherever he falls: he takes the first corner, and the flies make haste to come.

Inspiration. I have found my advantage in going to a hotel with a task which could not prosper at home. I secured so a more absolute solitude.[1] . . . At home, the day is cut up into short strips. In the hotel, I forget rain, wind, cold, and heat.[2] At home, I remember in my library the wants of the farm, and have all too much sympathy. I envy the abstraction of some

---

[1] Much of this paragraph is omitted, as it is printed in full in "Inspiration" (*Letters and Social Aims*, pp. 288, 289).

[2] In his lecturing journeys Mr. Emerson found it important to establish a rule (only broken in the case of especial

scholars I have known. . . . All the conditions must be right for my success, slight as that is. What untunes is as bad as what cripples or stuns me.

Therefore, I extol the prudence of Carlyle, who, for years, projected a library at the top of his house, high above the orbit of all housemaids, and out of earshot of doorbells. Could that be once secured, — a whole floor, — room for books, and a good bolt, — he could hope for six years of history, and he kept it in view till it was done. . . . And George Sand's love of heat agrees with mine. Even the steel pen is a nuisance.[1]

The capital rule must not be forgotten of " *une*

friends) to decline private hospitalities and go to a hotel, where his first demand was, "Now make me red-hot." He also could command his time to revise or supplement his manuscript.

[1] Mr. Emerson, when at home, wrote almost always with a quill pen. When the second storey of the house was enlarged, a few years before this time, a little room was made over the new bedroom with one pleasant window looking southward towards Walden woods. It was hard to find, in a remote corner of the garret. Mr. Emerson called it his "den" and occasionally used it under stress of circumstances. But in its construction another possible use as a hiding-place for a fugitive slave had been in the minds of Mr. and Mrs. Emerson, for

demi-heure par jour de lecture suivie et sérieuse," or, as Van Helmont says, "study of Eternity."

And the first rule for me would be to defend the morning, keep all its dews on. Goethe thanks the flies that waked him at dawn as the Musagetes.

And where shall I find the record of my brag of places, favourite spots in the woods and on the river, whither I once went with security for a poetic mood?

In my paper on " Civilization," I omitted an important trait, namely, the increased respect for human life. The difference between the Oriental nations, on one side, and Europe and America, on the other, lies mainly herein. The Japanese in France are astonished, 't is said, at the vast apparatus and expense of a capital trial [examples of Eastern slaughter referred to]. Remember General Scott's maxim, too, about the sacrifice of one life more than necessity requires.

at that time he told his children, when " the Building of a House" was the subject given them for a school composition, to be sure to say, " No house now is complete without such a hiding-place."

The French say that "the special characteristic of English art is the absence of genius." — *Apud* M. CHESNEAU.

Inspiration. Aunt Mary wrote, "How sad, that atmospheric influences should bring to dust the communions of Soul with the Infinite!" — meaning, how sad that the atmosphere should be an excitant. But no, she should be glad that the atmosphere and the dull rock itself should be deluged with deity, — should be theists, Christian, Unitarian, poetic.

Dr. S. Hawtry, Master of Eton, says, "I refer to another feature which an Eton education calls into existence, — I mean a kind of serenity and repose of character; this will be at once recognized as a well-known characteristic of free-minded English gentlemen, and I think Eton has its full share in perpetuating this characteristic in an age in which there is much vieing with, much outrunning and outwitting one another." This is not irony in Dr. Hawtry, though it reads so on this side the water.

Of Paris, Renan writes, after saying that the provincial academies of France have no original studies, — "*Cette brillante Alexandrie sans succursales m'inquiète et m'effraie. Aucun atelier de travail intellectuel ne peut être comparé à Paris: on dirait une ville fait exprès pour l'usage des gens d'esprit : mais qu'il faut se défier de ces oasis au milieu d'un désert. Des dangers perpétuels les assiégent. Un coup de vent, une source tarie, quelques palmiers coupés, et le désert reprend ses droits.*"

When Renan speaks of France, Macaulay or any Englishman of England, or any American of America, I feel how babyish they are. I suppose hardly Newton, or Swedenborg, or Cervantes, or Menu, can be trusted to speak of his nationality.

The grief of old age is, that, now, only in rare moments, and by happiest combinations or consent of the elements, can we attain those enlargements and that intellectual *élan*, which were once a daily gift.

Men are good where they have experience, but not off their beat. Hence Dr. Robert Hare and Mr. S———, and many other men reckoned of excellent sense, tumble helplessly into mesmeric spiritism, and prove its most credulous dupes, because here they have no guide. It is in government as it is in war. It was said many officers can manœuvre a regiment or a division, who could not get a hundred thousand men in or out of Hyde Park, without confusion. So in government. There is plenty of administrative skill in trade and civil affairs, management of railroads and factories, which is at once at a loss and unequal to the disposition of the affairs of an empire.

A good text was that medical observation suggested by the distemper of the cattle at Chenery's and elsewhere,—namely, that men carry the seeds of diseases in their constitutions latent, and which remain latent, during much, perhaps during the whole, of their life. But if it happen that the patient loses, from any cause, his normal strength, instantly these seeds begin to ripen, and the disease, so long latent, becomes acute, and conquers him.

June.

I have more enjoyed, in the last hours of finishing a chapter, the insight which has come to me of how the truths really stand, than I suffered from seeing in what confusion I had left them in my statement.

St. Francis rode all day along the border of

the Lake of Geneva, and, at night, hearing his companions speak of the lake, inquired, "What lake?" — MORISON's *Life of St. Francis*.

It is a tie between men to have read the same book.[1] . . .

Great men are the universal men, men of the common sense, not provincial; Raffaelle not a mannerist. Everybody would paint like Raffaelle, if everybody could paint at all.

[*Reserves.*] "We can never compete with English in manufactures, because of the low price of labour in Europe," — say the merchants, day by day. Yet this season, half or two thirds of our labourers are gone to the war, and we have reaped all the hay by the use of the horse-mower and the horse-rake; the wheat, by McCormick's reaper; and, when the shoemakers went, then, by the use of the new pegging-machine and scrap-machine, we make six hundred pairs of shoes every day at Feltonville, and can let Weymouth send away one hundred

[1] The rest of the passage is found in the "Address at the Opening of the Concord Public Library" (*Miscellanies*, pp. 507, 508).

shoemakers to the war in the regiment that has just departed. We make horseshoes by machine as well as Pittsburg. We can spare all the whalemen to the navy, for we draw oil out of the rocks in Pennsylvania; we can spare the Cuba sugar, for we made seven million gallons of sorghum molasses in 1860, though the article was not known here in 1850.

In that theme of *Inspiration*, 't is to be noted that we use ourselves, and use each other: some perceptions — I think the best — are granted to the single soul.

Kings. "*Quand la bonne foi serait bannie de la terre, elle devrait se retrouver dans le cœur des rois,*" said the French King John, who was taken prisoner at Poitier.

Manners. Their vast convenience I must always admire. The perfect defence and isolation which they effect makes an insuperable protection. Though he wrestle with you, or swim with you, lodge in the same chamber, sleep in the same bed, he is yet a thousand miles off, and can at any moment finish with you. Manners seem to say, "You are you, and I am I."

Old age[1] brings along with its uglinesses the comfort that you will soon be out of it, — which ought to be a substantial relief to such discontented pendulums as we are. To be out of the war, out of debt, out of the drouth, out of the blues, out of the dentist's hands, out of the second thoughts, mortifications, and remorses that inflict such twinges and shooting pains, — out of the next winter, and the high prices, and company below your ambition, — surely these are soothing hints. And, harbinger of this, what an alleviator is sleep, which muzzles all these dogs for me every day? Old age; — 'tis proposed to call an indignation meeting.

Man. The body borrows the elements of its blood from the whole world, and the mind its belief.

The tradition is never left at peace, but must be winnowed again by the new comers. "Every age has another sieve, and will sift it out again."

[1] The following page should have been printed in *Solitude and Society*, in the chapter called "*Old Age.*" (R. W. E.'s note.)

Our Democratic party shows itself very badly in these days, simply destructive, and "would tear down God from Heaven if they could."

Talk with Alcott last night. Men have no scale. Talents warp them. They don't see when their tendency is wrong; don't discriminate between the rank of this and that perception. A gossiping, rambling talk, and yet kept the line of American tendencies. The English and French are still thirty or forty years back in theology. What questions do bishops and universities discuss? We have silently passed beyond all such Debateable Lands.

Want of scale appears in this; Each of the masters has some puerility, as Carlyle his proslavery whim; Tennyson, English class feeling; University men, Churchmen, not humanity, heroism, truth. Our faculties are of different ages —the Memory is mature, sometimes the Imagination adult, and yet the Moral Sense still swaddled and sheathed. Yet on the credit of their talent, these masters are allowed to parade this baby faculty, all fits and folly, in the midst of grown company.

We have freedom, are ready for truth, but we have not the executive culture of Germany.

They have good metaphysics,— have made surveys, sounding every rod of way, set their foot on every rock, and where they felt the rock they planted a buoy and recorded it. Kant, Hegel, Schelling are architects. Scope is not sufficient. We have scope, but we want the Copernicus of our inward heaven. Let us be very mum at present about American literature. One of these ages, we too will set our feet on Andes' tops.

We lack repose. As soon as we stop working, or active thinking, we mope: there is no self-respect, no grand sense of sharing the Divine presence. We are restless, run out and back, talk fast, and overdo.

Nothing in the universe so solid as a thought.

An Indian came to the white man's door and asked for rum. "Oh, no," said the farmer, "I don't give rum to Indians, they steal my pigs and chickens." "Oh, me no steal; me good Indian." "But good Indians don't ask for rum," replied the farmer. "Me no good Indian; me dam rascal."

Use of Towns I considered in an old Journal in many points. But we are far from having the best æsthetics out of them. The French and

Italians have made a nearer approach to it. A town in Europe is a place where you can go into a *café* at a certain hour of every day, buy *eau sucrée*, or a cup of coffee, for six sous, and, at that price, have the company of the wits, scholars, and gentlemen fond of conversation. That is a cheap and excellent club, which finds and leaves all parties on a good mutual footing. That is the fame of the "Café Procope," the "Café Grec" of Rome, the "Café de Trinità" of Florence, and the principle of it exists in every town in France and Italy. But we do not manage it so well in America. Our clubbing is much more costly and cumbersome.

The test of civilization is the power of drawing the most benefit out of cities.

The young men in America take little thought of what men in England are thinking or doing.[1] . . . It may be safely affirmed that when the highest conception, the lessons of religion, are imported, the nation is not culminating, has not genius, but is servile.[2] . . .

'T is a good word of Niebuhr in speaking of

[1] See "Social Aims" (pp. 103, 104).
[2] See "Character" (*Lectures and Biographical Sketches*, p. 111).

the respect which somehow the "oracles" obtained in the ancient world, — "Did man, in those early periods, stand nearer to Nature?" See Lieber's *Reminiscences*.

In Italy a nobleman said to Niebuhr, "I understand the present Pope is not even a man of family." "Oh," replied Niebuhr, "I have been told that Christ himself was not a man of family; and St. Peter, if I recollect well, was but of a vulgar origin. Here in Rome we don't mind these things."

[Certain family events occurring in this year may be mentioned. Mr. Emerson's elder brother, William, on whom his early responsibilities and long years of assiduous professional work had worn heavily, came to Concord with his wife for the summer. The year had for them been one of grief and anxiety. William, the eldest son, a young man of charming personality, scholarly habit, and a promising student of law, had died of consumption a few months after his marriage. John Haven, the second son, gave his services, medical and surgical, to help care for the wounded during Grant's Wilderness campaign in May and June. Charles, the youngest, after serving as a private in the New York Seventh

Regiment, was commissioned a lieutenant in a New York regiment in 1862, and later served successively on the staffs of General Banks and General Emory in Louisiana and Virginia.]

Various powers: power of getting work out of others, which Napoleon had.

When I go to talk with Alcott it is not so much to get his thoughts as to watch myself under his influence. He excites me, and I think freely. But he mistakes me, and thinks, if J[ames?] is right, that I come to feed on him.

It is mortifying that all events must be seen, by wise men even, through the diminishing lens of a petty interest. Could we have believed that England should have disappointed us thus? — that no man in all that civil, reading, brave, cosmopolitan country, should have looked at our revolution as a student of history, as philanthropist, eager to see what new possibilities for humanity were to begin, — what the inspirations were: what new move on the board the Genius of the World was preparing? No, but every one squinted; lords, ladies, statesmen, scholars, poets, all squinted, — like Borrow's Gypsies when he read St. John's Gospel. *Edinburgh,*

Quarterly, Saturday Review, Gladstone, Russell, Palmerston, Brougham, nay, Tennyson; Carlyle, — I blush to say it; Arnold. Everyone forgot his history, his poetry, his religion, and looked only at his shop-till, whether his salary, whether his small investment in the funds, would not be less; whether the stability of English order might not be in some degree endangered. No Milton, no Bacon, no Berkeley, no Montesquieu, no Adam Smith was there to hail a new dawn of hope and culture for men, to see the opportunity for riddance of this filthy pest which dishonoured human nature; to cry over to us, "Up, and God with you! and for this Slavery, — off with its head! We see and applaud; the world is with you; such occasion does not come twice. Strike for the Universe of men!" No; but, on the other hand, every poet, every scholar, every great man, as well as the rich, thought only of his pocket-book, and to our astonishment cried, "*Slavery forever! Down with the North! Why does not England join with France to protect the slaveholder?*" I thought they would have seized the occasion to forgive the Northerner every old grudge; to forget their dislike of his rivalry, of his social short-comings; forget, in such a moment, all petty disgusts and would see in him the honoured instrument of Heaven to destroy this rooted poison tree of five thousand years.

We shall prosper, we shall destroy slavery, but by no help of theirs. They assailed us with mean cavils, they sneered at our manners, at our failures, at our shifts, at the poverty of our treasury, at our struggles, legal and municipal, and irregularities in the presence of mortal dangers. They cherished our enemies, they exulted at the factions which crippled us at home; whenever the allies of the rebels obstructed the great will and action of the Government, they danced for joy.

They ought to have remembered that great actions have mean beginnings; poor matters point to rich ends.

Alas, for England; she did not know her friends. 'Tis a bad omen for England, that, in these years, her foreign policy is ignominious, that she plays a sneaking part with Denmark, with France, with Russia, with China, with America.

August 31.

High School. Beginning of term. Whole number, 32; Present to-day, 22; Class in Arithmetic begin alligation; 1st Latin begin Cicero;

2d, begin Cæsar; 3d, begin Viri Romæ, 12 in class; Greek, Xenophon; French, 2 in class; Geometry, 1 scholar; Natural Philosophy, 10 scholars; Bookkeeping, 6 scholars.

Remember Madden's rule to Dr. Johnson about having fruit enough in an orchard, — " Enough to eat, enough to lay up, enough to be stolen, and enough to rot on the ground."

Among " Resources," too, might be set down that rule of my travelling friend, " When I estimated the costs of my tour in Europe, I added a couple of hundreds to the amount, to be cheated of, and gave myself no more uneasiness when I was overcharged here or there."

So Thoreau's practice to put a hundred seeds into every melon hill, instead of eight or ten.

Affirmative. John Newton said, " The best way to prevent a bushel being filled with chaff, is to fill it with wheat." Trench " On the study of words." — *Past and Present of the English Language.*

When a man writes descriptions of the sun as seen through telescope, he is only writing autobiography, or an account of the habit and defects of his own eyes.

Henry Thoreau found the height of the cliff[1] over the river to be 231.09 feet.

September 21.

Hon. Lyulph Stanley, Wendell Phillips, and Agassiz, Channing, and Alcott here.

Agassiz is really a man of great ability, breadth, and resources, a rare and rich nature, and always maintains himself, — in all companies, and on all occasions. I carried him to Mrs. Mann's, and, afterwards, to Bull's,[2] and, in each house he gave the fittest counsel in the best way. At the Town Hall, he made an excellent speech to the farmers, extemporaneous, of course, but with method and mastery, on the question of the location of the Agricultural College, urging the claims of Cambridge. Judge French[3] followed him with a very good state-

---

[1] Overlooking "Fairhaven Bay" on the South Branch of the Concord River.

[2] The producer of the Concord grape.

[3] Henry F. French, first President of the Massachusetts Agricultural College at Amherst, and father of the sculptor, Daniel Chester French, who, ten years later, made the bronze

ment of the history of the affair from the beginning until now.

Agassiz thinks that, if he could get a calf elephant, and young enough, that is, before birth, he should find the form of the mastodon: that if he could get a tapir calf before birth, he should find the form of the megatherion. But, at present, these are practical impossibilities, as they require hundreds of dissections; hundreds, that is, of live subjects.

September 24.

Yesterday with Ellery walked through "Becky Stow's Hole,"[1] dry-shod, hitherto a feat for a muskrat alone. The sky and air and autumn woods in their early best. This year, the river meadows all dry and permeable to the walker. But why should Nature always be on the gallop? Look now and instantly, or you shall never see it: not ten minutes' repose allowed. Incessant whirl. And 't is the same with my companion's genius. You must carry a stenographic press in your pocket to save his commentaries on things and men, or they are irrecoverable. I

Minute-Man who guards the North Bridge in Concord, and now (1913) is finishing the marble statue of Emerson.

1 A sphagnum swamp, in which some remarkable plants grew.

tormented my memory just now in vain to restore a witty criticism of his, yesterday, on a book.

> Though Love recoil, and Reason chafe,
> There came a voice without reply,
> 'T is man's perdition to be safe,
> When for the Truth he ought to die.[1]

The American Nationality is now within the Republican Party. Hence its serenity. In like manner, in view of all the nationalities of the world, the battle of humanity is now in the American Union, and hence the weakness of English and European opposition.

Napoleon's word, that in twenty-five years the United States would dictate the politics of the world, was a little early; but the sense was just, with a Jewish interpretation of the "forty days" and "seventy weeks." It is true that if we escape bravely from the present war, America will be the controlling power.

[Grieved at his friend's wilful hostility towards our country in its struggle for integrity

---

[1] See the Quatrain "Sacrifice" (*Poems*, p. 296). The last two lines are a quotation from a sermon by Caleb Vines, a Puritan, preached at St. Margaret's, Westminster, before the Honourable House of Commons, November 30, 1642.

and freedom, Mr. Emerson wrote to Carlyle, September 26, these words: —

"I have, in these last years, lamented that you had not made the visit to America which in earlier years you projected.... It would have made it impossible that your name should be cited for one moment on the side of the enemies of mankind. Ten days' residence in this country would have made you the organ of the sanity of England and of Europe to us and to them, and have shown you the necessities and aspirations which struggle up in our Free States, which, as yet, have no organ to others, and are ill and unsteadily articulated here.... Ah! how gladly I would enlist you, with your thunderbolt, on our part! How gladly enlist the wise, thoughtful, efficient pens and voices of England!... Are English of this day incapable of a great sentiment? Can they not leave cavilling at petty failures and bad manners, and at the dunce part (always the largest part in human affairs) and leap to the suggestions and finger-pointings of the gods, which, above the understanding, feed the hopes and guide the wills of men? This war has been conducted over the heads of all the actors in it." *Carlyle-Emerson Correspondence*, vol. ii, pp. 285, 286.]

'T is a defect in our manners that they have not yet reached the prescribing a term to visits.[1] . . .

What a pity that Beauty is not the rule, since everybody might have been handsome as well as not. Or, if the moral laws must have their revenge, like Indians, for every violation, what pity that everybody is not promoted on the battle-field, as our generals are; that is, instantly embellished by a good action. My servant squints and steals: I persuade her to better behaviour: she restores the long-lost trinkets, embroidered purse, and, at the same time, the *strabismus* should be healed.

Manners. What a harness of buckram wealth and city life put on our poets and literary men, even when men of great parts. Alcott complained to me of want of simplicity in Lowell, Holmes, Ward, and Longfellow: and Alcott is the right touchstone to test them; true litmus to detect the acid. Agassiz is perfectly accessible, has a brave manliness which can meet a peasant, a mechanic, or a fine gentleman with

[1] The whole passage may be found in "Social Aims" (p. 91).

equal fulness. Henry James is not spoiled; Bryant is perfect; New York has not hurt him. Whittier is unspoiled. Wasson is good company for prince or ploughman. Rowse also. I should be glad if James Lowell were as simply noble as his cousin Frank Lowell, who, my wife once said, "appeared like a King." C—— T—— has perfect manners. Charles Newcomb and Channing are saved by genius. Thoreau was with difficulty sweet. A—— W—— has never left her broad humanity, and suggests so much that is told of Madame Récamier.

But in all the living circle of American wits and scholars is no enthusiasm. Alcott alone has it. "Enthusiasm a delight, but may not always be a virtue," wrote Aunt Mary. The enthusiast will not be irritated, sour, and sarcastic.

Wealth of Nature the only good. 'T is vain to accuse scholars of solitude, and merchants of miserliness: they are really so poor that they cannot help it. Poverty is universal. "Ah, blessed Ocean, 't is good to find enough of one thing." Genius delights because of its opulence. We scorn the poor *littérateurs* who hide their want by patchwork of quotations and borrowings; and the poor artist, who, instead of the rapid drawing on a single conception, laboriously etches after his model with innumerable stipplings. What a saving grace is in poverty and solitude, that the obscure youth learns the practice instead of the literature of his Virtues! One or two or three ideas are the gods of his Temple, and suffice him for intellect and heart for years. They condescend to his shoeshop, or his hoe and scythe and threshing-floor.

The solitary worshipper knows the essence of the thought: the scholar in society sees only its fair face.

Aunt Mary writes: "After all, some of the old Christians were more delivered from external things than the (modern) speculative, who are anxious for society, books, ideas, — and become sensitive to all that affects the organs of thought. A few single grand ideas, which become objects, pursuits, and all in all!"

Aunt Mary and her contemporaries spoke continually of angels and archangels, with a good faith, as they would have spoken of their parents, or their late minister. Now the word palls, — all the credence gone.

The War at last appoints the generals, in spite of parties and Presidents. Every one of us had his pet, at the start, but none of us appointed Grant, Sherman, Sheridan, and Farragut, — none but themselves. Yet these are only shining examples; the fruit of small powers and virtues is as fixed. The harvest of potatoes is not more sure than the harvest of every talent.

Great difference in life of two consecutive days. Now it has grip, tastes the hours, fills the horizon; and presently it recedes, has little possession, is somnambulic.

We read often with as much talent as we write.

The retrospective value of a new thought is immense. 'T is like a torch applied to a long train of powder.[1]

A page of Aunt Mary's gives much to think of the felicity of greatness on a low ground of condition, as we have so often thought a rich Englishman has better lot than a king. "No fair object but affords me gratification, and with common interests." Again, she writes, "they [probably the common farming people about

[1] This passage is printed in *Natural History of Intellect* (p. 21).

her] knew by hearsay of apes of men, vampire despots, crawling sycophants."

Criticism. I read with delight a casual notice of Wordsworth in the *London Reader*, in which, with perfect aplomb, his highest merits were affirmed, and his unquestionable superiority to all English poets since Milton, and thought how long I travelled and talked in England, and found no person, or none but one, and that one Clough, sympathetic with him, and admiring him aright, in face of Tennyson's culminating talent, and genius in melodious verse. What struck me now was the certainty with which the best opinion comes to be the established opinion. This rugged, rough countryman walks and sits alone, assured of his sanity and his inspiration, and writes to no public, — sneered at by Jeffrey and Brougham, branded by Byron, blackened by the gossip of Barry Cornwall and De Quincey, down to Bowring, — for they all had disparaging tales of him, — yet himself no more doubting the fine oracles that visited him than if Apollo had brought them visibly in his hand: and here and there a solitary reader in country places had felt and owned them; and now, so few years after, it is lawful in that obese material England, whose vast strata of population are nowise converted or altered, yet to affirm unblamed, unresisted, that this is the genuine, and the rest the impure, metal. For, in their sane hours each of the fine minds in the country has found it, and imparted his conviction, so that every reader has somewhere heard it on the highest authority : —

"And thus the world is brought
To sympathy with hopes and fears it heeded not."

English genius is more truly shown in the drawings in *Punch* than in all their water-colour and Royal Academy exhibitions; just as their actors are dreary in tragedy, and admirable in low comedy.

Criticism. Dr. Holmes, one day, said to me that he disliked scientific matter introduced into (literary) lectures, "it was meretricious."

Prodigality of Nature. She can afford millions of lives of men to make the movement of the earth round the sun so much as "suspected." [1] ... How much time a man's poetic

[1] This sentence occurs in "Poetry and Imagination" (*Letters and Social Aims*, pp. 23, 24). Much of what

experiences cost him. He abandons business and wealth for them. How much time Love costs him!

> "The time I lost pursuing
> The light which lies
> In woman's eyes
> Has been my heart's undoing."

Ah, yes, but if his love was well directed, it has been his mind's upbuilding.

How often I have to say that every man has material enough in his experience to exhaust the sagacity of Newton in working it out. We have more than we use. We know vastly more than we digest. I never read poetry, or hear a good speech at a caucus, or a cattle-show, but it adds less stock to my knowledge than it apprises me of admirable uses to which what I knew can be turned. I write this now on remembrance of some *structural* experience of last night,—a painful waking out of dreams as by violence, and a rapid succession of quasi-optical shows following like a pyrotechnic exhibition of architectural or grotesque flourishes, which indicate magazines of talent and invention in our struc-

follows is printed in "Resources" (*Letters and Social Aims*, pp. 139, 140).

ture, which I shall not arrive at the control of in my time, but perhaps my great-grandson will mature and bring to day.

October 9.

Yesterday at Mr. George L. Stearns's, at Medford, to meet Wendell Phillips, and Mr. Fowler of Tennessee. The conversation political altogether, and though no very salient points, yet useful to me as clearing the air, and bringing to view the simplicity of the practical problem before us. Right-minded men would very easily bring order out of our American chaos, if working with courage, and without by-ends. These Tennessee slaveholders in the land of Midian are far in advance of our New England politicians. They see and front the real questions. [One] point would seem to be absolute — Emancipation, — establishing the fact that the United States henceforward knows no colour, no race, in its law, but legislates for all alike, — one law for all men. . . .

It was good in Fowler, his marked though obscure recognition of the higher element that works in affairs. We seem to do it, — it gets done; but for our will in it, it is much as if I claimed to have manufactured the beautiful skin and flavour of my pears.

Certain memorable words, expressions that flew out incidentally in late history, as, for example, in Lincoln's letter, "To all whom it may concern," are caught up by men,— go to England, go to France,— reëcho thence with thunderous report to us, and they are no longer the unconsidered words they were, but we must hold the Government to them; they are powers, and are not to be set aside by reckless speeches of Seward, putting all afloat again.

October 12.

Returned from Naushon, whither I went on Saturday, the 8th, with Professor Goldwin Smith, of Oxford University, Mr. Charles B. Sedgwick,[1] John Weiss, and George C. Ward.

Mr. Forbes at Naushon is the only "Squire" in Massachusetts, and no nobleman ever understood or performed his duties better. I divided my admiration between the landscape of Naushon and him. He is an American to be proud of. Never was such force, good meaning, good sense, good action, combined with such domestic lovely behaviour, and such modesty and persistent preference of others. Wher-

[1] Of Syracuse, an admirable man and member of Congress.

ever he moves, he is the benefactor. It is of course that he should shoot well, ride well, sail well, administer railroads well, carve well, keep house well, but he was the best talker also in the company, — with the perpetual practical wisdom, seeing always the *working* of the thing, — with the multitude and distinction of his facts (and one detects continually that he has had a hand in everything that has been done), and in the temperance with which he parries all offence, and opens the eyes of his interlocutor without contradicting him.[1] I have been proud of many of my countrymen, but I think this is a good country that can breed such a creature as John M. Forbes.

There was something dramatic in the conversation of Monday night between Professor Goldwin Smith, Forbes, and Ward, chiefly, — the Englishman being evidently alarmed at the near prospect of the retaliation of America's standing in the identical position soon in which England now and lately has stood to us, and play-

[1] This description by Mr. Emerson of his friend Mr. Forbes, whose services throughout the war in every sort had been important and admirable (although he never allowed his name to get into the papers), is printed, though without his name, in *Letters and Social Aims* (p. 103).

ing the same part towards her. Forbes, a year ago, was in Liverpool and London entreating them to respect their own neutrality, and disallow the piracy, and the blockade-running, and hard measure to us in their colonial ports, etc. And now, so soon, the parts were entirely reversed, and Professor Smith was showing us the power and irritability of England and the certainty that war would follow, if we should build and arm a ship in one of our ports, send her out to sea, and *at sea* sell her to their enemy, which would be a proceeding strictly in accordance with her present proclaimed law of nations. Forbes thinks the Americans are in such a temper toward England that they will do this if the opportunity occurs. When the American Government urged England to make a new treaty to adjust and correct this anomalous rule, the English Government refused. And 't is only ignorance that has prevented the Rebel Confederacy from availing themselves of it.

Mr. Smith had never heard of J. J. Garth Wilkinson; nor had the Trollopes heard of Elizabeth Sheppard,[1] nor scarcely any English, fifteen years ago, of Browning.

[1] Author of *Charles Auchester* and *Counterparts*.

At Naushon, I recall what John Smith said of the Bermudas, and I think as well of Mr. Forbes's fences,[1] which are cheap and steep. "No place known had better walls or a broader ditch."

What complete men are Forbes, Agassiz, and Rockwood Hoar!

I came away from Naushon saying to myself of John Forbes, how little this man suspects, with his sympathy for men, and his respect for lettered and scientific people, that he is not likely ever to meet a man superior to himself!

The dire, τὸ δεινόν, is that which I used to long for in orators. I can still remember the imposing march of Otis's eloquence, which, like Burke's, swept into it all styles of address, all varieties of tone and incident, and in its skirts "far flashed the red artillery."

In modern eloquence what is more touching or sublime than the first words of Lafayette's speech in the French Assembly in 1815 (?), "When, after so many years silence [the whole Consulate and Empire], I raise a voice which the friends of liberty will still recognize," etc.

[1] Buzzards Bay and the Vineyard Sound.

Nemesis is that recoil of Nature, not to be guarded against, which ever surprises the most wary transgressor (of the Laws). Not possibly can you shut up all the issues.

Ste.-Beuve notes, in 1838, the charming letters of Lafayette to his wife, just published.

The Age, and the Hour. The party of virility rules the hour, the party of ideas and sentiments rules the age.

October 19.

Yesterday, as I passed Shannon's field, robins, blackbirds, bluebirds, and snowbirds (*fringilla hiemalis*) were enjoying themselves together.

NEW YORK, *October* 20.

Bryant has learned where to hang his titles, namely, by tying his mind to autumn woods, winter mornings, rain, brooks, mountains, evening winds, and wood-birds. Who speaks of these is forced to remember Bryant. [He is] American. Never despaired of the Republic. Dared name a jay and a gentian, crows also. His poetry is sincere. I think of the young poets that they have seen pictures of mountains, and sea-shores, but in his that he has seen mountains and has the staff in his hand.

It occurred in talking with Henry James yesterday, who attached a too exclusive originality to Swedenborg, that he did not seem to recognize the eternal co-presence of the revolutionary force. The revolutionary force in intellect is never absent. Such persons as my poor Platonist Taylor in Amesbury; Jones Very; and the shoemaker, ———, at Berwick; Tufts in Lima (or Cuba), New York, are always appearing in the deadest conservatism; — in an age of antiquaries, representing the most modern times; — in the heart of papacy and toryism, the seed of rebellion; — for the world is ever equal to itself, and centripetence makes centrifugence.

October 25.

Power of certain states of the sky. There is an astonishing magnificence even in this low town, and within a quarter of a mile of my doors, in the appearance of the Lincoln hills now drest in their coloured forest, under the lights and clouds of morning, as I saw them at eight o'clock. When I see this spectacle so near, and so surprising, I think no house should be built quite low, or should obstruct the prospect by trees.

America makes its own precedents. The imperial voice of the Age cannot be heard for the tin horns and charivari of the varlets of the hour, such as the London *Times*, *Blackwood's*, and the *Saturday Review*. But already these *claqueurs* have received their cue— I suppose it was hinted to them that the American People are not always to be trifled with; they are ending their home war, and are exasperated at English bad behaviour, and are in force to destroy English trade. Speak them fair;— and *The Times* has just discovered what "temper, valour, constancy, the Union has shown in the War," and what a noble "career of honour and prosperity lies before her," etc.

When a lady rallied Adam Smith on his plain dress, he pointed to his well-bound library, and said, "You see, Madam, I am a beau in my books." The farmer in this month is very patient of his coarse attire, and thinks, "at least, I am a beau in my woods."

October 30.

At Club, yesterday, we had a full table, Agassiz, Hoar, Hedge, Cabot, Holmes, Appleton, Peirce, Norton, Forbes, Ward, Sumner, Whipple, Woodman, Dwight, Emerson; Andrew (who, with Brimmer and Fields, was elected yesterday); and, for guests, Mr. C. G. Loring, Sterry Hunt, and Mr. Godkin, the English correspondent of the *Daily News*.

Before the War, our patriotism was a firework, a salute, a serenade, for holidays and summer evenings, but the reality was cotton thread and complaisance. Now the deaths of thousands and the determination of millions of men and women show it real.

> Rich are the sea-gods, who gives gifts but they?
> All hidden gems are theirs.
> What power is theirs, they give it to the wise, —
> For every wave is wealth to Dædalus,
> Wealth to the cunning artist who can work
> The wave's immortal sinew.[1]

November 18.

The way that *young woman*[2] keeps her school

---

[1] This addition to the earlier lines of "Seashore," written at Pigeon Cove, probably came in a walk on the south shore beach on the beautiful island of Naushon, where Mr. Emerson could not resist the beauty of the pebbles.

[2] Miss Eliza Hosmer, daughter of Mr. Emerson's farmer friend and neighbour, Edmund Hosmer, often referred to in the earlier journals.

was the best lesson I received in the Preparatory School to-day. She knew so much, and carried it so well in her head, and gave it out so well, that the pupils had quite enough to think of, and not an idle moment to waste on noise or disorder. 'T is the best recipe I know for school discipline.

November 26.

Agassiz, Brimmer, Cabot, Holmes, Hoar, Fields, Dana, Norton, Sumner, Whipple, Emerson, at the Club; and Senator Wilson, M. Laugel and M. Duvergne d'Hauranne guests. I promised Sumner to attend to the question of the Academy.

Cows are dull, sluggish creatures, but with a decided talent in one direction — for extracting milk out of meadows : — mine have a genius for it, — leaking cream, "larding the lean earth as they walk along." Wasps, too, for making paper. Then what soothing objects are the hens!

Bryant.[1] His sincere, balanced mind has the enthusiasm which perception of Nature inspires,

[1] This passage was written for the Bryant Festival which was held in New York on November 8. It seems probable that Mr. Emerson took part in it.

but it did not tear him; only enabled him; gave him twice his power; he did not parade it, but hid it in his verse. His connection with party *usque ad aras*.[1] "True bard, but simple," I fear he has not escaped the infirmity of fame, like the presidential malady, a virus once in, not to be got out of the system: he has this, so cold and majestic as he sits there, — has this to a heat which has brought to him the devotion of all the young men and women who love poetry, and of all the old men and women who once were young. 'T is a perfect tyranny. Talk of the shopmen who advertise their drugs or cosmetics on the walls and on the palisades and huge rocks along the railways; — why, this man, more cunning by far, has contrived to levy on all American Nature and subsidized every solitary forest and Monument Mountain in Berkshire or the Katskills, every waterfowl, every partridge, every gentian and goldenrod, the prairies, the gardens of the desert, the song of the stars, the Evening Wind, — has bribed every one of these to speak for him, so that there is scarcely a

[1] *Even to the altars*, a Latin version of a Greek expression for devotion, though Mr. Emerson, in his quatrain "Pericles," makes the altar a bound beyond which right service may not go (*Poems*, p. 296).

feature of day and night in the country which does not — whether we will or not — recall the name of Bryant. This high-handed usurpation I charge him with, and on the top of this, with persuading us and all mankind to hug our fetters and rejoice in our subjugation.

(From ML)

INTRODUCTION TO LECTURE ON "EDUCATION," IN COURSE ON "AMERICAN LIFE"

(Read at the Melodeon, November, 1864 [1])

I congratulate my countrymen on the great and good omens of the hour; that a great portion of mankind dwelling in the United States have given their decision in unmistakeable terms in favor of social and statute order, that a nation shall be a nation, and refuses to hold its existence on the tenure of a casual *rencontre* of passengers, who meet at the corner of a street, or on a railroad, or at a picnic, — held by no bond, but meeting and parting at pleasure; that a nation cannot be trifled with, but involves interests so dear and so vast that it is intolerable crime to treat them with levity; they shall be

[1] Soon after Lincoln had been elected President for a second term.

held binding as marriage, binding as contracts of property, binding as laws which guard the life and honour of the citizen. The people, after the most searching discussion of every part of the subject, have decided that the unity of the nation shall be held by force against the forcible attempt of parties to break it. What gives commanding weight to this decision is that it has been made by the people sobered by the calamity of the War, the sacrifice of life, the waste of property, the burden of taxes, and the uncertainties of the result. They protest in arms against the attempt of any small or any numerous minority of citizens or states to proceed by stealth or by violence to dispart a country. They do not decide that if a part of the nation, from geographic necessities or from irreconcileable interests of production and trade, desires separation, no such separation can be. Doubtless it may, because the permanent interest of one part to separate will come to be the interest and good will of the other part. But, at all events, it shall not be done in a corner, not by stealth, not by violence, but as a solemn act, with all the forms, with all deliberation, and on the declared opinions of the entire population concerned, and with mutual guaranties and compensations.

I need not go over the statistics of the Country: those colossal lines are printed on your brain. These lines of land subject to one law are almost astronomical measures, containing a pretty large fraction of the planet. These grand material dimensions cannot suggest dwarfish and stunted manners and policy. Everything on this side the water inspires large and prospective action. America means opportunity, freedom, power; and, very naturally, when these instincts have not been supported by adequate mental and moral training, they run into the grandiose, into exaggeration and vapouring. This is odious, but inevitable. The inhabitants of the Great Republic are taxed with rudeness and superficiality. It was said of Louis XIV that his gait was becoming in a king, but, in a private man, would have been an insufferable strut. Still, when we are reproached with vapouring by people of small home territory, like the English, I often think that ours is only the gait and bearing of a tall boy, a little too large for his trousers, by the side of small boys. They are jealous, quicksighted about their inches.

But let us call bad manners by the right name. . . . Don't take any pains to praise good people. I delight in certain dear persons, that they need no letters of introduction, knowing well that, wherever they go, they are hung all over with eulogies. If there is any perception in the company, these will be found out as fountains of joy.

Power of criticism. Laugel said, the other day, that the French Emperor censures and prohibits newspapers, but never meddles with books. But now I am glad to see Laboulaye, in his critique on the *Life of Julius Cæsar*, toss his Emperor Napoleon on his horns, and with invulnerable propriety.

"The late good and wise first Lord Ravensworth used to say, 'there was nothing grateful but the earth; you cannot do too much for it: it will continue to pay tenfold the pains and labour bestowed upon it.'" — BEWICK's *Life*.

Victor Cousin said, in conversation about the Encyclical Letter, that "the Pope had missed an opportunity of keeping still, which would never occur again."

[As in previous volumes, a few of Mr. Emerson's favorite authors, from his early youth steadily recurring in the lists of the first volumes (as Homer, Plato, Plutarch, Montaigne, Bacon, Shakspeare, Milton, Herbert, Swedenborg, Wordsworth, and others), are not given in this list. In spite, however, of the frequent mention of Plotinus, Proclus, and the other Neoplatonists, and of the Oriental Scriptures and poets, these names will appear, as showing when Mr. Emerson was reading them. Carlyle and Goethe will also be mentioned.

It often happens that an allusion to an author may be in a passage not included in the selections here printed.]

Authors or Books quoted or referred to in Journal for 1864

Menu; Aristotle; Zeno;

Suetonius; Ossian; Mahomet;

Walter Mapes; Dante; William of Ockham; Arthurian Legends; Chronicle of the Cid;

Chaucer; Boccaccio; Philippe de Comines; Savonarola; Machiavelli; Copernicus; Michel Angelo, *Sonnets;* Guicciardini:

Cervantes; Galileo; Van Helmont; Captain John Smith; Drummond of Hawthornden;

Clarendon; D'Herbelot, *Bibliothèque Orientale*; Pepys; Scougal;

Swift; Berkeley; Chesterfield; Hervey, *History of George II*; Montesquieu;

Kant; James Otis; Goethe, *Correspondence*, also translation of Romaic poem "Charon"; Sir N. W. Wraxall, *Our Own Times*; Bewick, *Life*; Fichte; William Blake; Lafayette, *Letters to his Wife*; Hegel *apud* J. Hutchison Stirling;

Josiah Quincy; Jeremiah Day; Burns; Schelling; Niebuhr; Sir R. Wilson, *Private Journal*; Brougham; Berthollet; Nesselrode; Moore; Sir William Napier; Legardie, *Causeries Parisiennes*;

Adam Smith; Palmerston; De Quincey; Schopenhauer; E. C. Hawtrey, *On Eton*; "Barry Cornwall" (B. W. Procter); Bowring; Earl Russell; Bryant; Alfieri; Carlyle; Alcott;

Francis Lieber, *Reminiscences*; Horace Bushnell; George Sand; Sainte-Beuve, *Nouveaux Causeries* and *Portraits Contemporains*; Hawthorne; Hans Andersen; W. L. Garrison; John Sterling; Rev. F. H. Hedge;

Agassiz; Whittier; Longfellow; R. C. Trench, *English Past and Present*; Napoleon III, *Life of Cæsar apud* Laboulaye; Gladstone; Tennyson; Cardinal Manning;

Holmes; Rev. James Freeman Clarke; Henry James; Harriet Beecher Stowe; Dr. J. J. Garth Wilkinson; Jones Very; Henry Ward Beecher; Rev. Edwin Hubbell Chapin;

Thoreau; W. E. Channing; Mommsen, *History of Rome;* Clough; Matthew Arnold; Thomas W. Parsons, *Translation of Dante;* Julia Ward Howe; James Hutchison Stirling, *The Secret of Hegel;*

Ernest Renan, *Vie de Jésus;* T. W. Higginson; Goldwin Smith; David A. Wasson;

Taine; Elizabeth Sara Sheppard; Theodore H. Hittell, *Adventures of " Grizzly Bear Adams ";* F. B. Sanborn; James A. C. Morison, *Life of St. Francis;* James Kendall Hosmer; *Punch,* and *Revue des Deux Mondes.*

JOURNAL

LECTURING AFAR
END OF THE WAR
LINCOLN
DUTIES OF THE HOUR
UNIVERSITY CULTURE
WILLIAMSTOWN ADDRESS
INTELLECT. MANNERS
DR. JACKSON
STAR-GAZING
CASS AND TRACY
CARLYLE

JOURNAL LVI

1865

(From Journals KL, DL, ML, XO, and IT)

[THE war was drawing to a close, yet no one dared hope the end was so near; the times were hard, and the winter severe. Mr. Emerson went West in January, lectured in Pittsburgh, in Ohio, and apparently gave short courses in Chicago and Milwaukee. In his letters he spoke of "bitter weather."]

(From KL)

CONCORD, *February* 13, 1865.

Home from Chicago and Milwaukee. Chicago grows so fast that one ceases to respect civic growth: as if all these solid and stately squares which we are wont to see as the slow growth of a century had come to be done by machinery as cloth and hardware are made, and were therefore shoddy architecture without honour.

'T was tedious, the squalor and obstructions of travel; the advantage of their offers at

Chicago made it necessary to go; in short, this dragging of a decorous old gentleman out of home and out of position to this juvenile career was tantamount to this,—"I'll bet you fifty dollars a day that you will not leave your library, and wade and ride and run and suffer all manner of indignities and stand up for an hour each night reading in a hall"; and I answered, "I'll bet I will." I do it and win the $900.

[In the beginning of Spring, a happy event had happened in Mr. Emerson's family. William Hathaway Forbes (elder son of John Murray Forbes), a major in the Second Massachusetts Cavalry, had been taken in the previous May in hand-to-hand fight with Mosby's guerrillas, when pinned down by his dying horse. He was held prisoner at Columbia, South Carolina, escaped in late autumn, and was retaken, but soon after released on parole. In March he became engaged to Mr. Emerson's younger daughter Edith, and was exchanged just in time to rejoin his regiment as lieutenant-colonel, and he was present at Lee's surrender.]

Wilkinson always an affirmative writer; radiant, intellectual, humane, brave as such are.

April 10.

General Hooker, in his order from his headquarters at Cincinnati, assuming command of the Department of the Northwest, says to every officer and soldier, "No one will consider the day as ended, until the duties it brings have been discharged."

I value the fortnightly *Publishers' Circular*, mainly for its Paris correspondence, containing, as it does, biography of literary men in Paris, and showing the identity of literary life in Paris with our own, scattering the illusion that overhangs Paris in the eyes and reports of frivolous travellers, and showing there just such a coarse and vindictive Bohemia as New York is for dissipated young men of talent.

'T is far the best that the rebels have been pounded instead of negociated into a peace. They must remember it, and their inveterate brag will be humbled, if not cured. George Minott used to tell me over the wall, when I urged him to go to town meeting and vote, that "votes did no good; what was done so would n't last, but what was done by bullets would stay put." General Grant's terms certainly look a little too easy, . . . and I fear that the high tragic historic justice which the nation, with severest consideration, should execute, will be softened and dissipated and toasted away at dinner-tables. But the problems that now remain to be solved are very intricate and perplexing, and men are very much at a loss as to the right action. If we let the Southern States into Congress, the Northern Democrats will join them in thwarting the will of the Government. And the obvious remedy is to give the negro his vote. And then the difficult question comes, — what shall be the qualification of voters? We wish to raise the mean white to his right position, that he may withstand the planter. But the negro will learn to write and read (which should be a required qualification) before the white will.

To be amused. People go into the church, as they go into the parlour, to be amused. The frivolous mood takes the most of the time, as the frivolous people make the majority. And Cicero said of the Greeks, and Eastern provinces, that they gave themselves to art for forgetfulness and the consolation of servitude; — *oblectamenta et solatium servitutis.*

The thunderbolt strikes on an inch of ground, but the light of it fills the horizon.[1]

I should say of Samuel Hoar, Senior, what Clarendon writes of Sir Thomas Coventry, that "he had a strange power of making himself believed, the only justifiable design of eloquence."

"The mind of Locke will not always be the measure of Human Understanding." — SAMPSON REED.

There is no police so effective as a good hill and wide pasture in the neighbourhood of a village, where the boys can run and play and dispose of their superfluous strength and spirits, to their own delight and the annoyance of nobody.

Criticism, Illusion of words. There are really few people who distinguish, on reading, a page full of words from a page full of new experience. They are satisfied with the first, if it is in harmony with their habitual opinions. They say it is good, and put it in my hands, or will read

[1] See *Poems*, Appendix, "The Poet" (p. 334).

it to me, and are discontented if I slight it. But they never take it up again, because it makes no impression on their memory; whilst they do remember and return to the page of real experiences, and thus vindicate the critic.

For "Inspiration," the experience of writing letters is one of the best keys to the *modus* of it.[1] . . .

Immortality. The path of spirits is in silence and hidden from sense. Who knows where or how the soul has existed, before it was incarnated in mortal body? Who knows where or how it thinks and works when it drops its fleshly frame? Like those asteroids, which we call shooting stars, which revolve forever in space, but sweeping for a moment through some arc of our atmosphere and heated by the friction, give out a dazzling gleam, then pass out of it again on their endless orbit invisible.

President Lincoln.[2] Why talk of President

[1] This passage is printed in "Inspiration" (*Letters and Social Aims*, p. 281).

[2] On the Nineteenth of April, Concord's great day, instead of the customary celebration, the people gathered in the

Lincoln's equality of manners to the elegant or titled men with whom Everett or others saw him? A sincerely upright and intelligent man as he was, placed in the Chair, has no need to think of his manners or appearance. His work day by day educates him rapidly and to the best. He exerts the enormous power of this continent in every hour, in every conversation, in every act; — thinks and decides under this pressure, forced to see the vast and various bearings of the measures he adopts: *he* cannot palter, he cannot but carry a grace beyond his own, a dignity, by means of what he drops, e. g., all his pretension and trick, and arrives, of course, at a simplicity, which is the perfection of manners.

May 6.

In reading Mark Antonine last night, it was pleasant to be reminded, by some of his precepts, of a living example in a dear person near me.

We are such vain peacocks that we read in

old church in sorrow for the death of the great President who had bravely and wisely borne the burden of the War. Mr. Emerson made an address, printed in the "Miscellanies." The following passage, probably written earlier, does not appear in that speech.

an English journal, with joy, that no house in London or in Paris can compare with the comfort and splendour at Delmonico's in New York. But I was never in Delmonico's.

Lafayette. "*Le bien et le mal de la Révolution paraissaient en général separés par la ligne que j'avais suivie.*"

Bonaparte said one day in a sally (*sortie*) to the Council of State, "*Tout le monde en France est corrigé: il n'y a qu'un seul homme qui ne le soit pas, Lafayette! Il n'a jamais reculé d'une ligne. Vous le voyez tranquille; eh bien? Je vous dis, moi, qu'il est tout prêt à recommencer.*"

Saint-Beuve . . . vindicates the noble unique fidelity of Lafayette, but finds in him credulity. . . . And Sumner, who read here in Concord a lecture on Lafayette, is of all Americans the one who is best entitled by his own character and fortunes to read his eulogy.

"*La netteté est le vernis des maîtres.*" — VAUVENARGUES.

Boileau asks Molière, "Where the devil do you get your rhyme?" For inspiration has unknown resources; has cunning also.

If I were successful abroad in talking and

dealing with men, I should not come back to my library and my work, as I do. When the spirit chooses you for the Scribe to publish some Commandment, if it makes you odious to men, and men odious to you, you shall accept that loathsomeness with joy.

The moth must fly to the lamp; the man must solve those questions, though he die.

Talk with Alcott; assured him that character was the result of pagan morals. All the victories of religion belong to the moral sentiment.[1] ... The parson calls it Justification by Faith. All the victories, all the convictions, all the anxieties of Revivals are the old Eternal fact of remorse for wrong, and joy in the Right.

It is becoming to the Americans to dare in religion to be simple, as they have been in government, in trade, in social life; and they have rightly pronounced Toleration,— that no religious test shall be put. They are to abolish laws against atheism.

They are not to allow immorality; they are to be strict in laws of marriage; they are to be just to women, in property, in votes, in personal

[1] Several omitted sentences are printed in "Character" (*Lectures and Biographical Sketches,* pp. 113, 114).

rights; and they are to establish the pure religion, Justice, Asceticism, Self-devotion, Bounty.

They will lead their language round the globe, and they will lead religion and freedom with them. . . .

It was his tender conviction of this power and presence that made Jesus a light in the world, and the spirit that animated him is as swift and puissant to-day.

Scientific men with their Atheism, like the French savants, appear to me insane men with a talent; and the cure would be the opening of the moral sentiment.

There is far more than bare works: there is faith also; that is, the raptures of goodness are as old as history, and new with this morning's sun. The language and the legends of Arabia and India and Persia are of the same complexion as the Christian. *Vishnu Purana* bear witness — Socrates, Zeno, Menu, Zertusht, Confucius, Rabia are as tender as St. Francis, St. Augustine, and St. Bernard.

We say there exists a Universal Mind which imparts this perception of duty, opens the interior world to the humble obeyer. . . . It has been imparted in all ages. Religion is the homage to this presence.

Admirable fairness of Elizabeth Hoar's mind. I think no one who writes or utilizes his opinions can possibly be fair. She will see finer *nuances* of equity which you will never see if untold. She applied the Napoleon *mot*, " Respect the burden," so well to Lincoln, as to [the attitude of] Wendell Phillips.

And one may say, there is a genius for honesty, as well as for poetry, and nobody can anticipate the directness and simplicity of the true man.

The best in argument is not the accosting in front the hostile premises, but the flanking them by a new generalization which incidentally disposes of them.

It should be easy to say what I have always felt, that Stanley's *Lives of the Philosophers*, or Marcus Antoninus, are agreeable and suggestive books to me, whilst St. Paul or St. John are not, and I should never think of taking up these to start me on my task, as I often have used Plato or Plutarch. It is because the Bible wears black cloth. It comes with a certain official claim against which the mind revolts. The book has its own nobilities — might well be charming, if it was left simply on its merits, as the others; but this " you must,"— " it is your duty," repels. 'T is like the introduction of martial law into Concord. If you should dot our farms with picket lines, and I could not go or come across lots without a pass, I should resist, or else emigrate. If Concord were as beautiful as Paradise, it would be detestable at once.

When divine souls appear, men are compelled by their own self-respect to distinguish them.

Whenever the moral sentiment is affirmed, it must be with dazzling courage. As long as it is cowardly insinuated, as with the wish to show that it is just what the Church receives to-day it is not imparted and cannot be owned

May 28.

In the acceptance that my papers find among my thoughtful countrymen, in these days, I cannot help seeing how limited is their reading. If they read only the books that I do, they would not exaggerate so wildly.

Select books, select anecdotes, select discoveries, select works of art, select men and women. The most accomplished man should bring his contemporaries to the high culture by pointing out these with insight and reverence.

The graduate at the University should know

"the famed lines Pythagoras devised
For which a hecatomb he sacrificed";[1]

should know Archimedes's *Eureka!*[2] should know Newton's binomial theorem inscribed on his tomb, as well as his optical, and astronomic, and chemical insights; should know Da Vinci's cartoon, and Michel Angelo's Pisan soldiers; should know Brunelleschi's dome, and Michel's; should know Columbus's guess, and its grounds; should know Alfred's rough hints of English freedom; Roger Bacon's inventions; and, as far as possible, the history of the magnetic compass; should know the Homeric Controversy; should know the wonderful illumination thrown on all history in our own day by the scholars of the Sanscrit; should know the history of the Mahabharata; should know the history of Zoroaster, what, and who, and when was he (See Nicholas Grimvald's *Verses on Zoroaster*); should know how the decimal zero was invented.

In literature, there are many curiosities of the

[1] The relation of the hypothenuse of a right-angled triangle to the sides.

[2] That is, the story of how he chanced on the discovery of the law of specific gravity.

second or third order which should be known, as the *Imitation of Christ*, of À Kempis; or of Gerson; as the *Farce of Patelin;* as the *Song of Roland;* as the *Mariage de Figaro*, and the *Marseillaise* of Rouget; so, in England, the *Sonnets* of Shakspeare; the *Paradise of Dainty Devices;* specially, too, the *Morte d'Arthur*.

I must think that Carlyle's humour and demoniac fun, telling the story in a gale, bantering, scoffing, now at his hero, now at the enemy, always, too, at the learned reporters he has been consulting, will affect all good readers agreeably; for it is a perpetual flattery to the wise reader, a tête-à-tête with him, abusing the whole world as mad dunces;— all but you and I, reader!—

[The rest of the Journal KL is devoted to the poem "May-Day."]

(From DL)

June (?).

America shall introduce pure religion. Ethics are thought not to satisfy affection. But all the religion we have is the ethics of one or another holy person.[1] . . .

[1] The rest of this long passage is printed in "Sovereignty of Ethics" (*Lectures and Biographical Sketches*, pp. 212, 213).

July.

Our young soldiers. These dedicated men! who knew on what duty they went, and whose fathers and mothers said, "We gave him up when he enlisted." We see the dawn of a new era, worth to the world the lives of all this generation of American men, if they had been demanded.[1]

It is commonly said of the War of 1812 that it made the nation honourably known; it enlarged our politics, extinguished narrow sectional parties. But the states were young and unpeopled. The present war, on a prodigiously enlarged scale, has cost us how many valuable lives; but it has made many lives valuable that were not so before, through the start and expansion it has given. It has fired selfish old men to an incredible liberality, and young men to the last devotion. The journals say it has demoralized many rebel regiments, but also it has *moralized* many of our regiments, and not only so, but *moralized* cities and states. It added

[1] These two sentences are found in the short speech Mr. Emerson made at the Commemoration exercises on July 21, when Harvard University assembled and did honour to her surviving soldiers.

to every house and heart a vast enlargement. In every house and shop, an American map has been unrolled, and daily studied, and now that peace has come, every citizen finds himself a skilled student of the condition, means, and future, of this continent.

I think it a singular and marked result that the War has established a conviction in so many minds that the right will get done; has established a chronic hope for a chronic despair.

This victory the most decisive. This will stay put. It will show your enemies that what has now been so well done will be surely better and quicker done, if need be, again.

America. The irresistible convictions of men are sometimes as well expressed by braggart lips, or in jeers, that sound blasphemous; — and that word "manifest destiny," which is profanely used, signifies the sense all men have of the prodigious energy and opportunity lying idle here. The poor Prussian or Austrian or Italian, escaping hereto, discovers that he has been handcuffed and fettered and fast-tied all his lifetime, with monopolies and duties at every toll-gate on his little cart of corn, or wine, or straw, or on his cow, or ox, or donkey; and padlocked lips, padlocked mind, no country, no education, no vote, — but passports, police, monks, and foreign soldiers.

July 23.

Notes for Williamstown.[1] Returns the eternal topic, the praise of intellect. I gain my point, gain all points, whenever I can reach the young man with any statement which teaches him his own worth. Thus, if I can touch his imagination, I serve him; he will never forget it. If I can open to him for a moment the superiority of knowledge to wealth or physical power. Especially works on me at all times any statement of Realism, and, old as my habit is of thrumming on this string, I must continue to try it, till in a manlier or a divine hour, I can see the truth, and say it.

It occurred the other day, with a force not retained, that the advocate of the good cause finds a wealth of arguments and illustrations on his way. He stands for Truth, and Truth and Nature help him unexpectedly and irresistibly at every step. All the felicities of example, of imagery, of admirable poetry, old religion, new

[1] Mr. Emerson addressed the Society of the Adelphi at Williams College on July 31.

thought, the analogies of science, throng to him and strengthen his position. Nay, when we had to praise John Brown of Ossawatomie, I remember that what a multitude of fine verses of old poetry fitted him exactly, and appeared to have been prophetically written for the occasion.

One drug needs another drug to expel it, — if feasts, then wine; after wine, coffee; and after coffee, tobacco; if vanity, then pride; if anger, then war, sword, and musket. But temperance is strength, and essence is religion. To Be is to live with God.

Miss Peabody tells me that Jones Very one day said to her, "To the preëxistent Shakspeare wisdom was offered, but he declined it, and took only genius."

Enfant du peuple. That fair, large, sound, wholesome youth or maid, whom we pick out in a whole street full of passengers as a model of native strength, is not to be raised by rule in schools or gymnasia. It is the Vermont or New Hampshire farm, and a series of farmers labouring on mountain and moor, that produced this rare result. When a good head for ciphering, trade, and affairs is turned out, he drifts to the city counting-room, or perhaps to the law-school, and brings thither a constitution able to supply resources to all the demand made on him, and easily goes ahead of all competitors, has a firm will, cool head, and in the sequel, plants a family which becomes marked through two or three generations for force and beauty, until luxury corrupts them, as it had destroyed those whom they displaced.

August 13.

A disaster of this year has been the loss of six or seven valuable pear trees by the pear-blight. I think, in preceding years, single boughs have withered and died, but these have not attracted much notice; but now I cut off half of each tree with its coppery leaves and the mournful smell of the sick bark, and shall not save them so.

The difference between writers is that one counts forms, and the other counts powers. The gazetteer, in describing Boston, reckons up the schools, the churches, and the missionary societies; but the poet remembers the alcoves of the Athenæum, or the Bates Library; certain wise and mannered men, certain fair women, and the happy homes in which he saw them. The friend, — he is the power that abode with us; and the book, which made night better than day, — that may be well counted.

In the *Revue des Deux Mondes* I found a paper on the Future Life which suggested the thought that one abstains — I abstain, for example — from printing a chapter on the immortality of the soul, because, when I have come to the end of my statement, the hungry eyes that run through it will close disappointed; — *That is not here which we desire;* — and I shall be as much wronged by their halting conclusion as they feel themselves by my shortcomings.[1] . . .

"*Michel Angelo fut la conscience de l'Italie.*" — A. DUMESNIL.[2]

August 24.

Yesterday called on Forceythe Willson[3] at

[1] This sentence, less personally stated, is found in "Immortality" (*Letters and Social Aims*, pp. 345, 346).

[2] With this sentence for a text, follows a similar passage on the loneliness and unpopularity of great souls to that printed in "Progress of Culture" (*Letters and Social Aims*, pp. 216, 217).

[3] The strange and moving poem "The Old Sergeant," published in the West, attracted the attention of Mr. Lowell

Cambridge, went into the city with him, to the Athenæum and Union Club.

In how many people we feel the tyranny of their talent as the disposer of their activity. In Wendell Phillips, now the " *seul homme d'état* in America," I feel that his patriotism or his moral sentiment are not primarily the inspiration of his career, but this matchless talent of debate, of attack, of illustration, of statement, — this talent which was in him, and must be unfolded ; that drove him, in happy hours, under most fortunately determining auspices, into the lists, where kings were to be competitors, and nations spectators.

The conduct of intellect must respect nothing so much as preserving the sensibility.[1] . . .

Manners. There are things whose hour is always a little over or not quite come, as, for

and Mr. Emerson. After a fruitless search to learn of the man and his residence, Lowell found that he was his next-door neighbour on Mount Auburn Street. He proved to be a young man, and, though of commanding stature and physique, with a sensitive and kindly shyness reminding one of Hawthorne. His other notable war poem was "In State," printed in the *Atlantic.* Mr. Willson died in 1867.

[1] The passage is printed in *Natural History of Intellect* (p. 43).

example, the rule that you shall not go out to dine too well dressed; which means, that a certain slovenliness fits certain persons, but requires perfect *aplomb* and clear, sensible manners and conversation. Cold scholars cannot afford these liberties.

Under a commanding thought, all people become as graceful as if they were asleep. That knows how to lay the hands and the feet, as, long since, it knew how to make them.

Scotus Erigena, sitting at the table of Charles the Bald, when the King asked him how far a *Scot* was removed from a *sot*, answered with Irish wit, "By a table's breadth."

The old sharper said "his conscience was as good as ever it was; he had never used it any."

September 30.

Yesterday, at our Cattle-Show, I saw a man sitting in the Town Hall so like to the late President Lincoln, in the whole head, that I called the attention of Rev. Mr. Reynolds to him, who at once recognized the fact. It was Elijah Wood of this town. The view was in profile, and he had his hand against his face, covering it a little, and so probably increasing the likeness.

Nature is very rich in patterns, but cunningly; not so rich as she seems, and so repeats herself. Cousins of fourth and fifth degree have sometimes striking resemblance, and are therefore both repetitions of the common ancestor. Robert Winthrop, when young, strongly resembled the portrait, in the Historical Society's Rooms, of Governor Winthrop. Indeed, I suppose the cunning artist does not quite repeat her type until after four or five generations when all the rememberers are gone, and she can just duplicate every face of the fifth back generation, without risk of confusion or discovery. But I don't think even this interval will be safe now, Art having circumvented her with the photograph, which will force her to invent new varieties, or lose her reputation for fertility.

Mr. Benjamin Peter Hunt [1] said that a young man of good position in Philadelphia went to the war, and accepted the colonelcy of a colored regiment. On his return lately to Philadelphia,

[1] Mr. Emerson's pupil at the Chelmsford Academy, and valued friend later in Philadelphia.

all his acquaintances cut him. Judge Hoar said to me that he had long ago made up his mind that the cutting was to be from the other side; that this country belonged to the men of the most liberal persuasion.

Now in the time of the Fugitive Slave Law, when the best young men who had ranged themselves around Mr. Webster were already all of them in the interest of freedom, and threw themselves at once into opposition, Mr. Webster could no longer see one of them in the street; he glared on them, but knew them not; his resentments were implacable. What did they do? Did they sit down and bewail themselves? No; Sumner and his valiant young contemporaries set themselves to the task of making their views not only clear but prevailing. They proclaimed and defended them and inoculated with them the whole population, and drove Mr. Webster out of the world. All his mighty genius, which none had been so forward to acknowledge and magnify as they, availed him nothing; for they knew that the spirit of God and of humanity was with them, and he withered and died as by suicide. Calhoun had already gone, as Webster, by breaking his own head against the nature of things.

Potentiality. In estimating nations, 'tis well to remember the sovereign nature which often remains when the actual performance is inferior. Thus, in England, what destroying criticism we can read or make on its education, its literature, its science, its politics! And yet the force of that race may still any day turn out a better man than any other.

Theodore will buy a hat, a soft hat, or a beaver, for summer or winter. In his choice, he looks about him in the street, or he remembers that this friend or that reputable citizen wears one of a certain form or colour which is becoming. One good instance suffices him and guides to a certain extent his choice. But he does not consider that it is always character, personal force, of some kind in the individual he thinks of that makes the hat he wears so proper and perfect in its place.

Beware of the Minor Key. Despair, whining, low spirits, only betray the fact that the man has been living in the low circle of the senses and the understanding. These are exhaustible, and he has exhausted them, and now looks backward and bewails them.

In Stirling's *Secret of Hegel* —

"The intellectual power from words to things
Went sounding on a dim and perilous way."

Carlyle is to be defended plainly as a sincere man who is outraged by nothing so much as sentimentalism, or the simulating of reform, and love of Nature, and love of truth. Therefore he detests "Progress of Civility," "Enlightenment," "New Ideas," "Diffusion of Knowledge," and all shallow insincerities coming under such names.

November 5.

We hoped that in the peace, after such a war, a great expansion would follow in the mind of the Country; grand views in every direction, — true freedom in politics, in religion, in social science, in thought. But the energy of the nation seems to have expended itself in the war, and every interest is found as sectional and timorous as before. . . .

WILLIAMSTOWN, *November* 14.[1]

I saw to-night in the observatory, through Alvan Clark's telescope, the Dumb-Bell nebula

[1] The address which Mr. Emerson had made to the Society of the Adelphi at Williams College in July seems to have led

in the Fox and Goose Constellation; the four double stars in Lyra; the double stars of Castor; the two hundred stars of the Pleiades; the nebula in (Perseus?). Mr. Button, Professor Hopkins's assistant, was our star-showman, and Stanbrough and Hutton, who have been my committee of the "Adelphic Union," inviting me here, carried me thither. I have rarely been so much gratified.

Early in the afternoon Professor Bascom carried me in a gig to the top of the West Mountain, and showed me the admirable view down the valley in which this town and Adams lie, with Greylock and his attendant ranges towering in front. Then we rose to the crest, and looked down into Rensselaer County, New York, and the multitude of low hills that compose it,— this was the noted Anti-Rent country,— and beyond, in the horizon, the mountain range to the west.

---

to his being asked to lecture there in the autumn, probably before the Lyceum. But when he came, a spontaneous movement of the students, which pleased him, led to his staying there a day or two and reading other papers to them. One of these students, Mr. Charles J. Woodbury, talked much with Mr. Emerson and after his death published his memories and notes in a remarkable and charming little book, *Talks with Emerson* (The Baker and Taylor Co., New York).

Of all tools, an observatory is the most sublime. And these mountains give an inestimable worth to Williamstown and Massachusetts. But, for the mountains, I don't quite like the proximity of a college and its noisy students. To enjoy the hills as poet, I prefer simple farmers as neighbours.

The dim lanthorn which the astronomer used at first to find his object-glasses, etc., seemed to disturb and hinder him, preventing his seeing his heavens, and, though it was turned down lower and lower and lower, he was still impatient, and could not see until it was put out. When it had long been gone, and I had looked through the telescope a few times, the little garret at last grew positively lightsome, and the lamp would have been annoying to all of us.

What is so good in a college as an observatory? The sublime attaches to the door and to the first stair you ascend;— that this is the road to the stars. Every fixture and instrument in the building, every nail and pin, has a direct reference to the Milky Way, the fixed stars, and the nebulæ, and we leave Massachusetts and the Americas and history outside at the door, when we come in.

December 10.

Dr. Jackson shone in the talk on Thanksgiving Day,[1] explaining many things so successfully, — the possibility of the balloon by the aid of gun-cotton (one of whose principal merits, he asserted, was, that it does not foul the barrel or engine as powder does); the ocean telegraph, which he thinks far less practicable, and certainly less desirable to us than the Siberian. Then the fact that the patents of the telegraph companies do not really protect the monopoly, for what is patented they no longer use, as, the system of "marks on paper," of Morse's patent; for the telegraph is everywhere conducted without paper, being read by the ear. He thinks the United States Post-Office should take possession of the telegraph as part of the postal arrangement, pay a compensation to the companies, and give its use to the people at a cent a word, and so save the immense transportation of letters, by this

[1] Dr. Charles T. Jackson, Mrs. Emerson's brother, who came with his large family to the Thanksgiving gathering at Concord, was the life of the occasion. Mr. Emerson sat at one end of the long table and he at the other. Mrs. Ripley always counted on sitting beside him to learn from him of all the wonders of advancing science, and his ready wit and skill as a *raconteur* gave pleasure to all.

imponderable correspondence. He told the story of the Rumford Medal voted to Ericsson by the American Academy, and the money voted to Roper and Company for valuable improvements on Ericsson; from which last he anticipates very great practical benefit. The union, or double-union, engine:— I. T. Williams told me, the other day, that ninety-seven per cent of caloric was wasted in all attempts to use caloric for force in mechanics. Dr. Jackson says much is lost, but nothing like so much. He knew Amory's chimney which burns the smoke. Its advantage is demonstrable, yet it is not used, resembling thus Boyden's turbines, which pretend to save ninety-seven per cent of the power of a waterfall, and, being tested, were found to do what they claimed, yet are not used.

It seems to be a fixed rule in the planting and growth of settlements, that the men follow the waters. Thus, on each side of a height of land, the people will go to the market that is downstream.

I. T. Williams told me that the last time he saw Albert H. Tracy, he told him that when he and Cass were in Congress they became very intimate, and spent their time in conversation on the Immortality of the Soul,[1] and other intellectual questions, and cared for little else. When he left Congress, they parted, and though Mr. Cass passed through Buffalo twice, he did not come near him, and he never saw him again until twenty-five years afterward. They saw each other through open doors at a distance, in a great party at the President's House in Washington. Slowly they advanced towards each other as they could, and at last met, said nothing, but shook hands long and cordially. At last Cass said, "Any light, Tracy?" "None," answered Tracy; and then said, "Any light, Cass?" "None," replied he. They looked in each other's eyes, gave one shake more each to the hand he held, and thus parted for the last time.

When I was a senior in college, I think, Samuel Barrett, whom I had known in Concord, was about to be ordained in the Chambers Street Church and I called upon him in his room in college — I think he must have been a proctor. We talked about the vices and calamities of the time, — I don't recall what the grim

[1] This story is given here, although printed in "Immortality," because of the added interest given by the names.

shadows were, or how we came on them, — but when I rose to go, and asked him what was the relief and cure of all this, he replied with cheerful ardour, "Nothing but Unitarianism." From my remembrance of how this answer struck me, I am sure that this antidote must have looked as thin and poor and pale to me then, as now.

Carlyle. I have neglected badly Carlyle, who is so steadily good to me. Like a Catholic in Boston, he has put himself by his violent anti-Americanism in false position, and it is not quite easy to deal with him. But his merits are overpowering, and when I read *Friedrich*, I forget all else. His treatment of his subject is ever so masterly, so original, so self-respecting, so defiant, allowing himself all manner of liberties and confidences with his hero, as if he were his hero's father or benefactor; that he is proud of him, and yet checks and chides, and sometimes puts him in the corner, when he is not a good boy; that, amid all his sneering and contempt for all other historians, and biographers, and princes, and peoples, the reader yet feels himself complimented by the confidences with which he is honoured by this free-tongued, dangerous companion, who discloses to him all his secret opinions, all his variety of moods, and varying estimates of his hero and everybody else. He is as dangerous as a madman. Nobody knows what he will say next, or whom he will strike. Prudent people keep out of his way. If genius were cheap, we should do without Carlyle; but, in the existing population, he cannot be spared.

(From XO)

Reaction. Its power is as the need. Systole and diastole of the heart, ebb and flow of tide, centripetal and centrifugal, horse down-hill and up-hill; so the assailant makes the strength of the defence. Therefore, we ought to pray, Give us a good enemy, — like the Southerner who exasperates the too good-natured North into resistance; or like President Johnson, who outrages his opponents and mortifies his friends.

Illusion. "We know all things as in a dream, and are again ignorant of them according to vigilant perception." — PLATO, in *Sophist*.

The first illusion that is put upon us in the world is the amusing miscellany of colours, forms, and properties. Our education is through surfaces and particulars. Nature masks under ostentatious sub-divisions and manifold particulars the poverty of her elements, and the rigid economy of her rules. And, as infants are occupied wholly with surface-differences, so multitudes of adults remain in the infant or animal estate, and never see or know more.

Moral sentiment. As the flower precedes the fruit, and the bud the flower, so, long before the opinion, comes the instinct that a particular act is unfriendly, unsuitable, wrong. We are wonderfully protected.

(From IT)

Memory. If we pierce to the origin of knowledge, and explore the meaning of memory, we might find it some strange mutilated roll of celestial papyrus, on which only a disjointed jumble of universal traditions, of heavenly scriptures, of angelic biographies, were long ago written, — relics of a foreworld.

The Past will not sleep. It works still. With every new fact a ray of light shoots up from the long-buried years.

Authors or Books quoted or referred to in Journal for 1865

Vedas; *Vishnu Purana*; Zertusht (Zoroaster); Confucius;

Pythagoras; Zeno; Archimedes;

Persius; Martial; Marcus Aurelius; St. Augustine; Mahomet; Scotus Erigena; King Alfred;

Chanson de Roland; *Morte d'Arthur*; St. Bernard; St. Francis of Assisi;

Chaucer; Thomas à Kempis, *Imitation of Christ*; Jean de Gerson, *De Consolatione Theologiæ*;

Savonarola; Michel Angelo; Vittoria Colonna; Ochino; Reginald Pole;

Calderon; Clarendon; De Retz; Thomas Stanley, *History of Philosophy*; Locke; Spinoza; Boileau; Newton;

Chesterfield; Duclos; Vauvenargues; Beaumarchais, *Le Mariage de Figaro*; Goethe, *Correspondence with the Grand Duke of Weimar*; Lafayette; Rouget de l'Isle, *Marseillaise*; Friedrich Augustus Wolf and others, *Homeric Controversy*; Von Gentz; John Dalton; Cuvier; Novalis (von Hardenberg); Malte Brun;

Lewis Cass; Daniel Webster; Manzoni; Lamartine; Michelet, *Renaissance*; Carlyle, *Frederick the Great*; Alcott;

Sampson Reed; Victor Hugo; Sainte-Beuve, *Portraits littéraires*; Dr. Charles T. Jackson; Abraham Lincoln; Benjamin Peirce; Charles Sumner; Wendell Phillips; Henry James, *Substance and Shadow*; Dr. J. J. Garth Wilkinson; Henry Wilson; Henry Ward Beecher; Jones Very;

Matthew Arnold; Thomas W. Parsons, Translation of *Dante*; James Hutchison Stirling, *The Secret of Hegel*; A. Dumesnil; Frank Bird; Ernest Renan; Goldwin Smith; Lanfrey; Forceythe Willson.

JOURNAL

TASKS. SENSE. MANNERS

CRITICISM. LOVE

LAWS OF MIND

POLARITY. READING'S TEMPTA-
TION

WAR CLARIFIES

HEGEL

AMERICA'S MORAL BASIS

THE CAMP ON MONADNOC

ATLANTIC CABLE

VISIT TO AGASSIZ

HINDOO THEOLOGY

UNIVERSE OF THOUGHT

ANALYZED SOUND

JOURNAL LVII
1866

(From Journals DL, LN, and ML)

[EARLY in January Mr. Emerson set forth for his lecturing tour in the West. He no longer had the difficult task of arranging this, which was done for him, by some agency,— a great relief and advantage. The conditions of travel were now more comfortable, yet the work was arduous. He was away from home till February 19, lecturing in New York, Pennsylvania, Ohio, Indiana, Illinois, Michigan, and Wisconsin. However, he almost invariably returned rather refreshed and stimulated by his winter's experiences in the advancing West.]

Vox immissa volat; litera scripta manet.[1]

(From DL)

January 5, 1866.

I thought, last night, as so often before, that when one has a task before him in which liter-

[1] The uttered word flies away, the written character abides.

ary work becomes *business*, — undertaken, that is, for money, — any hearing of poetry or any intellectual suggestion (as e. g. out of J. Hutchison Stirling's book lately) brings instant penitence, and the thoughts revert to the Muse, and, under this high invitation, we think we will throw up our undertaking, and attempt once more this purer, loftier service. But if we obey this suggestion, the beaming goddess presently hides her face in clouds again. We have not learned the law of the mind, cannot control and bring at will or domesticate the high states of contemplation and continuous thought. "Neither by sea nor by land canst thou find the way to the Hyperboreans." Neither by idle wishing, nor by rule of three or of thumb. Yet I find a mitigation or solace of the alternative which I accept (of the paid lectures, for instance) by providing always a good book for my journey, as Horace, or Martial, or the *Secret of Hegel*, some book which lifts quite out of prosaic surroundings, and from which you draw some lasting knowledge.

In the *Funeral* of Steele, Sable, the Undertaker, reproaches the too cheerful mute, "Did I not give you ten, then fifteen and twenty shillings a week to be sorrowful? And the more I give you, I think the gladder you are."

February.

Common sense; — Lord Mansfield or any great lawyer an example of it, though they call it *law*. And Beau Brummel even surprised other fops by having this basis: as, when he was asked what scents he used for his linen, replied, "Country air and country washing."

Love. The maiden only need consider that she passes securely through ten or a dozen appearances, as in the street, or at an evening party. The lover will do all the rest; since he is ever working up, enriching, enhancing her image and attributes, with the smallest aid from her; so that thus there are two working on her part, and none on his.

The power of manners is a principal agent in human affairs. The rich and elegant and the strong-willed not so much talk down as look down and silence the well-disposed middle class. 'T is fine that the scholar or the red republican defies these people, or writes against them: he cannot get them out of his thoughts. When he meets them in the street, he cannot deny them his bow, and when he meets them in clubs or in drawing-rooms, he prizes their attentions, and easily leaves his own set on any advances from theirs. In England Sir Robert Peel and Thackeray are only two out of manifold examples. I myself always fall an easy prey to superior manners. I remember how admirable in my youth were to me the Southern boys. Andrew Johnson, wont to look up to the planters as a superior race, cannot resist their condescensions and flatteries, and, though he could not be frightened by them, falls an easy victim to their caresses. This result was explicitly foretold by Moncure D. Conway and Frederick Douglass.

The remedy of this political mischief should be to train a youth in poverty to a nobler style of manners than any palace can show him, by Plato and Plutarch, by the Cid, and Sidney, and George Herbert, and Chaucer.

Quick people touch and go, whilst heavy people insist on pounding. 'T is in vain to try to choke them off and change the conversation to avoid the slaughter-house details. Straightway they begin at the beginning, and thrice they slay the slain; society shall be distressing, and there's an end of it.

"*Ce que dit le ruisseau ; Toujours, toujours, partout, dans tout, pour tout, toujours.*"
GEORGE SAND.

(From ML)

Criticism. Best masters for the young writer and speaker are the fault-finding brothers and sisters at home, who will not spare him, but will pick and cavil, and tell the odious truth.

Education. He who betaketh him to a good tree hath good shade; for the Cid knew how to make a good knight, as a good groom knows how to make a good horse.

Talk of Columbus or Newton. I tell you the babe just born in the hovel yonder is the beginning of a revolution as great as theirs.

I am far from thinking it late. I do not despond at all whilst I hear the verdicts of European juries against us. Renan says so and so. That does not hurt us at all. Arnold says thus or thus: neither does that touch us. I think it safer to be so blamed, than praised. Listen to every censure in good part. It does not hit the quick since we do not wince. And if you do wince, that is best of all. Set yourself instantly to mend the fault, and thank the critic as your benefactor. And Ruskin has several rude and some ignorant things to say.

University. But be sure that scholars are secured, that the scholar is not quite left out; that the Imagination is cared for and cherished; that the money-spirit does not turn him out; that Enthusiasm is not repressed; and Professor Granny does not absorb all. Teach him Shakspeare. Teach him Plato; and see that real examiners and awards are before you.

In the college, 'tis complained, money and the vulgar respectability have the same ascendant as in the city. What remedy? There is but one, namely, the arrival of genius, which instantly takes the lead, and makes the fashion at Cambridge.

Charles XII said to Swedenborg, of the Mathematics, "He who knew nothing of this science did not deserve to be considered a rational man"; — "a sentiment," adds Swedenborg, "worthy of a king."

Koran. "Paradise, whose breadth equalleth the Heavens and the earth."

"Hell is a circle about the unbelieving."

"Only the law of God it is which has no antecedent, and in which no change can be discovered."

"Sleeping are men, and when they die, they wake."

"The saint's best blush in Heaven is from his heart-blood's red."

Always falls on his feet. When one of Napoleon's favorite schemes missed, he had the faculty of taking up his genius (*esprit*), as he said, and of carrying it somewhere else.

SAINTE-BEUVE.

Ever since Pericles, there has not been a young lover in all civil nations but has found his affection met and celebrated by the beautiful shining of the Evening Star. 'T is everywhere the symbol of warm and tender joy. But does aught of that glorious and penetrating power belong to the planet itself, as known to the astronomer? I must read [how] Herschel, or Leverrier, or whoever has best computed its elements describes it,— but I shall find it chaotic and uninhabitable for a human race. The poetic and moral enchantment is wholly subjective, we know.

[Beginning in the middle of April, Mr. Emerson was to give in Boston a series of lectures — *Philosophy of the People:* I. Seven Metres of Intellect; II. Instinct, Perception, Talent; III. Genius, Imagination, Taste; IV. Laws of Mind; V. Conduct of Intellect; VI. Relation of the Intellect to Morals. The extracts from ML (Moral Law) are mostly notes for these. A summary of this course may be found in the Appendix to Cabot's *Memoir*, vol. ii, pp. 791-796.]

March.

Laws of the mind. I have first to keep the promise of the last lecture, by treating *Common Sense*, which, one would say, means the shortest line between two points, — how to come at a practical end, — and requires indispensably an act of *your* mind and not a quotation. But things are rarely seen by direct light, but only by the reflex light of others' opinion and culture, and a new opinion drawn from the thing itself is almost as astonishing as if, in the dark, the faces of our friends should become luminous, and show by inward light.

LAWS OF MIND

1. Identity. One law consumes all diversity.
2. Flowing or Transition, endless ascension.
3. Individualism or Bias. I want the world, but on my terms.
4. Subjectiveness. All is as I am.
5. Detachment. Cell makes cell, and animal animal, and thought opens into thought.

Dr. Johnson said: "To temperance every day is bright, and every hour propitious to diligence."

"A man can do anything, if he will doggedly set himself at work to it," etc.

Intellect. "I have wandered," says Aunt Mary, "into Brown's idea of knowing nothing of mind but thoughts."

The Celestial Mind incapable of offence, of haste, of care, of inhospitality, of peeping, of memory, incapable of embarrassment, of discourtesy, treating all with a sovereign equality.

Aunt Mary wrote: "Religion, that home of genius, will strengthen the mind as it does the character."

Immortality. "As a proof of endless being we may rank that novelty which perpetually attends life. On the borders of the grave the hoary sage looks forward with an invariable elasticity of mind or hope. After millions of years, when on the verge of a new existence, (for such is the nature of created existences to be forever new to life,") etc. Aunt Mary's letters.

Van Helmont says, "The soul understands in peace and rest, and not in doubting." 'T is the faith of Swedenborg and of Pascal, that piety is an essential condition of science.

I should like to know what power to believe in immortality any one could possess who had not already a revelation of it in the phenomena of intellect.

(From LN)

" When the wind bloweth strong, hoist thy sail to the top,
    'T is joyous in storm not to flinch.
  Keep her full! keep her full! none but cowards strike sail,
    Sooner founder than take in an inch."
                    CODE OF THE VIKINGS.

March 26.

I often think of uses of an Academy, though they did not rapidly appear when Sumner proposed his bill; and perhaps if it was national, and must meet in Washington, or Philadelphia, — even New York would be a far-away place for me, — such benefits as I crave, it could not serve. But to-day I should like to confide to a proper committee to report on what are called the "Sentences of Zoroaster," or the "Chaldaic Oracles"; to examine and report on those extraordinary fragments, — so wise, deep, — some of them poetic, — and such riddles, or so frivolous, others, — and pronounce shortly, but advisedly, what is their true history.

Zoroaster has a line saying that "violent deaths are friendliest to the health of the soul." Attribute that among his good fortunes to Lincoln. And in the same connection remember the death of Pindar.

Can identity be claimed for a being whose life is so often vicarious or belonging to an age or generation? He is fallen in another; he rises in another.

Polarity. Every nature has its own. It was found, that, if iron ranged itself north and south, nickel or other substance ranged itself east and west; and Faraday expected to find that each chemic element might yet be found to have its own determination or pole; and every soul has a bias or polarity of its own, and each new. Every one a magnet with a new north.

Not Niebuhr only lost his power of divination, but every poet has on the hills counted the Pleiads, and mourned his lost star. Ah, the decays of memory, of fancy, of the saliency of thought! Who would not rather have a perfect remembrance of all he thought and felt in a certain high week, than to read any book that has been published?

When I read a good book, say, one which opens a literary question, I wish that life were 3000 years long. Who would not launch into this Egyptian history, as opened by Wilkinson, Champollion, Bunsen, but for the *memento mori* which he reads on all sides? Who is not provoked by the temptation of the Sanscrit literature? And, as I wrote above, the Chaldaic Oracles tempt me.[1] But so also does Algebra,

---

1 Many of these, with other extracts from the Oriental Scriptures, were printed by Mr. Emerson in the *Dial*. Their age and authenticity as teachings of Zoroaster (Zertusht) are doubtful.

and astronomy, and chemistry, and geology, and botany. Perhaps, then, we must increase the appropriation, and write 30,000 years. And, if these years have correspondent effect with the sixty years we have experienced, some earnest scholar will have to amend by striking out the word "years" and inserting "centuries."

It is plain that the War has made many things public that were once quite too private. A man searches his mind for thoughts, and finds only the old commonplaces; but, at some moment, on the old topic of the days, politics, he makes a distinction he had not made; he discerns a little inlet not seen before. Where was a wall is now a door. The mind goes in and out, and variously states in prose or poetry its new experience. It points it out to one and another, who, of course, deny the alleged discovery. But repeated experiments and affirmations make it visible soon to others. The point of interest is here, that these gates once opened never swing back. The observers may come at their leisure, and do at last satisfy themselves of the fact. The thought, the doctrine, the right, hitherto not affirmed, is published in set propositions, in conversation of scholars, and at last in the very choruses of songs.

The young hear it, and, as they have never fought it, never known otherwise, they accept it, vote for it at the polls, embody it in the laws. And this perception, thus satisfied, reacts on the senses to clarify them, so that it becomes more indisputable. Thus it is no matter what the opposition may be of presidents or kings or majorities, but what the truth is as seen by one mind.

I copy a scrap copy of my letter sent to Mrs. C. T., when in Europe (perhaps never sent), which I pick up to-day: —

"I have let go the unreturning opportunity which your visit to Germany gave me to acquaint you with Gisela Von Arnim, and Herman Grimm her husband, and Joachim the violinist, — and I who prize myself only on my endurance, that I am as good as new when the others are gone, — I to be slow, derelict, and dumb to you, in all your absence! I shall regret this as long as I live. How palsy creeps over us with gossamer first, and ropes afterwards! And you have the prisoner when you have once put your eye on him, as securely as after the bolts are drawn. — How strange that Charles Newcomb, whose secret you and I alone have, should come to write novels. Holmes's genius is all that is new, — nor that to you. The worst is that we can do without it. Grand behavior is better, if it rest on the axis of the world."

Hegel [1] seems to say, Look, I have sat long gazing at the all but imperceptible transitions of thought to thought, until I have seen with eyes the true boundary. I know what is this, and that. I know it, and have recorded it. It can never be seen but by a patience like mine added to a perception like mine. I know the subtile boundary, as surely as the mineralogist Haüy knows the normal lines of his crystal, and where the cleavage must begin. I know that all observation will justify me, and to the future metaphysician I say, that he may measure the power of his perception by the degree of his accord with mine. This is the twilight of the gods, predicted in the Scandinavian mythology.

[1] Mr. Emerson was reading *The Secret of Hegel,* sent him by J. Hutchison Stirling (of Leith, Scotland), a book in which he took much interest.

Hegel's definition of liberty was, *the spirit's realization of itself.*

Hafiz can only show a playing with magnitudes, but without ulterior aim.

Hafiz fears nothing; he sees too far; he sees throughout.

American Politics. I have the belief that of all things the work of America is to make the advanced intelligence of mankind in the sufficiency of morals practical; since there is on every side a breaking up of the faith in the old traditions of religion, and, of necessity, a return to the omnipotence of the moral sentiment, that in America this conviction is to be embodied in the laws, in the jurisprudence, in international law, in political economy. The lawyers have always some glaring exceptions to their statements of public equity, some reserve of sovereignty, tantamount to the Rob Roy rule that might makes right. America should affirm and establish that in no instance should the guns go in advance of the perfect right. You shall not make *coups d'état*, and afterwards explain and pay, but shall proceed like William Penn, or whatever other Christian or humane person who treats with the Indian or foreigner on principles of honest trade and mutual advantage. Let us wait a thousand years for the Sandwich Islands before we seize them by violence.

Fame is ever righting itself. In the jangle of criticism, Goethe is that which the intelligent hermit supposes him to be, and can neither be talked up nor down.

Beauty in Life. It is peremptory for good living in houses in a cultivated age, that the beautiful should never be out of thought. It is not more important that you should provide bread for the table, than that it should be put there and used in a comely manner. You have often a right to be angry with servants, but you must carry your anger and chide without offence to beauty. Else, you have quarreled with yourself as well as with them.

June 14.

But the surprise and dazzle of beauty is such, that I thought to-day, that if beauty were the rule, instead of the exception, men would give up business.

(From a loose sheet)

Thus lofty, thus universal is the principle which we call Grace in nature; not lodged in certain lines or curves, not contained in colour-boxes, or in rare and costly materials, but in every stroke in which it is found, presenting a kind of miniature of the world. Herein, in its central character, we see our concern in it. The perception of Beauty is an office of the Reason — and therefore all men have property in it.

(From LN)

Deity. In the speed of conversation L. said, "Poor God did all he could to make them so, but they steadily undid," etc. It recurs now as an example of the organic generalization. The speaker casts the apparent or hypothetical order of things into a word and names it God; but, in the instant, the mind makes the distinction or perceives the eternal and ever-present of the Perfect, still whole and divine before him, and God quits the name of *God*, and fills the universe as he did the moment before.

Bias. Seven men went through a field, one after another. One was a farmer, he saw only the grass; the next was an astronomer, he saw the horizon and the stars; the physician noticed the standing water and suspected miasma;

he was followed by a soldier, who glanced over the ground, found it easy to hold, and saw in a moment how the troops could be disposed; then came the geologist, who noticed the boulders and the sandy loam; after him came the real-estate broker, who bethought him how the line of the house-lots should run, where would be the drive-way, and the stables. The poet admired the shadows cast by some trees, and still more the music of some thrushes and a meadow lark.

[Some extracts attributed to Taliessin, the Welsh bard, precede this.]

I suspect Walt Whitman had been reading these Welsh remains when he wrote his "Leaves of Grass." Thus Taliessin sings: —

"I am water, I am a wren;
  I am a workman, I am a star;
  I am a serpent;
  I am a cell, I am a chink;
  I am a depositary of song, I am a learned person."

Single speech Poets. Hogg only wrote "Kilmeny"; Sampson Reed, "Genius"; Forceythe Willson, "The Old Sergeant" ballad; Matthew Arnold, "Thyrsis"; S. Ferguson, "Song of the Anchor"; Wolfe, "Burial of Sir John Moore"; Rouget de l'Isle, "Marseillaise"; Halleck, "Marco Bozzaris"; Messenger, "Old wine, old books"; Henry Taylor, "Philip Van Artevelde"; Daniel Webster, "Speech against Hayne"; Lord Caernarvon, "Speech on Lord Danby's Impeachment . . ."; Henry Kirke White, "Herb Rosemary"; Pollok, "Oceana"; W. C. Bryant, "Waterfowl"; George Borrow, single verse in "Svend Vonved"; Raleigh, (if "Soul's Errand" is taken, nothing is left but) "Pilgrimage."

Read Aunt Mary's MSS. yesterday — many pages. They keep for me the old attraction; though, when I sometimes have tried passages on a stranger, I find something of fairy gold; — they need too much commentary, and are not as incisive as on me. They make the best example I have known of the power of the religion of the Puritans in full energy, until fifty years ago, in New England. The central theme of these endless diaries is her relation to the Divine Being; the absolute submission of her will, with the sole proviso, that she may know it is the direct agency of God (and not of cold laws of contingency, etc.), which bereaves and humiliates her. But the religion of the diary, as of the class it represented, is biographical; it is the culture, the poetry, the mythology, in which they personally believed themselves dignified, inspired, judged, and dealt with, in the present and in the future. And it certainly gives to life an earnestness, and to Nature a sentiment, which lacking, our later generation appears frivolous.

[Mr. Emerson's son and daughter Ellen, one of their cousins, and some friends were camping on the rocky plateau of Monadnoc for a week. Miss Keyes, daughter of Hon. John S. Keyes, of Concord, later became Mrs. Edward W. Emerson.]

July 2.

I went with Annie Keyes and Mr. Channing on Wednesday, 27th June, to Troy, N. H., thence to the Mountain House in wagon, and, with Edward and Tom Ward[1] who had come down to meet us, climbed the mountain. The party already encamped were Moorfield Storey, Ward, and Edward, for the men; and Una Hawthorne, Lizzie Simmons, and Ellen E. for the maidens. They lived on the plateau just

[1] Thomas Wren Ward, son of Mr. Emerson's friend, Samuel Gray Ward.

below the summit, and were just constructing their one tent by spreading and tying India-rubber blankets over a frame of spruce poles large enough to hold the four ladies with sleeping space, and to cover the knapsacks. The men must find shelter, if need is, under the rocks. The mountain at once justified the party and their enthusiasm. It was romance enough to be there, and behold the panorama, and learn one by one all the beautiful novelties. The country below is a vast champaign, — half cleared, half forest, — with forty ponds in sight, studded with villages and farmhouses, and, all around the horizon, closed with mountain ranges. The eye easily traces the valley followed by the Cheshire Railroad, and just beyond it the valley of the Connecticut River, then the Green Mountain chain: in the north, the White Hills can be seen; and, on the east, the low mountains of Watatic and Wachusett. We had hardly wonted our eyes to the new Olympus, when the signs of a near storm set all the scattered party on the alert. The tent was to be finished and covered, and the knapsacks piled in it. The wanderers began to appear on the heights, and to descend, and much work in camp was done in brief time. I looked about for a shelter in the rocks, and not till the rain began to fall, crept into it. I called to Channing, and afterwards to Tom Ward, who came, and we sat substantially dry, if the seat was a little cold, and the wall a little dripping, and pretty soon, a large brook roared between the rocks, a little lower than our feet hung. Meantime, the thunder shook the mountain, and much of the time was continuous cannonade.

The storm refused to break up. One and another adventurer rushed out to see the signs, and especially the sudden torrents, little Niagaras, that were pouring over the upper ledges, and descending upon our plateau. But everybody was getting uncomfortably wet, the prospect was not good for the night, and, in spite of all remonstrance on the part of the young ladies, I insisted that they must go down with me to the " Mountain House," for the night. All the four girls at last were ready, and descended with Storey and me, — thus leaving the tent free to be occupied by Mr. Channing, Tom Ward, and Edward. The storm held on most of the night, but we were slowly drying and warming in the comfortable inn.

Next day, the weather slowly changed, and we climbed again the hill, and were repaid for all mishaps by the glory of the afternoon and evening. Edward went up with me to the summit, up all sorts of Giant stairs, and showed the long spur with many descending peaks on the Dublin side. The rock-work is interesting and grand;—the clean cleavage, the wonderful slabs, the quartz dikes, the rock torrents in some parts, the uniform presence on the upper surface of the glacial lines or scratches, all in one self-same direction. Then every glance below apprises you how you are projected out into stellar space, as a sailor on a ship's bowsprit out into the sea. We look down here on a hundred farms and farmhouses, but never see horse or man. For our eyes the country is depopulated. Around us the arctic sparrow, *Fringilla nivalis*, flies and peeps, the ground-robin also; but you can hear the distant song of the wood-thrushes ascending from the green belts below. I found the picture charming, and more than remunerative. Later, from the plateau, at sunset, I saw the great shadow of Monadnoc lengthen over the vast plain, until it touched the horizon. The earth and sky filled themselves with all ornaments, — haloes, rainbows, and little pendulums of cloud would hang down till they touched the top of a hill, giving it the appearance of a smoking volcano. The wind was north, the evening cold, but the camp-fire kept the party comfortable, whilst Storey, with Edward for chorus, sang a multitude of songs to their great delectation. The night was forbiddingly cold, — the tent kept the girls in vital heat, but the youths could hardly keep their blood in circulation, the rather, that they had spared too many of their blankets to the girls and to the old men. Themselves had nothing for it but to rise and cut wood and bring it to the fire, which Mr. Channing watched and fed; and this service of fetching wood was done by Tom Ward once to his great peril during the night. In pitching a formless stump over into the ravine, he fell, and in trying to clear himself from the stump now behind him, flying and falling, got a bad contusion.

[At Commencement, Mr. Emerson received the degree of Doctor of Laws from Harvard University.]

I see with joy the Irish emigrants landing at Boston, at New York, and say to myself, There they go — to school.

Hazlitt, Lovelace's editor, says, "Wither's song, 'Shall I, wasting in despair,' is certainly superior to the 'Song to Althea.'" — I will instantly seek and read it.

I have read it, and find that of Lovelace much the best.

There is this to be said in favor of drinking, that it takes the drunkard first out of society, then out of the world. The Turk is for the late centuries "the sick man," and sick, it is said, from his use of tobacco, which the great Turks of Mahomet's period did not know.

The scatterbrain, Tobacco. Yet a man of no conversation should smoke.

In classes of men, what a figure is Charles Lamb! so much wit lodged in such a saccharine temperament.

What a saint is Milton! How grateful we are to the man of the world who obeys the *morale*, as in humility, and in the obligation to serve mankind. True genius always has these inspirations.

Humanity always equal to itself; the religious understand each other under all mythologies, and say the same thing. Homer and Æschylus in all the rubbish of fables speak out clearly ever and anon the noble sentiments of all ages.

CALVINISM. THE CABLE

Calvinism was as injurious to the justice as Greek myths were to the purity of the gods. Yet noble souls carried themselves nobly, and drew what treasures of character from that grim system.

We want heat to execute our plans.[1] . . . What said Bettine to Goethe? "Go to ruin with your sentiments! 'T is the senses alone that work in art, as in love, and nobody knows this better than you."

I find it a great and fatal difference whether I court the muse, or the muse courts me: That is the ugly disparity between age and youth.

July 30.

This morn came again the exhilarating news of the landing of the Atlantic telegraph cable at Heart's Content, Newfoundland, and we repeat the old wonder and delight we found on the Adirondac, in August, 1858.[2] We have grown more skilful, it seems, in electric machinery, and may confide better in a lasting success. Our political condition is better, and, though dashed

---

[1] The rest of the paragraph is found in "Inspiration" (*Letters and Social Aims*, p. 276).

[2] See "The Adirondacs," in *Poems* (pp. 190-193).

by the treachery of our American President, can hardly go backward to slavery and civil war. Besides, the suggestion of an event so exceptional and astounding in the history of human arts is, that this instant and pitiless publicity now to be given to every public act must force on the actors a new sensibility to the opinion of mankind, and restrain folly and meanness.

Old light (polarized) is much better than new. The indirect and reflex ray sometimes better than the direct. Quotation has its utilities. On a lower stage, see the history of quotation. Leave the great wheat-countries, the Egypts, and Mississippi Valleys, and follow the harvest into the bakers' shops and pedlers' carts.

When the Quakers settled in France (in the early part of the French Revolution) asked of the National Assembly to be released from military duty, Mirabeau (President) replied, "The Assembly will in its wisdom consider your requests, but, whenever I meet a Quaker, I shall say, 'My brother, if thou hast a right to be free, thou hast a right to prevent any one from making thee a slave: as thou lovest thy fellow-creature, suffer not a tyrant to destroy him: it would be killing him thyself.'"

"The hero of the Daityas, armed with his club, rushed against Nrisimha. But, like the insect which falls in the fire, the Asura disappeared, absorbed by the splendor of his enemy."
— *Bhagavat Purana.*

What fanatics in politics we are! There are far more important things than free suffrage; namely, a pure will, pure and illumined.

August 12.

Last night, in conversation with the New York ladies, Alcott appeared to great advantage, and I saw again, as often before, his singular superiority. As pure intellect, I have never seen his equal. The people with whom he talks do not even understand him. They interrupt him with clamorous dissent, or what they think verbal endorsement of what they fancy he may have been saying, or with, "Do you know Mr. Alcott, I think thus and so," — some whim or sentimentalism; and do not know that they have interrupted his large and progressive statement, do not know that all they have in their baby brains is spotty and incoherent, that all that he sees and says is like astronomy, lying there real and vast, and every part and fact in eternal connection with the whole, and that they ought to sit in silent gratitude, eager only to hear more, to hear the whole, and not interrupt him with their prattle. It is because his sight is so clear, commanding the whole ground, and he perfectly gifted to state adequately what he sees, that he does not lose his temper, when his glib interlocutors bore him with their dead texts and phrases. Another, who sees in flashes, or only here and there a land-mark, has the like confidence in his own truth, and in the infinitude of the soul, but none in his competence to show it to the bores; and if they tease him, he is silent.

Power is not pettish, but want of power is. Alcott's activity of mind is shown in the perpetual invention and felicity of his language; the constitutionality of his thought, apparent in the fact that last night's discourse only brought out with new conviction the old fundamental thoughts which he had when I first knew him.

The moral benefit of such a mind cannot be told. The world fades: men, reputations, politics shrivel: the interests, power, future of the soul beam a new dayspring. Faith becomes sight.

Maya (Illusion) of the Hindoos. Rudra says, "O thou, who, always unalterable, createst, conservest, and destroyest this universe, by the aid of Maya, that energy in numerous forms which, powerless when it reposes in thy bosom, makes believe that it is distinct from thee, and gives to the world an apparent reality." — *Bhagavat Purana*, vol. ii, p. 127.

Maya. The assistants said: "In the road of birth, where is no shelter; — which great miseries make difficult; where the god of death presents himself as a frightful reptile; where they have before their eyes the mirage of objects; where the opposite affections (of pleasure and pain) are precipices; where they fear the wicked as ferocious beasts; where grief is like a fire in the forest; — how should a caravan of ignorant beings, loaded with the heavy burden of the body and the soul, tormented by desire, — how, O God who givest asylum, should it ever arrive at thy feet?"

The Veda says: "The world is born of Maya."

"*Brahma qui n'a pas de qualités.*"

"*Cet être exempt d'attributs et de personnalité, qui est à la fois ce qui existe et ce qui n'existe pas*" (*pour nos organes*). — Vol. ii, p. 111.

There is a maxim which those who know the Veda repeat in all places; this:—"An action done in conformity to the law, becomes invisible, and does not reappear." Equivalent this to Novalis's saying: "Of the Wrong we are always conscious: of the Right never."

William Forbes writes wisely, "Difficulties exist to be surmounted,"—a right heroic creed.[1]

Gifts. Flowers grow in the garden to be given away. Everybody feels that they appeal to finer senses than his own, and looks wistfully around in hope that possibly this friend or that may be nobler furnished than he to see and read them,

[1] Mr. Emerson was already aware that his strength began to fail. His poem "Terminus," written in the previous year, was an admission of this. His book contracts were not properly remunerative. He saw that he could not continue his distant lecturing, the chief source of income, and his wife's invested property was unremunerative, through the dishonesty of her agent. All this his good son-in-law had discovered, and strove to win his permission to take such action as would ensure his receiving his real dues. He found Mr. Emerson reluctant because of his modesty and the difficulties with which the way seemed beset. But Colonel Forbes's affectionate zeal, clear head and energy won. He saved Mrs. Emerson's property just in time, and much increased Mr. Emerson's receipts from his books.

COLONEL WILLIAM HATHAWAY FORBES

or at least a better naturalist. Especially they are sent to ceremonies and assemblies sacred or festal or funereal, because, on occasions of passion and sentiment, there may be higher appreciation of these delicate wonders.

August 31.

Visited Agassiz by invitation, with Lidian and Ellen, and spent the day at his house and on the Nahant rocks. He is a man to be thankful for, always cordial, full of facts, with unsleeping observation, and perfectly communicative. In Brazil he saw on a half-mile square 117 different kinds of excellent timber,— and not a saw-mill in Brazil. A country thirsting for Yankees to open and use its wealth. In Brazil is no bread: manioca in pellets the substitute, at the side of your plate. No society, no culture; could only name three men, — the Emperor, M. Coutinho, and M. Couteau. . . . For the rest, immense vulgarity; and, as Longfellow said, the Emperor wished he could swap places with Agassiz, and be a professor,— which Agassiz explained thus, that the Emperor said; "Now you, when you leave your work, can always return into cultivated society, I have none."

Agassiz says, the whole population is wretchedly immoral, the colour and features of the people showing the entire intermixing of all the races. Mrs. Agassiz found the women ignorant, depressed, with no employment but needlework, with no future, negligent of their persons, shabby and sluttish at home, with their hair about their ears, only gay in the ballroom; the men well dressed.

I can find my biography in every fable that I read.

In the history of intellect no more important fact than the Hindoo theology, teaching that the beatitude or supreme good is to be attained through science: namely, by the perception of the real and unreal, setting aside matter, and qualities, and affections or emotions and persons, and actions, as Maias or illusions, and thus arriving at the contemplation of the one eternal Life and Cause, and a perpetual approach and assimilation to Him, thus escaping new births or transmigration.

Truth is the principle, and the moral of the Hindoo theology, — truth as against the Maya which deceives Gods and Men; Truth the principle, and Retirement and Self-denial the means of attaining it. And they stop at no extreme in the statement.

Nobility. The extreme example of the sentiment, on which the distinction of rank rests, is not to be found in Spain, Germany, or England, but in India, where poverty and crime do not interrupt or diminish the reverence for a Brahmin. In India, a Brahmin may be very poor, and perform daily menial tasks for the English, as porters or servants, but the natives still kneel to him, and show him the highest respect. — Mr. Dall testified this fact to me on his return from India.

Self-respect always commands. I see it here in a family little known, but each of whose members, without other gifts or advantages above the common, have that, in lieu of all: teaching that wealth, fashion, learning, talent, garden, fine house, servants, can be omitted, if you have quiet determination to keep your own way with good sense and energy. The best of it is that the family I speak of do not suspect the fact.

Anquetil Duperron. What a counterpart to all the Bohemianism we attribute to Parisian *littérateurs*, is the address of Anquetil Duperron to the Indian Brahmins.

Louis XVI sent one to Anquetil Duperron with 3000 francs in a leathern bag: his friend set it down beside the chimney, and departed. As soon as he was gone, Anquetil snatched it up, ran out, and threw it at the heels of his friend, who found the bag arrived at the bottom of the staircase before him. The Society of Public Instruction, later, voted him a pension of 6000 francs. Anquetil returned the order, saying he had no need of it. When very near his end, he said to his physician, "I am going to set out on a voyage much more considerable than all those I have already made, but I do not know where I shall arrive."

The year 1866 has its memorabilia in the success of Atlantic Cable; in the downfall of Austria; in the checking of Napoleon and of Maximilian; in Agassiz's South American science. (Shall I say in the possession taken by the American Government of the Telegraph in the postal service? for I thought a public statement meant that.)

The promise of literature amazes, for none reads in a book in a happy hour without suggestion of immensities on the right hand and on the left — without seeing that all recorded experience is a drop of dew before the soliciting universe of thought.

Thought is more ductile than gold, more expansive than hydrogen gas; nations live on one book, and, in active states, one thought, one perception, discloses endless possibilities. It is ever as the attention, as the activity of the mind, and not as the number of thoughts or sensations, that the result is.[1]

Egypt. "Know that the gods hate impudence." Inscription on the temple of Sais.

A poem in praise of Rameses II says of the tower which he built, —

> "The sunlight beams in its horizon,
> and sets within it.
>
> . . . . . .
>
> "The Nile
> Coming all along the heaven."

---

[1] Compare in "Celebration of Intellect": "Keep the Intellect Sacred. Revere it. Give all to it. Its oracles countervail all. Attention is its acceptable prayer." (*Natural History of Intellect*, p. 130.)

Hafiz's poetry is marked by nothing more than his habit of playing with all magnitudes, mocking at them. What is the moon or the sun's course or heaven, and the angels, to his darling's mole or eyebrow? Destiny is a scurvy night-thief who plays him or her a bad trick. I might and perhaps will collect presently a few examples, though, as I remember, they occur *passim* in the "Divan." But I am always struck with the fact that mind delights in measuring itself thus with matter, — with history. A thought, any thought, pressed, followed, opened, dwarfs nature, custom, and all but itself.

The fancy carries out all the sentiments into form, and makes angels in the sky, and organizes remorse into a Judgment Day, and the universe at court; and so we have painted out our heaven and hell.

But I do not know but the sad realist has an equal or better content in keeping his hard nut. He sees the eternal symmetry, the world persisting to be itself, the unstooping morals of Nature, and says, "I can trust it." There is no fancy in my innate, uniform essential perception of Right, unique though million-formed or -faced. Through all processes, through all enemies, the result is Benefit, Beauty, the aim is the Best. I can well omit this parish propensity of casting it in small, in creeds, in *Punch* pictures, as the popular religions do, into Westminster Catechisms; Athanasian creeds; Egyptian, Christian, Mahometan or Hindoo paradises and hells. I will not be the fool of fancy, nor a child with toys.

The positive degree is manly, and suits me better: the truth is stranger and grander than the gayest fable. I cling to astronomy, botany, zoölogy, as read by the severe Intellect, and will live and die assured that I cannot go out of the Power and Deity which rule in all my experience, whether sensuous or spiritual.

Fame. I confess there is sometimes a caprice in fame, like the unnecessary eternity given to these minute shells and antediluvian fishes, leaves, ferns, yea, ripples and raindrops, which have come safe down through a vast antiquity, with all its shocks, upheavals, deluges, and volcanoes, wherein everything noble in art and humanity had perished, yet these snails, periwinkles, and worthless dead leaves come staring and perfect into our daylight. — What is Fame, if every snail or ripple or raindrop shares it?

It were good under the head of Greatness to collect signal examples of those high steps in character by which a good greatness is dwarfed in the presence of a higher strain, and this again by another. Aunt Mary's history and letters would give many suggestions; as, e. g., her definition of fame, her confidence that she "would, in spite of all failures, know one day what true friendship is, for the love of superior virtue is mine own gift from God": again; "That greatest of all gifts, however small my power of receiving, the capacity, the element to love the all-perfect, without regard to personal happiness — happiness —'t is itself!"

All greatness is in degree, and there's more above than below. Thus, what epic greatness in Dante's Heaven and Hell, revealing new powers in the human mind! What majestic power again in Swedenborg's Heaven and Hell! What again in the popular Calvinism of the last two centuries! Each of these war against the other. Now read the Indian theory: "As to Heaven and Hell, they are inventions of Maya, and are therefore both imaginary," etc.

It costs nothing to a commander to command: and everybody, the most powerful, finds himself some time also in the hands of his commander, it may be a woman, or a child, or a favorite; but usually it is another man organically so related to you that he easily impresses and leads your will, neutralizes your superiorities; — perhaps has less general ability than his victim, but is superior where the victim is weak, and most desires to be strong. But this locally stronger man has his dragon also, who flies at his throat, and so gives the first his revenges.

Thus every one has his master, and no one is stronger than all the others.

Dr. Jackson[1] said he was at Pulpit Rock, Lake Superior, when he heard music, like rhythmical organ or vocal chanting, and believed it to come from some singers. But going on a little further, it ceased; in another direction, heard it again, and by and by perceived that it was the beating of the waves on the shore deprived of its harshness by the atmosphere. He has never seen the subject treated scientifically, he thinks,

[1] Dr. Charles T. Jackson in 1844 and 1845 explored the unbroken wilderness on the shores of Lake Superior, examined its geology and made known its mineral resources, on which he made a report in 1850.

except in a paper on Sound by Dr. Wollaston.[1]

(From ML)

September.

My idea of a home is a house in which each member of the family can on the instant kindle a fire in his or her private room. Otherwise their society is compulsory and wasteful to the individual.

---

[1] Mr. Emerson turned his brother-in-law's story of this strange experience to good account in his poem "May-Day." (Compare *Poems,* p. 179.)

When going across the Plains to California in an emigrant caravan, in July, 1862, while straying alone among some large cottonwood trees with little underbrush, about forty rods away from our camp close by the upper North Platte River, not far from Fort Laramie, I heard suddenly wonderful music, not far away, which I could not account for: it was low, but rather sad, and seemed to come from many instruments, yet was indistinct. It was like no natural noise.

It was wholly unlike Indian music and no human settlement was near, except our camp. On my return thither I asked about the music. No one had heard it.

The day was cold and cloudy with a strong "Norther," following very hot weather. We were close by the broad, rushing Platte, troubled by the fresh wind, as were the great trees. After my return home I heard my uncle Dr. Jackson tell of his experience at Lake Superior, which I thought explained my own. He spoke of the phenomenon (perhaps quoting Dr. Wollaston) as "Analyzed Sound." *Edward W. Emerson.*

There may be two or three or four steps, according to the genius of each, but for every seeing soul there are two absorbing facts, — *I and the Abyss.*

September 15.

I think the preacher had better first secure his acre and his independence. Then let him know that the secrets are all disclosed in household talk — let him know that in every act and expression of men he can divine all the logical sequences or concomitants.

Speak the affirmative, which is always good. Then you lose no time. You grow, whether the deacons like you or not, and are presently in a position to dictate to them and to the people.

The old psalms and gospels, mighty as ever, showing that what people call religion is literature: this man knew how to put his statement, and the people said, Thus saith the Lord.

Men and Women. Man's conclusions are reached by toil. Woman arrives at the same by sympathy. He studies details. She catches by instinct the character. I suppose women feel about men who huddle them aside in the press as geniuses feel about energetic workers, namely, that they see through these noisy masters. In the company of superior women we all know that we are overlooked, judged, and sometimes sentenced. They are better scholars than we, and if not now, yet better twenty years later. Their organic share is education. They are by sympathy and quickness the right mediators between those who have knowledge and those who want it.

Man is a rude bear when men are separated in ships, in mines, in colleges, in monasteries. Conversation descends; manners are coarse. Let women sail as passengers, and all is righted. Taste, beauty, order, grace; life is respectable, and has elevated aims. Now she has been rightly drawn into interest in missions and various humanities, and at last the putting an end to Slavery.

Woman could not refuse to take part. That organization in this country was, you know, an education. The Executive Committee was composed of *Men and Women* and continued so until the end was reached. One truth leads in another. That cause was an education, a university, and it compelled a constant inquisition into Human Rights. And Woman has learned to ask for all her rights — and that of the vote. 'T is the right remedy at the right moment. Every truth leads in another truth.

As Parry, as [others], in their several explorations in the Arctic, came out each on the *SEA*, so the independent thinkers, like Behmen, like Spinoza, came out each on an adamantine Necessity: the theories of the students were weathercocks, but this inevitable result was final.

(From LN)

The progress of invention is really a threat. Whenever I see a railroad I look for a republic. We must take care to induct free trade and abolish custom-houses, before the passenger balloons begin to arrive from Europe, and I think the Railroad Superintendent has a second and deeper sense when he inscribes his legend over the ways, — "Look out for the Engine!"

The Unexpected. Wealth is chiefly convenient for emergencies. Day by day, every family gets well enough through its common routine, the poor as the rich. Only now and then comes a pinch, a sudden and violent call for means; as, a marriage, or a sickness, or a visitor, or a journey, or a subscription that must be met; then it is fortunate and indispensable to have new power. But emergencies are in the contract. They will and must occur to every susceptible person. Therefore you must set your daily expense at the famine-pitch, live within your income all the year round, to be ready with your dollars for these occasions.

October 12.

To writers. If your subject does not appear the flower of the world at this moment, you have not yet rightly got it.[1] . . .

Every word in the language has once been used happily. The ear caught by that felicity retains it.[2] . . .

October 24.

Dreams. I have often experienced, and again last night, in my dreams, the surprise and curiosity of a stranger or indifferent observer to the trait or the motive and information communicated. Thus some refractory youth, of whom I had some guidance or authority, expressed very frankly his dissent and dislike, disliked my way of laughing. I was curious to understand the objection, and endeavoured to penetrate and appreciate it, and, of course, with the usual misfortune, that, when I woke and at-

[1] See "Poetry and Imagination" (*Letters and Social Aims*, pp. 33, 34).

[2] Printed in "Imitation and Originality" (*Letters and Social Aims*, p. 193).

tempted to recover the specification, which was remarkable, it was utterly forgotten. But the fact that I, who must be the author of both parts of the dialogue, am thus remote and inquisitive in regard to one part, is ever wonderful.

October 25.

Success in your work, the finding a better method, the better understanding that insures the better performing, is hat and coat, is food and wine, is fire and horse and health and holiday. At least, I find that any success in my work has the effect on my spirits of all these.

What his right hand achieveth. I like my neighbour T.'s[1] manners; he has no deference, but a good deal of kindness, so that you see that his good offices come from no regard for you, but purely from his character.

I don't know but I value the name of a thing, that is, the true poet's name for it, more than the thing. If I can get the right word for the moon, or about it,—the word that suggests to me and to all men its humane and universal

[1] Probably Mr. Augustus Tuttle, whose farm was a half-mile below on the Turnpike.

beauty and significance, — then I have what I want of it, and shall not desire that a road may be made from my garden to the moon, or that the gift of this elephant be made over to me.

Cunning egotism. If I cannot brag of knowing something, then I brag of not knowing it. At any rate, Brag.

Theresa made herself useful and indispensable to all her neighbours as well as inmates, by being always in possession of a matchbox, an awl, a measuring-tape, a mucilage-pot, a corkscrew; microscope, reading-glass, and opera-glass.

The Negro, thanks to his temperament, appears to make the greatest amount of happiness out of the smallest capital.

AUTHORS OR BOOKS QUOTED OR REFERRED TO IN JOURNAL FOR 1866

The *Vedas;* Zoroaster (?), *Chaldean Oracles;* Pindar; Cicero, description of Demosthenes;

Taliessin, *apud* Nash; Mahomet; Hafiz; Chaucer;

Scaliger; Sir Walter Raleigh, *The Soul's Er-*

rand, Pilgrimage; Sir Philip Sidney; Van Helmont; Edward, Lord Herbert of Cherbury; Richard Lovelace, *To Althea;* Pascal; Newton; Steele, *The Funeral;*

Lord Mansfield; Duclos; Niebuhr; Sir William Herschel; Goethe, "Song of the Parcæ" in *Iphigenia, Musagetes;* John Marshall; Anquetil Duperron; Hegel, *apud* J. H. Stirling; Varnhagen von Ense; James Hogg; Robert Brown; Charles Lamb;

Rev. W. E. Channing; Daniel Webster, *Speech against Hayne;* Henry Kirke White, *The Herb Rosemary;* Bettine Brentano, *Goethe's Correspondence with a Child;* Sir Thomas Fowell Buxton; Sir Robert Peel;

Halleck, *Marco Bozzaris;* Champollion; Faraday; Bunsen; Charles Wolfe, *Burial of Sir John Moore;* Bryant, *To a Waterfowl;* Carlyle; Robert Pollok, *The Ocean;*

Henry Taylor, *Philip van Artevelde;* George Ripley; Sampson Reed, *Genius;* George Borrow's translation of ballad *Svend Vonved;* Sainte-Beuve; George Sand; Samuel Ferguson, *Forging of the Anchor;* John Sterling, *Alfred the Harper;* J. S. Mill; Robert H. Messenger, *Give me the Old;* Dr. C. T. Jackson; Tennyson; Gladstone.

JOURNAL

THE WEST
MORAL LAW. THE NEWNESS
NATIONALITY
MARY MOODY EMERSON
PROGRESS OF CULTURE
MRS. RIPLEY'S DEATH
QUOTATION AND ORIGINALITY
THE PREACHER
FALSE POSITION OF ENGLISH AUTHORS
THE FREEZING MISSISSIPPI

JOURNAL LVIII

1867

(From Journals ML, LN, and NY)

[THE winter brought its usual task, and Mr. Emerson went westward in January, lecturing in nine States and not returning home until after the middle of March. He visited Kansas for the first time, and took great pleasure in Minnesota. From Fond du Lac, Wisconsin, he wrote to a friend in Chicago, "Such a citizen of the world as you are should look once at these Northern towns which I have seen under the perhaps too smiling face of the mildest, best winter weather. . . . Minneapolis would strongly attract me, if I were a young man, — more than St. Paul; — and this town [Fond du Lac] is a wonderful growth and shines like a dream, seen this morning from the top of Amory Hall."

At the time of the celebration of the centenary anniversary of Emerson's birth, Mr. B. J. Brown wrote in the *Daily Leader* of Menominee, Wisconsin, reminiscences of Mr. Emerson's visit to Saginaw, Michigan. As president of the Library

Association, Mr. Brown called upon Mr. Emerson at the hotel. He wrote: —

"The enduring impression of greatness, majesty, and power which this interview with him left upon me was something akin to that which I experienced upon the first glimpse of the ocean. The tones of his voice long lingered in my ear." . . .

Mr. Brown told Mr. Emerson of the new railroad that was to be (though the work had hardly begun) from Lake Superior to Puget Sound.

"Emerson felt the greatest interest in the project, and it needed slight sympathy and appreciation to kindle into speech the thoughts which at the moment evidently engrossed him. It strongly appealed to his imagination and his feelings, and nothing in his lecture on the following evening approached the lofty and sustained eloquence . . . in which he clothed the subject.

"At some time during the day he told me of an opinion he had once heard Chief Justice Shaw deliver upon a question connecting itself with the law of highways, and how admirable it had seemed to him. Professedly seeking to relate simply what the great chief justice had said, he so transmuted it in the alembic of his own imagination as to invest the subject of the common roads of the country with a dignity which linked it to the movement of the tides and of the planets in their courses."]

(From ML)

WASHINGTON, IOWA, *February* 13, 1867.

In riding in an open sleigh, from Oshkosh to Ripon, in a fiercely cold snowstorm driving in my face, I blessed the speed and power of the horses. Their endurance makes them inestimable in this rough country. They seem left out of doors in the snow and wind all day. Around this square before the house, I counted just now twenty horses tied. Some of them seem to stand tied all day. Last night, just before going to bed, I looked out; — there stood two or three at that hour, — the farmers perhaps listening to the railroad men in the court-house, or sitting round the bar-room fire.

Mrs. Carr gave me a speech of Red Jacket, that compares with my old one from him about time. When the young men were boasting of their deeds, he said, " But the sixties have all the twenties and forties in them."

As soon as these people have got a shanty built to cover them, and have raised one crop of wheat, they want a railroad, as the breath of life; and, after one railroad, then a competing railroad. The first, because a railroad station is an instant market for the wheat; a second, because the first charges its own rates for freight, which takes half the price out of their crop, or, as much money to get it from their farm to Chicago as it costs to get it from Chicago to New York. And the second road underbids the first, and every new road underbids that. So that a web of roads has the like effect as the first creation of railways produced on the factories, which formerly turned out their new stocks only in spring and autumn, when the traders came to New York and Boston, for their semi-annual supply. But the new roads enabled them to come often, and therefore the factories could sell and the traders buy, all the year round, so that it required less capital to be a country trader. Now a market at each station makes a small New York near to every farm. Then, socially, in spring, and in much of winter, the people of Indiana, Illinois, etc., are confined to their sidewalks or the rail. Off these, they stick at once in bottomless universal quagmire, and, as here and now in a thaw, the melting snow makes a river of each run; in the vast level the poor water does not know where to go, and drowns, as yesterday here, a fine span of horses, because a boy in crossing a brook caught his wheel on a stone, and only saved his own life by climbing from his wagon on to a tree.

Mr. Brown of Saginaw tells me that "Men that live by their own labour are almost always moral people."

Thomas Taylor and Winckelmann would have preferred, to all meeting-houses and churches, to have restored the old native service of the temples on whose ruins these had been constructed, and to have worshipped, with Horace for the psalm-book, chanting, "*Mercuri facunde nepos Atlantis*," or, "*Sic te diva potens Cypri*," with tibia and theorbus and lyre, to all the psalters and all the organs of the Romish or the English congregations.

Eloquence. "But what astonishes, what surprises you?" "To hear an Athenian talk two hours together, hold us silent and immovable as the figures of Hermes before our doors, and find not a single one among us that can carry home with him a thought or an expression." — LANDOR, *Works*, vol. i, p. 88.

This passage reminds me of my own experience in hearing in old times Jonathan Phillips's speech at a Unitarian meeting in Dr. Channing's church.

Christ preached the greatness of man: We preach the greatness of Christ. The first is affirmative; the last negative.

We measure religions by their civilizing power. Christianity gains and thrives against worldly interests. So does Buddhism, Stoicism, and every high enthusiasm.

The mind is true: though the premises are false, the conclusions are right. And this self-reliance which belongs to every healthy human being is proof of it, — proof that not a petty egoism, but the soul of the world is in him, and, in proportion as it penetrates his miserable crust of partiality, it saith, 'Here am I, here is the Whole.' Therefore we require absoluteness in every soul, — absoluteness in the orator, — in the poet, — in the hero, — in all manners; and if they have it not, they simulate it.

The just pride of a man consists herein, that the recognition of him by others is nowise necessary to him.

Those persons who constitute the natural aristocracy — i. e., sacred persons — are not found in the actual aristocracy or only on its edge; as the chemical energy of the spectrum is found to be greatest just outside of the spectrum.

The intellectual power is not the gift, but the presence of God. Nor do we reason to the being of God, but God goes with us into Nature, when we go or think at all. Truth is always new and wild as the wild air, and is alive. . . .

"This world is no place for the man who doth not worship, and where, O Arjoon! is there another?" — *Bhagavat Geeta.*

When we come into the world, a wonderful whisper gives us a direction for the whole road; much as if one should hear from a skilful guide, on starting out on a journey, that, to come at the point he sought, he should follow the setting sun. This whisper wonderfully impresses us, and is temperament, taste, bearing, talent. 'T is like the card of the compass, which arranges itself with the poles of the world. But having made and moulded the constitution, the Creator contents himself, and is ever dumb.

He that made the World lets that speak, and does not employ a town-crier, etc., etc.

After much experience, we find literature the best thing, and men of thought, if still thinking, the best company. I went to England, and after allowing myself freely to be dazzled by the various brilliancy of men of talent; — in calm hours, I found myself no way helped, my sequins were all yellow leaves. I said, I have valued days, and must still, by the number of clear insights I get, and I must estimate my company so. Then I found I had scarcely had a good conversation, a solid dealing man with man, in England. Only in such passages is a reason for human life given; and every such meeting puts a mortal affront on kings and governments, by showing them to be of no account. Of course, these people, these and no others, interest us, — the dear and beautiful beings, who are absorbed in their own dream. Let us, then, have that told: let us have a record of friendship among six, or four, or two, if there be only two, of those who delight in each other only because both delight in the Eternal laws: who forgive nothing to each other: who, by their joy and homage to these laws, are made incapable of conceit, which destroys the fine wits. Any other affection between men than this geometric one of relation to the same thing is a mere mush of materialism.

And the Spirit drove him apart into a solitary place. — This does the spirit for every man.

He or That which in despair of naming aright, some have called the *Newness*, — as the Hebrews did not like to pronounce the word, — he lurks, he hides, he who is success, reality, joy, power,[1] — that which constitutes Heaven, which reconciles impossibilities, atones for shortcomings, expiates sins or makes them virtues, buries in oblivion the crowded historical past, sinks religions, philosophies, nations, persons to legends, reverses the scale of opinion, of fame; reduces sciences to opinion, and makes the thought of the moment the key to the universe, and the egg of history to come.

'T is all alike, — astronomy, metaphysics, sword, spade, pencil, or instruments and arts yet to be invented, — this is the inventor, the worth-giver, the worth. This is He that shall come; or, if He come not, nothing comes: He

[1] This expression occurs in "Works and Days" (*Society and Solitude*, p. 175).

that disappears in the moment when we go to celebrate Him. If we go to burn those that blame our celebration, He appears in them. The Divine Newness. Hoe and spade, sword and pen, cities, pictures, gardens, laws, bibles, are prized only because they were means He sometime used. So with astronomy, music, arithmetic, castes, feudalism, — we kiss with devotion these hems of his garment, — we mistake them for Him; they crumble to ashes on our lips.

Every innovation grows out of a thought, which hastens to embody itself in practical rules. These rules require much controversy, sifting, and amendment, to make them work well in practice, and the sentiment in which all agreed, the mother of all the rules, is soon overlaid and forgotten in the debate. But that also got expression at first.

The rules become national, and fill the world with noise, and the sentiment passes for rhetoric. But the rules are changed every year, grow aged very soon, whilst the sentiment is immortal, and can at any time provide itself with new codes.

Swedenborg was never quite ideal. The eye must be achromatic, but Swedenborg sees all amiss with this prismatic blur of misplaced gaudiness. Why do his images give no pleasure?

Milton anticipated Swedenborg when he wrote in *Paradise Lost*, Book v, —

> "What if Earth
> Be but the shadow of Heaven, and things therein
> Each to the other like, more than on earth is thought?"

I am so purely a spectator that I have absolute confidence that all pure spectators will agree with me, whenever I make a careful report. I told Alcott that every one of my expressions concerning "God," or the "soul," etc., is entitled to attention as testimony, because it is independent, not calculated, not part of any system, but spontaneous, and the nearest word I could find to the thing.

"Over the soul can and will God allow no one to rule but Himself alone." — MARTIN LUTHER.

The moral sentiment is pure vision, and what is Religion? Religion is the architecture of the sentiment. The sentiment never rests in vision, but wishes to be enacted. It does not pause,[1] . . .

[1] For the rest of this paragraph, see "Character" (*Lectures and Biographical Sketches*, p. 103).

Man is architectural; always goes to precipitate the particles held in solution by his thought into a form which obeys and represents the thought: aims always to turn his tent into a house; his camping ground into an estate, — garden and field; these lightning flashes of the Divine Soul into a good house-lamp, or, better, if he can, into an annual and perennial Sun.

I affirm that in all men is this majestic perception and command which we call moral sentiment:[1] ... It is the truth itself. It is foolish cavil to say, — What? you will adore yourself?

I find that all men are perishing, frivolous ghosts before this dread Imperturbability which dwells in the heart of every person. Don't be deceived by outsides. That is the stupendous mystery with which we are always familiar, but passes all explanation, that, in the rubbish of whims and appetites and sins of all these poor personalities, resides, at bottom, this sublime Universality.

The Soul, as it obeys the inward law, reveres it, comes to feel that the listening after any saint or prophet were an impiety against this immediate revelation.

[1] What follows is found in "Character" (*Lectures and Biographical Sketches*, pp. 97, 98).

Morals. The moral sentiment . . . it is absolute and in every individual the law of the world. . . . It is found that the instinct of the brute creation has a certain faint coincidence with morals. The moral element is the Reason of things applied to human action.

We do not cite Archimedes to establish the equality of the radii of the circle, nor Pythagoras for the law of the hypothenuse, nor Newton for laws of light, nor Rumford for those of heat, though these may first have announced certain propositions. Once announced, they are accepted by all and stand forevermore on the nature of things, though they were successively enunciated by these men. It had been vain to enunciate them if they had not been first true in the Mind, and the true geometer passes over these perished announcers to the eternal nature of which they, as he, are the vehicles. So we do not attribute, except in the pleasing acts of imagination, authority to Moses or to Jesus or other moralists, as soon as we have seen that their lessons are really true in Nature ; then we lose the words and the saint in the riches of the soul from which he spoke, and which is perfect to-day.

It is not to be disputed that every opinion,

every motive, every idea, plants itself in a man who becomes its representative and name for his age or ages, as Solon or Lycurgus, as Homer, Euclid, Aristotle, as Jesus, as Mahomet, as Cæsar, as Brutus, as Washington, as Calhoun.

It is doubtful whether London, whether Paris, can answer the questions which now rise in the mind. Sainte-Beuve says, "*J'ai l'idée qu'on est toujours de son temps, et ceux-là mêmes qui en ont le moins l'air.*"

Nationality. We Americans have got suppled into the state of melioration. We have lived fast in ten years; in four years last past.[1] . . .

Things once not possible are probable now. Women dispose of their own property. Women will vote. Women lecture, preach, are physicians, artists.

Stand where you are, and make the best of it. I cannot find any bar in the way of social life here.[2] . . . I see, too, happy homes, and true

[1] Most of what follows is printed in "Resources" (*Letters and Social Aims*, pp. 141, 142).

[2] See "Fortune of the Republic" (*Miscellanies*, p. 535).

gentlemen to live and die for, and friends to die with.

Nationality is often silly. Every nation believes that the Divine Providence has a sneaking kindness for it; as, "God has been received a burgher of Berne." . .

America. I thought at Chapin's lecture, — It is not a question whether we shall be a nation, or only a multitude of people; but whether we shall be the new nation, the leading Guide and Lawgiver of the world, as having clearly chosen and firmly held the simplest and best rule of political society.

The office of America is to liberate, to abolish kingcraft, priestcraft, caste, monopoly, to pull down the gallows, to burn up the bloody statute-book, to take in the immigrant, to open the doors of the sea and the fields of the earth, — to extemporize government in Texas, in California, in Oregon, — to make provisional law where statute law is not ready. This liberation appears in the power of invention, the freedom of thinking, in readiness for reforms.[1] . . .

The human race is immortal: oppressed here,

[1] See "Fortune of the Republic" (*Miscellanies*, p. 527).

they step aside into taverns or solitudes, and are free there. In the quiet of cottages, or of friendship, or of pot-houses, they see the passing of so many gods, whether Jove, or Hertha, or Thor, or Christ, or Allah, which live longer or shorter terms, and then die;— but the good human race outlives them all, and forever in the heart abides the old sovereign Sentiment requiring justice and good will to all, and rebuilds the decayed temples, and with new names chants again the praise of Eternal Right.

How shall it inaugurate its own ritual in the new age? It has the Sunday, which is the wisdom and necessity of mankind; for inspiration, for solitude, for society.[1]

The *morale* is the source of inspiration; it shall inspire whom it will to uplift and persuade men, will write hymns and meditations and histories that edify and provoke us.

(From LN)

March.

Lessing said of the astronomers, "It is easier for them to meet disaster than at sea, — and they make glorious shipwreck who are lost in seeking worlds."

[1] Compare "Character" (*Lectures and Biographical Sketches*, p. 117).

Universities. The treatises that are written on university reform may be acute or not, but their chief value to the observer is the showing that a cleavage is occurring in the hitherto firm granite of the past, and a new era is nearly arrived.

Books. The advantage of the old-fashioned folio was, that it was safe from the borrowers.

Gladly the boy learns that the 5 line in the Multiplication Table goes to tune of "Yankee Doodle."

If a man happens to have a good father, he needs less history: he quotes his father on each occasion, — his habits, manners, rules. If his father is dull and unmentionable, then his own reading becomes more important.

Colour. At Nantasket Beach, I cannot but approve the taste which clothed the emperors in purple, when I see the wet porphyry pebbles.

Culture is partial. I know so well that frequent unhappy figure with educated eyes, and uneducated body.

The good writer seems to be writing about himself, but has his eye always on that thread of the universe which runs through himself, and all things.

The word *miracle*, as it is used, only indicates the savage ignorance of the devotee, staring with wonder to see water turned into wine, and heedless of the stupendous fact of himself being there present.[1] If the water became wine, became fire, became a chorus of angels, it would not compare with the familiar fact of his own perception. Here he stands, a lonely thought, harmoniously organized into correspondence with the Universe of Mind and Matter.

April 10.

Yesterday at the funeral of George L. Stearns.[2] Rode to Mount Auburn in a carriage with Mr. Alcott and Mr. P——, and had long conversation on Swedenborg. Mr. P——, intelligent and well-versed on Swedenborg; but his intel-

[1] The beginning of the paragraph is printed in the "Sovereignty of Ethics" (*Lectures and Biographical Sketches*, p. 200).

[2] Major George L. Stearns, of Medford, a merchant of Boston, and, during the war, a most devoted patriot. Mr. Emerson's notice of him is printed in *Lectures and Biographical Sketches*.

ligence stops, as usual, at the Hebrew symbolism. Philosopher up to that limit, but there accepts the village church as part of the sky. In a day not far off this English obstinacy of patching the ecliptic of the Universe with a small bit of tin will come to an end.

[On the Nineteenth of April — Concord's proud day — of this year, a granite obelisk was dedicated, on the Common, in honour of the soldiers connected with the town who lost their lives in the recent war. Mr. Emerson made the address which is printed in the *Miscellanies*.]

You complain that the Negroes are a base class. Who makes and keeps the Jew or the Negro base, who but you, who exclude them from the rights which others enjoy?

If I were rich, I should get the education I have always wished by persuading Agassiz to let me carry him to Canada: and Dr. Gray to go to examine the trans-Mississippi Flora; and Wyman should find me necessary to his excavations; and Alvan Clark should make a telescope for me too; and I can easily see how to find the gift for each master that would domesticate me with him for a time.

I thought, as the train carried me so fast down the east bank of the Hudson River, that Nature had marked the site of New York with such rare combination of advantages, as she now and then furnishes a man or woman to a perfection in all parts, and in all details, as if to know the luxuriant type of the race; — finishing in one what is attempted or only begun in a thousand individuals.

The length and volume of the river; the gentle beauty of the banks; the country rising immediately behind the bank on either side; the noble outlines of the Katskills; the breadth of the bays at Croton (?) and Tarrytown (?); then, West Point; then, as you approach New York, the sculptured Palisades; — then, at the city itself, the meeting of the waters, the river-like Sound; and the Ocean at once, — instead of the weary Chesapeake and Delaware Bays.

Mr. Justice Maule requested Sir Cresswell Cresswell, then at the bar, "to remember that his opponents were vertebrate animals," and "that his manner to them would be offensive from God Almighty to a black beetle." — *Pall Mall Gazette.*

May 1.

[The new volume of poems, *May-Day*, was just printed, and here in the Journal is a list of fifty friends and relatives to whom Mr. Emerson sent it on May-Day.

On May 3, Mr. Emerson read "The Rule of Life" to the Radical Association in Boston, the substance of which was later incorporated in "The Sovereignty of Ethics" and "The Preacher."]

Nature sings, —

> He lives not who can refuse me,
> All my force saith, Come and use me.
>
> A May-day sun, a May-day rain,
> And all the zone is green again.

Why is Collins's "Ode to Evening" so charming? It proves nothing, it affirms nothing; it has no thought, no fable, no moral. I find it pleases only as music. It is as if one's head, which was full of the sights and sounds of a summer evening, should listen to a few strains of an Æolian Harp, and find it restoring to him those sights and sounds. 'T is good whistling.

[On May 30, Mr. Emerson made a short address at the meeting for the organization of the Free Religious Association in Boston (See *Miscellanies*, p. 475).]

Aunt Mary read Tasso in 1826. The story hurries her along, but she has " too little imagination now to relish the inventions, and all the time thinks of Homer's Iliad. Alas! how narrow the limits of human invention. The *Paradise Lost* gains in the comparison, yet had *that* never been, were it not for these. The moderns write better, but the readers are too wise to enjoy as in an unphilosophical age. A few pulsations of created beings, a few successions of acts, a few lamps held out in the firmament, enable us to talk of *time*, make epochs, write histories,—to do more—to date the revelations of God to man. But these lamps are held to measure out some of the moments of eternity, to divide the history of God's operations in the birth and death of nations,—of worlds. It is a goodly name for our notions of breathing, suffering, enjoying, acting. We personify it. We call it by every name of fleeting, dreaming, vapouring, imagery. Yet it is nothing. We exist in eternity; dissolve the body, and the night is gone, the stars are extinguished, and we measure duration by the number of our thoughts, by the activity of reason, the discovery of truths, the acquirement of virtue, the approach to God."

Immortality. The longest life is but a morning; but where is the Day?

July 2.

I happen to-day to fall upon a line in Æschylus, *Seven against Thebes*, which says so long ago what Dr. Holmes talked of at the last Club, — the alleged standing up of the hair in terror.

$$\text{Τριχὸς δ' ὀρθίας πλόκαμος ἵσταται} \quad \text{(line 564)}.$$

In old Boston, a feature not to be forgotten was John Wilson, the town crier, who rung his bell at each street corner, — "Lost! a child strayed this morning from 49 Marlborough Street; four years old; had on check apron," etc. "Auction! Battery-March-Square, "etc., etc. He cried so loud that you could not hear what he said, if you stood too near.

Pindar, in the First Olympic Ode, speaks with the robust courage of a prize-fighter of his own skill in verse, and as only Kepler and Shakspeare (in the Sonnets) have done among the moderns. There is the like stoutness in his bust. Wordsworth, however, has shown a stout heart, and Landor, but none compare with Kepler.

Reading. I suppose every old scholar has had the experience of reading something in a book which was significant to him, but which he could never find again. Sure he is that he read it there; but no one else ever read it, nor can he find it again, though he buy the book, and ransack every page.

Classic. Mrs. Barbauld's *Hymns for Children* are also classics, as well as Pope and Dryden.

[On Commencement Day Mr. Emerson was chosen an Overseer of Harvard University, and on the following day, July 18, for the second time, after thirty years' interval, delivered the Phi Beta Kappa Address. It is printed, with some changes, under the name " The Progress of Culture," in *Letters and Social Aims*.]

The good augury of our larger dedication to natural science in this century is not so much for the added material power which it has yielded (though that is conspicuous and we cannot have too much) as for the intellectual power it evokes, and, shall I say, the sublime delight with which the intellect contemplates each new analogy appearing between the laws of Nature and its own law of life. Newton, habitually regarding a particular fact in Nature as an universal fact, — what happens in one place, at one time, happens in all places at all times, — happens to see an apple fall, and says to himself, "What is the moon but a bigger apple falling also to the earth?[1] What is the earth but a much bigger apple falling to the sun? I see the law of all Nature. Every atom falls to every atom." Then comes the farther thought, Herein I am apprised that this universal material attraction is only a particular example of a more universal law, — we will call it Centrality, — which holds for mind as well as matter.

Identity and Centrality, the one law for atom and sphere, for atom and universe, is indignantly denied by children, whether two years old or a hundred, and is affirmed by those

[1] Compare a similar passage in "Progress of Culture," the Phi Beta Kappa oration (*Letters and Social Aims*, p. 222).

whose eyes are opened. Every breath of air is the carrier of the Universal mind. The child sees the single fact; the philosopher sees in it only the eternal identity.

I cannot yet say accurately what is the analogon of each cosmical or chemical law; Swedenborg, or a possible Swedenborg, can; but I affirm with perfect security that such analogon for each material law observed exists in the spiritual nature, and that, better than the satisfaction in arriving at the formula of the chemic law, is the spasm (shall I say) of pleasure which pervades the intellect in recognizing, however dimly, the instant perception of its equal holding through heaven, as well as through earth. The laws below are sisters of the laws above.[1]

Medical Use of Friendship. Linnæus cured his gout by wood-strawberries, but when Kalm returned from America, Linnæus was laid up with severe gout. But the joy in his return, and the curiosity to see his plants, restored him instantly, and he found his old friend as good as the treatment by wood-strawberries.

When I see my friend, his eyes testify of

[1] This last sentence occurs in "Progress of Culture" (*Letters and Social Aims*, p. 223).

much more good than his speech, for he leaves me to learn from others the benefits he has just conferred. Great are the Silences and the Influences.

(From NY)

Mrs. Sarah Alden (Bradford) Ripley was of so fine a nature that she could well afford to busy herself in any possible household chore. No dust nor grime could stick to the pure silver.

[Mrs. Ripley died in Concord in the summer of 1867. Mr. Emerson had known and prized her from the time of her marriage to his kind and helpful half-uncle Samuel Ripley, in whose school at Waltham, of which she was a great part, he had, as a boy, studied and given some small help. Rev. Mr. Ripley, after his retirement, moved back to his birthplace, the Old Manse in Concord, but died very soon. Mrs. Ripley lived there with her daughters until her death, more than twenty years later, and she and her brother, George P. Bradford, were constant and welcome visitors to Mr. and Mrs. Emerson at their home. Mr. Emerson wrote of her, —]

At a time when perhaps no other woman read Greek, she acquired the language with ease, and read Plato,—adding soon the advantage of German Commentators. After her marriage, when her husband, the well-known clergyman of Waltham, received boys in his house to be fitted for College, she assumed the advanced instruction in Greek and Latin, and did not fail to turn it to account by extending her studies in the literature of both languages. . . . She became one of the best Greek scholars in the country, and continued in her latest years the habit of reading Homer, the tragedians, and Plato.

But her studies took a wide range in mathematics, in natural philosophy, in psychology, in theology, as well as in ancient and modern literature. She had always a keen ear open to whatever new facts, astronomy, chemistry, or the theories of light and heat, had to furnish. Any knowledge, all knowledge, was welcome. Her stores increased day by day. She was absolutely without pedantry. Nobody ever heard of her learning until a necessity came for its use, and then nothing could be more simple than her solution of the problem proposed to her.

The most intellectual gladly conversed with one whose knowledge, however rich and varied, was always with her only the means of new ac-

MRS. SARAH ALDEN (BRADFORD) RIPLEY

quaintance. . . . She was not only the most amiable, but the tenderest of women, wholly sincere, thoughtful for others. . . . She was absolutely without appetite for luxury or display or praise or influence, with entire indifference to trifles.

(From LN)

Charles Newcomb has wonderful power of illustration of his refinements of sentiment by means of household experiences; e. g., "As the youth, sleeping with his brother, feels how much he is not to him." "Bacon, at home in his reflections. When intellectual, then is he himself, as a childless woman, restless except when making bread, and is then happy and singing."

Original power in men is usually accompanied with assimilating power.[1] . . .

Read Parsons's Dante. The translation appears excellent, most faithful, yet flowing and elegant, with remarkable felicities, as when

Per tutti i cerchi dello Inferno scuri

is rendered, —

"Through all the dingy circles down in hell."

[1] For the rest of this long passage, see "Quotation and Originality" (*Letters and Social Aims*, pp. 190, 191).

But Dante still appears to me, as ever, an exceptional mind, a prodigy of imaginative function, executive rather than contemplative or wise. Undeniable force of a peculiar kind, a prodigy, but not like Shakspeare, or Socrates, or Goethe, a beneficent humanity. His fames and infamies are so capriciously distributed, — what odd reasons for putting his men in inferno! The somnambulic genius of Dante is dream strengthened to the tenth power, — dream so fierce that it grasps all the details of the phantom spectacle, and, in spite of itself, clutches and conveys them into the waking memory, and can recite what every other would forget. What pitiless minuteness of horrible details! He is a curiosity like the mastodon, but one would not desire such for friends and contemporaries, abnormal throughout like Swedenborg. But at a frightful cost these obtain their fame. Dante a man to put in a museum, but not in your house. Indeed I never read him, nor regret that I do not.[1]

"And two I saw there leaning back to back
Propped like a pair of dishes put to warm."

[1] This is a characteristic expression of Mr. Emerson's aversion of the negative and the dismal. Of course this refers to the *Inferno* alone.

Dante says,—

"'Living I am, and thou, if craving fame,
  Mayst count it precious,' this was my reply,
'That I with other notes record thy name.'"
                    (PARSONS.) *Inf.*, Canto XXXII.

"For 't is no task wherewith to be amused
 The bottom of the Universe to paint."

"*Quotation and Originality*" (subsequent to printing). Leibnitz predicted the Zoöphytes (*Penhoen*); Kant the Asteroids; Swedenborg, Uranus; Goethe found the true theory of colours; Kenelm Digby the same theory in 1580. Columbus nor Cabot not the first discoverer of America; *Linnæus* did not find the Sexes in plants so soon as Van Helmont by 100 years.

Will not an age or a man come, when it will be thought impertinent to say of him, as soon as he is dead, *Poor* Mr. A, or B, or C?

There is no saying of Rochefoucauld which is so bitter a satire on humanity as our religious Dr. Johnson's, when some one lamented the death of a friend: "We must either outlive our friends, you know, or our friends must outlive us; and I see no man who would hesitate about the choice."

Johnson, with his force of thought and skill of expression, with his large learning and his true manliness, with his piety and his obstinate narrow prejudices, and withal his rude impulses, is the ideal or representative Englishman.

Note also the sharp limitations of his thought. I never can read a page of Piozzi without being reminded of Aunt Mary.

September 1.

Struggled hard last night in a dream to repeat and save a thought or sentence spoken in the dream; but it eluded me at last: only came out of the pulling, with this rag, —

> "his the deeper problem,
> But mine the better ciphered."

[In September Mr. Emerson read "The Preacher" to a company assembled at the house of Rev. J. T. Sargent in Boston.]

Buckminster, Channing, Everett, Taylor, Beecher, Bushnell, Chapin, it is they who are necessary, and the opinions of the floating crowd of no importance whatever. A vivid thought brings the power to paint it, and, in proportion to the depth of its source, is the force of its projection. I am happy and enriched. I go away invigorated, assisted in my own work, however different from his, and shall not forget to come again for new impulses.

At the present day, thoughtful people must be struck with the fact that the old religious forms are outgrown; as shown by the fact that every intellectual man is out of the old church: all the young men of intelligence are on what is called the radical side. How long will the people continue to exclude these, and invite the dull men? Beecher told me that he did not hold one of the five points of Calvinism in a way to satisfy his father. The good Heaven is sending every hour good minds into the world, and all of them at maturity, on opening, discover the same expansion, the impatience of the old cramps, and a bias to the new interpretation. If you hold them in the old used-up air, they suffocate. Would you in new Massachusetts have an old Spain?

The laws of Nature are simple to poverty, but their applications immense and innumerable.

I wish to find in my preacher that power to illuminate and warm and purify, which I know in the fiery souls which have cheered and lifted my life, and, if possible, that power to clothe every secret and abstract thought in its corresponding material symbol. Seas and mountains, timber and metals, diamonds and fossils, interest the eye, but it is only with some preparatory or predicting charm; their real value comes only when I hear their meaning made plain in the spiritual truth they cover.

In that Newtonian experiment we wrote of above, there is the surprise and delight of finding identity, which the deep mind always anticipates. The child is perpetually amused by a new object, by a chip, or a wad of wool, or a rope or a bed-key,— each of a hundred subjects, if before unseen, amuses him for a few moments, and he is long in learning, as the man is long in learning, that each is the old toy in a new mask.

Naturel. M. S. said, on hearing the parts at Commencement, that she did not care so much for the improvement the speakers showed, as for how much of the boy they had kept.

The beauty of the landscape is in proportion to the quantity of light: from tragic to celestial.

Butler told Fox he had never read Smith's *Wealth of Nations*. "Neither have I," replied Fox. "There is something in all these subjects which passes my comprehension; something so wide that I could never embrace them myself, or find any one who did. 'Peace to the strepent horn.'"

Neither can I comprehend the west wind; but I open my bay, when it blows, or lift the anchor, and go to sea, because I know it is the right wind for fair weather.

Another example of Stirling's *Zymoses* is the dramatic ξύμοσις in Elizabethan age, and the metaphysical, in Germany, in the nineteenth century.

September.

Ralph[1] looks as if he was afraid that all these beautiful things would vanish before he had time to see them.

And now for my fagots of letters! It occurs

---

[1] Ralph Emerson Forbes, Mr. Emerson's first grandchild, then fifteen months old, and undoubtedly on the study floor at the time playing with an assortment of things from his grandfather's drawers.

that in my doctrines of "Classes" it cannot be forgotten how each passes to every person under different categories. In Boston, I pass for a scholar, but to my friend "Ras," only in connection with the cows, and my name is *moo*.

October 31.

William Forbes says that little Ralph puts on his Society-face when he sees his new-born sister in the cradle, and gives her a condescending kiss.

The god of Victory is said to be one-handed, but Peace gives victory to both sides.

Style. Matthew Arnold has the true critical perception and feeling of style, and has shown more insight on that subject than any contemporary. See his "Celts" and his "Homer."

Earl Grey said, in the old Reform discussion, in 1832, when questioned by the Tories, how far he should carry his principle, if the reformers should pull down the House of Lords, etc.? — "I shall stand by my order."[1] Carlyle and his followers now stand as the Tories did. And in their zeal to stand by the aristocratic order, one

[1] This anecdote is told by Mr. Emerson in "The Man of Letters" (*Lectures and Biographical Sketches*, p. 251).

wishes to ask them, — "But, if your order stands for injustice, do you not belong to a higher order?" Carlyle might well be allowed the liberty of genius of riding his hobby very hard, — of riding into the Inferno, if he will, — sure that he has the palm-branch of Poets in his hand, and the power of genius will bring him safely back. But under the attraction and prestige of his name, Tennyson, and Ruskin, and Kingsley, men of talent, but far inferior to him in character, venture to follow their party or *society*-proclivities also, and subscribe to the infamous Eyre-fund. This is a grave misfortune to themselves, and to their society, which follows them. The like wrongs are found here, and our society needs a crusade preached by our Peter Hermits.

Holmes, in his lecture to the Medical College, said that Dr. James Jackson's Preface to his *Letters to a Young Physician* compared well with the three famous prefaces, namely, Calvin's to his *Institutes*, Casaubon's to Polybius, and President De Thou's to his History.

'T is very certain that when the deluge comes in, it will not mind our garden-fences nor Boston or Portland, nor New York, but only the Alleghanies and the Andes, or, the lines where the pent-up fires are hottest, and the crust of the globe thinnest.

Mr. Grattan, English Consul, said at the Dickens dinner in Boston, that "the chairman's four *Vices* were as good as the four cardinal virtues of any other man." Holmes, Hillard, Ellis Grey Loring, and T. J. Stevenson, were the vice-presidents.

I rarely take down Horace or Martial at home, but when reading in the Athenæum, or Union Club, if I come upon a quotation from either, I resolve on the instant to read them every day. But,—at home again, homely thoughts.

Quotation—yes, but how differently persons quote! I am as much informed of your genius by what you select as by what you originate. I read the quotation with your eyes, and find a new and fervent sense: thus Shakspeare's *Richard II* has always borrowed much of its interest from Edmund Kean's rendering: though I had that play only at second-hand from him through William Emerson, who heard him in London. When I saw Kean in Boston, he played nothing so high.[1] The reading of books is according to the sensibility of the scholar.[2] . . .

One remembers his friends by their favourite poetry or other reading, as I recall Shakspeare's "Make mouths at the invisible event," always from Aunt Mary's lips, and so many of Antoninus's and Milton's sentences.

The synthesis, the architecture, gives the value to all the stones. A thought contents me, but has little value to any other to whom I speak it. But, as soon as greater mental activity, or more scope, places that thought with its right foregoers and followers, and we have a right Discourse, we have somewhat impressive and powerful, and the worth of the solitary thought vastly enhanced.

Certain resemblances in Nature, or unexpected repetitions of form, give keen pleasure

[1] Mr. Emerson delighted in reading *Richard II* to his children, bearing Kean's rendering, as given by his brother, in mind.

[2] The rest of the paragraph is printed in "Quotation and Originality" (*Letters and Social Aims*, p. 194).

when observed; as the figure of the oak leaf on the under shell of the tortoise; the figure of the acanthus leaf in the flame of burning wood; or, better, as Ellery Channing said, that the oak wood burning gives again the form of the oak leaf. So the vegetable form of frost on the window pane suggesting the identity of vegetation with crystallization. So the piping of the hylas in the early days of April sounds at a little distance like the jingle of sleighbells. And Quatremère de Quincy's theory of Art is resemblance in the work to something of a different kind. And why not in the repetition in Nature of her scents, as of the orange in the little *Sarothra*;[1] of black birch and chequerberry.

In this old matter of originality and quotation, a few points to be made distinctly.

The apparently immense amount of debt to the old. . . . At first view, 't is all quotation, — all we have. But presently we make distinction: first, by wise quotation. Vast difference in the mode of quotation. One quotes so well that the person quoted is a gainer. The quoter's selection honours and celebrates the author. The quoter gives more fame than he receives aid. Thus Coleridge. Quoting is often merely of a

[1] False John's-wort.

suggestion which the quoter drew, but of which the author is quite innocent.

For good quoting, then, there must be originality in the quoter, — bent, bias, delight in the truth, and only valuing the author in the measure of his agreement with the truth, which we see, and which he had the luck to see first. . . . If another's words describe your fact, use them as freely as you use the language and the alphabet, whose use does not impair your originality. Neither will another's sentiment or distinction impugn your sufficiency. Yet in proportion to your reality of life and perception will be your difficulty of finding yourself expressed in others' words or deeds.

And yet — and yet — I hesitate to denounce reading, as aught inferior or mean. When visions of my books come over me, as I sit writing, when the remembrance of some poet comes, I accept it with pure joy, and quit my thinking, as sad lumbering work; and hasten to my little heaven, if it is then accessible, as angels might. For these social affections also are part of Nature and being, and the delight in another's superiority is, as Aunt Mary said, "my best gift from God." For here the moral nature is involved, which is higher than the intellectual.

The new knowledge is nothing but the old knowledge new vamped and painted.

"The illusion of knowing." (*Aunt Mary.*)

December.

[Mr. Emerson records the following guests from oversea who visited him during the autumn.]

September 11. Mr. H. Lee Warner, of St. John's College, Cambridge, England.

October. Viscount and Lady Amberley.

November 23. Mr. Cowper, Earl Morley, and Lord Camperdown with letter from Froude. Hon. Mr. Stratt and Mr. J. R. Holland with letter from Mrs. Ward. Rev. Leslie Stephen and his wife, who is Thackeray's daughter.

[Notwithstanding the first two months of the year having been spent in the West, lecturing, Mr. Emerson's calls carried him again thither in the last month. Beginning in Erie, Pennsylvania, on the 5th, before the New Year came in he had spoken in Illinois, Iowa, Ohio, and Missouri. He fulfilled his engagements at all sacrifice of comfort and even at serious risk, as this extract from a letter written to his family shows: —]

December 17.

Yesterday morning in bitter cold weather I had the pleasure of crossing the Mississippi in a skiff with Mr. ———, we the sole passengers, and a man and a boy for oarsmen. I have no doubt they did their work better than the Harvard six could have done it, as much of the rowing was on the surface of fixed ice, in fault of running water. But we arrived without other accident than becoming almost fixed ice ourselves; but the long run to the Tepfer House, the volunteered rubbing of our hands by the landlord and clerks, and good fire restored us.[1]

AUTHORS OR BOOKS QUOTED OR REFERRED TO IN JOURNAL FOR 1867

Bhagavat Geeta; Vishnu Purana; Lycurgus; Solon; Pythagoras; Confucius; Pindar; Æschylus, *Seven against Thebes* ; Socrates; Aristotle; Euclid of Alexandria; Archimedes; Cæsar;

Martial; Marcus Aurelius; Dante; Luther; Kepler; De Thou, *Historia Sui Temporis*; Casaubon; Calvin; Van Helmont;

---

[1] It should be remembered that Mr. Emerson was sixty-four years old.

Sir Kenelm Digby; Clarendon; La Rochefoucauld; George Fox; Bossuet; Spinoza; Newton; Leibnitz;

Linnæus; Diderot; Winckelmann; Collins, *Ode to Evening;* Kant; Lessing; Washington; Hester Lynch Piozzi, *Anecdotes of Dr. Johnson;* Anna Letitia Barbauld; Goethe; Benjamin Thompson (Count Rumford);

Charles Butler, *Reminiscences;* Thomas Taylor; Belzoni; Calhoun; Buckminster; Channing; Sir W. E. Parry, *Arctic Voyages;* Everett; Edward Taylor; Gerrit Smith; Michelet, *Bible de l'humanité;* Alcott;

Bushnell; Sainte-Beuve; Agassiz; Holmes; Tennyson; Asa Gray; Charles Kingsley; Beecher; Edwin H. Chapin; Thomas W. Parsons, Translation of *Inferno;* Matthew Arnold, *On Translating Homer;* Ruskin; Max Müller, *The Science of Language;* Goldwin Smith, *Life of Pym.*

JOURNAL

BEAUTY
FREE TRADE. SUFFRAGE. PEACE
A WORLD RELIGION
UNITY AND EVOLUTION
TENNYSON. WILLIAM MORRIS
CALVIN AND BUDDHA
THE FORTUNE-TELLER
HEGEL AND METAPHYSICIANS
VISIT TO NEWPORT
MIDDLEBURY
VERMONT MOUNTAINS
HARVARD UNIVERSITY
LOWELL

JOURNAL LIX

1868

(From Journals LN and NY)

J'ai pris la vie par le côté poétique.
FRANZ WOEPKE.

[As usual, Mr. Emerson lectured, near and afar, during the winter and in the spring, but just what the tour was does not clearly appear. During his absence his brother William, who had lost his wife, and was now very feeble, came from New York to consult a Boston physician and was a guest for some time at his brother's house. He returned to New York, where he died in September.]

(From LN)

Sometimes you must speak, if only as Aunt Mary told me, when I was a boy, and quarrelled with Elisha Jones and Frank Barrett. Dr. Ripley sent for them one evening to come to the house, and there made us shake hands: Aunt Mary asked me, "Well, what did you say to them?" "I did not say anything." — "Fie on you! you should have talked about your thumbs, or your toes, only to say something."

Admirable chapter of Harriet Martineau, in her *Eastern Life, Present and Past*, vol. i, p. 230. One would think it had never been read, or that the minds of the readers had been instantly dipped in Lethe. It needs instant republication, and the advertisement to be cried in the churches. It plays into my chapter of "Quotation" to find this necessity of repetition. If man takes any step, exerts any volition, initiates anything, no matter what, it is law of fate that another man shall repeat it, shall simply echo it. The Egyptian legend got this tyrannical currency; ploughed itself into the Hebrew captives.

Free Trade. I have no knowledge of trade and there is not the sciolist who cannot shut my mouth and my understanding by strings of facts that seem to prove the wisdom of tariffs. But my faith in freedom of trade, as the rule, returns always. If the Creator has made oranges, coffee, and pineapples in Cuba, and refused them to Massachusetts, I cannot see why we should put a fine on the Cubans for bringing these to us, — a fine so heavy as to enable Massachusetts men to build costly palm-houses and glass conservatories, under which to coax these poor plants to ripen under our hard skies, and thus discourage the poor planter from sending them to gladden the very cottages here. We punish the planter there and punish the consumer here for adding these benefits to life.

Tax opium, tax poisons, tax brandy, gin, wine, hasheesh, tobacco, and whatever articles of pure luxury, but not healthy and delicious food.

Beauty unequally bestowed; — Yes, but the highest beauty is that of expression, and the same man is handsome or ugly as he gives utterance to good or base feeling. I noticed, the other day, that when a man whom I had always remarked as a handsome person was venting Democratic politics, his whole expression changed, and became mean and paltry.

That is, Nature distributed vulgar beauty unequally, as if she did not value it; but the most precious beauty she put in our own hands, that of expression.

Norton read, the other night, in his lecture, the decree of the Commune of Florence for the rebuilding of the Cathedral, but wholly without effect, from the omission (perhaps the scorn) of emphasis. It should be read with the cry of a herald.

"Each supreme," says Harriet Martineau of the statues of the Egyptian gods. And why not? and men also, as the sky is perfect and the sea; porphyry and marble and iron and bronze, each is perfect and best in its place to the architect, and Roman cement under the sea, and wood and glass.

A banker, Mr. Manger, told me that such is the promise of the investments of the undertakers of the Pacific Railroad, that vaster fortunes will be made in this country than were ever amassed by private men: that men now alive will perhaps come to own a thousand millions of dollars. 'T is well that the Constitution of the United States has forbidden entails, and the only defence of the people against this private power is from Death the Distributor.

I have lately had repeated occasion to regret the omission to ask questions — while there was yet time — of persons who alone could answer them; and now that these are dead, there is none living who can give me the information. To have been so easily near the witnesses, and to have neglected an opportunity which now the whole world could not restore!

I wish the American poet should let old times go and write on Tariff, Universal Suffrage, Woman's Suffrage; Science shall not be abused to make guns. The poet shall bring out the blazing truth that he who kills his brother commits suicide. The gold was not hid in the Black Mountains that one man should own it all. The telegraph shall be open as writing is to all men. The grape is fertile this year that men may be genial and gentle, and make better laws, and not for their set alone. Thus shall the harvest of 1868 be memorable. The laws shall sternly hold men to their best, and fools shall not be allowed to administer what requires all the wisdom of the wisest.

I read with interest this line in the second Book of Herodotus, "The Egyptians are the first of mankind who have defended the immortality of the Soul."

Extremes meet, and there is no better example than the haughtiness of humility. No aristocrat, no porphyrogenite, can begin to compare with the self-respect of the saint. Aunt Mary in her vision of her place in heaven looks very coolly at her "Divine Master." "I approached no nearer the person of my Divine Master — but the Infinite must forever and ever surround me. I had too proud a spirit, too elate, too complacent from constitution, maybe, ever to have that affinity to Jesus which his better, holier ones have."

It is simply the consciousness, however yet obscure and undefined, of resting on Deity, that destroys all other divinities, or so-called divinities, and can well afford to be disgraced and degraded in their presence.

Among the men who fulfil the part of the American Gentleman, I place gladly Theodore Lyman, who went in a right spirit to the War, and who now works so faithfully and beneficently in this charge of establishing the pisciculture in Massachusetts.[1]

I understood Dr. C. T. Jackson in talk yesterday to say that the balloon can never be relied on as a machine for travel, since the attempt to resist the wind and sail against it will tear the balloon to pieces; that there must be

[1] Colonel Theodore Lyman, of Brookline, a handsome, spirited and accomplished young officer on the staff of General Meade, after the war became a worker and helper of Agassiz at his Museum in Cambridge.

wings invented to fly against the wind; and that guncotton which is so light, and, especially, which does not soil the barrel, is the best force yet found. The reliance on a permanent west wind in the upper region of the atmosphere may hold only over the land, and not over the sea. In the region of the trade-winds, the balloon may be applicable. The project has ceased to be presumptuous, since the ocean telegraph has become a fact.

What a divine beneficence attaches to Andrew Johnson! In six troubles, and in seven, he has been an angel to the Republican party, delivering them out of their distresses.

"The eye altering alters all." The saint, with grand healthy perception, in the atheism of Byron reads the ciphers of Eternity, finds in heathen fables and mythology the veiled truths of theism. A great cosmical intellect is indifferent to the arts, may easily look at them as poor toys, as he would look at a child's picture-alphabet. The saint only cares that the naturalist detects design in Nature; himself is quite careless of the vaunted evidences. He has vision.

Obstructives of the present day are the Pope, with his Encyclical Letter, and his later demonstrations; Bishop of Orleans, Dupanloup; Bishop of Oxford; the State of New Jersey; Andrew Johnson.

March, 1868.

I hold it a proof of our high capabilities that Horatio Greenough was born in Boston.

Can any one doubt that if the noblest saint among the Buddhists, the noblest Mahometan, the highest Stoic of Athens, the purest and wisest Christian, Menu in India, Confucius in China, Spinoza in Holland, could somewhere meet and converse together, they would all find themselves of one religion, and all would find themselves denounced by their own sects, and sustained by these believed adversaries of their sects? Jeremy Taylor, George Herbert, Pascal even, Pythagoras, — if these could all converse intimately, two and two, how childish their country traditions would appear!

March 18.

I suppose that what Richard Owen told me in London of Turner's coming to him to ask him to give him the natural history of the mollusk on which the whale fed, he wishing to understand it *ab ovo* thoroughly, because he was going to paint "the Whaleship," was just that chance of suggestion which I sought for my "Song of Boston," in going down the harbour, to Nantasket, and in my visit not yet made to Bunker Hill Monument. We cannot give ourselves too many advantages, and a hint to the centre of the subject may spring from these pensive strolls around the walls.

Education. The Sunday-School man who said his class were already in the "Swiss Robinson," and he hoped by next term to get them into "Robinson Crusoe."

I have a problem for an engineer, this, — To what height must I build a tower in my garden that shall show me the Atlantic Ocean from its top? Where is the Coast Survey?

"You," said the Brahmin Mandanis to the King (Alexander the Great), "are the only man whom I ever found curious in the investigation of philosophy at the head of an army." — STRABO.

(From a loose sheet)

Man of Science. Common sense or law of bodies must be obeyed. But he finds limits to this, or, itself leading to contradictions, for matter is fluent, and has no solid bottom; mere bubbles at last.

Then the very mathematician and materialist is forced to a poetic result, — as *metamorphosis; "progressive or arrested development."* [1]

Unity. In vain he would keep up the bars of species or genera; the pedant becomes poet against his will; Cuvier must approximate to Geoffroy Saint-Hilaire in spite of himself. These dreadful Okens and Goethes will be born. Unity! Unity! There is this Mischievous Mind as tyrannical, nay, more tyrannic, than the other. *The Niagara currents in the mind.*

The Mind must think by means of Matter; find Matter or Nature the means and words of its thinking and expression. The world its school and university for Heaven or Thought.

---

[1] Mr. Emerson, in "Poetry and Imagination" (*Letters and Social Aims*, p. 7), speaks of "the electric word pronounced by John Hunter a hundred years ago, *arrested and progressive development*." The wonderful arrangement of the anatomical specimens in the museum of the *Jardin des Plantes* had suggested strange thoughts on evolution to Mr. Emerson in 1833. These and the above hint from John Hunter, with reading of Lamarck, had prepared Mr. Emerson in advance for Darwin's teaching.

[Here follows in the Journal a list of the committee appointed to visit the Greek department at Harvard College the following year, in which Mr. Emerson's name appears.]

(From NY)

Revolutions. In my youth, Spinoza was a hobgoblin; now he is a saint.

When I see tracts of blowing sand planted with pitch pine trees and held fast as if granite slabs had been laid on them, and by the annual fall of the leaves made slowly but surely into a fertile soil; . . . when I see the Japanese building a steam navy, and their men of rank sending children to America for their education; the Chinese, instead of stoning an ambassador if he steps out of the walls of Canton, now choosing Mr. Burlingame as their ambassador to Western courts; when I see a good spring of water found by a hazel-twig; and my message sent from Boston to London in sixty seconds.[1] The plough displaces the spade; the bridge displaces the ferryman; the press displaces the scrivener; the locomotive the coach; the telegraph the courier.

[1] This apparently unfinished sentence is a catalogue of "Revolutions" of the day.

Greatness. The appearance of a great man draws a new circle outside of our largest orbit, and surprises and commands us. It is as if to the girl fully occupied with her paper dolls a youth approaches and says, "I love you with all my heart; come to me." Instantly she leaves all, dolls, dances, maids, and youths, and dedicates herself to him; or, as California, in 1849, or the war in 1861, electrified the young men, and abolished all their little plans and projects with a magnificent hope or terror, requiring a whole new system of hopes and fears and means. Our little circles absorb and occupy us as fully as the heavens; we can minimize as infinitely as maximize, and the only way out of it is (to use a country phrase) to kick the pail over, and accept the horizon instead of the pail, with celestial attractions and influences, instead of worms and mud pies. Coleridge, Goethe, the new naturalists in astronomy, geology, zoölogy, the correlations, the social science, the new readings of history through Niebuhr, Mommsen, Max Müller, Champollion, Lepsius, astonish the mind, and detach it effectually from a hopeless routine. "Come out of that," they say; "you lie sick and doting, only shifting from bed to bed." And they dip the patient in this Russian bath, and he is at least well awake, and capable of sane activity. The perceptions which metaphysical and natural science cast upon the religious traditions are every day forcing people in conversation to take new and advanced position. We have been building on the ice, and lo! the ice has floated. And the man is reconciled to his losses when he sees the grandeur of his gains.

Henry Clapp said that Rev. Dr. O—— was always looking about to see if there was not a vacancy in the Trinity. He said that Greeley knew that he was a self-made man, and was always glorifying his maker. He said that T—— aimed at nothing, and always hit it exactly.

Goethe. Schiller wrote to Humboldt, in 1802, "If Goethe had only a spark of faith, many things here might be improved."

It takes twenty years to get a good book read. For each reader is struck with a new passage and at first only with the shining and superficial ones, and by this very attention to these the rest are slighted. But with time the graver and deeper thoughts are observed and pondered.

New readers come from time to time, — their attention whetted by frequent and varied allusions to the book, — until at last every passage has found its reader and commentator.

May 22.

Education. I am delighted to-day in reading Schwegler's account of Socrates, to have intelligent justice done to Aristophanes. The rogue gets his dues.

Go into the school or the college, and see the difference of faculty: Some who lap knowledge as a cat laps milk, and others very slow blockheads.

Cowley considered the use of a university for the cherishing of gifted persons.

[Here follow most of pp. 32, 33 in "Poetry and Imagination" (*Letters and Social Aims*).]

Tennyson's Saint Grail. Tennyson has abundant invention, but contents himself with the just enough; is never obscure or harsh in a new or rare word. Then he has marked virility, as if a surgeon or practical physiologist had no secrets to teach him, but he deals with these as Abraham or Moses would, and without prudery or pruriency. His inventions are adequate to the dignity of the fable. The gift of adequate expression is his; [Bacchic phrensy in *Maud*. A nightingale drunken with his overflowing melody, an animal heat in the verse, and its opulent continuations.[1]] The priest is astonished to find a holiness in this knight-errant which he himself never knew, and rubs his eyes. The fine invention of Tennyson is in crowding into an hour the slow creations and destructions of centuries. It suggests besides, in the coming and vanishing of cities and temples, what really befalls in long durations on earth. How science of Ethnology limps after these enchantments! Miracles of cities and temples made by Merlin, like thoughts.[2]

What I wrote on the last leaf concerning Tennyson is due perhaps to the first reading, — to the new wine of his imagination, — and I may not enjoy it, or rate it so highly again.

[1] The passage in brackets thrown in, a momentary remembrance, then the thread of the discourse is resumed and Mr. Emerson speaks of Percival and the Monk in the idyll.

[2] In the Journal the date January 1, 1870, follows this paragraph, but it does not appear how much was the later writing.

[Then Mr. Emerson writes into the Journal three years later, under date of October, 1871, the following sentence: —]

The only limit to the praise of Tennyson as a lyric poet is, that he is alive. If he were an ancient, there would be none.

May.

Dionysius the elder, when some one asked him if he was at leisure, replied, "May that never befall me."

Calvinism is the breath of a hot village of Teutonic peasants, exalted to the highest power, their notions of right and wrong, their loves and fears and hatreds, their notions of law and punishment and reward, — all acute but narrow, ignorant and revengeful, yet devout. Dr. Watts's Hymns are its exponent. I remember that Burnap in the Cambridge Divinity School used to say that Calvinism stood on three legs, — Dr. Watts's Psalms and Hymns, Milton's *Paradise Lost*, and the Westminster Catechism, — or was there not a fourth, King James's translation of the Bible?

I should say that the opposite pole of theology was the Hindoo Buddhism, as represented in the prayers of the Bhagavata Purana.

We had a story one day of a meeting of the Atlantic Club, when the copies of the new number of the *Atlantic* being brought in, every one rose eagerly to get a copy, and then each sat down, and *read his own article.*

Out of power a party is immensely strong; it stands for principles, and its opponents have nothing but possession. But the moment the radical or republican comes into place, he has then to consider not what should be, but also what can be, which he finds a very different and very difficult problem. "Did you give Athens the best laws?" "No," replied Solon, "but the best it would receive."

Old and New. We read the English and foreign news with relish, the American with disrelish. We read of Socrates, Antoninus, and Menu gladly; not so gladly of our hodiernal churches.

When I remember how easily and happily I think in certain company, — as, for instance, in former years, with Alcott, and Charles Newcomb, earlier with Peter Hunt, though I must look far and wide for the persons and conditions, which yet were real, — and how unfavorable my daily habits and solitude are for this success, and consider also how essential this commerce is to fruitfulness in writing,—I see that I cannot exaggerate its importance among the resources of inspiration.

Gurney[1] seemed to me, in an hour I once spent with him, a fit companion. Holmes has some rare qualities. Horatio Greenough shone, but one only listened to him; so Carlyle. Henry Hedge, George Ward especially, and if one could ever get over the fences, and actually on even terms, Elliot Cabot. But I should like to try George E. Tufts,[2] my brilliant correspondent of three letters; and William B. Wright, of the "Highland Rambles." There is an advantage of being somewhat *in the chair* of the company, — a little older and better-read, — if one is aiming at searching thought. And yet, how heartily I could sit silent, purely listening, and receptive, beside a rich mind!

[1] Ephraim Wales Gurney, beloved professor of Latin at Harvard College, and later dean. He died in his prime. He was chosen a member of the Saturday Club shortly before his death.

[2] A man whose letters interested Mr. Emerson so much that once, while staying at Saratoga, he went on a journey in quest of him, but in vain. He was an original thinker, a mechanic, crippled by some disease.

May 30.

Heard Weiss speak on the platform of the Free Religious Society, and was struck with his manhood. Use and opportunity with such rare talent would have made him a great orator. He makes admirable points, but has the fault of lingering around a point, and repeats it, and dulls it. But sincerity and independence and courage, — in short, manhood, — he has, which the audience heartily enjoys, and tamer speakers learn a good lesson. He at least vindicates himself as a man, and one of great and subtle resources.

How important an educator has Scott been!

In the Board of Overseers of the College, the committee on honorary degrees reported unfavourably on all but the commanding names, and instantly the President and an ex-President pressed the action of the Corporation, acknowledging that these men proposed for honours were not very able or distinguished persons, but it was the custom to give these degrees without insisting on eminent merit. I remember that Dr. Follen, in his disgust at the Reverend and Honourable Doctors he saw in America, wished to drop the title and be called *Mister*.

Who listens to eloquence makes discoveries. A man who thought he was in earnest hears, and finds out that he was not. How we then feel that we could wash the feet of the speaker for the right.

C. J. Fox said, if he had a boy, he would make him write verses, the only way of knowing the meaning of words. — *Recollections*, of SAMUEL ROGERS.

What Landor said of Canning is truer of Disraeli, that "he is an understrapper made an overstrapper."

June 16.

In reading these fine poems of Morris, I see but one defect, but that is fatal, namely, that the credence of the reader no longer exists. I wrote thus last night, after reading "King Acrisius," but this evening I have read "The Proud King," wherein the fable is excellent, and the story fits this and all times.

Beauty is in great part a moral effect. It comes to serenity, to cheerfulness, to benignity, to innocence, to settled noble purpose. It flees from the perplexed, the self-seeking, the cowardly, the mean, the despairing, the frivolous, and the stupid. Self-respect, how indispensable to it! A free and contented air.

The roots of to-day are in yesterday and the days and days before. Why is this girl always unaccountably cheerful? Only because the due letter was written and posted yesterday, the valise of her brother's clothes went by the express, and he must have received them hours ago, and there is time this forenoon for all that is to be done. So with the weeks and the months. 'T is her habit, and every day brings the gay acknowledgment of these petty fidelities, by letter or by the faces of all whom she meets.[1]

The Youth gets on obscurely well enough from day to day, but once he chances to meet a young man who tells him something. He rolls it over in his mind for a day or two and must go back to him. The friend has told him his fortune; he has given him his character; he now sees somewhat he never saw, though the same things were close beside him. Every talk with that youth interests him, and all his life has a new look, whilst with him. He does not

[1] A tribute to his daughter Ellen.

care longer for the old companions; they are tame and superficial; he wants a witch, he wants an interpreter, a poet, a sympathizer; he has heard of books, and finds one at last that reminds him of his friend. This also is a dear companion.

Dreary are the names and numbers of volumes of Hegel and the Hegelians, — to me, who only want to know at the shortest the few steps, the two steps, or the one taken. I know what step Berkeley took, and recognize the same in the Hindoo books. Hegel took a second, and said, that there are two elements, something and nothing, and that the two are indispensable at every subsequent step, as well as at the first. Well, we have familiarized that dogma, and at least found a kind of necessity in it, even if poor human nature still feels the paradox. Now is there any third step which Germany has made of like importance and renown? It needs no encyclopædia of volumes to tell. I want not the metaphysics, but only the literature of them.[1] . . .

Enchantments. There are inner chambers of

[1] See for the substance of what follows *Natural History of Intellect* (p. 13).

poetry, which only poets enter. Thus loosely we might say, Shakspeare's Sonnets are readable only by poets, and it is a test of poetic apprehension, the value which a reader attaches to them. But also the poem, —

"Let the bird of loudest lay
On the sole Arabian tree," etc., etc., —

and the "Threnos" that follows it, if published for the first time to-day anonymously, would be hooted in all journals; and yet such a poem comes but once in a century, and only from a genius. I prize Beaumont and Fletcher's song, "Fountain heads and pathless groves," etc., in the same way.[1] . . .

We think we have a key to the affair if we can find that Italian artists were at Agra four centuries ago, and so the Taj is accounted for. Or, if Greeks were in Egypt earlier than we had found, and ties of one race can be detected, the architectural race that built in both lands. But the wonder is the one man that built one temple; and after that, the creation of two temples, or two styles, or twenty, is easy to accept.

[1] What follows is printed in "Poetry and Imagination" (*Letters and Social Aims*, pp. 55, 56).

Yea and Nay. We go to the artist's studio, and see his plans. They do not satisfy this *exigeant* eye, which yet knows not what it wants, only knows that these drawings do not content it. But any number of Nays does not help us in the smallest degree. Nothing will but the blessed appearance from any quarter of a plan of genius that meets all the conditions, and delights us, and we all say, *That is it*. The Cabots built the Athenæum;[1] Billings went into it and said, this hall and staircase want greatness, and drew his plans. The Committee and the Cabots assented at once, and Billings was added to the Cabots as one of the architects.

NEWPORT, *July*.

Seashore

Here chimes no clock, no pedant calendar,
My waves abolish time, dwarf days to hours,
And give my guest eternal afternoon.

July 13.

I have seen Sarah Clarke and her friends at Newport, with great pleasure and content, — at least with as much as so bad a traveller and visitor as I can find.[2] The land and water have

[1] The Athenæum Library in Boston on Beacon Street.

[2] Mr. and Mrs. Emerson had a happy week or more with their friend, Miss Clarke (his pupil in the Boston school for

the unfailing charm of the sea, which abolishes time, makes it all "afternoon," or vacation, and always tells us how far we are from Nature, and that the first poetry is not yet written.

As I was told in Venice that there were plenty of people who never stirred out of it to the main land, and, as my Mrs. Holbrook, with whom I went from Boston to Malta, never went on deck or saw the sea; so it is in seaports; the wharves are practically as far from the ocean as are the mountains. A boy born in Boston may often wander with boys down to the wharves, see the ships, boats, and sailors, but his attention is occupied by the rough men and boys, very likely by the fruit ships and their cargoes, specially the molasses casks. His eye may never get beyond the islands and the lighthouse to the sea. He remains a cockney, and, years later, chances to visit far from his town the shore where the ocean is not hidden by ships and the wharf population, but fills the horizon. Its chill breath comes to him a snuff of defiance, he

young ladies, where he assisted and succeeded his brother William). She was an artist, sister of Rev. James Freeman Clarke. The presence of Mrs. Helen Hunt, some of whose poems Mr. Emerson valued, added much pleasure to their stay.

realizes its wonder for the first time, and now first beholds the maker of cities and of civilization and may come to understand how Greece came to exist, and Tyre, and England.

Newport. The admirable sites for building and the combination of so many advantages point plainly to its future as the attractive waterside in the country. My chief acquisition was the acquaintance of Mrs. Helen Hunt, Sarah Clarke's friend, and her poetry I could heartily praise. The sonnet " Thought " and " Ariadne's Farewell " were the best, but all had the merit of originality, elegance, and compression.

Mrs. Hunt wished me to admire George Eliot's "Spanish Gypsy," but on superficial trial by hearing passages, I refused. It was manufactured, not natural, poetry. Any elegant and cultivated mind can write as well, but she has not insight into Nature, nor a poetic ear. Such poetry satisfies readers, and scholars, too, at first sight, — does not offend, — conciliates respect, and it is not easy to show the fault. But let it lie awhile, and nobody will return to it. Indeed, time, as I so often feel, is an indispensable element of criticism. You cannot judge of Nahant, or Newport, or of a gallery, or a poem, until you have outlived the dismay or overpowering of a new impression.

I took a volume of Wordsworth in my valise, and read for the first time, I believe, carefully "The White Doe of Rylstone," a poem in a singularly simple and temperate key, without ornament or sparkle, but tender, wise, and religious, such as only a true poet could write, honouring the poet and the reader.

August 16.

Came home last night from Vermont with Ellen. Stopped at Middlebury on the 11th, Tuesday, and read my discourse on *Greatness, and the good work and influence of heroic scholars*.[1] On Wednesday spent the day at Essex Junction, and traversed the banks and much of the bed of the Winooski River, much admiring the falls, and the noble mountain peaks of Mansfield and Camel's Hump (which there appears to be the highest), and the view of the Adirondacs across

---

[1] This address, of the same title as the last lecture of the course which Mr. Emerson gave in the autumn in Boston, was probably not quite identical with the essay "Greatness" in *Letters and Social Aims*, and very probably contained matter which now appears in "The Scholar" and the "Man of Letters" in *Lectures and Biographical Sketches*.

the Lake. In the evening, took the stage to Underhill Centre, and, the next morning, in unpromising weather, strolled away with Ellen towards the Mansfield Mountain, four miles off; and, the clouds gradually rising and passing from the summit, we decided to proceed towards the top, which we reached (with many rests at the Half-Way House and at broad stones on the path) a little before 2 o'clock, and found George Bradford[1] at the Mountain House. We were cold and a little wet, but found the house warm with stoves.

After dinner, Ellen was thoroughly warmed and recruited lying on a settee by the stove, and meanwhile I went up with Mr. Bradford and a party to the top of "the Chin," which is the highest land in the State, — 4400 feet. I have later heard it stated 4389 feet. Lake Champlain lay below us, but was a perpetual illusion, as it would appear a piece of yellow sky, until careful examination of the islands in it and the Adirondac summits beyond brought it to the earth for a moment; but, if we looked away an instant, and then returned, it was in

[1] George Partridge Bradford, Mr. Emerson's valued friend, refined, sensitive, and affectionate, a scholar and teacher, Mrs. Ripley's brother.

GEORGE PARTRIDGE BRADFORD

the sky again. When we reached the summit, we looked down upon the "Lake of the Clouds," and the party which reached the height a few minutes before us had a tame cloud which floated by a little below them.

This summer, bears and a panther have been seen on the mountain, and we peeped into some rocky caves which might house them. We came, on the way, to the edge of a crag, which we approached carefully, and lying on our bellies; and it was easy to see how dangerous a walk this might be at night, or in a snow-storm. The White Mountains, it was too misty to see; but "Owl's Head," near Lake Memphremagog, was pointed out. Perhaps it was a half-mile only from the House to the top of "the Chin," but it was a rough and grand walk. On such occasions, I always return to my fancy that the best use of wealth would be to carry a good professor of geology, and another of botany, with you. In the House were perhaps twenty visitors besides ourselves. A Mr. Taylor, of Cincinnati, — a very intelligent gentleman, — with excellent political views, Republican and free-trader; George Bartlett was there with a gay company of his friends, who had come up from Stowe, where he had given a theatrical entertainment of amateurs, the night before.[1] In the evening, they amused us mightily with charades of violent fun.

The next morning a man went through the house ringing a large bell, and shouting "Sunrise," and everybody dressed in haste, and went down to the piazza. Mount Washington and the Franconia Mountains were clearly visible, and Ellen and I climbed now the *Nose*, to which the ascent is made easy by means of a stout rope firmly attached near the top, and reaching down to the bottom of the hill, near the House. Twenty people are using it at once at different heights. After many sharp looks at the heavens and the earth, we descended to breakfast. I found in this company . . . [many] agreeable people.

At 9.30 A. M. Ellen and I, accompanied for some distance by George Bradford, set forth on our descent, in the loveliest of mornings, and, parting from him at one of the galleries, ar-

[1] George Bradford Bartlett, of Concord, son of the admirable village doctor Josiah Bartlett, and nephew of Mr. Bradford. When failing eyesight obliged him to leave business he used his gift as an actor and manager of private theatricals often for charitable purposes (as for the Sanitary Commission during the War). His fame spread widely, and summer hotels welcomed him, for his wit, his picnics, games and charades greatly helped their seasons.

rived safely at the Half-Way House, — there to find a troop of our fellow-boarders of the "Underhill House" just mounting their horses to climb the mountain. They advised us to take a little forest path to the "Mossy Glen," before we continued our journey from this point, which we did, and found a pretty fall. Returning to the Half-Way House, which is empty, and only affords at this time a resting-place for travellers and a barn for horses, we resumed our walk, and arrived (without other event than a little delay among the raspberries) at Mr. Prouty's Hotel at Underhill, say at 1.30; dined, re-packed our trunk, and took a wagon to Stowe, thence the stage-coach to Essex Junction, and thence the train, which brought us to Burlington, where we spent the night; and, the next morning, the Rutland and Burlington train, which brought us safely to Westminster, Massachusetts, where Ellen took a wagon for Princeton, and I continued my railroad ride to Concord, arriving at 6.30 in the evening.

[On August 21, the City of Boston gave a banquet in honor of the Chinese Embassy and the recently ratified treaty with China, negotiated by our minister to that country, also its ambassador to ours, Mr. Burlingame. Mr. Emerson made a short address on the occasion which is printed in the *Miscellanies*.]

University. The University question divides people with some rancour, which blinds the eyes, and I hope will be avoided, in consideration of the gravity of the subject. We might as well come to it after a late dinner in the strength of wine, as to hope to treat it wisely on the strength of party and passion.

The general uneasiness and movement in the public in regard to education shows a certain cleavage.

Evils of the College —

It does not justify itself to the pupil.

It does not open its doors to him.

Balks him with petty delays and refusals.

The instructors are in false relations to the student.

Instead of an avenue, it is a barrier.

Let him find good advice, but of a wise man, sympathetic, a patron of the youth on entering the gate.

It gives degrees on time, on the number of dinners eaten ("eat your terms"), not on examination.

It gives foolish diplomas of honour to every old clergyman, or successful gentleman, who lives within ten miles.

Ball and boat clubs do not hurt, but help the morals of the students.

If the college falls behind the culture of the people, it is instantly ridiculous.

For my report on the Greek Committee I must not forget to insert my opinion on examinations; — that whenever one is on trial, two are on trial; the examiner is instructed whenever the pupil is examined.

At Monadnoc, the final cause of towns appears to be to be seen from the mountains.

Nature

Day by day for her darlings to her much she added more;
In her hundred-gated Thebes every chamber was a door,
A door to something grander, — loftier walls, and vaster floor.

J. T. Williams said that he told a friend of Evarts that he considered Evarts the best candidate for the United States Senate from New York, and should labor for his election. Afterwards he met Evarts, who came up to him and thanked him for the kind expression he had used. After Evarts had entered the President's Cabinet, Williams saw him again and told him that his new action had lost him the opportunity forever. He would never be United States Senator from New York. Evarts said, No, he was quite mistaken, and that he was now secure of being the man, *whichever party prevailed*; for, said he, unquestionably the Democratic party will carry the next election in New York.

> " Advances
> With rapturous lyrical glances,
> Singing the song of the Earth,
> Singing hymns to the gods."

Is it Goethe's?

France is a country of method and numerical order, the palace of arithmetic; everything is centralized, and, by a necessity of their nature, the French have introduced the decimal system of weights and measures, and made it perfect. They measured the first degree of the meridian, Picard's. They published the first national dictionary of the language. In the Revolution, they abolished the chronology of the world, and began with the year one. "*On se contentait de vivre au jour en jour.*" — *Biographie Générale.*

The only place where I feel the joy of eminent domain is in my woodlot. My spirits rise whenever I enter it. I can spend the entire day there with hatchet or pruning-shears making paths, without a remorse of wasting time. I fancy the birds know me, and even the trees make little speeches or hint them. Then Allah does not count the time which the Arab spends in the chase.

Ah, what a blessing to live in a house which has on the ground-floor one room or one cabinet in which a Worcester's Unabridged; a Liddell and Scott; an Andrews and Stoddard; Lemprière's Classical; a "*Gradus Ad Parnassum*"; a Haydn's *Dictionary of Dates* ; a *Biographie Générale;* a Spiers' French, and Flügel's German Dictionary, even if Grimm is not yet complete, — where these and their equivalents, if equivalents can be, are always at hand, — and yet I might add, as I often do, — ah! happier, if these or their substitutes have been in that house for two generations or for three, — for Horace's metres and Greek literature will not be thoroughly domesticated in one life. A house, I mean, where the seniors, who are at fault about school questions, can inquire of the juniors with some security of a right answer. This is one of my dreams for the American house.

[During October and November, Mr. Emerson gave a course of six lectures in Boston. The subjects were: — I, Art; II, Poetry and Criticism; III, Historic Notes of Life and Letters in New England; IV, Leasts and Mosts; V, Hospitality, Homes; VI, Greatness.]

The distinction of the poet is ever this force of imagination which puts its objects before him with such deceptive power that he treats them as real.[1] . . .

Single speech. "Laodamia" is almost entitled to that eminence in Wordsworth's literary performance. That and the "Ode on Immortality" are the best.

'T is really by a sentence or a phrase or two that many great men are remembered. Zoroaster has three or four, and Marcus Aurelius only as many.

George Tufts wrote me, —

"Life is a flame whose splendor hides its base."

[1] The rest of the passage is found in "Poetry and Imagination" (*Letters and Social Aims*, p. 44).

Mediocre books. There are the sound stomachs and the sick; the farmer and the butcher minister to the sound, the physician and the confectioner to the sick. The well can look at the sun, and use all his light and heat; the sick only what is reflected and shaded. It is the same in literature. Strong minds ask principles, direct *aperçus*, and original forms. The sick public want what is secondary, conventional, and imitations of imitations. There is need of Shakspeare and Hegel, and also of Martin Tupper (if that is his name) and McCosh.

In the perplexity in which the literary public now stands with regard to university education, whether studies shall be compulsory or elective; whether by lectures of professors, or whether by private tutors; whether the stress shall be on Latin and Greek, or on modern sciences, — the one safe investment which all can agree to increase is the library. A good book can wait for a reader hundreds of years. Once lodged in the library, it is unexpensive and harmless while it waits. Then it is a good of the most generous kind, not only serving the undergraduates of the college, but much more the alumni, and probably much more still, the scattered community of scholars.

Ours is the *zymosis*[1] of Science. The heavens open, and the earth, and every element, and disclose their secrets. The large utterance of the gods which in every organism Nature retains, the great style, the fate or invariable adherence to its qualities and methods, and the unity of system which reigns through all the innumerable and immense parts, — we are daily learning; and what beams of light have shone upon men now first in this century! The Genius, Nature, is ever putting conundrums to us, and the *savants*, as in the girls' game of "Twenty Questions," are every month solving them successively by skilful, exhaustive method. This success makes the student cheerful and confident, and his new illumination makes it impossible for him to acquiesce in the old barbarous routine, whether of politics, or religion, or commerce, or social arrangements. Nature will not longer be kinged, or churched, or colleged, or drawing-roomed as before.

A man never gets acquainted with himself, but is always a surprise. We get news daily of the world within, as well as of the world outside, and not less of the central than of the sur-

[1] State of fermentation.

face facts. A new thought is awaiting him every morning.

I often think how hard it is to say with sweetness your thought, when you know that it affronts and exasperates your audience. It is even difficult to write it for such readers without leaving on the line some bitterness. But the French do this, and the French alone, with perfect equanimity in their excellent *Revue des Deux Mondes*.

John Hunter was so far from resting his mind in society, that he felt real fatigue in the midst of company where the conversation *n'avait pas de suite*. (*Biographie Générale*.)

His museum cost him £70,000. The Government bought it for £15,000, after long negotiation. Pitt said, "'Tis not a time to buy anatomical pieces, when I want money to buy powder."

"Don't ask me," he said to his pupils, "what I thought a year ago on this or that; ask me what I think to-day." He, Hunter, first used the expression "*arrested development*," which plays so important a part in modern science.

November 11.

Yesterday was well occupied in accompanying William Robert Ware to the church he is building for the First Church Society, on Berkeley Street. It has a completeness and uniformity of strength, richness, and taste, perfect adaptation to its present purpose, and an antiquity in all its ornamentation that give delight. It seemed to threaten ruin to the Radical Club, retroaction in all people who shall sit down in its sumptuous twilight. I lamented for my old friend Dr. Frothingham his loss of sight, once more, that he could not enjoy this faultless temple. I looked through all the details of the drawings for the Alumni Hall at Ware's office, which conciliate the eye very fast, and the capital suggestion that the Dining-Hall shall be used for daily Commons, if properly accepted and followed up, will go far to remove every point of objection on the old ground that this vast expense is for three or four days only in the year. In his Technologic Chambers, he showed me a multitude of interesting fragments of art, casts mainly, from Trajan's Column, from English, French, and Italian churches, a head from a statue at Rheims Cathedral of the thirteenth [16th?] century by John of Bologna (?) which gives, what I always seek, when I see new sculpture — decisive proof of a master. Ware believes the Romans were their own artists, and not Greeks; confirmed by specimens of Etruscan art which he saw.

December 9.

In poetry, tone. I have been reading some of Lowell's new poems, in which he shows unexpected advance on himself, but perhaps most in technical skill and courage. It is in talent rather than in poetic tone, and rather expresses his wish, his ambition, than the uncontrollable interior impulse which is the authentic mark of a new poem, and which is unanalysable, and makes the merit of an ode of Collins, or Gray, or Wordsworth, or Herbert, or Byron, — and which is felt in the pervading tone, rather than in brilliant parts or lines; as if the sound of a bell, or a certain cadence expressed in a low whistle or booming, or humming, to which the poet first timed his step, as he looked at the sunset, or thought, was the incipient form of the piece, and was regnant through the whole.

Wordsworth is manly, the manliest poet of his age. His poems record the thoughts and emotions which have occupied his mind, and which he reports because of their reality. He has great skill in rendering them into simple and sometimes happiest poetic speech. Tennyson has incomparable felicity in all poetic forms, and is a brave, thoughtful Englishman; exceeds Wordsworth a hundredfold in rhythmic power and variety, but far less manly compass; and Tennyson's main purpose is the rendering, whilst Wordsworth's is just value of the dignity of the thought.

I told Ware that I prize Michel Angelo so much that, whilst I look at his figures, I come to believe the grandiose is grand. Thomas Gray in poetry has relations to Michel Angelo, and the like question between the grandiose and grand is suggested in reading his odes.

An Englishman has firm manners. He rests secure on the reputation of his country, on his family, his education, and his expectations at home. There is in his manners a suspicion of insolence. If his belief in the Thirty-nine Articles does not bind him much, his belief in the fortieth does;—namely, that he shall not find his superiors elsewhere. Hence a complaint you shall often find made against him here, that, whilst at his house he would resent as unpermissible that a guest should come to a seven o'clock dinner in undress, he bursts into yours in shooting-jacket. Well, it is for the company to put him in the wrong by their perfect politeness.

When I find in people narrow religion, I find narrow reading.

Remarkable [New England] families were: The three Jackson brothers, — Dr. James, Judge Charles, and Patrick; the three Lowell brothers, John, Rev. Dr. Charles, and Francis Cabot Lowell; the four Lawrences, Abbott, Amos, Luther, William; the Cabots; the three Hunts, William, Richard, and Leavitt (William Hunt tells me also of his brother John, in Paris); the Washburns, three governors, I believe.

Culture is one thing, and varnish another. There can be no high culture without pure morals. With the truly cultivated man, — the maiden, the orphan, the poor man, and the hunted slave feel safe.

There are so many men in the world that I can be spared to work a great while on one chapter;— so long that, when at last it is finished and printed and returns to me, I can read it without pain, and know that others can.

Farming. Marshall Miles said to me that he wants to come home to his old farm, and thinks he shall, presently; "for it is what you get out of the earth that is pure gain, but what we get by speculating, each on the other, is not."

A chapter on the intellect should begin low by examples; as Thales and his shadow of the pyramid; or Haüy and his finding the laws of cleavage in crystals, — and so instructing the lapidary how to cut; and plenty of other illustrations how the laws of real nature are turned into rules of thumb; and, if I understood them, that law of the "catenary" (is it?) of Hooke's:[1] and the corollaries of Chladni's central discovery of music on the steel filings (for which see Tyndall *On Sound*); and if I could understand it again, the related suggestion of the form of the skeleton of mammals by Dr. Wyman from the iron filings on [a paper over] the magnet.

[1] That the curve of a hanging chain, if reversed, will give a safe model for an arch.

Mrs. Sarah Alden Ripley said that the farmers like to be complimented with thought.

Authors or Books quoted or referred to in Journal for 1868

Menu; *Bhagavat Geeta; Vishnu Purana;* Pythagoras; Confucius; Æschylus; Herodotus; Aristophanes; Strabo; Marcus Aurelius; Hafiz; Tycho Brahe; Cudworth; Pascal; Spinoza; Robert Hooke; Dr. Isaac Watts, *Hymns and Spiritual Songs;*

Jonathan Edwards; Franklin; Gray; Collins, *Ode to Evening;* John Hunter; Niebuhr; Washington; John Adams; William Vincent, *Voyage of Nearchus;* Haüy; Herder; Geoffroy Saint-Hilaire; Goethe;

James Madison; Chladni, *Acoustics;* Alexander Hamilton; Schiller; Samuel Rogers, *Recollections;* Cuvier; Hegel; Oken;

Rev. W. E. Channing; De Quincey; Keats; Champollion; Balzac; Alcott;

Harriet Martineau, *Eastern Life;* Dupanloup; Sainte-Beuve, *Portraits Contemporains;* Richard Owen, *Paleontology;* Frederic H. Hedge; Disraeli; Tennyson, *The Holy Grail;* O. W. Holmes; Martin Tupper;

Lepsius; John Bright; James McCosh; Hay on *Etruscan Pottery;* Jeffries Wyman, *Symmetry and Homology in Human Limbs;* Mommsen; W. E. Channing; Schwegler, *History of Philosophy;* Matthew Arnold, *Thyrsis;* Lowell; Charles K. Newcomb; "George Eliot," *The Spanish Gypsy;* Tyndall, *On Sound;* Max Müller;

Charles Eliot Norton; John Weiss; Taine, *Nouveaux essais de critique;* Ephraim Wales Gurney; William Morris, *King Acrisius, The Proud King;* Mrs. Helen Hunt, *Thought, Ariadne's Farewell.*

JOURNAL

CELTIC BARDS AND MORTE D'ARTHUR
TONE IN POETRY
FRIENDS
RICHARD HUNT
READINGS TO CLASS
COLLEGE MARKING
JUDGE HOAR
CHARLES SUMNER
HESIOD. HUMBOLDT. AGASSIZ
POETRY. GOOD WRITING

JOURNAL LX

1869

(From Journals NY and ML)

[IN January, Mr. Emerson seems to have made a shorter lecturing trip than usual, going no farther West than Cleveland.]

(From NY)

In this proposition lately brought to me by a class, it occurs that I could by readings show the difference between good poetry and what passes for good; that I could show how much so-called poetry is only eloquence; that I could vindicate the genius of Wordsworth, and show his distinctive merits. I should like to call attention to the critical superiority of Arnold, his excellent ear for style, and the singular poverty of his poetry, that in fact he has written but one poem, "Thyrsis," and that on an inspiration borrowed from Milton. A topic would be this Welsh genius (and Arnold, too, has been attracted to that) which I recognized to-day in reading this new translator, Skene, and which I find, as long ago, far more suggestive, contagious, or I will say, more inoculating the reader with poetic madness, than any poet I now think of, except Hafiz. I can easily believe this an idiosyncrasy of mine, and, to describe it more accurately, I will add that I place these as not equal, but *of like kind* in genius and influence with the Zoroastrian sentences, and those of the *Bhagavat Geeta* and the *Vishnu Purana*.

There is always a height of land which, in a walk for pleasure or business, the party seek as the natural centre, or point of view; and there is in every book, whether poem or history, or treatise of philosophy, a height which attracts more than other parts, and which is best remembered. Thus, in *Morte d'Arthur*, I remember nothing so well as Merlin's cry from his invisible, inaccessible prison. To be sure, different readers select by natural affinity different points. In the proposed class, it would be my wish to indicate such points in literature, and thus be an "old guide," like Stephen, who shows, after ten years' daily trudging through the subterranean holes, the best wonders of the Mammoth Cave.

The gripe of Byron has not been repeated, and the delightful romance which came from Scott to young America has not. Tennyson has finer, more delicate beauty and variety, but does not possess men as the others did. Tennyson has a perfect English culture, and its petulance.

Homer has this prerogative, that he never discovers in the Iliad a preference to the Greeks over the Trojans.

It were good to contrast the hospitality of Abu Bekr in the *Sahara* with that of Admetus in Euripides's *Alcestis*. That of the Arab is at once noble, yet human; that of the king in the play is overstrained to absurdity.

I have said above that tone, rather than lines, marks a genuine poem. Wolfe's

"Not a drum was heard, not a funeral note,"

is an example, so is Sterling's "Dædalus," so "Dinas Emlinn" of Scott, and Scott always has that merit; and Byron's Incantation in "Manfred," and the whole of [the poem] charms, in spite of its shallowness, by that unity; and Beaumont and Fletcher's "Melancholy." I think the vice of the French, their notorious incapacity of poetic power, is the total want of this music, which all their brilliant talent cannot supply. Voltaire could see wholes as well as parts, and his testimony to French unpoeticalness is distinct. "*Si le roi m'avait donné*," etc., has right tone, and that little carol is still their best poem. Many poems owe their fame to tone, as others to their sense.

But Victor Hugo has genius in *Le Semeur*, and the *star*-piece, which I have saved. And, I must repeat, that one genial thought is the source of every true poem. I have heard that a unity of this kind pervades Beethoven's great pieces in music. And why, but because tone gives unity?

In the matter of religion, men eagerly fasten their eyes on the differences between their own creed and yours; whilst the charm of the study is in finding the agreements and identities in all the religions of men.

The few stout and sincere persons, whom each one of us knows, recommend the country and the planet to us. 'Tis not a bad world this, as long as I know that John M. Forbes or William H. Forbes and Judge Hoar, and Agassiz, and my three children, and twenty other shining creatures whose faces I see looming through the mist, are walking in it. Is it the thirty millions of America, or is it your ten or twelve units that encourage your heart from day to day?

Of immortality, I should say that it is at least equally and perhaps better seen in little than in large angles. I mean, that in a calm and clear state of mind, we have no fears, no prayers, even; that we feel all is well. We have arrived at an enjoyment so pure, as to imply and affirm its perfect accord with the nature of things, so that it alone appears durable, and all mixed or inferior states accidental and temporary.

The managers of the public conventions, political and other, understand well that they must set the fire going by ready popular speakers, like Wilson, and Russell, and Swift, who will crackle and kindle, and afterwards they may venture to pile on the slow anthracite of argumentative judges and political economists; kindlings first, and then hard coal.

Shakspeare. I think, with all due respect to Aubrey, and Dyce, and Delia Bacon, and Judge Holmes, that it is not by discovery of contemporary documents, but by more cunning reading of the Book itself, that we shall at last eliminate[1] the true biography of Shakspeare.

[On March 1, Mr. Emerson read before the Woman's Club an account of his aunt, Mary Moody Emerson, with some extracts from her letters and journal. (See *Lectures and Biographical Sketches*.)]

Montaigne says that "Socrates's virtue does seem to have been ever on the rack to perform its actions, but to have done them naturally and gracefully. 'T was a better born virtue than other men's."

In my visit to New York I saw one remarkable person new to me, Richard Hunt,[2] the architect. His conversation was spirited beyond any that I could easily remember, loaded with matter, and expressed with the vigour and fury of a member of the Harvard boat or ball club relating the adventures of one of their matches; inspired, meantime, throughout, with fine theories of the possibilities of art. Yet the tone of

[1] As has been said before, Mr. Emerson always used eliminate as *bring out*, instead of *leave out*.
[2] Brother of William Morris Hunt, the painter.

his voice and the accent of his conversation so strongly reminded me of my rural neighbour Sam Staples as to be in ludicrous contrast with the Egyptian and Greek grandeurs he was hinting or portraying. I could only think of the immense advantage which a thinking soul possesses when horsed on a robust and vivacious temperament. The combination is so rare of an Irish labourer's nerve and elasticity with Winckelmann's experience and cultivation as to fill one with immense hope of great results when he meets it in the New York of to-day.

[Mr. Emerson's friend, James T. Fields, the genial publisher and author, and his son-in-law, Colonel William H. Forbes, did him the friendly office of arranging for him a "Class," to whom he read, in Chickering Hall, on ten Saturday afternoons in the spring, his favourite pieces of prose or verse, with some short introduction. Among the subjects were, Chivalry (extracts from Old Chronicles); Chaucer; Shakspeare; Ben Jonson and Lord Bacon; Herrick; Donne; Herbert; Vaughan; Marvell; Milton; Johnson; Gibbon; Burke; Cowper; Wordsworth.

These readings were much enjoyed by the Class, but, in this wealth of material and the limits of an hour, many things that Mr. Emerson wished to read were not included, as appears from the following entry, which yet tells of many that were.]

(From ML)

March 21, 1869.

Readings at Chickering Hall. Yesterday finished the Tenth Reading at Chickering Hall. Many good things were read in these ten Saturdays, and some important passages that had been selected were not read. Read nothing of Byron but the lines, "I twine my hopes of being remembered," etc., from "Childe Harold"; nothing of Sterling but "Alfred the Harper"; nothing of Wordsworth but "Helvellyn," "Dion," and verses from the "Ode"; nothing from Coleridge, prose or verse. From Scott, I read the Abbot and Bruce in *Lord of the Isles;* "Helvellyn"; "Look not thou when beauty's charming." Read nothing from Blake but "Persecution." From Gray, nothing. From Campbell, nothing. From Clough, Thoreau, Channing, Brownell, Mellen, Longfellow, Arnold, Willis, Sprague, nothing. Of Moore, nothing.

I had designed to read some pages on the art of writing, on Language, Compression, etc.;

but with the exception of a page or two on *the dire*, τὸ δεινόν, omitted them. Little searching criticism was given. I meant to show some *inspired prose* from Charles K. Newcomb, Sampson Reed, Mary Moody Emerson, etc., but did not.

I meant to have one Ethical Reading, and one Oriental: but they came not. Nothing from Goethe except the "Song of the Parcæ" in *Iphigenia*. Nothing from Horatio Greenough. Did not read the proposed hymns of Watts, and Barbauld, or Sir Thomas Browne. I designed to read from Montaigne, of "Friendship," of "Socrates," but did not. From Goethe, *West - Östlichen Divan*. From Coleridge, *Lay Sermons*, *Literary Biography*, *Friend*. From Plutarch's *Morals;* Synesius; Plotinus. From James Hogg, read only "Kilmeny"; had wished to read "The Witch of Fife." Of Samuel Ferguson, should have read "Forging of the Anchor"; of Frederic H. Hedge, should have read *Lines in the Dial;* and from Brownell, "The Old Cove"; and from Ellen Hooper, "Sweep Ho!"

What selections from Plato I might read! e. g., *Theages*, and the beginning and end of *Phædon*, and the naïvetés of the *Apology*. Carlyle's portrait of Webster in letter to me. Story of Berthollet, and examples of Courage; Fra Cristoforo, in *I Promessi Sposi*. And, in American Poets remember Sarah Palfrey's "Sir Pavon," and Helen Hunt's "Thought."[1] Eugène Fromentin on Arab Hospitality; Lord Carnarvon's speech in the House of Lords on the impeachment of the Earl of Danby; Faryabi, in D'Herbelot; The Cid's arraignment of his sons-in-law before the Cortes; Romeo, in Cary; Lord Bacon's "Young Scholar," "Ships of Time," Speech for Essex; Earl of Devonshire, from Coleridge's "Puritan Soldier"; *Lay Sermons;* Story of Marvell's refusal of royal bounty. Gibbon's Conception and Conclusion of the *History*. Hobbes's definition of Laughter (not read); Hobbes's barbarous society (not read); John Quincy Adams's Peroration; Behmen, *Life of Christ*. Milton, Prose and Poetry. Charles K. Newcomb, of Swedenborg and Brook Farm; Dr. Johnson, "Iona"; Hindoo Books; Chivalry, Lord Herbert; Chief Justice Crewe; Merlin in *Morte d'Arthur;* the lion story; "Celinda"; Cid; Horn of Roland in *Chanson de Roland;* Voltaire on French Poetry; Nie-

[1] Most of what is above and what follows are reminders for another year.

buhr's *View of Poetry;* Creation of new characters; Pepys's notices of Shakspeare and Clarendon.

Poetry. "Dædalus," unread; Wordsworth,

"The intellectual power from words to things
    Went sounding on, a dim and perilous way";

"Russian Snow," not read; Beaumont and Fletcher, "Melancholy," "Lines on *An Honest Man's Fortune*"; Speech of Caratach in *Bonduca*, Scene I; Gray and Collins — inimitable skill in perfectly modern verse; had digested their classics. Jones Very's two poems, "The Strangers" and "Barberry Bush," with notes of Jones Very. William Blake's "Persecution," and Allingham's "Touchstone"; Clough; Henry Kirke White's "Herb Rosemary"; Waller's "Rose," and Bayly's "Round my own lovely Rose," and Mrs. Hemans's "Nightingale"; Hogg's "Witch of Fife"; Tennyson's "Memory"; Byron's "Shipwreck," and "Out upon Time"; Bryant's "Waterfowl." . . .

Coup-de-force poetry, Everett; Lapidary or gem-carving; Eloquent; Biblical; Sculpturesque, M. Angelo; *Vers de Société*, Daniel Webster.

The Mountain

> Seemed, though the soft sheen all enchants,
> Cheers the rough crag and mournful dell,
> As if on such stern forms and haunts
> A wintry storm more fitly fell.

Et vocatus et non vocatus Deus aderit. Invoked or uninvoked, the God will be present.

Who was the king to whom the sophist wished to teach the art of memory, and who replied, that he would give him a greater reward if he could teach him to forget?

No more irreconcilable persons brought to annoy and confound each other in one room than are sometimes actually lodged by Nature in one man's skin.

Memory. It sometimes occurs that memory has a personality of its own, and volunteers or refuses its information at *its* will, not at mine. I ask myself, Is it not some old aunt who goes in and out of the house, and occasionally recites anecdotes of old times and persons, which I recognize as having heard before, — and she being gone again, I search in vain for any trace of the anecdotes?

March 29.

Alcott came, and talked Plato and Socrates, extolling them with gravity. I bore it long, and then said, that was a song for others, not for him. He should find what was the equivalent for these masters in our times; for surely the world was always equal to itself, and it was for him to detect what was the counter-weight and compensation to us. Was it natural science? Was it the immense dilution of the same amount of thought into nations? I told him to shut his eyes, and let his thoughts run into reverie or whithersoever, — and then take an observation. He would find that the current went outward from man, not to man. Consciousness was upstream.

Bunsen's physiognomy, as I remember him in London, suggested not a noble, but the common German scholar, with marked sentimentalism, or, as we commonly say, *gushing;* and these prayers, and violent conventicle utterances to which he runs in his correspondence and diary, betray that temperament. Yet he had talent and generosity, and appears to have been highly useful.

May 5, died Philip Physick Randolph, son of the late Jacob Randolph, M. D.[1]

[On May 17, Mr. Emerson read a paper on Religion at the house of the Rev. J. T. Sargent; and on May 28, spoke at the second annual meeting of the Free Religious Association.]

God had infinite time to give us; but how did He give it? In one immense tract of a lazy millennium? No, but He cut it up into neat succession of new mornings, and, with each, therefore, a new idea, new inventions, and new applications.

"The door of intercourse is closed between those confined and those unconfined by space," say the Ali Ilahi An. — DABISTAN.

The religions are the amusements of the intellect.

June.

Yesterday, Saturday, June 12, the committee on scale of merit and discipline met at Dr. Walker's in Cambridge. Present, Dr. Walker, Professor Runkle, Theodore Lyman, and I. Rev. Mr. Hale alone was absent. Dr. Walker

[1] A young man of high and serious mind living in Philadelphia, valued by Mr. Emerson.

gave some details of the manner in which the scale is made up, and stated that the Faculty were for the most part contented with it as it stands, and do not wish any alteration. He added that there is question and inconvenience in regard to elective studies. For the poor men, it is matter of grave importance that they shall have rank sufficient to obtain a scholarship, that is, an income; and when elective studies are proposed, they do not choose that which they wish to learn, but that which will give the most marks, that is, highest rank. It was stated that the idle boys would choose botany, or some other study which cost no thought and little attention, and it was not quite fair that for such idle reading they should receive equally high marks with those who elected severer studies as trigonometry, or metaphysics, or advanced studies in Greek. Mr. Lyman said the state of study was much superior at present to that which he remembered when in college, and alluded to the performance of young Hill at the examination.

Some of the professors, as Mr. Lowell and Mr. Peirce, Senior, do not keep a daily account of merits of the students, but make up a general average, each in a way of his own. It was suggested that whilst each teacher should keep a daily record of the quality of recitations, he should by no means present that in his final report, but should correct it by his growing knowledge of the depth of real merit of the student, as shown to him by his proficiency and power, or his want of success, as made known in decisive strokes from time to time.

It is the necessary result of the existing system the mixing of the record of deportment with that of scholarship, and thus degrading a good scholar, if by neglect of prayers or recitations he had incurred a "public admonition," or raising the rank of a dull scholar if he was punctual and in deportment blameless.

President Hosmer, of Antioch College, tells me that there they do not mark for merit; and that, for discipline they organize the students in the Dormitory into a Society for noting and resisting all breaches of order. The students have a president and other officers, and when any disturbance occurs they examine, and vote perhaps to recommend the expulsion of the offenders, — which the College Government then considers and decides.

At present, the friends of Harvard are possessed in greater or less degree by the idea of making it a University for men, instead of a College for boys.

One would say that this better moral record should only serve to give the casting vote in favour of good behaviour, where the marks for scholarship were equal.

I think every one who has had any experience in marking a series of recitations has found how uncertainly his 6, and 7, and 8 are given. His first attempt will be worthless except in the extreme numbers, and can only be approximately trustworthy in a great number of days.

July 1.

Judge Hoar, in his speech at the Alumni dinner at Cambridge yesterday, was a perfect example of Coleridge's definition of genius, "the carrying the feelings of youth into the powers of manhood"; and the audience were impressed and delighted with the rare combination of the innocence of a boy with the faculty of a hero.

(From loose sheets of uncertain date)

Charles Sumner.[1] Clean, self-poised, great-

[1] It is possible that this tribute to Sumner may have been written much earlier during President Johnson's administration, when Sumner was striving to prevent any Reconstruction

hearted man, noble in person, incorruptible in life, the friend of the poor, the champion of the oppressed. Of course, Congress must draw from every part of the country swarms of individuals intent only on their private interests, eager only for private interests who could not love his stern justice. But if they gave him no high employment, he made low work high by the dignity of honesty and truth. But men cannot long do without faculty and perseverance, and he rose, step by step, to the mastery of all affairs entrusted to him, and by those lights and upliftings with which the Spirit that makes the Universe rewards labour and brave truth. He became learned and adequate to the highest questions, and the counsellor of every correction of old errors and of every noble reform. How nobly he bore himself in disastrous times! Every reform he led or assisted. In the shock of the war his patriotism never failed.

A man of varied learning and accomplishments. He held that every man is to be judged by the horizon of his mind, and Fame he defined as the shadow of excellence, but that which follows him, not which he follows after. A

measures that would keep the franchise from the coloured people and fail to secure their equal rights as citizens.

tragic character, like Algernon Sydney; a man of conscience and courage, but without humour. Fear did not exist for him.

Sumner has been collecting his works. They will be the history of the Republic for the last twenty-five years, as told by a brave, perfectly honest, and well-instructed man with social culture and relation to all eminent persons. Diligent and able workman, without humour, but with persevering study while reading, excellent memory, high sense of honour, disdaining any bribe, any compliances, and incapable of falsehood. His singular advantages of person, of manners, and a statesman's conversation, impress every one favourably. He has the foible of most public men, the egotism which seems almost unavoidable at Washington. I sat in his room once at Washington whilst he wrote a weary succession of letters, — he writing without pause as fast as if he were copying. He outshines all his mates in historical conversation and is so public in his regards that he cannot be relied on to push an office-seeker, so that he is no favourite with politicians. But wherever I have met with a dear lover of the Country and its moral interests, he is sure to be a supporter of Sumner.

It characterizes a man for me that he hates Charles Sumner: for it shows that he cannot discriminate between a foible and a vice. Sumner's moral instinct and character are so exceptionally pure that he must have perpetual magnetism for honest men; his ability and working energy such, that every good friend of the Republic must stand by him. Those who come near him and are offended by his egotism, or his foible (if you please) of using classic quotations, or other bad taste, easily forgive these whims, if themselves are good; or magnify them into disgust, if they themselves are incapable of his virtue. And when he read one night in Concord a lecture on Lafayette we felt that of all Americans he was best entitled by his own character and fortunes to read that eulogy.

Every Pericles must have his Creon; Sumner had his adversaries, his wasps and backbiters. We almost wished that he had not stooped to answer them. But he condescended to give them truth and patriotism, without asking whether they could appreciate the instruction or not.

A man of such truth that he can be truly described: he needs no exaggerated praise.

Not a man of extraordinary genius, but a man

of great heart, of a perpetual youth, incapable of any fraud, little or large; loving his friend, and loving his Country, with perfect steadiness to his purpose, shunning no labour that his aim required; and his works justified him by their scope and thoroughness.

He had good masters, who quickly found that they had a good scholar. He read law with Judge Story, who was at the head of the Law School of Harvard University, and who speedily discovered the value of his pupil, and called him to his assistance in the Law School.

He had great talent for labour, and spared no time and no research to make himself master of his subject. His treatment of every question was faithful and exhaustive and marked always by the noble sentiment.

(From NY)

July 26.

This morning sent my six prose volumes, revised and corrected, to Fields and Company for their new edition in two volumes.

Landor says, "A single man of genius hath never appeared in the whole extent of Austria, an extent several thousand times greater than our city (Florence); and this very street has given birth to fifty." — *Works*, vol. i, p. 191.

"Annibal Caracci said to his scholar, *What you do not understand, you must darken*." — LANDOR.

At Walden, the other day, with George Bradford, I was struck, as often, with the expression of refinement which Nature wears often in such places; — the bright sunshine reflected by the agreeable forms of the water, the shore-line, and the forest, the soft lapping sound of the water.

At my Club, I suppose I behave very ill in securing always, if I can, a place by a valued friend, and, though I suppose (though I have never heard it) that I offend by this selection, sometimes too visible, my reason is that I, who rarely see, in ordinary, select society, must make the best use of this opportunity, having, at the same time, the feeling that

"I could be happy with either,
Were the other dear charmer away."

I am interested not only in my advantages, but in my disadvantages, that is, in my fortunes proper; that is, in watching my fate, to notice, after each act of mine, what result. Is it prosperous? Is it adverse? And thus I find a pure entertainment of the intellect, alike in what is called good or bad.

In Xenophon's *Banquet*, Critobulus says, "I swear by all the gods, I would not choose the power of the Persian King in preference to beauty."

Washington City. I notice that they who drink for some time the Potomac water lose their relish for the water of the Charles River, the Merrimack, and the Connecticut. But I think the public health requires that the Potomac water should be corrected by copious infusions of these provincial streams. Rockwood Hoar retains his relish for the Musketaquid.

Sumner cites Cato as saying "that Kings were carnivorous animals."

In looking into Hesiod's *Works and Days*, I am reminded how much harm our clocks and almanacs do us by withdrawing our attention from the stars, the annual winds, and rains, habits of animals, and whatever primary observations of Nature the ancient nations relied on. Their year was throughout religious and imaginative.

"Sit in the shade, and drink moreover dark-hued wine— Pour in three cups of water first and add the fourth of wine." — HESIOD.

"You, Perses, flattered much the bribe-swallowing judges. Fools, they know neither how much half exceeds the whole, nor how great advantage is in mallow and asphodel." — Bohn's HESIOD, p. 76.

"Sow stripped, plough stripped, and reap stripped, if thou wouldst gather the works of Ceres." — Idem, p. 95.

The same periodicity — shall I say — reigns in fable, and brings the wildest curve round to a true moral, as works in electricity, gravitation, and the crystal. And this is also expressed in tone and rhythm.

[The Boston Society of Natural History celebrated, on September 14, the Centennial Anniversary of the birth of Alexander von Humboldt. Mr. Emerson was invited to speak, and an abstract of his remarks is printed in the *Miscellanies*. Some additional sentences are given in what follows.]

September.

Humboldt one of those wonders of the world like Aristotle, like Crichton, like Newton, appearing now and then as if to show us the possibilities of the *genus Homo*, the powers of the eye, the range of the faculties; whose eyes are natural telescopes and microscopes and whose faculties are so symmetrically joined that they have perpetual presence of mind, and can read Nature by bringing instantly their insight and their momentary observation together; whilst men ordinarily are, as it were, astonished by the new object, and do not on the instant bring their knowledge to bear on it. Other men have memory which they can ransack, but Humboldt's memory was wide awake to assist his observation. Our faculties are a committee that slowly, one at a time, give their attention and opinion, — but his, all united by electric chain, . . . You could not lose him. He was the man of the world, if ever there was one. You could not lose him; you could not detain him; you could not disappoint him. The tardy Spaniards were months in getting their expedition ready and it was a year that he waited; but Spain or Africa or Asia were all harvest-fields to this armed eye, to this Lyncæus who could see through the earth, and through the ocean, who knew how mountains were built, and seas drained. . . .

Agassiz never appeared to such advantage as in his Biographical Discourse on Humboldt, at the Music Hall in Boston, yesterday. What is unusual for him, he read a written discourse, about two hours long; yet all of it strong, nothing to spare, not a weak point, no rhetoric, no falsetto; — his personal recollections and anecdotes of their intercourse, simple, frank, and tender in the tone of voice, too, no error of egotism or of self-assertion, and far enough from French sentimentalism. He is quite as good a man as his hero, and not to be duplicated, I fear. I admire his manliness, his equality always to the occasion, to any and every company, — never a fop, never can his manners be separated from himself.

I never could get beyond five steps in my enumeration of intellectual powers; say, Instinct, Perception, Memory, Imagination (including Fancy as a subaltern), Reasoning or Understanding. Some of the lower divisions, as Genius, Talent, Logic, Wit, and Humour, Pathos, can be dealt with more easily.

The person who commands the servant successfully is the one who does not think of the manner, solely thinking that this thing must be done. Command is constitutional.

October 19.

Carried to Fields and Company to-day the copy of the four first chapters of my so-called new book, *Society and Solitude*.

I read a good deal of experimental poetry in the new books. The author has said to himself, "*Who knows but this may please, and become famous? Did not Goethe experiment? Does not this read like the ancients?*" But good poetry was not written thus, but it delighted the poet first; he said and wrote it for joy, and it pleases the reader for the same reason.

October 21.

I wish I could recall my singular dream of last night with its physics, metaphysics, and rapid transformations, — all impressive at the moment, that on waking at midnight I tried to rehearse them, that I might keep them till morn. I fear 't is all vanished. I noted how we magnify the inward world, and emphasize it to hypocrisy by contempt of house and land and man's condition, which we call shabby and beastly. But in a few minutes these have their revenge, for we look to their chemistry and perceive that they are miracles of combination of ethereal elements, and do point instantly to moral causes.

General Wayne was the commissioner of the Government who first saw the importance of the nook of land at the foot of Lake Michigan round which the road to the northwest must run, and managed to run the boundary line of Illinois in such manner as to include this swamp, called Chicago, within it.

Aunt Mary held a relation to good society not very uncommon. She was strongly drawn to it as to the reputed theatre for genius, but her eccentricity disgusted it, and she was quite too proud and impulsive to sit and conform. So she acquiesced, and made no attempt to keep place, and knew it only in the narratives of a few friends like Mrs. George Lee, Mrs. Mary Schalkwic, Miss Searle, etc., with whom she had been early intimate, and who for her genius tolerated or forgave her oddities. But her sympathy and delight in its existence daily appear through all her disclaimers and fine scorn.

Good writing. All writing should be selection in order to drop every dead word. Why do you not save out of your speech or thinking only the vital things, — the spirited *mot* which amused or warmed you when you spoke it, — because of its luck and newness? I have just been reading, in this careful book of a most intelligent and learned man, any number of flat conventional words and sentences. If a man would learn to read his own manuscript severely, — becoming really a third person, and search only for what interested him, he would blot to purpose, — and how every page would gain! Then all the words will be sprightly, and every sentence a surprise.

I will tell you what it is to be immortal, — this, namely, that I cannot read Plutarch without perpetual reminders of men and women whom I know.

Dr. Hedge tells us that the Indian asked John Eliot, "Why God did not kill the devil?" One would like to know what was Eliot's answer.

December 8.

The scholar wants not only time but *warm time*, good anthracite or cannel coal to make every minute in the hour avail.

"Harmony latent is of greater value than that which is visible." — HERACLITUS.

Calvinism. There is a certain weakness in solemnly threatening the human being with the revelations of the Judgment Day, as Mrs. Stowe winds up her appeal to the executors of Lady Byron. An honest man would say, Why refer it? All that is true and weighty with me has all its force now.

We meet people who seem to overlook and read us with a smile, but they do not tell us what they read. Now and then we say things to our mates, or hear things from them, which seem to put it out of the power of the parties to be strangers again.[1] Especially if any one show me a stroke of courage, a piece of inventive wit, a trait of character, or a pure delight in character when shown by others, henceforward I must be that man's or that woman's debtor, as one who has discovered to me among perishing men somewhat more clean and incorruptible than the light of these midnight stars. Indeed, the only real benefit of which we are susceptible is (is it not?) to have man dignified for us.

[1] This sentence occurs in *Social Aims* (p. 89).

"To declare war against length of time." — SIMONIDES.

Compensation of failing memory in age by the increased power and means of generalization.

I asked Theodore Lyman on Saturday how it was exactly with Agassiz's health. He said "that no further paralysis had appeared, and that he seemed not threatened. It was not apoplexy, but a peculiarity of his constitution, — these turns of insensibility which had occurred. It was *hysteria*." I replied that I had often said that Agassiz appeared to have two or three men rolled up into his personality, but I had never suspected there was any woman also in his make. Lyman replied that he had himself seen hysteria oftener in men than in women.

AUTHORS OR BOOKS QUOTED OR REFERRED TO IN JOURNAL FOR 1869

Zoroaster; Hesiod, *Works and Days*; Simonides; Heracleitus; Euripides, *Alcestis*; Xenophon, *Banquet*; Cato the Elder;

Proclus; *Arthurian Romances*; *Dabistan*;

James ("the Admirable") Crichton; Sir Philip Sidney, *Life of*, by Lord Brooke; De

Retz; Aubrey; Sprat, *Death of Cromwell, apud*
Johnson; Addison, *Cato*; Voltaire;

Winckelmann; Humboldt; Rev. W. E.
Channing; Varnhagen von Ense; Haydon;
Chevalier Bunsen; Alexander Dyce; Alcott;

Victor Hugo, *Le Semeur*; Agassiz; Tennyson; Crabbe Robinson, *Diary*; *La Cité Antique*;

Charles Sumner; Harriet Beecher Stowe,
Lady Byron Vindicated; Fromentin, *Un Été
dans le Sahara*; W. Ellery Channing, *Poems*;
Matthew Arnold, *Poems*; M. H. Cobb, *Outward Bound*; O. W. Holmes, Jr.

See also the list of authors and poems and
passages quoted in the readings on pages 282–
285.

JOURNAL

MEMORY. DREAMS

THOREAU. ALVAH CROCKER

SAMPSON REED

METAPHYSICIANS

PLUTARCH. HIS MORALS

NANTASKET BEACH

MARY MOODY EMERSON

MOUNT WASHINGTON. THE NOTCH

IMAGINATION. CHIVALRY

HARVARD MEMORIAL HALL

FOREIGN CULTURE

THE PILGRIMS

JOURNAL LXI

1870

(From Journals NY and ST)

[DURING January, Mr. Emerson was preparing his preface to a new translation, by Professor William Watson Goodwin, of *Plutarch's Morals*. This, by the kindness of Messrs. Little and Brown, the publishers, is included in the works (*Lectures and Biographical Sketches*).]

(From NY)

February 3, 1870.

The last proof-sheet of *Society and Solitude* comes back to me to-day for correction.

Mr. Charles P. Ware tells Edward that the night before the Cambridge Commemoration Day he spent at Mr. Hudson's room, in Cambridge, and woke from a dream which he could not remember, repeating these words, —

And what they dare to dream of, dare to die for.

He went to the Pavilion Dinner, and there heard Mr. Lowell read his poem, and when he came to the lines: —

"Those love her best who to themselves are true
And what" —

Ware said, "Now I know what's coming, — but it won't rhyme;" and Mr. Lowell proceeded, —

"they dare to dream of, dare to do."

[No mention of lectures is found until the spring, except before Lyceums in neighboring towns, and one in Philadelphia, February 7, an excursion always pleasant, for there Mr. Emerson met his old schoolmates of his Boston boyhood, Rev. William H. Furness and Mr. Samuel Bradford.]

February 24.

Bettine, in Varnhagen's *Diary*, reminds me continually of Aunt Mary, though the first is ever helping herself with a lie, which the other abhorred. But the dwelling long with grief and with genius on your wrongs and wrongdoers, exasperating the offender with habitual reproaches, puts the parties in the worst relation and at last incapacitates the complaining woman from seeing what degree of right or of necessity there is on the side of her offender, and what good reason he has to complain of her wrath and insults.

This ever-increasing bias of the injured party has all the mischief of lying.

February 27.

At Club yesterday, Lowell, Longfellow, Cabot, Brimmer, Appleton, Hunt, James, Forbes, Fields. Erastus Bigelow[1] was a guest.

How dangerous is criticism. My brilliant friend[2] cannot see any healthy power in Thoreau's thoughts. At first I suspect, of course, that he oversees me, who admire Thoreau's power. But when I meet again fine perceptions in Thoreau's papers, I see that there is defect in his critic that he should undervalue them. Thoreau writes, in his *Field Notes*, "I look back for the era of this creation not into the

[1] The inventor and improver of various looms, and writer on the Tariff.
[2] Probably Lowell. There is some reason to believe that Lowell, later, came to revise his superficial view in his chapter on Thoreau, which, however, unfortunately remains to amuse and prejudice his readers against Thoreau. When the criticism was written, Lowell probably founded it on *Walden*, in which Thoreau felt the need of giving the conventional religion, timid politics, and blindness to Nature of his fellow-citizens a shake. Of the beauty and height of his thought, as seen in the Journals — the Poet-Naturalist aspect — Lowell had little knowledge when that paper was written.

night, but to a dawn for which no man ever rose early enough." A fine example of his affirmative genius.

March 15.

My new book sells faster, it appears, than either of its foregoers. This is not for its merit, but only shows that old age is a good advertisement. Your name has been seen so often that your book must be worth buying.

I hate protection of trade in our politics, and now I recall in what Stillman said of the Greek war, — that the English opposition to the independence of Greece is merely out of fear of its depriving them of the Eastern trade.

A gentleman, English, French, or American, is rare; I think I remember every one I have ever seen.

March 16.

Musagetes. After the Social Circle had broken up, last night, and only two remained with me, one said that a cigar had uses. If you found yourself in a hotel with writing to do, — fire just kindled in a cold room, — it was hard to begin; but light a cigar, and you were presently comfortable, and in condition to work. Mr.

Simon Brown then said, that he had never smoked, but as an editor (of the *New England Farmer*) he had much writing, and he often found himself taking up a little stick and whittling away on it, and, in a short time, brought into tune and temper by that Yankee method.

Alvah Crocker gave me in the cars a history of his activity in the matter of the Fitchburg Railroad, beginning, I think, in 1837. He is the author of the road. He was a paper manufacturer, and could not get the material for making paper for less than eight cents a pound, — whilst in Boston and elsewhere it could be got for two, three, and four cents. He must find a way to bring Fitchburg nearer to Boston. He knew the country round him and studied the possibilities of each connection. He found he must study the nearest practicable paths to tidewater. No man but he had faith in the rivers; Nashua River.

After studying the Hoosac Mountains well, he decided that the mountain must be perforated. He must see Loammi Baldwin, who was the best engineer in the State. He could not get at that busy man. He knew that his own mother's dearest friend had been the lady who was now Mr. Baldwin's wife. To her he went, and told her who he was, and that he wished of all things to see Mr. Baldwin. The lady said, "I loved your mother dearly, but I know nothing of you; but for her sake, I will take care that you shall see him. Come here, say, next Sunday after dinner, about 3 o'clock, — that is the right time, and I will see that Mr. Baldwin shall answer all your questions." He did so.

Dream. The waking from an impressive dream is a curious example of the jealousy of the gods. There is an air as if the sender of the illusion had been heedless for a moment that the Reason had returned to its seat, and was startled into attention. Instantly, there is a rush from some quarter to break up the drama into a chaos of parts, then of particles, then of ether, like smoke dissolving in a wind; it cannot be disintegrated fast enough or fine enough. If you could give the waked watchman the smallest fragment, he could reconstruct the whole; for the moment, he is sure he can and will; but his attention is so divided on the disappearing parts, that he cannot grasp the least atomy, and the last fragment or film disappears before he could say, "I have it."

"*Aimer à lire, c'est faire un échange des heures d'ennui que l'on doit avoir en sa vie, contre des heures délicieuses.*" — MONTESQUIEU, *Pensées*.

March.

In "Clubs" I ought to have said that men being each a treasure-house of valuable experiences, — and yet the man often shy and daunted by company into dumbness, — it needs to court him, to put him at his ease, to make him laugh or weep, and so at last to get his *naturel* confessions, and his best experience.

The blinded Arago's "Ardent Age." —" Sa vieillesse est aussi remarquable que celle de M. de Humboldt, elle est même plus ardente." — VARNHAGEN, vol. x, p. 100.

I ought to have had Arago among my heroes in "Old Age," and Humboldt, and Agesilaus.

March 23.

On the 31st, I received President Eliot's letter signifying the acceptance of Carlyle's bequest of the Cromwellian and Friedrich books by the Corporation of Harvard College, and enclosing the vote of the Corporation. I wrote to Carlyle the same day enclosing the President's letter to me, and the record of their vote, and mailed it yesterday morning to him.[1]

"Study for eternity smiled on me."

Varnhagen says, "Goethe once said to me, 'How can the narrative be always right? The things themselves are not always right'"; and Varnhagen adds: "A microscopic history is not better than one seen with the natural, unarmed eye; — not the rightness of the now invisible littles, but the gross impression is the main thing." — VARNHAGEN, vol. x, p. 174.

At Wiesbaden, an Englishman being addressed by another guest at the table, called the waiter, and said to him aloud, "Waiter, say to that gentleman that I won't speak with him." This delighted Varnhagen, and he adds, "Worthy of imitation. Nothing more odious than *table d'hôte* conversation."

[1] For the account of the generous gift which Carlyle felt moved to make to the college, see the *Carlyle-Emerson Correspondence*.

The widow of General Charles Russell Lowell (sister of Colonel Robert G. Shaw) had visited Carlyle with a letter of introduction from Mr. Emerson, had talked freely with him about our war and sent him the *Harvard Memorial Biographies* to enlighten him on the cause and its heroes.

Musagetes. Goethe's fly. Read not in your official professional direction too steadily, — rather less and less, but, where you find excitement, awakening, for every surface is equally near to the centre. Every one has his own experience, — but I find the contrasts most suggestive.

[Under the new and more liberal dispensation of President Eliot's administration, courses of "University Lectures" were established, and Mr. Emerson was invited to give a course of sixteen in the Philosophical Department in April and May. These were: — I, Introductory, The Praise of Knowledge; II, Transcendency of Physics; III and IV, Perception; V and VI, Memory; VII, Imagination; VIII, Inspiration; IX, Genius; X, Common Sense; XI, Identity; XII, XIII, Metres of Mind; XIV, The Platonists; XV, Conduct of Intellect; XVI, Relation of Intellect to Morals.]

Identity. Bias. The best identity is the practical one, as in the pure satisfaction felt in finding that we have long since said, written, or done somewhat quite true and fit for ourselves.

Steffens relates that he went into Schelling's lecture-room at Jena (?). Schelling said, "Gentlemen, think of the wall." All the class at once took attitudes of thought; some stiffened themselves up; some shut their eyes; all concentrated themselves. After a time, he said, "Gentlemen, think of that which thought the wall." Then there was trouble in all the camp.

The scholar who abstracted himself with pain to make the analysis of Hegel is less enriched than when the beauty and depth of any thought by the wayside has commanded his mind and led to new thought and action; for this is healthy, and these thoughts light up the mind. He is made aware of the walls, and also of the open way leading outward and upward, whilst the other analytic process is cold and bereaving, and, — shall I say it? — somewhat mean, as spying.

The delicate lines of character in Aunt Mary, Rahel, Margaret Fuller, Sarah A. Ripley, need good metaphysic, better than Hegel's, to read and delineate.

There is one other reason for dressing well than I have ever considered, namely, that dogs respect it, and will not attack you in good clothes.

The strength of his moral convictions is the charm of the character of Fichte.

Autograph letters. Wise was the Turkish cadi who said, "O my friend, my liver, the questioner is one, and the answer is another."

I find Plutarch a richer teacher of rhetoric than any modern.

Plutarch quotes, as a true judgment, this, — "That this courteous, gentle, and benign disposition and behaviour is not so acceptable, so obliging, and delightful to any of those with whom they converse, as it is to those who have it." — PLUTARCH, *Morals*, vol. i, p. 59.

Old age. Here is a good text from Montesquieu: "*Les vieillards qui ont étudié dans leur jeunesse n'ont besoin que de se ressouvenir, et non d'apprendre. Cela est bien heureux.*" — *Pensées*, p. 232.

June 9.

I find Philip Randolph almost if not quite on a level with my one or two Olympic friends in his insight, — as shown in his manuscript, which I have been reading. He made that impression on me once and again in our interviews whilst he lived, and in his paper which was promised to the *North American Review*. But in these papers on science, philosophy, poetry, painting, and music, the supremacy of his faith purely shines.

How much it ever pleases me that this pure spiritualist was the best chess-player in Philadelphia, and, according to Evan Randolph's account to me, had beaten the best players in Paris!

Plutarch rightly tells the anecdote of Alexander (badly remembered and misrelated usually) that he wept when he heard from Anaxarchus that there was an infinite number of worlds; and his friends asking if any accident had befallen him, he replied, "Don't you think it a matter for my lamentation, that, when there is such a vast multitude of them, I have not yet conquered one?"—PLUTARCH, *Morals*, vol. i, p. 134.

Were I professor of rhetoric, I would urge my class to read Plutarch's *Morals* in English, and Cotton's Montaigne for their English style.

We think we do a great service to our country in publishing this book if we hereby force our public men to read the "Apophthegms of Great Commanders," before they make their speeches to caucuses and conventions. If I could keep the secret, and communicate it only to one or two chosen youths, I should know that they would by this noble infiltration easily carry the victory over all competitors. But as it was the desire of these old patriots to fill Rome or Sparta with this majestic spirit, and not a few leaders only, we desire to offer them to the American people.

The reason of a new philosophy or philosopher is ever that a man of thought finds that he cannot read in the old books. I can't read Hegel, or Schelling, or find interest in what is told me from them, so I persist in my own idle and easy way, and write down my thoughts, and find presently that there are congenial persons who like them, so I persist, until some sort of outline or system grows. 'T is the common course: ever a new bias. It happened to each of these, Heraclitus, or Hegel, or whosoever.

June 30.

I cannot but please myself with the recoil when Plutarch tells me that "the Athenians had such an abhorrence of those who accused Socrates that they would neither lend them fire, nor answer them any question, nor wash with them in the same water, but commanded the servants to pour it out as polluted, till these sycophants, no longer able to bear up under the pressure of this hatred, put an end to their own lives." — PLUTARCH, *Morals*, vol. ii, p. 96.

I find *Nouvelle Biographie Générale* a perpetual benefactor, — almost sure on every consultation to answer promptly and well. Long live M. le Docteur Hoefer! Just now he has answered fully on Plutarch, Suetonius, Amyot, but I dared not believe he would know Dr. Philemon Holland, — yet he answered at once joyfully concerning him; and even cites the epigram upon him: —

"Philemon with translations will so fill us
He cannot let Suetonius be Tranquillus."

July 14.

Here at Nantasket Beach, with Ellen, I wonder that so few men do penetrate what seems the secret of the innkeeper. He runs along the coast, and perceives that by buying a few acres, well chosen, of the seashore, which cost no more or not so much as good land elsewhere, and building a good house, he shifts upon Nature the whole duty of filling it with guests, the sun, the moon, the stars, the rainbow, the sea, the islands, the whole horizon,—not elsewhere seen, ships of all nations. All of these (and all unpaid) take on themselves the whole charge of entertaining his guests, and filling and delighting their senses with shows; and it were long to tell in detail the attractions which these furnish. Everything here is picturesque: the long beach is every day renewed with pleasing and magical shows, with variety of colour, with the varied music of the rising and falling water, with the multitudes of fishes, and the birds and men that prey on them; with the strange forms of the radiates sprawling on the beach; with shells; with the beautiful variety of sea-rolled pebbles,—of quartz, porphyry, sienite, mica, and limestone. The man buys a few acres, but he has all the good and all the glory of a hundred square miles, by the cunning choice of the place; for the storm is one of the grand entertainers of his company; so is the sun, and the moon, and all the stars of heaven, since they who see them here, in all their beauty, and in the grand area or amphitheatre which they need for their right exhibition, feel that they have never rightly seen them before.

The men and women who come to the house, and swarm or scatter in groups along the spacious beach, or in yachts, or boats, or in carriages, or as bathers, never appeared before so gracious and inoffensive. In these wide stretches, the largest company do not jostle one another. Then to help him, even the poor Indians from Maine and Canada creep on to the outskirts of the hotel to pitch their tents, and make baskets and bows and arrows to add a picturesque feature. Multitudes of children decorate the piazza, and the grounds in front, with their babble and games; and in this broad area every individual from least to largest is inoffensive and an entertaining variety. To make the day complete, I saw from the deck of our boat this morning, coming out of the bay, the English steamer which lately made the perilous jump on Minot's Ledge, and this afternoon I saw the turret monitor, *Miantonomoh*, sailing into Boston.

The parlours, chambers, and the table of the Rockland House were all good, but the supreme relish of these conveniences was this superb panorama which the wise choice of the place on which the house was built afforded. This selection of the site gives this house the like advantage over other houses that an astronomical observatory has over other towers, — namely, that this particular tower leads you to the heavens, and searches depths of space before inconceivable.

July 21.

I am filling my house with books which I am bound to read, and wondering whether the new heavens which await the soul (after the fatal hour) will allow the consultation of these.

I honour the author of the "Battle Hymn," and of "The Flag." She was born in the city of New York. I could well wish she were a native of Massachusetts. We have had no such poetess in New England.

August 7.

This morning I think no subject so fit for poetry as Home, the Massachusetts or the American Home.

I find my readings of Aunt Mary ever monitory and healthful as of old, and for the reason that they are moral inspirations. All the men and women whose talents challenge my admiration from time to time lack this depth of source, and are therefore comparatively shallow. They amuse, they may be inimitable; I am proud of them as countrymen and contemporaries; but it is as music or pictures, — and other music and pictures would have served me as well; but they do not take rank hold of me as consolers, uplifters, and hinderers from sleep. But the moral muse is eternal, and wakes us to eternity, — pervades the whole man. Socrates is not distant; Sparta is nearer than New York; Marcus Antoninus is of no age; Plotinus and Porphyry, Confucius and Menu had a deeper civilization than Paris or London; and the deeply religious men and women in or out of our churches are really the salt of our civilization, and constitute the nerve and tension of our politics in Germany, England, and America. The men of talent see the power of principle, and the necessity of respecting it, but they deal with its phenomena, and not with the source. It is learned and wielded as an accomplishment and a weapon.

As I have before written, that no number of *Nays* will help, — only one *Yea*, and this is moral. Strength enters according to the presence of the moral element. There are no bounds to this power. If it have limits, we have not found them. It domesticates. They are not our friends who are of our household, but they who think and see with us. But it is ever wonderful where the moral element comes from.

The Christian doctrine not only modifies the

individual character, but the individual character modifies the Christian doctrine in Luther, in Augustine, in Fénelon, in Milton. — Something like this I read in Lévêque or Antoninus.

September 2.

With Edward took the 7.30 A. M. train from Boston to Portland, thence to South Paris, where we took a carriage and reached Waterford, Mr. Houghton's inn, at 5 P. M. Thence, the next afternoon, to South Paris, carried by Mr. Wilkins, and took the train for Gorham, and thence immediately the stage to the Glen House, Mount Washington, where we arrived near 9 o'clock in the evening. Spent Sunday, September 4, and on Monday, September 5, at 8 o'clock, ascended the mountain in open carriage; descended in the railway [funicular] car, at 3, and reached the Crawford House. Next morning, September 6, took stage to Whitefield, arriving to dine, thence by railway to Plymouth, arriving at 9 P. M. Next morning, at 5 o'clock, took railroad, and arrived in Boston at 11.30 and home in an hour.

[To fill out this rather bald itinerary, it may be said that Mr. Emerson's family, seeing that the Philosophy course (sixteen lectures in a few weeks) had been a tax on his strength, betrayed him into a journey to Maine on the plea of showing to his son the village of Waterford, of which Mr. Emerson had a happy remembrance from the days long past when he went there to visit his Haskins relations, and his Aunt Mary. His consent was won, and reaching Waterford we climbed Bear Mountain and from its sheer cliff looked down into the blue lake below. Then he eagerly led the way to a broad brook whose clear waters, rushing over smooth ledges and boulders, had long delighted him in memory, and now gave like joy.

We were glad to find at Gorham, where we passed Sunday, Mr. James Bryce, now noted, who had lately brought his letter of introduction to Concord. Next morning he and young Emerson climbed the mountain, and Mr. Emerson followed in the stage from the great heat and moisture below into a fierce, cold snow-squall which blew almost dangerously on the top. We saw nothing but that, shivered through dinner, and gladly descended to Crawford's Notch, where Mr. Emerson had stayed with Ellen Tucker and her family some forty years before. — *E. W. Emerson.*]

Very much afflicted in these days with stupor: — acute attacks whenever a visit is proposed or made.

Montesquieu's prediction is fulfilled, "*La France se perdra par les gens de guerre.*" — *Pensées.*

September 24.

On Saturday, at the Club; present, Sumner, Longfellow, Lowell, Hoar, James, Brimmer, Fields, Estes Howe, Holmes, R. W. E., and, as guests, Mr. Catacazy, the Russian Minister, Hon. Samuel Hooper, and Henry Lee, Esq.

September 26.

Chivalry, I fancied, this afternoon, would serve as a good title for many topics, and some good readings which I might offer to the Fraternity [Course of Lectures] on December 6. George Ticknor, Hallam, and Renan (in his paper on the Paris Exposition) have each given me good texts; Fauriel has others; and the wonderful mythology and poetry of Wales, of Brittany, of Germany (in the *Nibelungenlied*), and Scott and Joinville and Froissart can add their stores. It might be called "Imagination" as well, and what we call chivalry be only a rich illustration. Every reading boy has marched to school and on his errands, to fragments of this magic, and swinging a cut stick for his broadsword, brandishing it, and plunging it into the swarm of airy enemies whom his fancy arrayed on his right and left.

The life of the topic, of course, would be the impatience in every man of his limits; the inextinguishableness of the imagination. We cannot crouch in our hovels or our experience. We have an immense elasticity. Every reader takes part with the king, or the angel, or the god, in the novel or poem he reads, and not with dwarfs and cockneys. That healthy surprise which a sunset sky gives to a man coming out on it alone, and from his day's work; or which the stars unexpectedly seen give.

(From ST)

October 2.

La portée, the range of a thought, of a fact observed, and thence of the word by which we denote it, makes its value. Only whilst it has new values does it warm and invite and enable to write. And this range or ulterior outlook appears to be rare in men;— a slight primitive difference, but essential to the work. For this possessor has the necessity to write,— 'T is easy and delightful to him; the other, finding no continuity, — must begin again uphill at every step. Now Plutarch is not a deep man, and might well not be personally impressive to his contemporaries; but, having this facile association in his thought, — a wide horizon to every fact or maxim or character which engaged him, every new topic reanimated all his experience or memory, and he was impelled with joy to begin a new chapter. Then there is no such chord in Nature for fagoting thoughts as well as actions, as *religion*, which means *fagoting*. Plutarch had a commanding moral sentiment, which, indeed, is common to all men, but in very unlike degree, so that in multitudes it appears secondary, as if aped only from eminent characters, and not native. But in Plutarch was his genius. This clear *morale* is the foundation of genius in Milton, in Burke, in Herbert, in Socrates, in Wordsworth, Michael Angelo, and, I think, also in many men who like to mask or disguise it in the variety of their powers, — as Shakespeare and Goethe. Indeed, we are sure to feel the discord and limitation in men of rare talent in whom this sentiment has not its healthy or normal superiority; as, Byron, Voltaire, Daniel Webster.

The writer is an explorer. Every step is an advance into new land.

Memory. The compensation of failing memory is,— the assistance of increased and increasing generalization.

"Old age stands not in years, but in directed activity."

Among my mnemonics I recorded that I went into France just three hundred years after Montaigne did. He was born, 1533; I visited it in 1833.

[During this year the Government of Harvard University determined that it should no longer discredit itself by conferring the degree of Master of Arts on any graduate who should have survived five years and have five dollars to pay into the treasury for receiving it. Mr. Emerson was appointed one of a Committee of Harvard teachers to prepare a plan for conferring that degree. He was also made one of the Committee to visit the Academic Department of the University.]

October 6.

To-day at the laying of the corner-stone of the "Memorial Hall," at Cambridge. All was well and wisely done. The storm ceased for us, the company was large, — the best men and the best women all there, — or all but a few ; — the arrangements simple and excellent, and every speaker successful. Henry Lee, with his uniform sense and courage, the Manager; the Chaplain, Rev. Phillips Brooks, offered a prayer, in which not a word was superfluous, and every right thing was said. Henry Rogers, William Gray, Dr. Palfrey, made each his proper Report. Luther's Hymn in Dr. Hedge's translation was sung by a great choir, the corner-stone was laid, and then Rockwood Hoar read a discourse of perfect sense, taste, and feeling, — full of virtue and of tenderness. After this, an original song by Wendell Holmes was given by the Choir. Every part in all these performances was in such true feeling that people praised them with broken voices, and we all proudly wept. Our Harvard soldiers of the war were in their uniforms, and heard their own praises, and the tender allusions to their dead comrades. General Meade was present, and "adopted by the College," as Judge Hoar said, and Governor Claflin sat by President Eliot. Our English guests, Hughes, Rawlins, Dicey, and Bryce, sat and listened.

"I bear no ill will to my contemporaries," said Cumberland. "After you, ma'am, in manners," said Swett. The only point in which I regret priority of departure is that I, as every one, keep many stories of which the etiquette of contemporariness forbids the airing, and which burn uncomfortably being untold. I positively resolve not to kill A. nor C. nor N. — but I could a tale unfold, like Hamlet's father.

Now a private class gives just this liberty which in book or public lecture were unparliamentary, and of course because here, at least, one is safe from the unamiable presence of reporters. Another point. I set great value in culture on foreign literature — the farther off the better — much on French, on Italian, on German, or Welsh — more on Persian or Hindu, because if one read and write only English, he soon slides into narrow conventions, and believes there is no other way to write poetry than as Pope or Milton. But a quite foreign mind born and grown in different latitude and longitude, — nearer to the pole or to the equator, — a child of Mount Hecla, like Sturluson, or of the Sahara, like Averroës, astonishes us with a new nature, gives a fillip to our indolence, and we promptly learn that we have faculties which we have never used.

How right is Couture's rule [1] of looking three times at the object, for one at your drawing, — of looking at Nature, and not at your whim; and William Hunt's emphasis, after him, on the mass, instead of the details! And how perfectly (as I wrote upon Couture long ago) the same rule applies in rhetoric or writing! Wendell Holmes hits right in every affectionate poem he scribbles, by his instinct at obeying a just perception of what *is* important, instead of feeling about how he shall write some verses touching the subject: and eminently this is true in Rockwood Hoar's mind, — his tendency to the integrity of the thing!

What a lesson on culture is drawn from every day's intercourse with men and women. The rude youth or maid comes as a visitor to a house, and at the table cannot understand half the conversation that passes, — so many allusions to books, to anecdotes, to persons, — hints of a song, or a fashion of the War, or the College, or the boatmen, or a single French or

[1] In his admirable *Méthode et entretiens d'atelier*.

Latin word to suggest a line or sentence familiar to inmates, unknown to the stranger, — so that practically 't is as if the family spoke another language than the guest. Well, there is an equal difference if their culture is better, in all their ways, and the like abbreviation by better methods, and only long acquaintance, that is, slow education, step by step, in their arts and knowledge can breed a practical equality. The like difference, of course, must appear in the father, the son, the grandson, and the great-grandson, if better opportunities of education are provided to each successor than his parent enjoyed.

Greatness. "They deride thee, O Diogenes!" He replied, "But I am not derided." — PLUTARCH, *Morals.*

But, *memo.* I must procure a Greek Grammar. O for my old Gloucester again!

A passage in the *Convito* of Dante testifies that he knew Greek too imperfectly to read Homer in the original. (See *Biographie Générale.*)

Objection to Metaphysics. The poet sees wholes, and avoids analysis. Ellery Channing said to me, he would not know the botanical name of the flower, for fear he should never see the flower again. The metaphysician, dealing, as it were, with the mathematics of the mind, puts himself out of the way of the Inspiration, loses that which is the miracle, and which creates the worship.

America. We get rid in this Republic of a great deal of nonsense which disgusts us in European biography. There a superior mind, a Hegel, sincerely and scientifically exploring the laws of thought, is suddenly called by a necessity of pleasing some king, or conciliating some Catholics, to give a twist to his universal propositions to fit these absurd people, and not satisfying them even by these sacrifices of truth and manhood; another great genius, Schelling, is called in, when Hegel dies, to come to Berlin, and bend truth to the crotchets of the king and rabble. Not so here. The paucity of population, the vast extent of territory, the solitude of each family and each man, allow some approximation to the result that every citizen has a religion of his own, — is a church by himself, — and worships and speculates in a new, quite independent fashion.

Plutarch treats every subject except Art. He is ingenious to draw medical virtue from every poison, to detect the good that may be made of evil.

An admirable passage concerning Plato's expression "that God geometrizes," in Plutarch's *Symposiacs*. (See especially in the Old Edition, vol. iii, p. 434.)

In the History of opinion, the pinch of falsehood shows itself, not first in argument and formal protest, but in insincerity, indifference, and abandonment of the church, or the scientific or political or economic institution, for other better or worse forms. Then good heads, feeling or observing this loss, formulate the fact in protest and argument, and suggest the correction and superior form. Rabelais, Voltaire, Heine, are earlier reformers than Huss, and Luther, and Strauss, and Parker, though less solemn and to less solemn readers.

Voltaire's Spinoza, — "*Je soupçonne, entre nous, que vous n'existez pas.*" — *Satires. Les Systèmes.*

It really appears that the Latin and Greek continue to be forced in education, just as chignons must be worn, in spite of the disgust against both, for fashion. If a wise traveller should visit England to study the causes of her power, it is not the universities in which he would find them; but Mr. Owen, Mr. Armstrong, Mr. Airy, Mr. Stephenson, Sir John Lubbock, Mr. Huxley, Mr. Scott Russell, Boulton, Watt, Faraday, Tyndall, Darwin. If any of these were college men, 't is only the good luck of the universities, and not their normal fruit. What these men have done, they did not learn there.

"Plato says that Time had its original from an intelligence." — PLUTARCH, *Morals*, vol. iii, p. 158.

The Greek text is, Πλάτων δὲ γεννητὸν κὰτ' ἐπίνοιαν, and Goodwin prints (vol. iii, p. 128) thus, — "that Time had only an ideal beginning."

Μισέω μνήμονα συμπόταν[1] (and I remember that Mr. Tom Lee complained of Margaret Fuller that she remembered things); "and the ancients used to consecrate Forgetfulness, with a ferula in hand, to Bacchus, thereby intimating that we should either not remember any irregularity committed in mirth and company, or

[1] I hate a fellow-reveller who remembers things.

should apply a gentle and childish correction to the faults." — *Idem*.

Plutarch loves apples like our Thoreau, and well praises them. — See *Morals*, vol. iii, p. 362.

Let a scholar begin to read something to a few strangers in a parlour, and he may find his voice disobedient, and he reads badly. Let him go to an assembly of intelligent people in a public hall, and his voice will behave beautifully, and he is another person, and contented.

A scholar forgives everything to him whose fault gives him a new insight, a new fact.

Peter Oliver,[1] in the *Puritan Commonwealth*, insists like a lawyer on the duty the Pilgrims owed to their Charter, and the presumed spirit and intent in which it was given. He overlooks the irresistible instruction which the actual arrival in the new continent gave. That was a greater king than Charles, and insisted on making the law for those who live in it. They could not shut their eyes on the terms on which alone they could live in it. The savages, the sands,

[1] Chief Justice of Massachusetts, 1771, until the evacuation of Boston by the Tories with whom he cast his lot.

the snow, the mutineers, and the French were antagonists who must be dealt with on the instant, and there was no clause in the Charter that could deal with these. No lawyer could help them to read the pitiless alternative which Plymouth Rock offered them, — Self-help or Ruin: come up to the real conditions, or die.[1]

November 30.

Judge W—— of Rhode Island was not a great man, and resented some slight he received from Tristram Burgess at the Bar, by asking him if he knew before whom he was speaking. He replied, "Yes, your honour; before the inferior Court of the inferior Bench of the inferior State of Rhode Island."

Mr. Weeden[2] told me, that his old aunt said of the people whom she knew in her youth that "they had to hold on hard to the huckleberry bushes to hinder themselves from being translated."

I delight ever in having to do with the drastic class, the men who can do things, as Dr. Charles

[1] Mr. Emerson was reading with reference to the address on Forefathers' Day in New York.

[2] Colonel William B. Weeden, of Providence, often Mr. Emerson's host when lecturing there.

T. Jackson; and Jim Bartlett,[1] and Boynton. Such was Thoreau. Once out of doors, the poets paled like ghosts before them. I met Boynton in Rochester, New York, and was cold enough to a popular and unscientific lecturer on Geology. But I talked to him of the notice I had read of repulsion of incandescent bodies, and new experiments. "O," he said, "nothing is plainer: I have tried it"; and, on my way to Mr. Ward's, he led me into a forge, where a stream of melted iron was running out of a furnace, and he passed his finger through the streamlet again and again, and invited me to do the same. I said, "Do you not wet your finger?" "No," he said, "the hand sweats a little and that suffices."

Parnassus.

So words must sparks be of those fires they strike.

I saw that no pressman could lay his sheets so deftly but that under every one a second sheet was inadvertently laid; and no bookbinder could bind so carefully but that a second sheet was bound in the book: then I saw that if the

[1] Son of the honoured physician of Concord for more than half a century. Mr. Bartlett was a mechanical engineer of importance in Detroit.

writer was skilful, every word he wrote sank into the inner sheet, and there remained indelible; and if he was not skilful, it did not penetrate, and the ink faded, and the writing was effaced.

Quotque aderant vates rebar adesse Deos.[1] — OVID.

AUTHORS OR BOOKS QUOTED OR REFERRED TO IN JOURNAL FOR 1870

Menu; Confucius; Heracleitus; Ovid; Suetonius; Marcus Aurelius; Plotinus; Porphyry; St. Augustine;

Averroës (Ibn Roshd); Snorre Sturluson; *Nibelungenlied;* De Joinville, *Chronicle of Saint Louis;* Froissart, *Chronicles;*

Huss; Luther; Michel Angelo; Rabelais; Amyot, Philemon Holland (translators of Plutarch's *Morals* into French and English respectively);

Thomas Stanley, *History of Philosophy;* Spinoza; Fénelon; Montesquieu, *Pensées;* Voltaire;

Peter Oliver, *The Puritan Commonwealth;* Matthew Boulton; James Watt; Goethe; Eckermann, *Conversations with Goethe;* Dumont,

[1] I will hold all bards that come my way to be gods.

Souvenirs sur Mirabeau; Fichte; Richter; Alexander von Humboldt; Hegel; Heinrich Steffens, Review of Schelling's Philosophy; Fauriel; Schelling; Hallam;

Varnhagen von Ense, *Tagebucher;* Arago; George Ticknor; Faraday; John G. Palfrey, *History of New England;* Carlyle; Heine;

George B. Airy; George Sand; Richard Owen; Strauss; John Scott Russell; O. W. Holmes; Charles Darwin; Margaret Fuller; Theodore Parker; Sir William Armstrong; J.W. Foster, *Geology;* Erastus B. Bigelow; Thomas Couture, *Méthode et entretiens d'atelier;* J. R. Lowell; Thoreau, *Field Notes;* Lévêque; Julia Ward Howe, *Battle Hymn of the Republic;*

Tyndall; William J. Stillman; Ernest Renan; Huxley, *Lay Sermons;* Sir John Lubbuck; Phillips Brooks; Hoefer, *Nouvelle Biographie Générale.*

JOURNAL

MUSEUM OF FINE ARTS
UNIVERSITY LECTURES
ORGANIC CHEMISTRY
MILL, PUSEY, FROUDE
JOHN MURRAY FORBES
THE CALIFORNIA EXCURSION
SPLENDORS OF THE AGE
CHANNING. BRET HARTE
POETRY IN SCIENCE
GEOFFROY SAINT-HILAIRE
SYMPATHY WITH BOYS
CULTURE IN ENGLAND AND HERE
BOYHOOD

JOURNAL LXII

1871

(From Journal ST)

[MR. EMERSON seems to have lectured in some Massachusetts towns; also at Buffalo, Cleveland, and New Brunswick, New Jersey, during January.

On February 3, he spoke by request at a meeting held for the purpose of organizing the Museum of Fine Arts in Boston.[1] In a letter of thanks, Mr. Martin Brimmer expressed his belief that the good effects of this speech in awakening substantial interest in the Museum soon appeared.

But through the winter Mr. Emerson had the serious task of preparing for a course of lectures on Philosophy for a new class at the University. According to Mr. Cabot, the lectures were mainly the same as those given in the previous Spring, except that "Identity" and "The Platonists" were omitted, but "Wit and Humour," "Demonology," and another on "The

[1] See *Boston Daily Advertiser* of February 4.

Conduct of the Intellect" were added. A large part of the new matter in this course was later used in "Poetry and Imagination," in *Letters and Social Aims*, the next published volume.]

January, 1871.

Old age. "Man is oldest when he is born, and is younger and younger continually." — TALIESSIN, *apud* Skene.

February 10.

I do not know that I should feel threatened or insulted if a chemist should take his protoplasm or mix his hydrogen, oxygen, and carbon, and make an animalcule incontestably swimming and jumping before my eyes. I should only feel that it indicated that the day had arrived when the human race might be trusted with a new degree of power, and its immense responsibility; for these steps are not solitary or local, but only a hint of an advanced frontier supported by an advancing race behind it.

What at first scares the Spiritualist in the experiments of Natural Science — as if thought were only finer chyle, fine to aroma — now redounds to the credit of matter, which, it appears, is impregnated with thought and heaven, and is really of God, and not of the Devil, as he had too hastily believed. All is resolved into Unity again. My chemistry, he will say, was blind and barbarous, but my intuition is, was, and will be true.

I believe that every man belongs to his time, if our Newtons and philosophers belong also to the next age which they help to form.

"Our progress appears great, only because the future of Science is hidden from us." — PHILIP RANDOLPH.

Of gravitation, John Mill said to Carlyle, "A force can act but where it is." "With all my heart," replied Carlyle, "but where is it?"

March 5.

Dr. E. B. Pusey of Oxford surprised me two or three days ago with sending me, "with greetings," a book, *Lectures on Daniel and the Prophets*, with the following inscription written on the blank leaf, —

> To the unwise and wise
> A debtor I.
> 'T is strange if true,
> And yet the old
> Is often new.

When in England, I did not meet him, but

I remember that, in Oxford, Froude one day, walking with me, pointed to his window, and said, "There is where all our light came from."

I ought also to have recorded that Max Müller, on last Christmas Day, surprised me with the gift of a book.

Coleridge says, "The Greeks, except perhaps in Homer, seem to have had no way of making their women interesting, but by unsexing them, as in the instances of the tragic Medea, Electra, etc. Contrast such characters with Spenser's Una, who exhibits no prominent feature, has no particularization, but produces the same feeling that a statue does, when contemplated at a distance.

'From her fair head her fillet she undight,
 And laid her stole aside: her angel's face
 As the great eye of Heaven shined bright,
 And made a sunshine in a shady place:
 Did never mortal eye behold such heavenly grace?'"

Greatness. Chateaubriand says that President Washington granted him an audience in Philadelphia, and adds, "Happy am I that the looks of Washington fell on me. I felt myself warmed by them for the rest of my life." Calvert gives the anecdote.

None is so great but finds one who apprehends him, and no historical person begins to content us; and this is our pledge of a higher height than he has reached. And when we have arrived at the question, the answer is already near.

April 7.

[Mr. Emerson's good friend Mr. John M. Forbes, hearing that he seemed worn and jaded by the strain of his Philosophy lectures, — two or more a week, — invited him to be his guest on an excursion in a private car to California. In the party, besides Mr. and Mrs. Forbes and their youngest daughter, were Colonel Forbes, with his wife (Mr. Emerson's daughter Edith), Mrs. George Russell, James B. Thayer (late Royall Professor of Law at Cambridge), Garth Wilkinson James, late the adjutant of Colonel Robert Shaw, and wounded on the slopes of Fort Wagner. Mr. Emerson's inborn reluctance to receive favours even from near friends, and his scruples about leaving his work, stood in the way, but at last he yielded to Mr. Forbes's tactful ingenuity of plea, and to his daughter's urgency, and went. The journey across the prairie, mountains, and desert (including a short stay at Salt Lake City and conversation with Brigham Young), the weeks in California in its spring freshness and sheets of flowers, were to Mr. Emerson an unforeseen delight and refreshment. The good friends in the party, with their tactful and affectionate care of him, each contributed to his pleasure, and his respect and admiration for the quality of his host grew with each day. Professor Thayer in a little volume gave a pleasant account of the journey.[1]

Mr. Emerson was enjoying the rest, and did little writing. But few notes of the trip occur.]

California Notes. Irrigation. Tea, impossible culture where labor is dear as in America. Silk (?) Wine is not adulterated; because grapes at one cent a pound are cheaper than any substitute.

Cape Donner. Golden Gate, named of old

[1] *A Western Journey with Mr. Emerson*, by James Bradley Thayer, Boston, 1884.

There is also in Mr. Emerson's letters to Carlyle, written after his return, a short mention of this journey and its pleasures and experiences, among others, the visit to Brigham Young. (*Carlyle-Emerson Correspondence*, vol. ii, pp. 343–345.)

In Mr. Cabot's *Memoir* (vol. ii, pp. 644–648) are extracts from Mr. Emerson's letters to his family from California.

from its flowers. Asia at your doors and South America. Inflamed Expectation haunting men. Henry Pierce's opinion of the need of check, calamity, punishment, to teach economy. Nickels [for] cents.

Mission Dolores. Flora. The altered Year. (See Hittel on California.)

John Muir. General Sumner.

Antelopes, prairie-dogs, elk-horns, wolves, eagles, vultures, prairie-hen, owls.

Sequoias generally have marks of fire: having lived thirteen hundred years must have met that danger, and every other, in turn. Yet they possess great power of resistance to fire. (See Cronise, pp. 507–508.)

Sarcodes Sanguinea, snow plant growing in the snow, a parasite from decayed wood; *monotropa*. *Cæanothus*; Wild lilac; Madrona; — *Arbutus Menziesii*; Manzanita; *Acrostaphylos glaucus*.

Black sand at Lake Tahoe, and carnelians. Mono Lake. Glaciers; Clarence King. Volcanic mountains, cones, Enneo County.

The attraction and superiority of California are in its days. It has better days, and more of them, than any other country.

Mount Shasta, 14,440 feet high, in northeastern corner of the State. Mount Whitney,

15,000 feet, in Tulare County. In Yosemite, grandeur of these mountains perhaps unmatched in the globe; for here they strip themselves like athletes for exhibition, and stand perpendicular granite walls, showing their entire height, and wearing a liberty cap of snow on their head.

Sequoia Gigantea, *Pinus Lambertiana*, Sugar pine, 10 feet diameter; 300 feet height; cones 18 inches. *Pinus Ponderosa*, yellow pine. *Pinus Albicaulis*.

May 12.

At the request of Galen Clark, our host at Mariposa, and who is, by State appointment, the protector of the trees, and who went with us to the Mammoth Groves, I selected a Sequoia Gigantea, near Galen's Hospice, in the presence of our party, and named it *Samoset*, in memory of the first Indian ally of the Plymouth Colony, and I gave Mr. Clark directions to procure a tin plate, and have the inscription painted thereon in the usual form of the named trees: and paid him its cost: —

> Samoset.
> 12 May
> 1871.

The tree was a strong healthy one; girth, at $2\frac{1}{2}$ feet from the ground, 50 feet.

What they once told me at St. Louis is truer in California, that there is no difference between a boy and a man: as soon as a boy is "that high" [high as the table], he contradicts his father. When introduced to the stranger, he says, "I am happy to make your acquaintance," and shakes hands like a senior.[1]

California is teaching in its history and its poetry the good of evil, and confirming my thought, one day in Five Points in New York, twenty years ago, that the ruffians and Amazons in that district were only superficially such, but carried underneath this bronze about the same morals as their civil and well-dressed neighbours.

Gifts. The pleasing humiliation of gifts.

The saying is attributed to Sir Isaac Newton that "they who give nothing before their death never in fact give at all."

[1] Mr. Emerson, by invitation, gave two lectures in San Francisco. Of his "Immortality" the *California Alta* of next day said that "An elegant tribute had been paid by Mr. Emerson to the creative genius of the Great First Cause, and a masterly use of the English language had contributed to that end."

We are sometimes startled by coincidences so friendly as to suggest a guardian angel: and sometimes, when they would be so fit, and every way desirable, nothing but disincidences occur. 'T is perhaps thus; the coincidence is probably the rule, and if we could retain our early innocence, we might trust our feet uncommanded to take the right path to our friend in the woods.[1] . . .

[Mr. Emerson reached home in the last week in May, much refreshed, and having had pleasure in the company of his good friends.

Perhaps on the journey, he wrote, at her request, the following]

Inscription for Mrs. Sarah Swain Forbes's Memorial Fountain:—

Fall, Stream! to bless. Return to Heaven as well:
So, did our sons, Heaven met them as they fell.[2]

What was the name of the nymph "Whom young Apollo courted for her hair"? That fable renews itself every day in the street and in the drawing-room. Nothing in nature is

[1] See *Natural History of Intellect* (p. 37).
[2] The roadside drinking-fountain is in Milton, on Adams Street, in front of the home of Mr. and Mrs. Forbes.

more ideal than the hair. Analyze it by taking a single hair, and it is characterless and worthless: but in the mass it is recipient of such variety of form, and momentary change from form to form, that it vies in expression with the eye and the countenance. The wind and the sun play with it and enhance it, and its coils and its mass are a perpetual mystery and attraction to the young poet. But the doleful imposture of buying it at the shops is suicidal, and disgusts.

Nature lays the ground-plan of each creature, — accurately, sternly fit for all his functions, — then veils it.

(From NY)

My Men.[1] Thomas Carlyle, Louis Agassiz, E. Rockwood Hoar, J. Elliot Cabot, John M. Forbes, Charles K. Newcomb, Philip P. Randolph, Richard Hunt, Alvah Crocker, William B. Ogden, Samuel G. Ward, J. R. Lowell, Sampson Reed, Henry D. Thoreau, A. B. Alcott, Horatio Greenough, Oliver Wendell Holmes, John Muir.

[1] This list seems an *extempore* recalling, not merely of near personal friends, but of men whose various powers had won Mr. Emerson's respect, from Thomas Carlyle, first met in 1833, to John Muir, his *genius loci* but a month before in the Sequoia forest.

[In June, Mr. Emerson had been chosen a member of the Massachusetts Historical Society, and on August 15, when the Society celebrated the Centennial Anniversary of Scott's birth, Mr. Emerson spoke. What he said is printed in *Miscellanies*.]

(From ST)

Scott said to Mr. Cheney, "Superstition is very picturesque, and I make it at times stand me in great stead; but I never allow it to interfere with interest or conscience." — LOCKHART, vol. viii, p. 81.

I think he spoke honestly and well, but his superstition was dearer to him and more comprehensive than he well knew: I mean that it made him a sterner royalist, churchman, and conservative than his intellect should allow.

Correlation of forces is an irrepressible hint which must compel the widest application of it. It gives unforeseen force to the old word of Cicero's *aliquid commune vinculum*, and we realize the correlation of sciences. But poetry correlates men, and genius, and every fine talent, and men the most diverse; and men that are enemies hug each other when they hear from that once hated neighbour the synonym of their own cherished belief.

The splendors of this age outshine all other recorded ages. In my lifetime have been wrought five miracles, — namely, 1, the Steamboat; 2, the Railroad; 3, the Electric Telegraph; 4, the application of the Spectroscope to astronomy; 5, the Photograph; — five miracles which have altered the relations of nations to each other. Add cheap postage; and the mowing-machine and the horse-rake. A corresponding power has been given to manufactures by the machine for pegging shoes, and the power-loom, and the power-press of the printers. And in dentistry and in surgery, Dr. Jackson's discovery of Anæsthesia. It only needs to add the power which, up to this hour, eludes all human ingenuity, namely, a rudder to the balloon, to give us the dominion of the air, as well as of the sea and the land. But the account is not complete until we add the discovery of Oersted, of the identity of Electricity and Magnetism, and the generalization of that conversion by its application to light, heat, and gravitation. The geologist has found the correspondence of the age of stratified remains to the ascending scale of structure in animal life. Add now, the daily predictions of the weather for the next twenty-four hours for North America, by the Observatory at Washington.

Poetry. "The newness." Every day must be a new morn. Clothe the new object with a coat that fits it alone of all things in the world. I can see in many poems that the coat is secondhand. Emphasis betrays poverty of thought, as if the man did not know that all things are full of meaning, and not his trumpery thing only.

'T is one of the mysteries of our condition that the poet seems sometimes to have a mere talent,— a chamber in his brain into which an angel flies with divine messages, but the man, apart from this privilege, commonplace. Wordsworth is an example (and Channing's poetry is apart from the man). Those who know and meet him day by day cannot reconcile the verses with their man.

> Ah, not to me these heights belong;
> A better voice sings through my song.

[In July, at the Commencement Dinner at Harvard College, it being the fiftieth year since Mr. Emerson graduated, Mr. William Gray, who presided, called upon him to speak. He did so, but what he said is not preserved.]

Rhetoric. All conversation and writing is rhetoric, and the great secret is to know thoroughly, and not to be affected, and to have a steel spring.

The English write better than we, but I fancy we read more out of their books than they do.

For *History of Liberty*.[1] There was a great deal of Whig poetry written in Charles and Cromwell's time: not a line of it has survived.

In certain minds Thought expels Memory. I have this example, — that, eager as I am to fix and record each experience, the interest of a new thought is sometimes such that I do not think of pen and paper at all, and the next day I puzzle myself in a vain attempt to recall the new perception that had so captivated me.

Channing's poetry does not regard the

[1] Mr. Emerson was moved, during the struggle against the encroachments of Slavery, to write a History of Liberty, and collected matter to this end, never reached, much of which appeared in his Anti-Slavery speeches and, in fragments, in the earlier volumes of his journal.

reader. It is written to himself; is his strict experience, the record of his moods, of his fancies, of his observations and studies, and will interest good readers as such. He does not flatter the reader by any attempt to meet his expectation, or to polish his record that he may gratify him, as readers expect to be gratified. He confides entirely in his own bent or bias for meditation and writing. He will write as he has ever written, whether he has readers or not. But his poems have to me and to others an exceptional value for this reason. We have not been considered in their composition, but either defied or forgotten, and therefore read them securely, as original pictures which add something to our knowledge, and with a fair chance to be surprised and refreshed by novel experience.

George Bradford said that Mr. Alcott once said to him, " that as the child loses, as he comes into the world, his angelic memory, so the man, as he grows old, loses his memory of this world."

October 18.

Bret Harte's visit. Bret Harte referred to my essay on Civilization, that the piano comes so quickly into the shanty, etc., and said, " Do you know that, on the contrary, it is vice that brings them in? It is the gamblers who bring in the music to California. It is the prostitute who brings in the New York fashions of dress there, and so throughout." I told him that I spoke also from Pilgrim experience, and knew on good grounds the resistless culture that religion effects.

October 21.

Ruskin is a surprise to me. This old book, *Two Paths*, is original, acute, thoroughly informed, and religious.

> " Wie der Fischer aus dem Meer
> Fische zieht die niemand sah."
>
> As the fisher from the sea
> Pulls the fish that no man saw.

Names should be of good omen, of agreeable sound, commending the person in advance, and, if possible, keeping the old belief of the Greeks, "that the name borne by each man and woman has some connection with their part in the drama of life." The name, then, should look before and after.

We have two or three facts of natural education: 1. First, the common sense of merciless dealing of matter with us, punishing us instantly for any mistake about fire, water, iron, food, and poison. 2. And this world perfectly symmetrical, so that its laws can be reduced to one law. 3. Then we have the world of thought, and its laws, like Niagara currents. 4. Then the astonishing relation between these two.

The necessity of the mind is poetic. . . . It is plain that Kepler, Hunter, Bonnet, Buffon, Geoffroy Saint-Hilaire, Linnæus, Haüy, Oken, Goethe, and Faraday were poets in science as compared with Cuvier.

The physicists in general repel me. I have no wish to read them, and thus do not know their names. But the anecdotes of these men of ideas wake curiosity and delight. Thus Goethe's and Oken's theory of the skull as a metamorphosed vertebra; and Hunter's "arrested development"; and Oersted's "correlation of forces"; and Hay's theory of the form of vases; and Garbett's and Ruskin's architectural theories; and Vitruvius's relation between the human form and the temple; and Peirce's showing that the orbits of comets (parabolics) make the forms of flowers; and Kepler's relation of planetary laws to music; and Franklin's kite.

Reality, however, has a sliding floor.

Look sharply after your thoughts. They come unlooked for, like a new bird seen on your trees, and, if you turn to your usual task, disappear; and you shall never find that perception again; never, I say,—but perhaps years, ages, and I know not what events and worlds may lie between you and its return!

In the novel, the hero meets with a person who astonishes him with a perfect knowledge of his history and character, and draws from him a promise that, whenever and wherever he shall next find him, the youth shall instantly follow and obey him. So is it with you, and the new thought.

> "For deathless powers to verse belong,
> And they like demigods are strong
> On whom the Muses smile."

In Twistleton's *Handwriting of Junius* (p. xiv) I find the quotation from Johnson, of Bacon's remark, "Testimony is like an arrow shot from a long bow: the force of it depends on the strength of the hand that draws it. Argument is like an arrow from a cross-bow, which has equal force, though shot by a child."

Tibullus (on Sulpicia) says of Venus: —

*Illam, quidquid agit, quoquo vestigia vertit,
Componit furtim, subsequiturque decor.*[1]

Then Twistleton's motto from Epicharmus is good —

Νοῦς ὁρῇ καὶ νοῦς ἀκούει, τἄλλα κωφὰ καὶ τυφλά.[2]

Geoffroy Saint-Hilaire is a true hero. Read his behaviour, in August, 1792, when his masters Lhomonde and Haüy, professors in his college of Cardinal-Lemoine, and all the rest of the professors were arrested and sent to the prison of Saint-Firmin. . . .

[Here follows the account of his repeated attempts, at desperate risk to himself, and his final success in accomplishing the escape of twelve of his friends.]

Saint-Hilaire was very ill in consequence of these exertions. Haüy wrote to him: "Leave your problems of crystals, rhomboids, and *dodécaèdres*; stick to plants, which are full of beauty;

[1] Whatsoe'er she does
Grace prompts unseen, and wheresoe'er she wanders
Attends her footsteps.
[2] The mind sees, the mind hears;
All other things are deaf and blind.

a course of botany is pure hygiene." He went with Bonaparte to Egypt, and saved the scientific results, by a brilliant stroke of heroism. In the debate in the Académie des Sciences, in 1830 (?), July 19, the contest between Cuvier and Geoffroy Saint-Hilaire broke out, and reminded of the old sects of philosophers who shook the world with their contests. The austere and regulated thinkers, men of severe science, took part with Cuvier; the bold minds ranged themselves with Geoffroy. What changes have come into the contests of Churches! The debates of the Œcumenical Council are only interesting to the Catholics and a few abnormal readers, interested as the billiard players in the contests of the billiard champions.

Culture. The wide diffusion of taste for poetry is a new fact. We receive twelve newspapers in this house every week, and eleven of them contain a new poem or poems, — all of these respectable, — perhaps one or two fit to clip from the paper, and put into your anthology. Many of these poems are quite as good as many of the pieces in Aikin's or Anderson's standard collections, and recall Walter Scott's reply when Tom Moore said, " Now, Scott, it seems to me that these young fellows write better poetry than we did, and nobody reads it. See how good this poetry is of so many young writers, and the public takes no note of them." Scott replied, "Egad, man, we were in the luck of time." Verses of conversation are now written in a hundred houses, or [for] "picnics" or "private theatricals," which would have made reputation a century ago, but are now unknown out of some family circle. Webster wrote excellent lines in an Album; Macaulay did the same, his "God": then Byrch's "Riddle on the Letter H."

George Bartlett's [1] wit and luck in the privatest "Game parties" are charming. Yet the public never heard of his name. Arthur Gilman, too. In England, in France, appear the Frères, Tom Taylors, Luttrells, Hendersons (Newton's Cotes, too, of whom but for Newton's one remark we should have never heard).

Yet good poetry is as rare as ever.

What a benediction of Heaven is this cheerfulness which I observe with delight,—which

[1] Mr. Bartlett has been mentioned in connection with the amusements at the hotel in the account of the Emerson visit to Mount Mansfield. When Mr. Emerson's children came home from a "game party" at Dr. Bartlett's house, Mr. Emerson always wished to hear George Bartlett's witty verses.

no wrath and no fretting and no disaster can disturb, but keeps its perfect key and heals insanity in all companies and crises.

"Little boys should be seen, and not heard": Very well, but Poets are not to be seen. Look at the foolish portraits of Herrick and Gray, one a butcher, and the other silly. The Greek form answered to the Greek character, but Poets are divided from their forms, — live an official life. Intellect is impersonal.

The father cannot control the child, from defect of sympathy. The man with a longer scale of sympathy, the man who feels the boy's sense and piety and imagination, and also his rough play and impatience and revolt, — who knows the whole gamut in himself, — knows also a way out of the one into the other, and can play on the boy, as on a harp, and easily lead him up from the Scamp to the Angel.

America. Oxford, working steadily now for a thousand years, — or the Sorbonne in France, — and a royal court steadily drawing for centuries men and women of talent and grace throughout the kingdom to the capital city, might give an impulse and sequence to learning and genius. And the history of this country has been far less friendly to a rich and polished literature than England and France. Count our literary men, and they are few, and their works not commanding. But if the question be not of books, but of men,— question of intellect, not of literature,— there would be no steep inferiority. For every one knows men of wit and special or general power, whom to compare with citizens of any nation. Edward Taylor lavished more wit and imagination on his motley congregation of sailors and caulkers than you might find in all France. The coarsest experiences he melted and purified, like Shakspeare, into eloquence. Wendell Phillips is a Pericles whilst you hear him speaking. Beecher, I am sure, is a master in addressing an assembly, though I have never heard such good speeches of his as I have read. Webster was majestic in his best days: and the better audience these men had, the higher would be the appreciation. Neither of them could write as well as he spoke. Appleton's wit is quite as good as Frère's or Selby's or Luttrell's, who shine in the biographies. And England has no Occasional Poet to surpass Holmes. Dr. Channing, I must believe, had no equal as a preacher in the world of his time. Then we have men of affairs, who would rule wherever there were men, — masters in commerce, in law, in politics, in society. Every civil country has such, but I doubt if any has more or better than we.

Add, that the Adamses have shown hereditary skill in public affairs, and Judge Hoar is as good a lawyer, a statesman, and an influence in public and in private, as any city could hope to find.

I pass over my own list of thinkers and friends [often referred to], and only add, that I believe our soil yields as good women, too, as England or France, though we have not a book from them to compare with *Allemagne*.[1] Yet Aunt Mary's journals shine with genius, and Margaret Fuller's conversation did.

[The burning of Chicago occurred in early October. Mr. Emerson had not meant to go on a far journey to lecture again, but could not resist the appeal to go there and speak, which he did, and incidentally lectured in other cities.]

Home again from Chicago, Quincy, Springfield, and Dubuque, which I had not believed I

[1] By Madame de Staël.

should see again, yet found it easier to visit than before, and the kindest reception in each city.

Authors or Books quoted or referred to in Journal for 1871

Epicharmus; Heracleitus; Vitruvius; Tibullus, *Elegia;* Iamblichus; Taliessin, *apud* Skene; Kepler; Robert Hooke; Newton; Roger Cotes;

Buffon; Linnæus; Gray; Bonnet; John Hunter; John Adams; Haüy; Henry McKenzie; Playfair; Goethe; Dugald Stewart; Mackintosh; John Quincy Adams; John Hookham Frère; Chateaubriand; Cuvier; Sir John Leslie; Geoffroy Saint-Hilaire;

James Hogg; Jeffrey; Oersted; Oken; Lord Brougham; Lord Cockburn; Rev. W. E. Channing; Chalmers; General Gourgaud; Daniel Webster; "Father" Edward Taylor; Robert Knox; John Wilson ("Christopher North"); De Quincey; Allan Cunningham;

Sir William Hamilton; Lockhart; Carlyle; Flourens, *Debat entre Cuvier et Geoffroy Saint-Hilaire;*

Rev. Edward B. Pusey, *Lectures on Daniel and the Prophets;* Macaulay; Cardinal Wiseman; Luttrell; Byrch, *Riddle on the Letter H;*

J. S. Mill; Dr. Charles T. Jackson; Benjamin Peirce; Holmes; Wendell Phillips; Beecher;

Dr. Jeffries Wyman, *Symmetry and Homology in Human Limbs;* Thomas G. Appleton; Tom Taylor; Froude; W. Ellery Channing, *Poems;* Ruskin, *The Two Paths;* Hay, *On Vases;* Tyndall, *On Sound;* Max Müller; Lacy Garbett, *Design in Architecture;* Charles Francis Adams;

Arthur Gilman; Twistleton, *The Handwriting of Junius;* Francis Bret Harte; John Muir; Cronise, *On Trees* (?)

JOURNAL

BALTIMORE AND WASHINGTON
BOSTON READINGS
CHILDHOOD'S MEMORIES
PARALLEL IN LITERATURE
OLD SUMMER STREET
AMHERST
BURNING OF THE HOME
FRIENDS TO THE RESCUE
FAILING HEALTH
ENGLAND. FRANCE. ITALY

JOURNAL LXIII

1872

(From Journal ST)

[IN January, Mr. Emerson gave a course of four lectures in Baltimore, and at Washington, where he was the guest of Senator Sumner, was asked to speak to the students (Freedmen) of Howard University. The address was partly *extempore*, but he probably, to help out the address, read them some sheets from his lecture on Books, to guide the reading of the more earnest and intellectual among them. The occasion was reported in all the papers,[1] and, after his return, Mr. Emerson was almost annoyed, but soon rather amused, by the many letters which he received. He told his family that the speech was "very poor; merely talking against time." In the course of it he praised George Herbert's *Poems* as "a Sunday book, and a Monday book, too," asked if it were in their library, and said he should have the privilege of giving it to them.

[1] There was a report in the *Boston Evening Transcript* January 22, 1872.

When he went to the bookstore in Boston to buy it he was told, "There is n't a Herbert to be had, Sir. Since your speech was published there has been such a demand for them that they are all sold out, and none left in Boston." However, he found one, and came home better pleased with the result of his speech than he had ever thought to be. Then more letters came, one suggesting that he should write on the subject of Books. Comparatively few persons had probably then read *Society and Solitude*, the volume published nearly two years before.

Mr. James T. Fields, who, with Colonel Forbes, had arranged the Saturday afternoon readings of English Prose and Verse in 1869, again kindly bestirred himself (Colonel Forbes having gone to Europe with his family) to have such another course. This plan was most successful, and the tickets were in great demand for the six Readings, in Mechanics' Hall, Boston, beginning in the middle of April. Mr. Emerson enjoyed sharing with an audience of friends, old and young, the pleasure that he had in these selections, made from his boyhood on. The poems and selections were of authors of various periods, and on widely differing themes. Mr. Emerson read his favorites, whether recent, or dear from the associations of his youth, not caring greatly whether all were illustrations of the short discourse at the beginning. As his memory was now imperfect, he, once at least, read a sheet which he had already read a few minutes before. His daughter Ellen, who had always accompanied him, was troubled at this and begged him always to read his lectures to her in advance. But he answered, "Things that go wrong about these lectures don't disturb me, because I know that everyone knows that I am worn out and passed by, and that it is only my old friends come for friendship's sake to have one last season with me."

The course, however, seems to have been very successful, and to have given great pleasure week by week to a large number of the best of Boston and the neighborhood.

What follows may have been some notes for the last of these readings, or possibly for some Sunday address to the Parker Society at the Music Hall.]

'T is becoming in the Americans to dare in religion to be simple, as they have been in government, in trade, in social life.

Christianity is pure Deism.

"Hunger and thirst after righteousness."

"The kingdom of God cometh not by observation"; is "received as a little child."

"God considers integrity, not munificence."
— SOCRATES.

Power belongeth unto God, but his secret is with them that fear him.

Schleiermacher said, "The human soul is by nature a Christian."

One thing is certain: the religions are obsolete when the reforms do not proceed from them.

You say, the Church is an institution of God. Yes, but are not wit, and wise men, and good judgment whether a thing be so or no, — also institutions of God, and older than the other?

Concord Lyceum. For that local lecture which I still propose to read at our Town Hall [remember to speak] concerning the hanging of private pictures, each for one month, in the Library, etc., etc.

Remember that a scholar wishes that every book, chart, and plate belonging to him should draw interest every moment by circulation: for

"No man is the lord of anything
 Till he communicate his part to others;
 Nor doth he of himself know them for aught

JOYS AS A CHILD

> Till he behold them formed in the applause
> Where they 're extended; where, like an arch, reverberates
> The voice again, or, like a gate of steel
> Fronting the sun, receives and renders back
> The figure and its heat."
>
> (*Troilus and Cressida.*)

When a boy I used to go to the wharves, and pick up shells out of the sand which vessels had brought as ballast, and also plenty of stones, gypsum, which I discovered would be luminous when I rubbed two bits together in a dark closet, to my great wonder; — and I do not know why luminous to this day. That, and the magnetizing my penknife, till it would hold a needle; and the fact that blue and gamboge would make green in my pictures of mountains; and the charm of drawing vases by scrawling with ink heavy random lines, and then doubling the paper, so as to make another side symmetrical, — what was chaos, becoming symmetrical; then halloing to an echo at the pond, and getting wonderful replies.

Still earlier, what silent wonder is waked in the boy by blowing bubbles from soap and water with a pipe!

Old Age. We spend a great deal of time in waiting.

> "No more I seek, the prize is found;
> I furl my sail, the voyage is o'er."

Whose lines? Mine, I believe, part of translation of some Latin lines for Mrs. Drury.

The good writer is sure of his influence, because, as he is always copying not from his fancy, but from real facts,— when his reader afterwards comes to like experiences of his own he is always reminded of the writer. Nor do I much care for the question whether the Zend-Avesta or the Desatir are genuine antiques, or modern counterfeits, as I am only concerned with the good sentences; and it is indifferent how old a truth is, whether an hour or five centuries, whether it first shot into the mind of Adam, or your own. If it be truth it is certainly much older than both of us.

Shakspeare. Parallax, as you know, is the apparent displacement of an object from two points of view;— less and less of the heavenly bodies, because of their remoteness,— and of the fixed stars, none at all. Well it is thus that we have found Shakspeare to be a fixed star.

Because all sorts of men have in three centuries found him still unapproachable. The merit of a poem is decided by long experience.

May 26, 1872.

Yesterday, my sixty-ninth birthday, I found myself on my round of errands in Summer Street, and, though close on the spot where I was born, was looking into a street with some bewilderment and read on the sign *Kingston Street*, with surprise, finding in the granite blocks no hint of Nathaniel Goddard's pasture and long wooden fence, and so of my nearness to my native corner of Chauncy Place. It occurred to me that few living persons ought to know so much of the families of this fast-growing city, for the reason, that Aunt Mary — whose manuscripts I had been reading to Hedge and Bartol, on Friday evening — had such a keen perception of character, and taste for aristocracy, and I heard in my youth and manhood every name she knew. It is now nearly a hundred years since she was born, and the founders of the oldest families that are still notable were known to her as retail-merchants, milliners, tailors, distillers, as well as the ministers, lawyers, and doctors of the time. She was a realist, and knew a great man or "a whale-hearted woman"—as she called one of her pets—from a successful money-maker.

If I should live another year, I think I shall cite still the last stanza of my own poem, "The World-Soul."[1]

Walk in the city for an hour, and you shall see the whole history of female beauty. Here are the school-girls in the first profusion of their hair covering them to the waist, and now and then one maiden of eighteen or nineteen years, in the moment of her perfect beauty. Look quick and sharply,—this is her one meridian day. To find the like again, you must meet, on your next visit, one who is a month younger to-day. Then troops of pleasing, well-dressed ladies, sufficiently good-looking and graceful, but without claims to the prize of the goddess of Discord.

[1] Spring still makes spring in the mind
    When sixty years are told;
  Love wakes anew this throbbing heart,
    And we are never old.
  Over the winter glaciers
    I see the summer glow,
  And through the wild-piled snowdrift
    The warm rosebuds below.

"No sign that our mighty rocks had ever tingled with earthquake," said John Muir.

He said he slept in a wrinkle of the bark of a Sequoia on the night after we left him.

June 12.

Sarah Clarke gratified us with her visit of twenty-six hours, ever the same peaceful, wise, just, and benevolent spirit, open, gentle, skilful, without a word of self-assertion. I regret that I did not recall and testify to her my oft recollection of her noble and oft-needed and repeated sisterly aid to Margaret Fuller, in old times, in her cruel headaches. We talked of many friends of both of us, but of Charles Newcomb it seems she knew nothing. Of Greenough she did not know much. I was glad, in describing his last visit to me, to add that he was one who to his varied perception added the rare one of τὸ δεινόν (the dire).

What proof of Goethe's wealth of mind like the *Sprüche?* . . .

July 11.

Yesterday read my paper on "Character" or "Greatness" to the "Social Union" comprising the four Classes at Amherst College. Stayed with Ellen at President Stearns's house, there finding Henry Ward Beecher, Judge Lord, and other gentlemen, with Miss Gleason, Miss Goodman, of Lenox, Miss Annie Lee, of Charlestown, and the daughters of President Stearns.

Visited the Boltwoods, and with Professor Charles U. Shepard,[1] went through his rich collection of minerals in the Walker Hall.

'T is easy to write the technics of poetry, to discriminate Imagination and Fancy, etc.; but the office and power which that word poetry covers and suggests are not so easily reached and defined. What heaven and earth and sea and the forms of men and women are speaking or hinting to us in our healthiest and most impressionable hours, — what fresh perceptions a new day will give us of the old problems of our own being and its hidden source; what is this Sky of Law, and what the Future hides.

Wednesday, July 24.

House burned.

[The above is all the record that Mr. Emerson

[1] A cousin of Mr. Emerson's, the professor of Anatomy at Amherst, and, in winter, at Charleston, South Carolina; also a geologist.

BURNING OF THE HOUSE

left of the temporary destruction of his home. By unhappy chance not one of their children was at hand to help their father and mother when, on a rainy morning, they were waked by the crackling of fire in the walls of their room. Their daughter Ellen was visiting friends at the seashore; Mrs. Forbes (Edith) was, with her husband and family, on the homeward voyage from England, and Edward, then convalescent from a surgical operation, had remained there, to pursue his medical studies. But the immediate neighbours, and soon a great number of the townspeople as well as the fire-company, were quickly on the spot, men and boys with great energy and courage saving property and fighting the fire, and women and girls sorting and gathering the household goods intelligently and quickly and saving them from the rain by carrying them to the houses near by. The occurrences at a fire in a village and the actions of kind-hearted but inexperienced neighbours have been a stock subject for ridicule in newspapers and stories, but here was an occasion when good sense and brave and affectionate neighbourly action reached a high-water mark, and never did the *town family*, as it used to exist in simpler days, and still in a measure remains, show forth more finely. The fire originated in the attic, almost surely from a kerosene lamp charring the timbers hot and dry from the summer. A woman, engaged the day before for domestic service, had apparently spent a part of the night in prowling among the chests and trunks there. When help began to arrive the house was filling with choking black smoke, making it hard to save furniture and clothing upstairs. By the time this was done and the falling ceilings drove out the men, the lower storey was so filled with smoke that, when the books in Mr. Emerson's study were remembered, they were *felt* there by brave boys, who rushed in, holding their breath, and pulled them out into baskets or blankets and all were saved; happily the manuscripts also.

Mr. and Mrs. Emerson, imperfectly clothed, wet by the rain, fatigued and worn by excitement, were taken home and cared for by Judge Keyes and his family, and the next day were welcomed to the Manse, — the ancestral home, dear to Mr. Emerson from his boyhood, — by his cousin, Miss Elizabeth Ripley. All sorts of exciting and some dangerous incidents occurred during the fire. When a hole chopped in the roof let out the smoke and let in the water which put out the fire, the roof and the top of the walls of the main house were ruined and the interior greatly damaged by smoke and water.

Mr. Cabot, in the *Memoir*, gives some account of the fire and its effects on Mr. Emerson, and he also prints in Appendix E of the second volume Dr. Le Baron Russell's moving story of the "friendly conspiracy," the instant and unsolicited action of friends old and new, some of them hardly known to Mr. Emerson, in testimony of affection and gratitude, to rebuild his house and send him abroad for rest and recreation meanwhile. There also, in Judge Hoar's letter to Dr. Russell, appears the Judge's happy and affectionate wit in presenting the matter to Mr. Emerson, as ambassador of his friends, in such a way that the gift was impossible to refuse, though Mr. Emerson pleaded for time to consider it, saying that thus far in life he "had been allowed to stand on his own feet."

Mr. Emerson seemed brave and cheerful during the fire, and for more than a week afterwards it looked as if he had suffered no harm. His daughter wrote that it did not seem as if that experience would seriously affect him. "There is no doubt," she wrote, "that it was a tragedy to him at the time, and that he suffered very much. Nothing ever showed me so distinctly how faithful he is never to mention himself, as this week has."

A room in the Court-House was secured for Mr. Emerson, to which his manuscripts and needed books were brought, and there he tried to work at the anxious and unwelcome task of preparing a new volume. This had been forced upon him by an English publishing-house who, otherwise, proposed to print earlier scattered works of his (from the *Dial* and elsewhere), but they consented to desist if in a very short time he would let them, in connection with his Boston publishers, bring out in England a new volume of his essays.

But, about a fortnight after the fire, Mr. Emerson began to be very unwell, and, though he kept about, a low feverish condition with cough and weakness came on. Growing no better, he went for a day or two to Rye Beach with his daughter and thence to Waterford, Maine. Improvement came slowly; he was distressed about the urgency of the publishers for the new volume on which he was quite unable to work. At Waterford he began to think that possibly the end of his life might be at hand, and to consider what would become of his manuscripts and journals, saying that, if his son were a scholar, they would be most valuable to him, "Otherwise they are worthless." He dreaded their falling into the hands of the wrong persons. His friend Mr. J. Elliot Cabot and Dr. Frederic H. Hedge were the only persons that he would consider, but he did not feel that he could ask either of them to leave their work for his, should his powers fail. It was explained to the publishers in London and here that it was absolutely out of the question for Mr. Emerson to do any work upon *Letters and Social Aims* until he had recovered his health by entire rest. Next year, Mr. Cabot most kindly arranged the material for it and prepared it for the press.[1]

Not long after the fire, Miss Emerson wrote to Dr. Edward H. Clarke, whom her father was about to consult, a letter telling of the failure of his memory and working powers, which now the family began to realize had been imperceptibly coming on him for five or six years,— Mr. Emerson had calmly recognized this in 1866, when he wrote "Terminus." The fire and subsequent illness had increased this trouble, and now *aphasia*, the difficulty of associating the fit word to the idea, appeared, though not at first seriously,

[1] See Mr. Cabot's preface to *Letters and Social Aims*.

and also being very variable according to the state of his health.]

NORWAY, MAINE, *August* 20.

Forgot, in leaving home, twenty necessities, — forgot to put Horace, or Martial, or Cicero's Letters, *La Cité Antique*, or Taine's *England*, in my wallet: forgot even the sacred chocolate satchel itself, to hold them or their like. Well, at the dear Vale,[1] eleven miles off yet, I may recall or invoke things as good. Yet I should there remember that letters are due . . . [to many dear friends who had joined in the generous provision for restoring the house and giving a restful vacation]. Perhaps I will venture on a letter of proposals of a voyage to Elliot Cabot, and a letter to the kindly Alexander Ireland[2] is more than due.

[Colonel William Forbes and his wife and children had returned from abroad, and Mr. Emerson, now recovered from his acute attack, joyfully accepted his daughter's invitation to spend a month with them on the Forbes's beau-

[1] The old home of the Haskins relatives and his Aunt Mary in Waterford.

[2] The loyal friend in Manchester, England, since 1833.

tiful island, Mrs. Emerson and their daughter Ellen going too.]

NAUSHON, *August* 31.

I thought to-day, in these rare seaside woods, that if absolute leisure were offered me, I should run to the college or the scientific school which offered best lectures on Geology, Chemistry, Minerals, Botany, and seek to make the alphabets of those sciences clear to me. How could leisure or labour be better employed? 'T is never late to learn them, and every secret opened goes to authorize our æsthetics. Cato learned Greek at eighty years, but these are older bibles and oracles than Greek. Certainly this were a good *pis aller* if Elliot Cabot and Athens and Egypt should prove an abortive dream.

I think one must go to the tropics to find any match to this enchanting isle of Prospero. It needs and ought to find its Shakspeare.[1] What dells! what lakelets! what groves! what clumps of historic trees of unknown age, hint-

[1] Rev. Edward Everett Hale once wrote an ingenious article showing the possibility of Prospero's island in *The Tempest* having been suggested to the poet by Gosnold's description of one of the group of Elizabeth Islands, which Mr. Hale thought preceded the presentation of the play.

ing annals of white men and Indians, histories of fire and of storm and of peaceful ages of social growth! Nature shows her secret wonders, and seems to have impressed her fortunate landlords with instant and constant respect for her solitudes and centennial growths. Where else do such oaks and beeches and vines grow, which the winds and storms seem rather to adorn than spoil by their hurts and devastations, touching them as with Fate, and not wanton interference? And the sea binds the Paradise with its grand belt of blue, with its margin of beautiful pebbles, with its watching herons and hawks and eagles, and its endless fleet of barques, steamers, yachts, and fishers' boats.

The island compels them — glad to be compelled — to be skilful sailors, yachtsmen, fishermen, and swimmers, thus adding all the charm of the sea to their abode, and adds the surprise and romance of hunting.

[It was not quite easy to persuade Mr. Emerson to go abroad for the winter and spring. The thought of seeing a few friends, old and new, in England, attracted him, but he always held himself as unfit for visiting and society, and now the limitations and growing infirmities of age were mortifying. Yet the thought of seeing the ancient Nile, and perhaps Greece, drew him, and at last he was persuaded to sail, in the last week in October, with his daughter Ellen, for Liverpool, leaving Mrs. Emerson with their daughter Mrs. Forbes. Mr. and Miss Emerson were met on arriving in England by his son Edward, then a student at St. Thomas's Hospital in London, whither, after a short rest at Chester, they went early in November. Edward then had to sail for home.

Mr. Emerson and his daughter were most affectionately welcomed on their arrival in London, and every delicate aid and guidance was given them by American friends who should be here mentioned. Colonel Henry Lee, who had in the winter lost two of his daughters by diphtheria in Florence, whose wife was ill, and his oldest son then struggling between life and death with typhoid fever, yet came daily to see them, and, keeping back his own troubles, cheered them with his friendly and witty talk; Mr. Charles Eliot Norton who, within a year, had lost his beautiful wife, was then resident in London with his family, and gave help and wise counsel as to planning the trip to France and Italy on the way to Egypt. His sister, too, gave sisterly help to Miss Emerson, who was temporarily lame; Rev. William Henry Channing, then a Unitarian preacher in Kensington, with affectionate zeal did everything possible to make their stay in London in their invalid condition easy and pleasant, as did also Mr. Moncure D. Conway, then minister of the South Place Ethical Society. Mr. Emerson had also the unexpected pleasure of meeting Charles K. Newcomb, the valued friend of many years ago.

Of English friends, first came Mr. Thomas Hughes, then Dean Stanley and Lady Augusta his wife, the admirable surgeon (soon after knighted) William MacCormac, who had taken care of young Emerson, and, best valued, Carlyle, though old, broken, and sad. In Chester, and in London, as far as his friends would allow, Mr. Emerson took great comfort in absence of responsibility and quiet, declared that "*idlesse* is the business of age. I love above all things to do nothing"; he said he never before had discovered this privilege of seventy years: also that he finds "there is a convenience of having a name, — it serves one as well as having a good coat." He began to eat better than he had for a long time, and made long nights, saying, "A warm bed is the best medicine, — and one gets such good sleep in this country, — good strong sleep." At the table he said, "The land of England desires much food in its inhabitants." When plans were made for him, he would smile and say, "Old age loves leisure." Nevertheless, in this short stay, though he felt reluctant to go into company, he enjoyed in moderation seeing the sights of London.

Mr. Norton, during the last year, as far as possible had sunk his own sorrows in cheering Ruskin and Carlyle, both sick and utterly downhearted, and had made himself much beloved by them. Carlyle said to him, speaking of a letter from Emerson acknowledging the last volumes of the completed *Frederick the Great*, "I have a letter received from him, after a long silence, and though there were few words in it that did not give me pain, it says the only thing that has been said about my book that was worth saying; and therefore, when I had read it through, I wrapped it up in a piece of paper and put it inside the book, and there it will stay till I am dead and it will fall into other hands than mine." This interesting sentence Miss Emerson, whose verbal memory was excellent, wrote in a letter to her sister soon after Mr. Norton's visit. It probably refers to Letter

CLV (January 7, 1866) of the *Carlyle-Emerson Correspondence*, and yet what is said of the pain-giving words might well refer to the letter from Emerson preceding it (CLIII, September 26, 1864), referring to Carlyle's perverse hostility to the North during the War. The last letters that passed between them were most friendly.

After staying but one week of chill and rainy November in London, Mr. Emerson and his daughter moved on to Canterbury — so attractive that he proposed they should send for Mrs. Emerson and settle there. However, after two days they went direct to Paris. There they had a happy week at the same hotel with Mr. and Mrs. James Russell Lowell and the charming Mr. John Holmes (brother of the Doctor), whose acquaintance Mr. Emerson had made fourteen years before at their Adirondac Camp. In Paris they were joined by the admirable Swiss travelling servant recommended to them by Dean Stanley, without whose services their farther journeyings would have been spoiled by cares and difficulties, thus avoided. They went thence by rail to Marseilles and Nice and by boat to Genoa, and thence again by boat to Leghorn. Making but short stays at Pisa and

Florence, they reached Rome on the last day of November.

The weather was fine, they met friends, and had especial good fortune in being the guests during their last week of Baron von Hoffman and his wife, who was the daughter of Samuel Gray Ward, of Boston, Mr. Emerson's early and valued friend. Their villa and garden high on the Cælian Hill were most beautiful and commanded a wonderful view of the Campagna and distant mountains. Under the Baron's admirable guidance they saw the ancient city to best advantage. Thence they went to Naples, and after four days sailed for Egypt. Christmas found them in Alexandria, and in the last days of the year they proceeded to Cairo.]

AUTHORS OR BOOKS QUOTED OR REFERRED TO IN JOURNAL FOR 1872[1]

Zend-Avesta; Heracleitus; Socrates; Cicero; Martial;
Taliessin; Saadi;

[1] Among these are given poems used by Mr. Emerson in his Readings, although by favourite authors not usually given in the yearly list.

Leonardo da Vinci; Vasari, *Life of Raphael;*
Spenser, *Muiopotmos;* Ben Jonson, *Ode to Himself;* John Fletcher, *Epilogue to An Honest Man's Fortune;* Waller, *Apology for having loved before;* Montrose, *Love Song;* Richard Lovelace, *To Althea;* Crashaw, *Sospetto d'Herode;*

Bishop Berkeley; Pope; David Lewis, *Lines to Pope;* Thomson, *Seasons;* John Wesley, Hymn, *O draw me, Father, after Thee;* John Hunter; Sir William Jones, translation of Hindu poem, *To Narayena;* Goethe, *Sprüche, West-Östlichen Divan;*

Schleiermacher; Wordsworth, *Sonnet to Schill, The Force of Prayer;* Scott, *Songs of the White Lady of Avenel;* Ballad, *Thomas the Rhymer;* Byron, *Murat* in *Ode to Napoleon, When coldness wraps this suffering clay;* Varnhagen von Ense; Boucher de Perthes, *De l'homme antédiluvien;* Josiah Conder, *The Modern Traveller;* Translations of Klephtic Ballads (from the *Dial*), *A Romaic Lochinvar,* and *Olympus and Kissarvos; Arab Ballad;*

Agassiz; Tennyson, *Maud;* Richard Monckton Milnes, *The Lay of the Humble;* Julia C. R. Dorr, *Outgrown;* Mrs. Caroline Tappan, *Lines to the Poet;* J. G. Saxe; Thoreau, *Inspiration;* Ruskin, *Sesame and Lilies;* J. R. Lowell;

Coventry Patmore; Herman Grimm, *Leben Raphaels*; Henry Timrod, *Ode to the Confederate Dead*; Edmund C. Stedman, *John Brown of Ossawatomie*; Helen Hunt, *Thought*.

JOURNAL

THE NILE
ROME, FLORENCE, PARIS
THREE WEEKS OF LONDON
OXFORD
RETURN HOME

JOURNAL LXIV

1873

(From Journal ST)

[IN spite of rest, friendly faces, and interesting scenes, the old feeling of the unprofitableness of travel for travel's sake, which has appeared so often in Mr. Emerson's writings, would assert itself, especially in the early part of the journey. His daughter records some of the "dismally witty remarks" that he made on the Delta as they passed through it to Cairo: "Could anything argue wilder insanity than leaving a country like ours to see this bareness of mud? — Look! there is some water, and see! there is a crowd of people. They have collected with a purpose of drowning themselves." Although he would have been quite willing to go home, he said that he would gladly spend a fortnight with Mr. Lowell in Paris, and desired to find in England Tennyson, Ruskin, and Browning before his return. Also, before leaving home, when Egypt was suggested, he said, "Yes, I should like to see the tomb of 'him who sleeps at Phylæ.'"

At Cairo, he was pleased to find Mr. Bancroft, and went about the city with him. Mr. Charles G. Leland and Mr. Augustus Julius Hare were also agreeable. General Charles Stone (formerly of the United States Army, then Chief-of-Staff of the Turkish force in Egypt) and his family showed great courtesy to Mr. Emerson and his daughter.]

SHEPHEARD'S HOTEL, CAIRO,
January, 1873.

Nothing has struck me more in the streets here than the erect carriage and walking of the Copts (I suppose them); better and nobler in figure and movement than any passengers in our cities at home.

On Tuesday, January 7, we sailed from Cairo for Philæ, in the dahabeah *Aurora*, with Mahmoud Bedowa, dragoman; a *reis* or captain, and his mate; ten oarsmen, two cooks, a factotum boy, a head waiter named Marzook, and second waiter Hassan, — in all eighteen: The company in the cabin were Mr. and Mrs. Whitwell, Miss May Whitwell, and Miss Bessie Whitwell, Miss Farquhar [a Scotch lady], Ellen, and I.

Egypt very poor in trees: we have seen hardly an orange tree. Palms are the chief tree along the banks of the river, from Cairo to Assuan; acacias, the fig. In Cairo, we had a banian with its boughs planting themselves around it under my window at Shepheard's Hotel.

Egypt is the Nile and its shores. The cultivated land is a mere green ribbon on either shore of the river. You can see, as you sail, its quick boundary in rocky mountains or desert sands. Day after day and week after week of unbroken sunshine, and though you may see clouds in the sky, they are merely for ornament, and never rain.

The Prophet says of the Egyptians, "It is their strength to sit still."[1]

Papyrus is of more importance to history than cotton.

All this journey is a perpetual humiliation, satirizing and whipping our ignorance. The people despise us because we are helpless

[1] Isaiah xxx, 7. Mr. Emerson, in quoting this, said to one of the party on the dahabeah, "The Yankee learns that strength for the first time when he comes to Egypt."

babies who cannot speak or understand a word they say; the sphinxes scorn dunces; the obelisks, the temple walls, defy us with their histories which we cannot spell. Every new object only makes new questions which each traveller asks of the other, and none of us can answer, and each sinks lower in the opinion of his companion. The people, whether in the boat, or out of it, are a perpetual study for the excellence and grace of their forms and motion. No people walk so well, so upright as they are, and strong, and flexible; and for studying the nude, our artists should come here and not to Paris. Every group of the country people on the shores, as seen from our dahabeah, look like the ancient philosophers going to the School of Athens.

In swimming, the Arabs show great strength and speed, all using what at Cambridge we used to call the "Southern stroke," alternating the right arm and the left.

All the boys and all the babes have flies roosting about their eyes, which they do not disturb, nor seem to know their presence. It is rare to find sound eyes among them. Blind beggars appear at every landing led about by their children.

From the time of our arrival at Cairo to our return thither, six weeks, we have had no rain; — unclouded summer on the Nile to Assuan and back, and have required the awning to be spread over us on the deck from 10 A. M. till late in the afternoon.

In Egypt the sandstone or limestone instructs men how to build, — stands in square blocks, and they have only to make a square door for tombs, and the shore is a pair or a series of steps or stairs. The lateen sail is the shadow of a pyramid; and the pyramid is the simplest copy of a mountain, or of the form which a pile of sand or earth takes when dropped from a cart. — I saw a crocodile in the Nile at a distance.

We arrived at Thebes 19th January; Esne (?), 24th; and at Assuan, 28th January; visited Philæ, on Wednesday, 29th January; arrived in Cairo Thursday, 13th February, making 38 days for our expedition and return.

The magnet is the mystery which I would fain have explained to me, though I doubt if there be any teachers. It is the wonder of the child and not less of the philosopher.[1] Goethe

[1] Mr. Charles Eliot Norton said that on the return voyage from England, in the following May, Mr. Emerson, as

says, "The magnet is a primary phenomenon, which we must only express in order to have it explained. Thereby is it then also a symbol for all besides for which we use to speak no word or name."

See Plutarch, *Morals*, vol. i, p. 156, old copy [edition].

Tuesday, January 28.

Met Mr. George L. Owen at Assuan, our party and his exchanging visits. I found him a very intelligent and agreeable companion. In the dahabeah in which we found him on the Nile, he shared the cabin with only one companion, Mr. Ralph Elliot.

[This meeting with Mr. Owen (also a second, soon after, in going down the Nile) was a very agreeable episode. Mr. Emerson's health was steadily improving, and with it his enjoyment.

At Cairo, Mr. Emerson and his daughter parted from their friendly travelling companions, took ship for Italy — in passing he enjoyed the sight of Crete, and its mountains, birthplace of Zeus, and after landing hastened on to Rome. They had little time for sight-

they walked the deck and spoke of the steersman, took from his own pocket his little compass, saying, "I like to hold the god in my hands."

seeing in eleven days, but received constant visits and kind attentions. Mr. Marsh, the American Minister, and his wife were very kind, and they saw their friends the Von Hoffmans; also the Storys, the Howitts, Lady Ashburton, Mr. Tilton the artist, Miss Sarah Clarke, and Dr. Wister, of Philadelphia.]

In Florence, I hoped to find Herman Grimm, who, as I had heard, was residing there to complete his *Life of Raffaelle*. Immediately on my arrival, I sent Curnex [the travelling servant] to the German bookstores to inquire his address. Neither of these knew of his presence in the city. In the street, I met Mr. Bigelow, our American Minister at Paris, and asked him for news of Grimm. He did not know that he was here. On my return to the Hotel du Nord, I found Mr. Bigelow's card saying that, immediately after leaving me, he had met Grimm in the street, and learned his address which he had written out for me on his card: and Grimm had also called and left his own. I went at once to Grimm, and was received and introduced to Gisela his wife, and invited them to dine with us that evening, which they did, to the great satisfaction of Ellen and me. He speaks English very well, and Gisela, who does not, talked with Ellen in German.

[Mr. Emerson had never met Grimm, although he and his wife (daughter of Bettine [Brentano] von Arnim) had corresponded with him occasionally for years. The meeting was very pleasant and fortunate, as Mr. Emerson and his daughter were to set out for Paris the next morning.

In Herman Grimm's *Essays* is a very interesting account of how he first became acquainted with Emerson's writings.

Grimm's comments to Miss Emerson on her father's appearance are interesting as showing not only the benefit of the Egyptian voyage, but what a wholesome looking man he was, even to the time of his last illness, and how much certain pictures belied him. His daughter, writing home from Florence, said, "Herman now began telling me of his pleasure in beholding Father, and said every photograph did him great injustice;—'they all represent a feeble old man of seventy; he looks a strong man of fifty. They look as if he were made of iron, of copper. He looks as if he were made of steel. He has a fine, sharp, manly face; and such bright colouring, which is all lost, of course, in the photographs.'"]

JOY OF A NEW CITY

[*March 16 to April.*]

In the Hotel de Lorraine, Rue de Beaune, Paris, where Ellen and I took rooms for some weeks during both our visits to Paris, we lived with James R. Lowell and his wife, and John Holmes, to our great satisfaction. There also I received, one evening, a long and happy visit from Mr. James Cotter Morison, who is writing the *Life of Comte*. At the house of Mr. Laugel, I was introduced to Ernest Renan; to Henri Taine; to Elie de Beaumont; and to some other noted gentlemen. M. Taine sent me, the next day, his *Littérature anglaise*, in five volumes.

The enjoyment of travel is in the arrival at a new city, as Paris, or Florence, or Rome,— the feeling of free adventure, you have no duties, — nobody knows you, nobody has claims, you are like a boy on his first visit to the Common on Election Day. Old Civilization offers to you alone this huge city, all its wonders, architecture, gardens, ornaments, galleries, which had never cost you so much as a thought. For the first time for many years you wake master of the bright day, in a bright world without a claim on you;— only leave to enjoy. This dropping, for the first time, the doleful bundle of Duty creates, day after day, a health as of new youth.

In Paris, your mere passport admits you to the vast and costly public galleries on days on which the natives of the city cannot pass the doors. Household cares you have none: you take your dinner, lunch, or supper where and when you will: cheap cabs wait for you at every corner,— guides at every door, magazines of sumptuous goods and attractive fairings, unknown hitherto, solicit your eyes. Your health mends every day. Every word spoken to you is a wonderful and agreeable riddle which it is a pleasure to solve, — a pleasure and a pride. Every experience of the day is important, and furnishes conversation to you who were so silent at home.

[Mr. Emerson now, as witnessed above, was greatly improved in health, and his memory and power of finding the right word in conversation had so far returned towards the normal that he no longer shrank from going into society.

He and his daughter arrived in London on Saturday, April 5, and went to comfortable lodgings. They remained in the city three weeks. On their previous stay, London had been comparatively empty of persons whom they would naturally have seen, but now friends and visitors were most attentive and they had little time for sight-seeing, as they had daily invitations to lunches and dinners. Of course the meeting with his oldest and best friend in England was what was foremost in Mr. Emerson's mind. Of the call on Carlyle Miss Emerson wrote, "He was in more amiable and cheerful humour than he had been a few days before when Father walked with him, and Father has been very happy in the remembrance of this call." Just before leaving London, she writes, "Father, after breakfast with Mr. Gladstone, spent the forenoon with Mr. Carlyle with real comfort, bade him good-bye, and then went to the Howards' and lunched with Mrs. Lewes."]

April.

In London, I saw Fergusson the architect; Browning the poet;[1] John Stuart Mill; Sir

[1] Miss Emerson writes of her father's "breakfasting at Lady Amberley's where he met Mr. Browning and was well pleased. They disagreed about Poetry: Mr. Browning praised Shelley." Mr. Emerson would never admit the claims of

Henry Holland; Huxley; Tyndall; Lord Houghton; Mr. Gladstone; Dean Stanley; Lecky; Froude; Thomas Hughes; Lyon Playfair; Sir Arthur Helps; the Duke of Argyle; the Duke of Cleveland; the Duke of Bedford; Sir Frederick Pollock; Charles Reade; Mr. Dasent; — with the Amberleys I paid a visit to Lord Russell at his house, and lunched there. I failed to see Garth Wilkinson, though I called on him twice, and he left his card twice at my door, in my absence. William H. Channing was, as always, the kindest of friends. Moncure Conway was incessant in his attentions, and William Allingham gave us excellent aid. George Howard, who will one day, I hope, be Earl of Carlisle, was the most attentive and generous of friends.

Mr. Thomas Hughes introduced me to the Cosmopolitan Club, which meets every Sunday and Wednesday night at 10 o'clock, and there I saw on two evenings very agreeable gentlemen, Sir Frederick Pollock, Fergusson, Lord Houghton, William Story, and others. Professor Tyndall procured me the privileges of the Athenæum, which is still the best of the great London Clubs; and also of the Royal

Shelley, except in the case of "The Skylark" and perhaps one or two more.

Institution, in Albemarle Street, where he presides since the death of Faraday.

Visited John Forster at his own house, Palace Gate House, Kensington, West.

[From London Mr. Emerson and his daughter went to Chester for a day or two, the guests of Lord and Lady Amberley, who showed them Tintern Abbey, and thence they went to Cyfarthra Castle to visit Mr. and Mrs. Crawshay.]

At Oxford [April 30 to May 3] I was the guest of Professor Max Müller,[1] and was introduced to Jowett and to Ruskin and to Mr. Dodgson, author of *Alice in Wonderland*, and to many of the University dignitaries. Prince Leopold was a student, and came home from Max Müller's lecture to lunch with us, and then invited Ellen and me to go to his house, and there showed us his pictures and his album, and there we drank tea. The next day I heard Ruskin's lecture, and we then went home with Ruskin to his chambers, where he showed us his pictures, and told us his doleful opinions

[1] This visit was much enjoyed. Professor Müller had invited Mr. Emerson to give two lectures, but he was not prepared to do so.

of modern society.[1] In the evening we dined with Vice-Chancellor Liddell and a large company.

[On May 3, the Emersons left Oxford for Warwick, where, after seeing the castle, they were met by Mr. E. F. Flower, an old friend, who took them to his home at Stratford-upon-Avon, where they spent ten days.

On Sunday, at the door of the church, they were met by the Clerk, who led them to seats in the chancel near Shakspeare's tomb.

Before sailing for home they made a short visit to Edinburgh, but no record appears in Journal or letters.

The presence of Mr. Norton and his family helped to make the homeward voyage pleasant. On the morning of Mr. Emerson's seventieth birthday his friend met him on deck and put into his hands the following verses.]

To R. W. Emerson

Blest of the highest gods are they who die
Ere youth is fled. For them their mother Fate,

---

[1] With Mr. Ruskin's constant jeremiades on the state of the world, and especially of England, Mr. Emerson was annoyed and displeased to such a point that he roundly rebuked him.

Clasping from happy earth to happier sky,
Frees life, and joy, and love from dread of date.
But thee, revered of men, the gods have blest
With fruitful years. And yet for thee, in sooth,
They have reserved of all their gifts the best ;—
And, thou, though full of days, shalt die in youth.

May 25, 1873. CHARLES E. NORTON.

[Mr. Emerson landed in Boston, May 27. Before sailing, his home in Concord had been burned, and now from the steamer he looked on his native city, which since his departure had been devastated by fire even to his birthplace, which was where the great establishment of C. F. Hovey & Co. now stands. That was in the autumn, and now the statelier building was rapidly advancing.

When he and his daughter got out of the cars at Concord, to their astonishment they found a large part of the population assembled there to greet them. They welcomed the two returned travellers with a cheer, echoed from the passengers in the train as it moved on. Then, as the reunited family entered the carriages, the local band played, and, escorted by the children of all the schools and many friends and neighbors, they drove home, passing under a welcoming triumphal arch. There stood the house among the trees, except for its freshness looking without and within as if nothing had ever happened. Mr. Emerson entered and saw; then turned, rapidly walked to the gate and said such words of joy and gratitude as his emotion would allow. The smiling crowd dispersed and he reentered his home to realize its restoration and greet his nearer friends.]

Egypt. Mrs. Helen Bell,[1] it seems, was asked "What do you think the Sphinx said to Mr. Emerson?" "Why," replied Mrs. Bell, "the Sphinx probably said to him, 'You're another.'"

For the writers on Religion, — none should speak on this matter polemically: it is the *Gai Science* and only to be chanted by troubadours.

Professor Max Müller has dedicated his new book to me, and sent me a copy. I have read it, and though I am too dull a scholar to judge of the correctness of his courageous deductions from resembling names, or to relish this as I did his earlier books, I respect and thank his erudition and its results.

[1] Daughter of Rufus Choate.

[Mr. Emerson was invited to make the Address at the opening of the Concord Free Public Library, in September, built and given to the town by one of its sons, William Munroe. The following paragraphs were written while he was preparing for this occasion. The Address is printed in *Miscellanies*.]

Be a little careful about your Library. Do you foresee what you will do with it? Very little, to be sure. But the real question is, What it will do with you? You will come here and get books that will open your eyes, and your ears, and your curiosity, and turn you inside out or outside in. You will find a book here that will tell you such news of what has been seen lately at the observatories in the sun and the other stars that you will not rest until you find a telescope to see the eclipse with your own eyes. 'T is only the other day that they found out what the stars are made of: what chemical elements, identical with those that are in our planet, are found in Saturn; what in the sun; and that human life could not exist in the moon.

They have just learned that Italy had people before the Romans, before the Etruscans, who made just such arrow-heads as we find in Concord, and all their tools were stone: Mr. Marsh told me he picked them up in Africa as in Vermont; and they find these all over the world,— and the world, instead of being six thousand years old, has had men on it a hundred thousand years.

All the new facts of science are not only interesting for themselves, but their best value is the rare effect on the mind, the electric shock; each new law of Nature speaks to a related fact in our thought: for every law of Chemistry has some analogon in the soul, and however skilful the chemist may be, and how much soever he may push and multiply his researches, he is a superficial trifler in the presence of the student who sees the strict analogy of the experiment to the laws of thought and of morals.

We read a line, a word, that lifts us: we rise into a succession of thoughts that is better than the book. The old saying of Montluc, that "one man is worth a hundred, and a hundred are not worth one," is quite as true of books.

Our reading sometimes seems guided. I open a book which happens to be near me,—a book I had not thought of before,— and, seeing the name of a known writer, I sit down to read the chapter, which presently fixes my attention as if it were an important message directly sent to me.

Darwin's *Origin of Species* was published in 1859, but Stallo, in 1849, writes, "animals are but fœtal forms of man."

Stallo quotes Liebig as saying, "The secret of all those who make discoveries is that they regard nothing as impossible." "The lines of our ancestry run into all the phenomena of the material world." — STALLO.

Theologic mysteries. Our theology ignores the identity of the worshipper; he has fallen in another, he rises in another. Can identity be claimed for a being whose life is so often vicarious, or belonging to an age or generation?

Harvard College. My new term as overseer begun at the close of Commencement Day, 1873, and ends at the close of Commencement Day, 1879.

Life. "We do not take into account what life is in the concrete, — the agreeable habit of working and doing, as Goethe names it, — the steadily engaging, incessant in-streaming of sensations into the bodily comfortableness." — HEGEL, *apud* Varnhagen.

[The latter half of the year was quietly passed in Concord by Mr. Emerson, except for a visit to his daughter Mrs. Forbes and her husband at Naushon. As the English publisher with whom he had had dealings, and, as it were, an enforced arrangement about a new volume (only suspended by his illness), had died, that matter was not troubling him.

On December 16, the Centennial Anniversary of the "Boston Tea Party," Mr. Emerson completed his poem "Boston," so long meditated, and, by request, read it at the celebration in Faneuil Hall.]

Authors or Books quoted or referred to in Journal for 1873

[The greater part of the authors mentioned in this list are included because Mr. Emerson met them upon his recent journey, principally in England.]

Kalevala of the Finns; Edward, Lord Herbert, *Autobiography*; Heeren, *Ancient World, Egypt*; Hegel; Stendhal (M. H. Bayle);

Sir Henry Holland; Elie de Beaumont; Thomas Carlyle; Earl Russell; George Bancroft; Richard Owen; Liebig; Francis W.

Newman; J. S. Mill; James Fergusson; R. M. Milnes; Gladstone; Charles Darwin; Vice-Chancellor Liddell; Dean Church;

Robert Browning; J. J. Garth Wilkinson; Dr. W. B. Carpenter; Charles Reade; Daniel Kirkwood, *Comets and Meteors;* Dean Stanley; Henry Lewes and Mrs. Lewes (George Eliot); Sir Arthur Helps; Jowett;

Dasent; Turgénieff; Froude; William W. Story; Lyon Playfair; Ruskin; J. R. Lowell; Alexander C. Fraser; Thomas Hughes; Max Müller; Stallo; Duke of Argyle; Sir Frederick Pollock; Dr. Hinton; Ernest Renan;

Charles G. Leland; Huxley, *Lay Sermons;* Charles E. Norton; William Allingham; Moncure D. Conway; Herman Grimm; Taine; Canon Liddon; Charles Flower; Professor Lecky; Smalley.

JOURNAL

DEATH OF SUMNER
ABEL ADAMS
FRANCIS C. LOWELL
CANDIDACY FOR LORD RECTORSHIP OF GLASGOW UNIVERSITY
PARNASSUS

JOURNAL LXV

1874

(From Journal ST)

[No longer pledged to far-away lecture engagements, but at home with his family, Mr. Emerson passed his days in his study looking over the sheets of manuscript still unprinted, which might or might not have done duty in lectures or occasional speeches, selecting and planning for their use, but making little progress, for arrangement of sibylline leaves, always difficult, was now almost impossible. He hardly realized this, but was under no pressure, and so undisturbed. He took pleasure in reading; he kept up his afternoon solitary walk, and enjoyed the monthly meeting with his friends at the dinner of the Saturday Club.

The Journal was almost entirely neglected. The following entry is the first, and must have been in latter March, after receiving the letter from Judge Hoar which follows it.]

Charles Sumner. For Sumner's merit, go back

to the dark times of 1850 and see the position of Boston and its eminent men.

WASHINGTON, *March* 11, 1874.

MY DEAR MR. EMERSON: —

Sumner is dead, as the telegraph will have told you before you receive this. He died at thirteen minutes before three this afternoon. I held his hand when he died; and, except his secretary and the attending physician, was the only one of his near friends who was in the room.

His last words (except to say "Sit down" to Mr. Hooper, who came to his bedside, but had gone out before his death) were these: "Judge, tell Emerson how much I love and revere him." I replied, "He said of you once that he never knew so *white* a soul."

During the morning, he had repeated to several persons, to me among the rest, "You must take care of The Civil Rights Bill." That was his last public thought.

Very sorrowfully and affectionately yours,
E. R. HOAR.

[Mr. Emerson, being asked for some lines that would be appropriate to be read or printed with regard to Senator Sumner, took these from his poem in memory of his own brother Edward Bliss Emerson. (See "In Memoriam E. B. E.," *Poems*.)]

> All inborn power that could
> Consist with homage to the good
> Flamed from his martial eye; . . .
> Fronting foes of God and man,
> Frowning down the evil-doer,
> Battling for the weak and poor.
> His from youth the leader's look
> Gave the law which others took,
> And never poor beseeching glance
> Shamed that sculptured countenance.

[Two notices of valued and early friends who died about this time follow. Mr. Abel Adams, of the firm of Barnard and Adams, was Mr. Emerson's parishioner, and neighbor in his Chardon Street housekeeping. He was also his business adviser, and was so troubled that the venture in Vermont and Canada Railroad stock turned out ill that he insisted on assuming the expenses of Edward Emerson in college, a great help to Mr. Emerson in the hard times of the war.]

I ought to have many notes of my pleasant memories of Abel Adams, one of the best of my friends, whose hospitable house was always open to me by day or by night for so many years in Boston, Lynn, or West Roxbury. His experiences as a merchant were always interesting to me. I think I must have somewhere recorded the fact, which I recall to-day, that he told me that he and two or three merchants had been counting up, in the Globe Bank, out of a hundred Boston merchants how many had not once failed, and they could only count three. Abel Adams was the benefactor of Edward W. E. in College, and of all of us in his last will.

September (?).

The death of Francis Cabot Lowell is a great loss to me. Now for fifty-seven years since we entered college together, we have been friends, meeting sometimes rarely, sometimes often; seldom living in the same town, we have always met gladly on the old simple terms. He was a conservative, I always of a speculative habit; and often in the wayward politics of former years, we had to compare our different opinions. He was a native gentleman, thoroughly true, and of decided opinions, always frank, considerate, and kind. On all questions his opinions were his own, and deliberately formed. One day he came to Concord to read to me some opinions he had written out in regard to the education now given at Cambridge. He did not leave the paper with me and I regret that I cannot recall its substance. However you might differ from him, he always inspired respect and love. I have never known a man of more simplicity and truth.

I heard gladly, long since, from Dr. Hobbs, of Waltham, what I had never heard from himself,—the story of Lowell's relation to the Chemical Mills in Waltham. His father, Mr. Frank Lowell, Senior, had founded them, and his son inherited in them an important interest. From whatever causes, the property had sadly depreciated. But Mr. Lowell undertook the charge of them himself, studied chemistry with direct reference to the work done in this mill, made himself master of all the processes required; corrected the mistakes; and against all advice stayed therein until its depreciated shares came up to par; then he sold his shares in the property and retired. A man of a quiet inward life, silent and grave, but with opinions and purposes which he quietly held and frankly stated, when his opinion was asked;—gently, but with a strong will, and a perseverance which at last carried his point. Mr. Henry Lee Higginson told me how scrupulously honest he was, how slow to avail himself of the right to take up mortgages, the terms of which had not been kept. Mr. H. thought him romantically honest. And his truth was of the like strain. He said to me, at his house, that when his Club had lately met there, several gentlemen expressed to him their satisfaction at being his guests; and this led him to say that he did not believe he had ever expressed to any man more regard for the person than he really felt. Exact and literal in affairs and in intercourse, he was the most affectionate parent, and his children's children filled the house with their joy.

His generosity was quiet, but sure and effective. Very strict in its direction, but ample in amount. He was the friend in need, silent but sure, and the character of the giver added rare value to the gift, as if an angel brought you gold. I may well say this, when I recall the fact that on the next day after my house was burned, he came to Concord to express his sympathy in my misfortune, and a few days afterward surprised me with a munificent donation from himself and his children which went far to rebuild it.

In college, I well remember the innocence of the youth when we first met; — and the perfect simplicity of his manners he never lost. Yet long years afterward I well remember that when we stood together to witness a marriage in the Stone Chapel, my wife inquired who was the gentleman who stood by me, and who looked so like a king; I was delighted by the perception.

I dearly prize the photograph taken from Rowse's drawing of his head, which is an admirable likeness, my gift from his daughter, Georgina Lowell. His daughter tells me that he thought he did not interest his acquaintances. I believe he always had their entire respect, and a friendship akin to love.

Fortunate in his birth and education, accustomed always to a connection of excellent society, he was never confounded with others by the facility of interest and neighbourhood, but remained as independent in his thought as if he had lived alone.

PARKER HOUSE,
Monday night, *November*.

The secret of poetry is never explained,— is always new. We have not got farther than mere wonder at the delicacy of the touch, and the eternity it inherits. In every house a child that in mere play utters oracles, and knows not that they are such. 'T is as easy as breath. 'T is like this gravity, which holds the Universe together, and none knows what it is.

"The arch is the parent of the vault, the vault is the parent of the cupola." — EDWARD A. FREEMAN.

The boy grew to man and never asked a question, for every problem quickly developed its law.

[In the Spring, Mr. Emerson had been surprised by an invitation from the Independent Club of the University of Glasgow to accept their nomination as candidate for the office of Lord Rector for that year, the duty involved being the delivery of the annual address. Mr. Emerson was pleased with the compliment, and, after some consideration, and consultation with near friends, sent his acceptance, but with little expectation of election—especially as Disraeli was the candidate of the Conservative body of students. The campaign, as shown by manifestoes, songs, etc., constantly sent to Mr. Emerson through the mail by his enthusiastic adherents, was conducted with great spirit and excitement. In November he was notified of the result. He had received more than five hundred votes, and Disraeli was chosen Lord Rector by a majority of some two hundred.

In December, the collection of poems, *Parnassus*, was published, which owes its existence to the urgency and activity through several years of Mr. Emerson's younger daughter. She loved to hear her father read poems and fragments collected through years in his "Black Anthology" (so called from its leather covers) and another. As his favourites were often hard to find, especially those from the older poets, and not in such collections as were at hand, the idea of publishing such a volume pleased him, when suggested, and he said, and, when urged again another year, repeated, "We must." Then the zealous school-girl began herself to seize occasions to bring volumes of the poets to her father in his study and insist on his choosing, and began herself to copy the favourites. This went on through several years until she became Mrs. Forbes, and then, whenever she was with her father either in Milton or Concord, she succeeded in commanding attention to the work, and herself had the copying done. Thus, when the lecturing ceased, there was more time to attend to the selections. It should be said also that Mr. Emerson became less exacting in his criticisms of newer verses. In the preface to *Parnassus* he gives in the first paragraph an account of his selection of poems from his early youth, followed by a short essay on the poets.]

AUTHORS OR BOOKS QUOTED OR REFERRED TO IN JOURNAL FOR 1874

Alexis, *Lines on Sleep;* Plotinus;

Dr. Charles R. Lowell; Charles Sumner; Edward A. Freeman, *Cathedral Architecture;* William Morris, *Proem to the Earthly Paradise;* Charles Warren Stoddard; Titus M. Coan, *The Tree of Life.*

JOURNAL

CABOT THE HELPER
MEETING OF OLD SCHOOLMATES
THE MINUTE MAN
LIFE AND THE CHILD
CARLYLE'S BIRTHDAY

JOURNAL LXVI
1875

(From Journal ST)

[THE flame of Mr. Emerson's powers of writing, faint in the last three years, now flickered to extinction in the journals of this and the following year. Yet the instinct of work remained, and he passed most of each day in his study still working at arranging his manuscripts, and his daughter Ellen helped him as far as she could. In the year before, the question of who should deal with his manuscripts when he was gone had been in his thought, and Mr. Cabot's name was the one which he wistfully mentioned, but felt that the favour was so great that he could not venture to ask it from his friend. But now the case became urgent, for the promised book was called for by the successors of the English publishers who had first wrung consent from Mr. Emerson by threatening to collect a book of old *Dial* papers, and other rejected material, out of copyright. So, with Mr. Emerson's permission, the matter was presented for Mr. Cabot's consideration. He consented with entire kindness to give what help he could, and thus lifted the last load from Mr. Emerson's shoulders. The relief was complete and rendered his remaining years happy. At last he could see and come near to the friend whom he had valued at a distance for years. Mr. Cabot's frequent visits, often for several days at a time, were a great pleasure. Just how large Mr. Cabot's share in preparing for the press *Letters and Social Aims* was he tells with entire frankness in the preface to that volume. Mr. Emerson furnished the matter, — almost all written years before, — but Mr. Cabot the arrangement and much of the selection. All was submitted to Mr. Emerson's approval, but he always spoke to his friend of the volume as "your book."

Early in the year his crony of the Boston school-boy days, Dr. William H. Furness, wrote to him begging him to accept an invitation to lecture in Philadelphia and to be his guest. In the affectionate letter in answer, given in full in Mr. Cabot's *Memoir*, Mr. Emerson writes: "Well, what shall I say in defence of my stolid silence at which you hint? Why, only this: . . . that the gods have given you some draught of their perennial cup, and withheld the same from me. I have, for the last two years, written nothing in my once diurnal manuscripts; and never a letter that I could omit. . . . Now comes your new letter with all your affectionate memories and preference fresh as roses. . . . I must obey it. My daughter Ellen, who goes always with my antiquity, insists that we shall. . . . My love to Sam Bradford." They went and the three playfellows had a happy reunion.

On March 18, Mr. Emerson read in Boston a lecture "True Oratory," probably nearly the same as the chapter "Eloquence" in *Letters and Social Aims*.

On the Nineteenth of April, the town celebrated the one hundredth anniversary of Concord Fight. President Grant and members of his Cabinet were present, the Governors of all the New England States with their escorting regiments, the Massachusetts General Court, the eminent writers of New England, and an immense concourse of people. At the end of the North Bridge (built anew for the occasion), where stood the American force, the bronze Minute Man made by Daniel C. French had been placed, and, when the throng arrived, Mr. Emerson unveiled it and made a short speech, the last he ever composed. Then, in the tent beyond, Lowell and Curtis delivered respectively the admirable Ode and Address.

Mr. Emerson's speech was not included in the *Works*. It is to be found in the Boston papers of the next day, the *Commonwealth* of April 27, and in the Concord pamphlet recording that celebration.]

In 1775, the patriotism in Massachusetts was so hot that it melted the snow, and the rye waved on the 19th April. Our farmers have never seen it so early. The very air and the soil felt the anger of the people.

It occurs that the short limit of human life is set in relation to the instruction man can draw of Nature. No one has lived long enough to exhaust its laws.

The delicacy of the touch and the eternity it inherits —

In every house a child that in mere play utters oracles, and knows not that they are such: 't is as easy as breathing. 'T is like gravity which holds the universe together, and none knows what it is.

[It should be mentioned that Mr. Emerson had been appointed a member of the sub-committee on Philosophy at Harvard University for the year.]

"Eichhorn would have the order of studies and the establishment of rigor therein in our universities increased. Others agreed. Then Schleiermacher quite simply said, he did not see how each must prescribe the way by which he came to his knowledge: the routine was in our ways of study so demolished, the rules of all kinds so heaped, that to him nothing seemed better to do than to pull down all the universities. 'And what to put in their place?' they asked: 'That would it find of itself at once, and quite rightly,' answered Schleiermacher." — VARNHAGEN VON ENSE. *Blätter aus der preussischen Geschichte*, v, 44.

December 5, 1875.
Thomas Carlyle's 80th birthday.

AUTHORS OR BOOKS QUOTED OR REFERRED TO IN JOURNAL FOR 1875

Gibbon, *Decline and Fall of the Roman Empire*; Eichhorn and Schleiermacher *apud* Von Ense; Charles Levigne, *Un Médecin de l'Ame*.

JOURNAL

CARLYLE MEDAL
UNIVERSITY OF VIRGINIA
LATIN SCHOOL CENTENARY
ALLINGHAM'S POEM

JOURNAL LXVII
1876
(From Journal ST)

ON Saturday, February 5, received through the post-office a pacquet containing a silver medal, on one face bearing the profile of Carlyle, with the name "Thomas Carlyle" inscribed; on the other face,

"In Commemoration
1875
December 4."

A card enclosed reads, "To R. W. Emerson from Alexander Macmillan" [London]; for which welcome and precious gift I wish to write immediately my thanks to the kind sender.

[In March, Mr. Emerson read a lecture in Lexington. An invitation from the Washington and Jefferson literary societies of the University of Virginia to give an address at their Commencement pleased him as a token from the South and he accepted it, and went with his daughter to Charlottesville in June. He was hospitably received, and read there "The Scholar" (in *Lectures and Biographical Sketches*).

On November 8, at a meeting of the Latin School Association in Boston, celebrating the hundredth anniversary of the reopening of the school after the evacuation of the city by the British, he gave his pleasant reminiscences of his school-days. His remarks were reported in the Boston papers of next day.

The year's journal, hardly begun, — or rather the journal of more than half a century, — closes with a poem of William Allingham, sent and signed by the Author, whom Mr. Emerson valued, enclosed between the leaves. It might seem, perhaps, a grateful tribute of a disciple to a master.]

POESIS HUMANA

What is the Artist's duty?
His work, however wrought,
Shape, color, word or tone
Is to make better known
(Himself divinely taught),
To praise and celebrate,
Because his love is great,
The lovely miracle
Of Universal Beauty.
This message would he tell.

This message is his trust,
Amidst the day's crude strife,
With all his heart and soul,
With all his skill and strength
Seeking to add at length, —
(Because he may and must, —)
Some atom to the whole
Of man's inheritance;
Some fineness to the glance,
Some richness to the life.

If he shall deal perforce
With evil and with pain,
With horror and affright,
He does it to our gain;
Makes felt the mighty course
Of law — whose atmosphere
Is beauty and delight;
Nay, these its very source.

His work, however small,
Itself hath rounded well,
Even like Earth's own ball
In softly tinted shell
Of air. His magic brings
The mystery of things;
It gives dead substance wings;
It shows in little, much;
And by an artful touch
Conveys the hint of all.

(From Ledgers of uncertain date)

[Mr. Emerson, with all the temperamental difficulty he found in arrangement of the abundant material received from Nature and man, had something of business method in his bookkeeping. Besides his Journals — day-books — he had also a few books which might be called ledgers, into which irregularly he copied, or wrote, good material according to subject. Such were IL (Intellect), PY (Poetry), PH (Philosophy), LI (Literature), TO (Tolerance?) and others less easily guessed.

The editors have ventured to give here a few concluding passages, of uncertain date, from some of these manuscripts, which they do not find among the journal selections, or in the *Works*.]

(From PH)

Idealism. Is it thought that to reduce the Divine mode of existence to a state of ideas is deducting with a high hand of idealism and unfastening the logic of the Universe? We are mammals of a higher element, and, as the whale must come to the top of the water for air, we must go to the top of the air, now and then, for thought.

The guiding star to the arrangement and use

of facts is in your leading thought. The heaven of Intellect is profoundly solitary, it is unprofitable, it is to be despised and rejected of men. If I recall the happiest hours of existence, those which really make a man an inmate of a better world, it is a lonely and undescribed joy, but it is the door that leads to joys ear hath not heard nor eye seen.

Each power of the mind is well in itself; as, perception, or memory : but we are first sensible of the miracle when these powers combine or interact. Mathematic combinations are potent only in the first degree, until powerful memory is joined to them; then you have Archimedes and Laplace.

Sensibility. The poorest place has all the wealth of the richest, as soon as genius arrives. . . . Ah, could I quicken your attention to your society by whispering to you its immense wealth of nature, and genius's possibility. There are persons who might take their seat on the throne of this globe without real or false shame.

The real estate of the Universe is Space and Matter; the proprietor is Intellect, and what belongs to Intellect, Will or Good Will.

Abnormal Minds. William Blake, Swedenborg, Behmen, and what other men of abnormal experience, — as, for example, some trustworthy second-sighted or forewarned seers or dreamers who are apprised in one country of the death or danger of their twin or brother in another country (if ever one could get a proven fact of this kind), — are important examples each to the metaphysician; Blake [also], who affirmed that he did not see the phenomenon, as the marble, the harp, or the cloud, but looked ever through it, and saw its meaning. The Zoroasters and Sibyls and oracular men to whom we owe some profoundest sentences are essential parts of our knowledge of the Human Mind, or the possible omnificence (latent but for these flashes) of the Intellect. The Hindu specimens have their value. Every such mind is a new key to the secret of Mind.

Wonder. The most advanced man in his most advanced moment — contemplating himself and Nature — sees how rude an idiot he is, how utterly unknown is the Cause and the Necessity, — its roots and its future all unknown, — a gigantic dream.

Divination. I think that not by analytic inspection, but by sympathy and piety, we correct our metaphysics. Thus Hegel and Kant have become possible by the extraordinary wealth of all natural sciences, which waked and tested every faculty of thought, and thus finer distinctions could be felt and expressed.

The analysis of Intellect and Nature which the grand masters, Heraclitus, Parmenides, Plato, Spinoza, Hume, Kant, Schelling, Hegel, have attempted are of primary value to Science, like the work of the great geometers and mathematicians, and cannot be spared or overpraised: they are dear to us as vindications of the sufficiency of the intellect, and pledges of future advances. They seem to the scholar to degrade all inferior and less ambitious observation as needless and of no worth. They freeze his invention and hope. They write *Ne plus ultra* on the dizzy pinnacle to which in the thin air their almost winged footsteps have climbed.

They have marked, once for all, distinctions which are inherent in the sound mind, and which we must henceforth respect.

The instinct that led Heraclitus and Parmenides and Lucretius to write in verse was just, however imperfect their success. The world lies so in heaps that it is not strange that there should yet be no painters, no Homer of our thoughts, far higher than the Homer of Greek thoughts.

Intellect. There is no age to Intellect. Read Plato at twenty or at sixty years, the impression is about equal.

The joy of the thinker in detecting his errors: — I have more enjoyed, in the last hours of finishing a chapter, the insight attained of how the truths really stand, than I suffer from seeing the confusion I had left in the statement.

Inspiration. Our music-box only plays certain tunes, and rarely a sweeter strain: but we are assured that our barrel is not a dead, but a live barrel, nay, is only a part of the tune, and changes like that. A larger dialectic conveys a sense of power and feeling of terror unknown; and Henry Thoreau said, "that a thought would destroy most persons," and yet we apologize for the power, and bow to the persons.

I want an electrical machine. Slumbering power we have, but not excited, collected, and discharged. If I should be honest, I should say, my exploring of life presents little or nothing of respectable event or action, or, in myself, of a personality. Too composite to offer a positive unity: but it is a recipiency, a percipiency. And I, and far weaker persons (if it were possible) than I, who pass for nothing but imbeciles, do yet affirm by our own percipiency the presence and perfection of Law, as much as all the martyrs.

A man's style is his mind's voice. Wooden minds, wooden voices. Truth is shrill as a fife, various as a panharmonium.

Transition. Transition the organic destiny of the mind.

The value of a trope is that the hearer is one. 'T is the great law of Nature, that the more transit, the more continuity; or, we are immortal by force of transits. We ask a selfish, selfsame immortality. Nature replies by steeping us in the sea which girds the seven worlds, and makes us free of them all. At any pitch, a higher pitch. What we call the Universe to-day is only a symptom or omen of that to which we are passing. Every atom is on its way onward. The universe circulates in thought. Every thought is fleeting. Our power lies in transition, there is said to be a certain infinite of power which is availed us in the power-press.

There's not only your talent, but your spirit. Easy to give your colour or character to any assembly, if your spirit is better than the speaker's. [My brother] Edward, with his wit, never failed to check any trifling with morals in his presence. 'T is impossible that the Divine Order be broken without resistance, and the remorses, wraths, indecisions, violence, and runnings away into solitude of men are the checks and recoils.

The wonder of the world in good hours — I might say whenever we go home from the streets — is, that so many men of various talent, including men of eminent special ability, do not recognize the supreme value of character. In history we appreciate it fully. We all read Plutarch with one mind, and unanimously take sides with Agesilaus in Sparta, with Aristides, Phocion, Demosthenes, in Athens, with Epaminondas in Thebes, and wonder how the Athenians could be such fools as to take such bravos as the Creons against these grave, just, and noble heroes. In Rome, we give our suffrages again to Scipio, Regulus, Paulus Æmilius, and Cato, and

Trajan, and Marcus Aurelius against their profligate rivals. In England, we know the worth of Sidney, Alfred, of More, of Burke. In America, we see the purity and exceptional elevation of Washington. And, at this moment, we see in the English Minister at the head of the Government the immense comfort and trust reposed in a competent minister of a high and blameless character.[1]

Nature. The secret of Nature glimmers to all eyes in these days, namely, that her ulterior meaning dwarfs all her wonders before the grandeur to which she leads us on. For she apprises man that he converses with reality, with the cause of causes, and her fairest pictures are only part of the immense procession of effects.

Mind and Nature. On this (unity) the emphasis of heaven and earth is laid. Nature is brute, but as this animates it, — only a language, a noun, for the poet. Nature always the effect; Mind the flowing cause. Nature, we find, is as is our sensibility; hostile to ignorance, — plastic, transparent, delightful to knowledge. Mind contains the law; History is the slow and atomic un-

[1] Probably Gladstone.

folding: the Universe, at last, only prophetic, or, shall we say, symptomatic of vaster interpretation and result.

(From TO)

'T is fine, that Hegel "dared not unfold or pursue the surprising revolutionary conclusions of his own method," but not the less did the young Hegelians consummate the work, so that quickly, in all departments of life, in natural sciences, politics, ethics, laws, and in art, the rigorous Dogma of Immanent Necessity exterminated all the old tottering, shadowy forms. 'T is like Goethe and Wordsworth disowning their poetry.

Room must be allowed for the skepticism. It was always in use that certain belligerent minds had a suicidal, a scorpion-sting-scorpion talent, as, it is said, the gastric juices sometimes eat up the stomach: so these have the whim to go behind the Institutions also, and ask the foundation of the foundation, "the guide of my guide," as M. R. asked me. And there is, as my brother Edward said, in boyhood, always "the other way"; or, as Shakspeare says, "A plague of opinion! a man can wear on both sides, like a leather jerkin."

They are all cracked; every one of them has

his egotism, or mania, or gluttony, or vulgarity, or flattery of some kind, as he has his rheumatism, or scrofula, or sixth toe, or other flaw in his body. All I want is his sanity, his specialty of acuteness, his fluency, his knack; and I should as soon think of asking after the old shoes of an observer as after his gluttonies, or his debts, or his conceit, or whatever infirmities. "Did the troops carry the battery?" "Sire, here is the list of the wounded." "Take that to the surgeon. Did they carry the battery? *Vive la France!*"

Allowance always for the exempts, who, by strong call of Nature, [haunt] the pond-sides, groping for plants (as Bishop Turpin for the talisman which Charlemagne threw into the pond): or, lost in the allurement of colour, mix pigments on a pallet; or study the surfaces and mantles and runes on seashells, heedless of France or England or Prussia, or what the Pope, the Emperor, the Congress, or the stock exchange, may do; or Carnot buried in his mathematics; or Kant in his climbing from round to round the steps of the mysterious ladder which is the scale of metaphysic powers. These are always justified sooner or later: point for point, the whole noisy fracas of politics or interest is truly and divinely recognized and counted for them, there in their spiritual coil or *cælum*. There is Sardinia, and London, Rome, and Vienna, and Washington, sternly abstracted into its salt and essence.

Transition. Ever the ascending effort. The Greeks and the Scandinavians hold that men had one name and the gods another for heaven, hell, water, cloud, and mountain. And the Edda, when it has named and dealt with the Asa and the Elfin, speaks of the "higher gods." See the ascending scale of Plato and especially of Plotinus.

Natural Sciences have made great stride by means of Hegel's dogma which put Nature, and thought, matter and spirit, in right relation, one the expression or externalization of the other. Observation was the right method, and metaphysics was Nature and subject to observation also. But (Hegel and all his followers) shunned to apply the new arm to what most of all belonged to it, to anthropology, morals, politics, etc. For this at once touched conservatism, church, jurisprudence, etc. Therefore the Natural Sciences made great progress and philosophy none. But Natural Science, without philosophy, without ethics, was unsouled. Presently Natural Science, which the governments have befriended, will disclose the liberalizing as well as the dynamic strength; then Natural Science will be presented as, e. g., geology, astronomy, ethnology, as contradicting the Bible. Difference of the two is: Natural Sciences, a circle, Morals and Metaphysics a line of advance; one the basis, the other the completion.

Not only Transition but Melioration. The good soul took you up, and showed you for an instant of time something to the purpose. Well, in this way, it educates the youth of the Universe, — warms, suns, refines each particle; then drops the little channel, through which the life rolled beatific, to the ground, — touched and educated by a moment of sunshine, to be the fairer material for future channels, through which the old glory shall dart again in new directions, until the Universe shall have been shot through and through, filled with light.

With this eternal demand for more which belongs to our modest constitutions, how can we be helped? The gods themselves cannot help us; they are just as badly off themselves.

Genius unsettles everything. It is fixed, is it? that after the reflective age arrives, there can be no quite rustic and united man born? Yes, quite fixed. Ah! this unlucky Shakspeare! and ah! this hybrid Goethe! make a new rule, my dear, can you not? and to-morrow Genius shall stamp on it with his starry sandals.

Genius consists neither in improvising, nor in remembering, but in both.

Writing should be like the settlement of dew on the leaf, of stalactites on the cavern wall, the deposit of flesh from the blood, of woody fibre from the sap. The poem is made up of lines each of which filled the sky of the poet in its turn; so that mere synthesis produces a work quite superhuman. For that reason, a true poem by no means yields all its virtue at the first reading, but is best when we have slowly and by repeated attention felt the truth of all the details.

Fame is a signal convenience. Do we read all the authors, to grope our way to the best? No, but the world selects for us the best, and we select from the best, our best.

Mankind have ever a deep common sense that guides their judgments, so that they are always right in their fames. How strange that Jesus should stand at the head of history, the first character of the world, without doubt, but the unlikeliest of all men, one would say, to take such a ground in such a world. Yet he dates our chronology. Well, as if to indemnify themselves for this vast concession to truth, they must put up the militia — Alexander, Cæsar, Napoleon, etc. — into the next place of proclamation. Yet 't is a pit to Olympus, this fame to that; or were by the place of Plato, Homer, Pindar, etc.

Thoughts. Against Fate, Thought; for, though that force be infinitely small, infinitesimal against the bulky masses of Nature, and the universal chemistry, 't is of that subtlety that it homeopathically doses the system.

Thought is nothing but the circulations made harmonious. Every thought, like every man, wears, at its first emergence from the creative night, its rank stamped on it: — this is a witticism, and this is a power. . . .

Thoughts come to those who have thoughts, as banks lend to capitalists and not to paupers. Every new thought which makes day in our souls has its long morning twilight to announce its coming. Add the aurora that precedes a beloved name.

The distinction of a man is that he thinks. Let that be so. For a man cannot otherwise compare with a steam-engine or the self-acting spinning-mule which is never tired, and makes no fault. But a man thinks and adapts. A man is not a man, then, until he have his own thoughts: that first; then, that he can detach them. But what thoughts of his own are in Abner or Guy? They are clean, well-built men enough to look at, have money, and houses and books, but they are not yet arrived at humanity, but remain idiots and minors.

[*Language.*] You can find an old philosopher who has anticipated most of your theses; but, if you cannot find the Antisthenes or the Proclus that did, you can find in *language* that some unknown man has done it, inasmuch as words exist which cover your thought.

Thus there is a day when the boy arrives at wanting a word to express his sense of relation between two things or two classes of things and finds the word *analogy* or identity of ratio. A day comes when men of all countries are compelled to use the French word *solidarité* to signify inseparable individualities.

(From IL)

Genius. Genius loves truth, and clings to it, so that what it says and does is not in a byroad visited only by curiosity, but on the great highways of the world, which were before the Appian Way, and will long outlast it, and which all souls must travel.

Genius delights in statements which are themselves true, which attack and wound any who opposes them.

They called Ideas Gods, and worshipped intellect. They dared not contravene with knacks and talents the divinity which they recognized in genius.

When the Greeks in the Iliad perceived that the gods mixed in the fray, they drew off.

Wonderful is the Alembic of Nature, through which the sentiment of tranquillity in the mind of the sculptor becomes, at the end of his fingers, a marble Hesperus: but the feeling manages somehow to shed itself over the stone, as if that were porous to love and truth.

Truth. Truth does not come with jangle and contradiction, but it is what all sects accept, what recommends their tenets to right-minded men. Truth is mine, though I never spoke it.

"Unquestionable truth is sweet, though it were the announcement of our dissolution." — H. D. Thoreau.

People value thoughts, not truths; truth, not until it has passed through the mould of some man's mind, and so is a curiosity, and an individualism. But ideas, as powers, they are not up to valuing. We say that the characteristic of the Teutonic race is, to prefer an idea to a phenomenon; and of the Celtic, to prefer the phenomenon to the idea. Higher is it to prize the power above the thought, i. e., above the idea individualized or domesticated.

Subjectiveness. Dangerously great, immoral even in its violence of power. The man sees as he is. Add the least power of vision, and the tyranny of duties slackens. I am afraid to trust you with the statement. The genius of Bonaparte gilds his crimes to us; but that is only a hint of what it was to him. It converts every obstruction into facilities and fuel of force; dwarfs into giants. His aim, so dim before, beams like the morning star, and every cloud is touched by its rays. . . .

Subjectiveness itself is the question, and Nature is the answer: the Universe is the blackboard on which we write. Philosophy is called the homesickness of the soul.

Automatic Action of Thought. There is a process in the mind analogous to crystallization in the mineral. I think of some fact. In thinking of it, I am led to more thoughts, which show themselves, first partially, and afterwards more fully. But in them I see no order. When I would present them to others, they have no beginning. Leave them now, and return later. Do not force them into arrangement, and by and bye you shall find they will take their own order, and the order they assume is divine.

Thought has its own foregoers and followers, that is, its own current. Thoughts have a life of their own. A thought takes its own true rank in the memory by surviving other thoughts that were preferred.

But also thought ranks itself at its first emergence.

Religion. Religion is the perception of that power which constructs the greatness of the centuries out of the paltriness of the hours.

Fancy and Imagination. Examples. Henry Thoreau writes, —

"The day has gone by with its wind, like the wind of a cannon ball, and now far in the west it blows; by that dim-colored sky you may track it." (June 18, 1853.)

"The Solidago Nemoralis now yellows the dry fields with its recurved standard a little more than a foot high, marching to the holy land, a countless host of crusaders." (August 23.)

Flight of eagle. "Circling, or rather looping along westward."

"And where are gone the bluebirds, whose warble was wafted to me so lately like a blue wavelet through the air?"

"The air over these fields is a foundry full of moulds for casting the bluebird's warbles." (Feb. 18, 1857.)

"The bird withdrew by his aërial turnpikes." (Oct. 5, 1857.)

Scholar's Creed. I believe that all men are born free and equal *quoad* the laws.

That all men have a right to their life, *quoad* the laws.

I believe in freedom of opinion religious and political.

I believe in universal suffrage,[1] in public schools, in free trade.

I believe the soul makes the body.

I believe that casualty is perfect.

(From EO)

Fate. The opinions of men lose all worth to him who observes that they are accurately predictable from the ground of their sect.

Well, they are still valuable as representatives of that fagot of circumstances, if they are not themselves primary parties. But even the chickens running up and down, and pecking at each white spot and at each other as ridden by chicken nature, seem ever and anon to have a pause of consideration, then hurry on again to be chickens. Men have more pause.

We are to each other results. As my perception or sensibility is exalted, I see the genesis of your action, and of your thought. I see you in your debt, and fountains; and, to my eye, instead of a little pond of life, you are a rivulet fed by rills from every plain and height in Nature and antiquity; and reviving a remote origin from the source of things.

---

[1] With the exception that known crime should withdraw the right of suffrage. [R. W. E.'s note.]

May and must. The *musts* are a safe company to follow, and even agreeable. If we are whigs, let us be whigs of Nature and Science, and go for the necessities. The must is as fixed in civil history and political economy as in chemistry. How much will has been expended to extinguish the Jews! Yet the tenacities of the race resist and prevail. So the Negro sees with glee, through all his miseries, his future possession of the West Indies (and of the Southern States of America) assured. For he accumulates and buys, whilst climate, etc., favour him, against the white.

Souls with a certain quantity of light are in excess, and, once for all, belong to the moral class,—what animal force they may retain, to the contrary, notwithstanding. Souls with less light, — it is chemically impossible that they be moral, what talent or good they have, to the contrary notwithstanding; and these belong to the world of Fate, or animal good: the minors of the universe, not yet twenty-one, — not yet voters, — not robed in the *toga virilis*.

Fate. We are talkative, but Heaven is silent. I have puzzled myself like a mob of writers before me in trying to state the doctrine of Fate for the printer. I wish to sum the conflicting impressions by saying that all point at last to an Unity which inspires all, but disdains words and passes understanding.[1] . . . The First Cause; as soon as it is uttered, it is profaned. The thinker denies personality out of piety, not out of pride. It refuses a personality which is instantly imprisoned in human measures.

> "It stands written on the Gate of Heaven Woe to him who suffers himself to be betrayed by Fate."
>
> HAFIZ.

I have heard that they seem fools who allow themselves to be engaged and compromised in undertakings, but that at last it appears quite otherwise, and to the gods otherwise from the first. I affix a like sense to this text of Hafiz: for he who loves is not betrayed, but makes an ass of Fate.

(From PY)

[*Man's Eastern Horizon.*] The men in the street fail to interest us, because at first view they seem thoroughly known and exhausted. As if an inventory of all man's parts and qualities had been taken. . . . But after the most exact

[1] Here follows the concluding passage of "Powers and Laws of Thought" (*Natural History of Intellect*, p. 64).

count has been taken, there remains as much more, which no tongue can tell. This remainder is that which genius works upon. This is that which the preacher, the poet, the artist, and Love, and Nature, speak unto, the region of power and aspiration. These men have a secret persuasion, that, as little as they pass for in the world, they are immensely rich in expectancy and power. The best part of truth is certainly that which hovers in gleams and suggestions unpossessed before man. His recorded knowledge is dead and cold. But this chorus of thoughts and hopes, these dawning truths, like great stars just lifting themselves into his horizon, they are his future, and console him for the ridiculous brevity and meanness of his civic life.

Psychology is fragmentarily taught. One man sees a sparkle or shimmer of the truth, and reports it, and his saying becomes a legend or golden proverb for all ages. And other men see and try to say as much, but no man wholly and well.

We see what we make. We can see only what we make. All our perceptions, all our desires, are procreant. Perception has a destiny.[1] . . .

[1] What follows is printed in "Poetry and Imagination" (*Letters and Social Aims*, p. 42).

[In the last six years of his life, after the journals had no entries save for a few memoranda, Mr. Emerson, though he wrote nothing, — could hardly answer a letter, — still, occasionally, when urged, read a discourse near home, among old friends. On these occasions his daughter always sat near him to make sure that the sheets of his manuscript did not get out of order, or even to prompt him, in case he mistook a word.

In April, 1877, he read his affectionate paper on his native city "Boston" at the Old South Church, and, a year later, in the same place, "The Fortune of the Republic."

In the Spring of 1879, he read "Eloquence" at Cambridge, and also "The Preacher" in The Divinity School Chapel, where, forty-one years before, he had startled his hearers with the Address which banished him from the University for so many years.

The School of Philosophy was established in Concord in that year by Mr. Alcott's friends, and there Mr. Emerson read "Memory," and in the following year, "Aristocracy," to its assembled company.

In 1880, it has been said, Mr. Emerson read his hundredth lecture to his townsfolk in The Concord Lyceum.

His last public reading was probably his paper on Carlyle (See *Lectures and Biographical Sketches*) before the Massachusetts Historical Society.

It is a pleasant circumstance to remember that in his last years Mr. Emerson took from the study shelves the volumes of his own printed works. They seemed new to him, and when his daughter came in, he looked up, smiling, and said, "Why, these things are really very good."

To readers of these journals — talks of a poet and scholar, who was also a good citizen of the Republic, with himself in varying moods — the words of the East Indian Mozoomdar may seem appropriate: —

"Yes, Emerson had all the wisdom and spirituality of the Brahmans. Brahmanism is an acquirement, a state of being rather than a creed."]

THE END

INDEX

INDEX

Abaddon, VII, 97.
Abandon, V, 239; VIII, 106.
Abandonment, continence and, VI, 203.
Abernethy on flies, II, 471.
Abolition cause, merits of, III, 469.
Abolition grows strong, III, 522.
Abolitionist, duties of, VI, 534–36; VII, 12; must be gentleman, IX, 148.
Abolitionists, VII, 221, 222.
Absoluteness, X, 186.
Abstract, the, is practical, V, 69.
Abuse, VIII, 100.
Academy Exhibition, VII, 488.
Accademia in Naples, III, 66.
Acceleration of thought, VIII, 53.
Acquaintances, II, 445; New York, VI, 163; intellectual, VII, 366; English, VII, 489; X, 415–17; new, IX, 261; manners of literary, X, 64, 65; French, X, 413.
Acquiescence, VI, 56.
Action, II, 62; and thought, I, 316, 317; and contemplation, II, 239–41; single-minded, III, 338; delight in heroic, IV, 320; and idea, VII, 554; physical and intellectual, IX, 88.
Actions, few, IV, 226.
Acton, walk with Thoreau, to, VIII, 40, 41.
Actual, the, V, 562.
Adam, fall of, IV, 287.
Adams, Abel, death of, X, 431, 432.
Adams, John, and Jefferson, funeral rites of, II, 113.
Adams, John, II, 216; on courage, his sayings, VIII, 228, 229.
Adams, John Quincy, II, 205; his eulogy on Monroe, II, 411; IV, 233; VI, 349, 350; compared with Webster, VI, 508; rules of, VIII, 353.
Adaptability in author, IX, 8.
Adaptiveness, VII, 61; 103.
Addison never knew nature, IV, 259.

Adirondac Club, IX, 159–61; IX, 193, 194.
Adirondacs, visit to, IX, 158–61.
Admiration, II, 378.
Adrastia, law of, VIII, 456.
Advance in truth, III, 224.
Advance necessary for truth, III, 477.
Advancing men humble, V, 318, 319.
Advantages, unsafe, IV, 34.
Adversity, education for, V, 70.
Advertisements, V, 356.
Æolus, royal, III, 10.
Æschylus, judging of, IV, 326; V, 437.
Æsthetic Club, IV, 292.
Affectation, IV, 222, 223.
Affinity, law of, VII, 301.
Affirmative, VI, 10; and David's inventory, VI, 126; ever good, VI, 135; the, IX, 41, 42.
Afternoon man, IV, 292, 293.
Agassiz, on embryos, VII, 557; lectures of, VII, 424; VIII, 341; and water, VIII, 425; IX, 80, 81; birthday of, IX, 95; IX, 149; 270; and Tiedemann, IX, 521; in Chicago, X, 11; speech of, at Saturday Club, X, 26; in Concord, X, 60; visit to, X, 161; on Humboldt, X, 300; health of, X, 305.
Age, sorrow and, V, 267, 268. *See also* Old Age.
Age, the reforming, IV, 465; trust your own, V, 293; our, our all, V, 323; our, living, the Creator's latest work, VI, 58–60; our, a renaissance, IX, 320; of bronze in England, VIII, 579.
Age, the, spirit of, II, 101; VIII, 7; art proper to, IV, 87, 88; IV, 137–39; what is? V, 306; alive, V, 351; eternity's fruit, V, 359, 360; service for cash — or grandeur? VII, 525, 526; VIII, 98; a critic, IX, 197; splendors of, X, 259. *See also* Present Age.

Ages, verdict of the, IV, 150.
Agent and reagent, VII, 324.
Agra, Taj, X, 249.
Agriculture, III, 125.
Agrippa, Cornelius and Robert Burton, VI, 291.
Aim, a grand, saves, V, 396, 397; in book, VII, 433; man's, VIII, 255, 256.
Akhlak-I-Jalaly, VII, 107.
Alboni, Hearing, VII, 443.
Alcott, A. B., III, 501; 573; V, 322; VI, 291, 301; VII, 222; IX, 119, 120; his *Record of a School*, III, 509; visit of, III, 559; journals of, IV, 11; writing of, IV, 61; 462; school of, IV, 69; thought of, his limitations, IV, 71, 72; school conversations of, IV, 75; symposium at house of, IV, 113, 114; his large thought, IV, 149; attack on, IV, 205; vision of, IV, 237; austerity of, IV, 334; views of, on a school, IV, 348; though possessed of one idea, large and human, IV, 403; the teacher, IV, 454; the believer, IV, 494; ray of oldest light, V, 51; and Margaret Fuller, visit of, V, 292; ground of, V, 388; and E. seeing law of compensation, VI, 74; English project of, VI, 169; described at length; his greatness and faults, VI, 170–78; fate of his book, VI, 217; English allies of, VI, 225; criticism of, VI, 386; the wandering Emperor, VI, 472; underprizes labor, VI, 544; community of, VII, 148; and his victims, VII, 179; on E.'s poems, VII, 234; senses of, VII, 309; visit of, to England, VII, 422; barriers of, VII, 498; Thoreau and, VII, 499; service of, incommunicable, VII, 524; schemes of, VII, 535; Channing and Thoreau on, VII, 552; the pencil and sponge, VIII, 70; parliament of, VIII, 96; and Platonic world, VIII, 303; visits his birthplace, VIII, 316; problem of, VIII, 362, 363; as companion, his strength and weakness, VIII, 396; expansion of, and trust in Nature, VIII, 413; courage of, VIII, 520; triumph of, at the Conversation, VIII, 562; his account of himself, VIII, 565; is never dazzled, IX, 35, 36; insight of, IX, 38, 39; on Fate, IX, 503, 504; like a Labrador spar, IX, 540; talk with, X, 10; 52; 99; New York ladies and, X, 157; on memory, X, 362.
Alcott, Junius, paper of, VI, 184.
Alcuin, VIII, 373.
Alexander, moonlight walk with Cranch and, III, 87.
Alexandria, II, 201; 203.
Alfieri, IV, 343; VII, 239, 240; on French, VIII, 521.
Alfred the Great, I, 206; VIII, 564; Asser and, VIII, 381.
Algebraic x, VIII, 419.
Ali Ben Abu Taleb, VIII, 6.
All. *See also* Each and All.
All in one; one tree a grove, IV, 485.
All, the, every violation and miracle melts into, IV, 56.
Allegory, history and, VIII, 251.
Allen, Judge, on juries, VII, 433.
Allingham, William, VIII, 207; his "Morning Thoughts," VIII, 161; poem of, X, 450, 451.
Alloy in men, IV, 180.
Allston, III, 487; V, 379; IX, 212; verses of, IV, 295; pictures of, V, 205; 219; strength of, VI, 501; methods of, VIII, 108.
Allyne, Dr., VII, 171.
Almanac, soul's, VII, 553.
Alpine flowers, II, 216.
Alterity, V, 569.
Alternation, IV, 478.
Amalgam, VII, 125–27.
America, I, 201, 202; VIII, 343; the spirit of, I, 160–62; a field for work, I, 245–48; young, I, 356; 388; pride in, III, 189; arts in, IV, 109; all races come to, IV, 138; lags and pretends, IV, 483, 484; lost in her area, VI, 119; seems trade and convention, VI, 390; free thought in, VI, 516; wants male principle, VII, 218; diffuse, unformed, VII, 286; democratic, VII, 477; unlearned, IX, 89; England and, IX, 571–73; and English behavior in Civil War, X, 78; speech on the

INDEX

Union, x, 84; opportunity of, x, 106; the leading guide of the world, x, 195; truth in, x, 337.
American artists, walk with, III, 90.
American clergy, IV, 413.
American conditions, v, 529.
American duties, x, 99.
American elementary education, English and, VII, 530.
American genius, unreal, v, 205; English and, x, 8.
American instability, VI, 330.
American politics, x, 144.
American seamen, III, 4.
American standards, v, 316.
American talents, x, 370, 371.
American thought; its obstacles, property, and imitation of Europe, IV, 89, 90; present, IV, 472.
American writers, pioneer, VI, 472.
American writing, untrained, VI, 105, 106.
American, verses on the travelling, III, 206; irresistible, VII, 294; Englishman and, VII, 405.
Americans, thin blood in, VI, 501; light-weight, VII, 254; idealistic, VII, 332, 333; underdosed, VIII, 398.
Amherst address, notes for, VIII, 572, 573.
Amherst professors, VIII, 576.
Amherst College, I, 273-77; x, 385.
Amici and his microscopes, III, 111.
Amiens, VII, 473.
Amusement, VII, 170.
Analogies, VIII, 493; Nature's, v, 327, 328.
Analogist, man an, IV, 28; 33.
Analogy, VIII, 271; IX, 176; hints of, IV, 303.
Analysis, v, 217; may be sublime, v, 327; important, x, 455.
Anaxagoras, II, 337-39.
Anaximander, II, 337.
Ancestry of E., II, 41.
Ancestry, our wild, III, 562; advantages of a pious, IV, 229-32.
Ancient poets, held sacred, III, 570.
Andover Seminary, I, 287.
Andrew, John A., IX, 377; 391.
Androcles, IX, 211.

Angelo, Michel, v, 299; 307; IX, 281; the Moses of, III, 99; homage to, III, 106; such men strengthen ideals, III, 252, 253; his Seventh Sonnet, III, 399, 400; giants of, created by Jewish idea, v, 348; and Raffaele, VIII, 63; poems of, IX, 170; his Third Sonnet, x, 35; and Thomas Gray, x, 268.
Angels, IV, 392.
Angle, a man's, VII, 333.
Animal food, v, 392.
Animal magnetism, IV, 311, 312; 488.
Animal share in writing, VIII, 496.
Animal spirits, VI, 447.
Animals, I, 224; v, 532; sermon subject, II, 471; visit to menagerie, III, 306; dreams and, III, 533.
Annals of thought, v, 191.
"Another State," v, 172.
Anquetil Duperron, x, 164.
Answer, unanswerable, VIII, 537.
Antagonisms, III, 304; balanced, VIII, 207.
Anthony, St., to the fishes, VIII, 27.
Anthropomorphism, II, 63.
Antigone, III, 569.
Antinomianism, IV, 449.
Antique, the, IV, 171; 197; no time in the, v, 434.
Antiquity, real, II, 503; sacred, VI, 127; cause and humility, VI, 104.
Anti-slavery conventions, VII, 17.
Anti-slavery, IX, 151.
Anti-Transcendentalists, VI, 125.
Antoine, Père, of New Orleans, VI, 351.
Apathy, IV, 400.
Apennine, Father; statue of, III, 125.
Aphorisms, II, 529.
Aplomb, IX, 531, 532.
Apocalypse, the, I, 335.
Appeal, Nature's, III, 227.
Appendages, men are, IV, 240.
Applause, IV, 289.
Apple-blossom, v, 396.
Apples, VII, 552; VIII, 238; and men, v, 64; and pears, IX, 466.
Appleton, Thomas G., VII, 416; 495.
Arabian quotations, IX, 408.

Arago, III, 170; quoted, IX, 109.
Arbor, VII, 307.
Arbors, VII, 295.
Arc and orbit, III, 343.
Archelaus, II, 339.
Archimedes, VII, 559; stark thinker, VIII, 382.
Architecture, V, 395; as imitation, III, 146; art and, reason makes them, IV, 102, 103; composition like, IV, 170, 171; gardens and, V, 27, 28.
Archytas, II, 341.
Arcueil, *Mémoires*, or *Transactions*, IX, 521.
Arethusa, Fountain of, III, 43.
Argument unprofitable, IV, 484.
Ariosto, III, 127.
Aristippus quoted, VII, 522.
Aristocracies, various, inevitable, VI, 457, 458.
Aristocracy, I, 311, 312; and idealism, V, 276, 277; Nature covers, VI, 462; in *Hamlet*, VII, 320; conditions of, VII, 321; real, VII, 335; a right, VII, 384, 385; degrees of, VIII, 216; now diffused, VIII, 576.
Aristocrats, natural, VI, 388.
Aristotle, III, 528; VII, 516; VIII, 49; his system an experiment, II, 285.
Armadillo-skinned man, VII, 377.
Arnim, Bettina von, V, 237; VI, 229; IX, 212, 213; in Varnhagen's Diary, X, 310.
Arnold, Matthew, X, 275; quoted, IX, 435; 480.
Arnold, Mr., on merchants, VIII, 275.
Arnott, Dr., VII, 412.
Aroma, V, 225.
Art, resemblance *versus* implied power, I, 29; and architecture, reason makes them, IV, 102, 103; strong from within, V, 182; power of, V, 488; direction of, VII, 33; miraculous, VII, 535; giants of, VIII, 252, 253; orders of architecture, IX, 323; two things in a picture, IX, 424, 425; definition of, IX, 528. *See also* Age, Beauty, Country, Disappointment, Dismal, English, Gods, Immortality, Landscape, Love, Plotinus, Reason, Selection, Strength, "Symposium," Thoreau.
Art galleries, VII, 478.
Artificial life, yet greatness always there, III, 325.
Artist, in society, VII, 457; chance of, to show beauty and law, VIII, 125, 126; mannered, IX, 578.
Artists, studios of, III, 84; the great, VII, 173.
Arts, correspondence of, III, 396; harmonious, III, 403; languishing, III, 501.
Ascendency, V, 536.
Ascension festival, III, 116.
Ascent, verse, IX, 87.
Asia, Bossuet on, I, 340–42.
Asia, verses, I, 380.
Asiatic genius, V, 570.
Asiatic Journal, the, IV, 318.
Aspirations for art, letters, and science an argument for immortality, II, 205.
Assaults, Western doctrine, VIII, 326.
Assemblée Nationale, VII, 469.
Asser and Alfred, VIII, 381.
Assessors, the soul's, VII, 426.
Association universal, VI, 300.
Astronomers, IX, 29.
Astronomy, VIII, 139; effect of, on religion, II, 489–91;|Herschel and, III, 197; overprized, IX, 16.
Asylum, beauty our, VII, 467.
Asylums of the mind: natural science, fancy, inventions, music, V, 120, 121.
At the Old Manse, verse, II, 208.
Atheist, theist or, V, 198.
Athenæum, The Boston, IV, 258; 317–20; V, 229.
Athenæum, a Concord, VI, 210.
Athenæum Club, the, VII, 483.
Athenians, the, VII, 548.
Athens, VIII, 26.
Atlantic, bridging the, VII, 245.
Atlantic Monthly, the, IX, 117, 118.
Atmosphere, VII, 312; an excitant, X, 46.
Attitude, IX, 543; your, VI, 168.
Audience, E.'s, IX, 33.

INDEX

Augustine, St., VIII, 97; *De Libero Arbitrio*, III, 500; a confession of, V, 180; on Memory and Plato, VII, 528, 529.
Auld Lang Syne, I, 342.
Aunt, A good, III, 409.
Aurora, V, 252.
Austen, Miss, novels of, IX, 336, 337.
Australia, women for, VII, 434.
Austria, X, 295.
Austrians in Venice, III, 135.
Author, pay of, IV, 9.
Authors, over-influence of, IV, 281; influence of, V, 391; our, VI, 47; pay of, VI, 249.
"Authority, One having," II, 296.
Autobiographies, diaries and, V, 516.
Autobiography, IX, 306; based on choice, VII, 264, 265.
Avarice, VI, 314.
Avernus, III, 72–74.
Axis, every man's, IV, 132.
Azores, III, 13.

Babcock, J. S., IX, 156.
Babe, the, VI, 184.
Baby. *See* E.'s children.
Bacon, Delia, belief of, VIII, 288; on Lord Bacon, VIII, 314, 315; and Hawthorne, IX, 90.
Bacon, Lord, II, 326; III, 414; VI, 43; the *Novum Organum*, I, 26, 27; his *Prima Philosophia*, II, 330, 332; quotations from, II, 410; juvenile critics of, IV, 429; his "*Leges legum*," VIII, 134; Delia Bacon on, VIII, 314, 315; Milton and, VIII, 408; Macaulay on, VIII, 483, 484; pivotal, VIII, 492; life of, explained, VIII, 492, 493.
Bacon, Roger, VIII, 349.
Bailey, VI, 286; his *Festus*, VII, 284.
Balance, V, 537.
Ball at the Governor's, III, 35.
Ball, Benjamin West, visit of, VI, 398, 399.
Ballad, *The Knight and the Hag*, I, 123–25.
Balloon, X, 232, 233.
Ballot or gun? VIII, 206.
Baltimore, lecturing in, VI, 335, 336.

Balzac, V, 371; VI, 231.
Bancroft, George, moral beauty, I, 346; his *History of the U.S.*, IV, 304, 305; on newspapers, IV, 410; and Bryant, VI, 315.
Bancroft, Mrs., VII, 348, 349.
Bandmann, X, 20.
Bangor sights and men, VII, 231, 232.
Banks, the, III, 217.
Barbarian voters, VII, 545.
Barbès and Blanqui; causes of uprising, VII, 462.
Barbour, John, *Bruce* of, III, 522.
Bard, IX, 472.
Bards; Thomas Taylor, Ossian, VIII, 361.
Bargain, a, V, 414.
Bargaining, VI, 270.
Baring, Lady Harriet, at dinner of, VII, 411.
Bar-keepers, IV, 20.
Barker, Anna, V, 278–80.
Barnard and Raby castles, VII, 387.
Barnwell and Upham, oratory of, I, 68.
Barren days, VII, 45, 46.
Barrett, Samuel, IX, 121.
Barrow, John, imitation of, I, 24.
"Barrows," natural, VII, 538.
Bartlett, Dr., bog of, IV, 342.
Bartlett, George, X, 255.
Bartlett, Robert, VI, 214.
Bassett, G. W., quoted, IX, 363.
Bat and ball, V, 410.
Bates, Joshua, VII, 405.
Bath, the, IX, 251.
Battery, man a, VIII, 280.
Battle, wind of, IX, 429.
Bayle, quoted, IX, 570.
Bead-eyes, III, 545.
Beards, V, 232.
Beast lingers in man, III, 318.
Beasts and man, IV, 381.
Beatitudes of intellect, IX, 221.
Beattie, VII, 311.
Beaumarchais, IX, 109.
Beautiful, the, everything its effort at, V, 121.
Beauty, I, 304; V, 118; immunity of, II, 252; embosomed in, IV, 23; a sword and shield, V, 223; cannot be held, V, 494; goes with truth, V, 537; found in work or worship,

VI, 30; in world of thought, VI, 123; flits before possession, VI, 202; demand of, VI, 445; and philanthropists, VII, 7; joy of, VIII, 178; and strength in poetry and art, VIII, 300, 301; spiritual causes under, IX, 279; and moral laws, X, 64; perception of, in life, X, 145, 146; highest, is of expression, X, 229; women and girls in the street, X, 384. *See also* Artist, Asylum, Book, Common Life, Faith, Hero, Infancy, Intellect, Lethe, Life, Moral, Sense, Sermons, Strength, Temperance, Universal, Winckelmann.

Beckford, T. A., his *Vathek*, VI, 444; his *Italy and Spain*, VI, 410-12.

"Becky Stow's Hole," X, 61.

Beecher, Henry Ward, X, 3; talk with, IX, 509; at Exeter Hall, IX, 570.

Beethoven, V, 19; 145; 506; his *Sinfonia Eroica*, IX, 68; homage from Goethe, IX, 213.

Beginnings, I, 315.

Behavior, fine, V, 442.

Behmen, Jacob, VII, 575; VIII, 551; his *Aurora*, III, 524; excellence of, VI, 517, 518; on the stars, VIII, 549.

Being, against seeming, IV, 299; and organizing, VI, 5, 6; and intellect, IX, 343.

Belief in our own work, VI, 126; and unbelief, VI, 482.

Believer, the, VIII, 543.

Bell, IV, 359.

Bell, The, poem, I, 238.

Benefits, doctrine of, V, 28, 29.

Benevolence, III, 416; God's, I, 191-95; 198-200.

Bentley, scholarship of, IV, 151.

Béranger, democracy of, VIII, 216.

Bereavement, III, 454; IV, 67, 68; 125.

Berkeley, Bishop, VII, 44.

Berkshire dream, the, III, 301.

Berth meditations, III, 4.

Berthollet, X, 7.

Beryl, VIII, 502.

Best, sifted by fame, II, 464; the, here and cheap, VII, 175; get the, VII, 549.

Best thought, speak your, III, 336.

Bettina. *See Arnim.*

Betting, VII, 495.

Bewick, *Life*, X, 85.

Bhagavat Geta, VII, 67, 68, 511; X, 187.

Bhagavat Purana, quoted, X, 157.

Bias, VIII, 226, 543; IX, 539; X, 22; seven men in a field, X, 146, 147.

Bible, the, IV, 24; VI, 168; educates, II, 176; your own, IV, 78; mandate for charity, IV, 357; misused, V, 4; only defect of, V, 140; primary, scriptures of the nations, V, 334, 335; a coming, VI, 425; and pagans, X, 100.

Bigelow, Erastus B., VIII, 341.

Big-endians and Little-endians, VIII, 62.

Biographie Générale, Nouvelle, X, 322.

Biographies for lectures, III, 387.

Biography, uses of, II, 279; a spiritual help, III, 440; interests not nations, IV, 421; individuals new, V, 208; history is, V, 223; autobiography, VII, 332.

Biot, III, 170.

Bipolarity, III, 355; VIII, 86.

Bird, singing, and talker, III, 304.

Bird songs, VIII, 77.

Birds, hawk and sea fowl, III, 283; at study window, VII, 199; on walk, IX, 43, 44.

Bird-while, a, IV, 453.

Birmingham, VII, 358.

Birmingham lustre, VII, 438.

Birthplace, VIII, 557.

Birthplace, E.'s, X, 383.

Black, Mrs. Rebecca, VI, 197, 198.

Black art, V, 151.

Blackbird, The, poem, I, 353.

Blackstone, on God's law, VIII, 133, 134.

Blagden, Rev. George, preaching of, III, 339.

Blake, H. G. O., walk with, V, 133.

Blake, William, quoted on Wordsworth, IX, 558; X, 23; quoted, IX, 575.

Blanqui, Barbès and; causes of uprising, VII, 462.

Blood, Thaddeus, on Concord Fight, III, 516; his memories of April, 1775, III, 534.

INDEX

Blood-fusions, VIII, 230.
Blouse, The, the day of, VII, 454.
Bluebird, IX, 275.
Boccaccio, III, 456; IV, 76.
Bodleian Library, VII, 423.
Body, and soul, I, 225–31; man a stranger in his, V, 52.
Boissier, Gaston, quoted, IX, 369.
Boldness the sign of spirit, VI, 205.
Bologna, III, 126.
Bonaparte, Jerome, III, 110.
Bonaparte, Napoleon, II, 407; IV, 421, 422; VI, 137; VIII, 204; the Simplon, III, 148; temperament, varied genius, IV, 437; rewards impersonality, IV, 463; and chapel bell, VI, 542; fortune of, VII, 11; between thought and matter, VII, 24; genius of, VII, 35; on Leonidas, VIII, 151; head of, VIII, 221; on Science, VIII, 451; his sense and admirable criticism, VIII, 456, 457; and Beethoven, IX, 68; his fortune turned, IX, 336; quoted, IX, 445; X, 98.
"Bonduca," V, 185, 186; 474.
Bonnets, women's, VIII, 40.
Bons-mots, X, 14.
Book, the proposed, II, 445; different to different men, III, 551; a human, V, 39; man and, V, 54; yielding to, VIII, 56; author can write but one, VIII, 486; written for beauty *versus* moral, IX, 317; twenty years for, X, 239; scholar's, circulating, X, 380.
Book-readers, V, 18.
Books, lists of, I, 32; II, 68; of wisdom, I, 392; of the centuries, II, 5, 6; and men, II, 13; justified, II, 411; each finds his own in, II, 465; convert action to thought, III, 286; are blessings, III, 490; of the future, III, 518; perusal or chance readings of, III, 536; mind has room for, V, 63; others', V, 37; fames, V, 63; secondary, V, 74; as gardens of delight, V, 189, 190; convicting, V, 258; of all time, V, 282–84; like divers and dippers, V, 406; beguile, V, 561; to read, VI, 282; the few great, VI, 300; relation of man to, VI, 300; that stir but do not feed, VI, 496; recommended, VII, 328, 329; advised by Carlyle, VII, 367; E.'s, survive, VII, 428; brought home, VII, 488; rainy day, VIII, 418; theft of, IX, 269; a little heaven, X, 221.
Bores, VI, 158.
Borromeo, St. Charles, III, 160.
Borrow, on Wales, IX, 471.
Bossuet, I, 340–42.
Boston, IX, 303; room in, III, 232; visit to, V, 231; bill of fare of, VI, 58; life in, in two acts, VI, 99; steam's lift to, VI, 270; meeting friends in, VI, 290; friends in, VI, 324; offerings of, VI, 512; societies of, VII, 267; adulation of Webster in, VIII, 111; the true, VIII, 223; low estate of, VIII, 364; false position of, VIII, 449; eminent names of, IX, 568; old, X, 203.
Boston Christianity, VII, 197.
Boston hymn, IX, 193.
Boston poem, VI, 249.
Bostonian and civilization, VII, 315.
Boswellism of travel, III, 340.
Boswellism, IV, 332, 333.
Botany, curiosity in, III, 482; with George B. Emerson, V, 3.
Botts, J. M., IX, 574.
Boucher, VIII, 347.
Boulogne, sails from, III, 171.
Boutwell, IX, 565.
Boy and alphabet, III, 289.
Boy, Nature leads the, VI, 252; and girl, IX, 300; sympathy with, X, 369.
Boyden, Uriah, VIII, 341.
Boynton, Dr., IX, 76; X, 342.
Boys, VII, 89, 86; and girls, V, 37; at baseball, VI, 191; ticket of admission, IX, 323.
Bradford, Dr. Gamaliel, his verses on E.'s poem, VIII, 442.
Bradford, George P., II, 444; III, 573; V, 35, 248; VII, 379; and Plymouth, III, 262; Charles Newcomb and, VI, 374; letter to, IX, 569.
Bradley, discovery of, IV, 362.
Brag, X, 176.
Brahma, IX, 57.
Brahmin, X, 163.

INDEX

Brant and Gansevoort, v, 170.
Brazer, Professor, Dr. Kirkland and, viii, 350, 351.
Brazil, x, 161, 162.
Brescia, iii, 140, 141.
Bridlington saddler, vii, 376.
Brig Jasper, the, iii, 3.
Briggs, Governor, viii, 112.
Brillat-Savarin, x, 31.
Brisbane, Albert, vi, 169, 355; on education, vii, 535.
British Museum, the, vii, 433, 434, 435.
Broadway, a symbol, iii, 355.
Brontë, Charlotte; her *Shirley*, viii, 109.
Brook, need of, vii, 531.
Brook Farm, vi, 34; 373, 374; 491; project does not attract, v, 473, 474; relations, vi, 391; difficulties, vi, 396; visit to, vi, 416, 417; pleasant, vi, 443.
Brooke, Lord, viii, 46; *Life of Sydney*, ix, 319.
Brookfield, i, 269, 270.
Brookfield [man], visit to, vii, 445, 446.
Brothers, vi, 165; viii, 307.
Brothers of E., ii, 42.
Brown, B. J., x, 181-83.
Brown, John, ix, 248, 251; in Concord, ix, 81-83; raid, ix, 238-40; Governor Wise and, ix, 245; Thoreau on, ix, 247, 248; execution of, ix, 253.
Brown, Dr. Samuel, vii, 388.
Browne, Sir Thomas, ii, 327; v, 146; quoted, ix, 295.
Browning, vi, 286; viii, 455.
Brownson, Orestes A., iv, 166; list, vi, 297.
Bruno, Giordano, extracts from, ii, 388.
Bryant, iii, 449; iv, 423; x, 76; Bancroft and, vi, 315; magic of, x, 80-82.
Buchner, ix, 112.
Buckminster, philosophic imagination, i, 323; all subjects good, ii, 304.
Buddha, icy light, vii, 110.
Buddhism, vi, 382; vii, 122; remorseless, vi, 318.
Buddhist hospitality, v, 408.

Bull, John, viii, 416.
Bull, Ole, Performance of, vi, 512.
Buller, Charles, vii, 411.
Bulletin, Nature's, is man, vi, 296.
Bulwer; his *Caxtons*, viii, 250.
Bunker Hill Monument Dedication, vi, 415, 416.
Bunsen, x, 287.
Bunsens, the, vii, 485.
Bunyan, iv, 421; verses of, iv, 367, 368.
Burglars, iv, 496.
Burke, i, 317-20; ii, 122; iii, 567; viii, 340; rhetoric of, v, 244; and Schiller believers, vi, 512; and Webster, vii, 234; growth of, vii, 262, 263; sayings of, viii, 528; quoted, ix, 372, 468.
Burnap, Rev. George Washington, on Dr. Watts and Dr. Doddridge, ii, 236, 237.
Burning, of the house, x, 386-89.
Burns, Robert, iii, 449; vi, 43; vi, 286; praise and criticism, ii, 428; and language, viii, 313.
Burnside, x, 4.
Burton, Robert, Cornelius Agrippa and, vi, 291.
Burton, Warren, letter to, bereavement, iv, 124, 125.
Business, men of, iii, 458; literary, x, 130.
Busybodies, vii, 29.
Butler, Joseph, on translations, ii, 130.
Buttrick, David, the market-man, iv, 373.
Byron, ii, 86; iii, 127; vii, 92, 285; death of, ii, 4; "The Gladiator," iii, 99; rooms of, iii, 108; failure of, vii, 163; feats of, viii, 36; suggested partnerships of authors, viii, 89.

Cable, Atlantic, x, 155.
Cabot, J. Elliot, x, 441, 442; quoted, ix, 58; on Art, ix, 549.
Cæsar, and Cicero, i, 332; poet's use of heroes, v, 187; in Britain, viii, 411.
Cadet at West Point, ix, 517.
Café, the, v, 527.
Cairo, x, 406.
Calculation, vi, 109.

INDEX

Calderon, IX, 67, 68.
Calhoun, J. C., VIII, 337.
California, VIII, 4, 7, 8; notes on, X, 352-55.
California people, X, 355.
Call to the Second Church, II, 261, 262.
Call, await your, III, 462; obey your, V, 476.
Calling, follow your, III, 232; V, 390.
Calm, II, 368; IV, 272; wind and, III, 7.
Calmness, godlike, V, 490.
Calvin, against, II, 33.
Calvinism, II, 420; III, 398; V, 245; X, 155; and Unitarianism, II, 424; strength of, and weak Unitarianism, III, 199, 200; dying, III, 323; early terrors from, IV, 286; five points of, VI, 387; power of, VIII, 32; three legs of, X, 242.
Calvinist, by temperament, VI, 208; inconvertible, VI, 377.
Cambridge jail, III, 231.
Cambridge, visit to, VII, 489.
Cameron, VII, 383.
Campbell, Thomas, II, 410; Moore on, II, 471; Elizabeth Hoar on life of, VII, 205.
Camper, IV, 205.
Camping, V, 345.
Candidacy, presidential, IX, 14.
Canning, Landor on, VII, 111.
Cannon, X, 33.
Canova, III, 133; on Phidias, VIII, 220.
Cant, IV, 246; V, 81, 149, 271; VIII, 346; of the day, VIII, 477.
Canterbury, I, 232.
Cants here and abroad, VIII, 550.
Capable men, III, 25.
Cape Cod, the visit to, VIII, 399-401.
Capital, man's, V, 408.
Capitol, the, IX, 395.
Capitoline, "The Gladiator" and Byron, III, 98.
Captain and scholar, III, 19.
Care and Caress, poem, I, 62.
Caricatures, IV, 450.
Carlyle, II, 524; 315, 472, 573; IV, 180, 181; VI, 400; VII, 285, 384; first reading of, II, 515; at Ecclefechan, visit to, his talk on persons and books, measure of his loyalty, III, 180-82; reports about Wordsworth and, III, 188; thoughts about, III, 190; Charles Emerson on, III, 557; wide genius of, his strength-worship, his style, IV, 195, 196; desired companionship of, IV, 258; nobility of, his acceptance, IV, 272-74; American edition of works of, IV, 346; letter of, IV, 389; love for, IV, 398, 399; his *French Revolution* — his astonishing style, IV, 405, 406; 410, 411; poverty of, IV, 446; Sterling and, V, 352; has power and wit, no philosopher, exhaustive, V, 440, 441; rhetoric of, V, 571; VII, 367; ignores dissenters and radicals, VI, 222; Milnes and, VI, 251; in *Past and Present*, VI, 387; on English woes, VI, 394, 395; manlike style of, VI, 410; portrait of, VII, 196, 197; medium of, VII, 216; exchange of pictures with, VII, 224, 225; welcome of, his wife and mother, his conversation, VII, 344-48; reputation of, VII, 367; views of, VII, 402-04; disciples of, VII, 437; on clubs, society, and Plato VII, 439, 440; no idealist, insular, intolerant, the voice of London, VII, 441-43; stands tests, VII, 561; refrains of, VIII, 95; his mirror of writing, VIII, 250; his *Life of Sterling*, VIII, 261, 262; step from Johnson to, VIII, 463; his *History of Frederick*, IX, 195, 196, 423, 424; Channing praises his history, IX, 204; insight of, IX, 465; projectile style of, IX, 529; protest to, X, 63; demoniac fun of, X, 104; hating sentimentalism, X, 116; his anti-Americanism, X, 122; perverse, X, 217; bequest to Harvard, X, 315; Norton and, X, 397.
Carlyle, medal, X, 449.
Carlyle, Mrs., tells of Goethe, III, 182.
Carnarvon, Earl, speech of, I, 328, 329.
Carnot, IX, 40.

INDEX

Carolina, Massachusetts dishonored by, VII, 13–15. *See also* South Carolina.
Carpenter, the, IV, 57.
Casella, song of, V, 61.
Cash payment, VII, 525.
Cass, Lewis, X, 121.
Casting composition, III, 446.
Cat, VII, 544.
Catalogue, value of, V, 190, 191.
Catania mule-ride to, its churches and museums, III, 49–53.
Catbird, VI, 208.
Cathedral, V, 29, 30.
Catholic Church, IX, 500.
Cause and effect, IV, 270; V, 62.
Cause, wait for strong, VII, 221; our, against Fugitive Slave Law, VIII, 215; a good, IX, 490.
Cavendish, V, 315, 316.
Cedar-birds, the fable of, IV, 352.
Censure, V, 33, 34, 69.
Centrality, X, 205.
Centre, each man a, IV, 295.
Century, the, its combinations and inventions, VIII, 344.
Ceremony baulks, IV, 236.
Chains, III, 399.
Chaise, Père la, III, 165.
Chaldean Oracles, V, 560; VI, 499, 500; VIII, 534.
Chalmers, VII, 396.
Champion boxer, VI, 82.
Change required for E., VII, 253.
Change, perpetual, IX, 482.
Channing, Dr. Ellery, sermon of, I, 290, 291; and inferior clergy, II, 202; on War, II, 456; Wordsworth speaks of, III, 183; visit of, IV, 236; strength of, VI, 271; letter on death of, VI, 284, 285.
Channing, William Ellery, VI, 46, 47, 492; VIII, 503; walk with, VI, 235, 236; VII, 506, 510, 531, 532, 536–40; to Marlboro' with, VIII, 130; walk with, VIII, 294, 295, 297, 298; VIII, 352, 485; IX, 110; X, 61; as a poet, VI, 357–59; VII, 230; humors of, VI, 422, 423; VIII, 352; his book on Rome, VII, 303; on Nature, VII, 330; on Herrick, VII, 532; talk with, VII, 538–40; as showman, VII, 540; and Thoreau on Alcott, VII, 552; November walk, VIII, 65; his criticisms, VIII, 74, 75; on goodness, VIII, 215; on Nahant and Truro, VIII, 252; on Hawthorne, VIII, 257; views of "the Arboretum," VIII, 297, 298; drive with, VII, 371–73; poetry of, VIII, 541; IX, 180; X, 361, 362; Ward quoted on, IX, 54; on frogs, IX, 105; on river with, IX, 106; on golden rod, IX, 185; advice on book, IX, 238; to White Pond with, IX, 523.
Channing, W. H., V, 56.
Channings, the, VI, 328.
Chapin, X, 4.
Chaos, advance from, VII, 131.
Character, no hiding, II, 300; not chance, tells, IV, 160, 161; above intellect, IV, 224; comes out, V, 458; counterpoise to surface distinctions, VI, 30–32; rich, VI, 507; men of, VII, 78; universal belief in, X, 458, 459. *See also* Self-Reliance, Greatness, and similar headings; Fate, Talent, Theocracy, War, Woman.
Chardon Street Convention, VI, 118.
Charity, IV, 342, 343; V, 111; common nature demands, IV, 452.
Charles II, manners, VII, 196.
Charleston, II, 196; tides of thought, II, 135, 136; at, good gifts of travel, II, 183–85.
Chartism, six points of, VII, 494.
Chartist meeting, the, VII, 414.
Chartists, VII, 402.
Chase, Salmon P., IX, 381.
Chaste attitude, III, 251.
Chastity, VII, 289; VIII, 236.
Chateaubriand, VIII, 402; imitation of, I, 75; of Washington, X, 350.
Chatel, Abbé; Eglise Catholique Française, III, 168.
Chaucer, V, 116; VIII, 349; X, 33; and Saadi, VI, 223; on poet and scholar, VIII, 238, 239.
Chauncy and Whitefield, I, 330.
Cheating, VII, 194.
Cheerfulness, III, 161; VIII, 554; IX, 562; X, 368; infants teach, VI, 276.
Cheering, IV, 360.
Cheering books, IX, 469.

INDEX 489

Chelmsford, IX, 235.
Chemistry, II, 288; human, IV, 133; the noblest, VII, 182; powers and limits, IX, 18; and moral science, IX, 31.
Cherokee "scream," the, IV, 426, 427.
Cherokees, the, IV, 424.
Chesterfield, VII, 358.
Chevelure, dangerous, VII, 509.
Cheyne Row, III, 230.
Chicago, X, 91, 371; birth of, IX, 76, 77.
Child, the, III, 325; civilizes the father, III, 511; parents and, IV, 134, 135; out of doors, IV, 298; lives with God, IV, 382; the sobbing, IV, 481; love of, V, 135; has poetry of life, V, 211; power of, V, 238; truth of, VI, 35; rules, VI, 468; early teaching of, VIII, 129; E.'s joys as a, X, 381.
Childhood, E.'s, VI, 305.
Children, VIII, 296; foreigners, V, 262; speech of, V, 435; precepts to, V, 528; directness of, VI, 35; E.'s, VI, 266; *versus* conversation, VI, 348; sacred, VI, 473; teachers of, VIII, 23; in Heaven's gardens, VIII, 465; wits of, X, 32.
Chinese reformers, VI, 458.
Chivalry, age of, Charles's remark, II, 87.
Chladni an Orpheus, VIII, 79.
Choate, Rufus, VII, 69; VIII, 112, 183, 184, 508; Webster and, VII, 87; on English and Fox, VIII, 558.
Choice abdication of, III, 337, 338.
Cholera times, value of death and life, II, 505, 506.
Christ, Jesus, II, 129; III, 413; IV, 213, 214; suspecting defects in, II, 323; love not by compulsion, II, 410; real love for, III, 223; stream and source, III, 324; influence of, III, 433; VI, 438; not final, III, 518; beautiful but incomplete, III, 531; a fellow-worshipper, IV, 129; message of, IV, 277; acted thought, IV, 435; human, IV, 444; love due to, IV, 496; reverence for what he represents, V, 7; true help of, V, 274; no institution, V, 389; history of, typical, V, 478; his command of silence, V, 491; love of, reasonable, V, 500; great defeat of, power of character, VI, 188; not yet portrayed, VIII, 52.
Christendom, renouncing soul's birthright the madness of, V, 272, 273.
Christian, gentleman and, V, 549.
Christianity, III, 415; value of, II, 78; and morals, II, 120; weighed by truth, II, 326; educates and frees, II, 510; truth precedes, II, 516; and slavery, III, 446, 447; and the English Church, Charles Emerson on, III, 547, 548; misrepresented, IV, 168; traces of demonology in, V, 163, 164; now insists on persons, not ideas, V, 454; old as creation, VII, 418; argument for, IX, 510.
Christians, dying, II, 317; savage, VIII, 523.
Church, the parish, IV, 443; desire for a fit, IV, 462; must respect the soul, V, 171; poverty of, V, 370; its office and benefit to the people, VI, 6-9; and trade, VIII, 334.
Church of St. Augustine, II, 175.
Church of England, VIII, 368.
Church of Rome, conversion to, IX, 243, 244.
Church bells of Boston, V, 281.
Church clock, the, V, 24.
Church-going, IV, 377.
Churches, III, 79; pictures, gardens, III, 94-96.
Churchman, transcendentalist and, VI, 380.
Church-member, lady turned, VI, 160.
Church-members, IX, 322.
Cicero, quotation, II, 422; quoted, IX, 362, 556.
Cid, the, VIII, 557; *Chronicle of*, VII, 307, 308.
Cipher, Nature's, V, 421.
Circles, little and greater, X, 238.
Circles, the poem, VII, 212, 213.
Circumstance, VIII, 4.
Circumstances in presence of soul, V, 312.
Circus, the, V, 402.
Cities, like shells, VI, 9.
Citizen, true, V, 357, 358.

City, joy of a new, X, 413.
City and country, V, 310.
City-builders, VIII, 145.
City founders, VIII, 223.
Civil history, IV, 125.
Civilization, II, 18; its triumphs treacherous, IX, 27, 28.
Clapp, Henry, quoted, X, 239.
Clare, poem of, VI, 168.
Clarendon, Lord, IV, 269; VIII, 405; on Falkland, IV, 264.
Clark, Galen, X, 354.
Clarke, James Freeman, on Hawthorne, X, 39.
Clarke, Sarah, V, 458; X, 385.
Class of 1821, meeting of, VII, 226, 227.
Classes, three, VI, 220, 221.
Classic and Romantic, IX, 24, 25, 26, 27.
Classic authors, supremacy of, VI, 268.
Classics, VI, 289.
Classification, IV, 100, 487; true, III, 294.
Classmates meeting, no disguises, VI, 37–39.
Clay, Cassius M., and Wendell Phillips, VII, 267, 268.
Clay, Henry, II, 53.
Clergy, VII, 413; in America, VI, 423.
Clerisy, the, or learned class, V, 337, 338.
Cleveland, Duke of, VII, 387.
Cliff, the, IX, 94; the day at, V, 423.
Climate, our happy, VII, 294; exhaustion of our, IX, 333.
Climbers, VIII, 24.
Clipper-ships, American, VIII, 370.
Clothes-pins, VI, 370.
Clouds, V, 450.
Cloud-shows, I, 26.
Clough, Arthur Hugh, meeting with, VII, 453; his *Bothie*, VII, 560; VIII, 16; in New England, VIII, 375–77; departure of, VIII, 388.
Club, Hedges', reaction from literary discussion, IV, 456, 457; for literature, VII, 255, 256; *des femmes*, VII, 456; *des clubs*, VII, 457; town and country, VIII, 10.

Clubs, IX, 103; value of, IX, 469.
Coal, man a, in the fire, IV, 18.
Coals to a market, VII, 338.
Coat, a, IV, 314, 315.
Coincidences, V, 107; X, 356.
Coke, VIII, 134; quoted, VIII, 135.
Colburn, Zerah, IV, 159.
Coldness as disguise, V, 348.
Coleman, his *Agriculture in Massachusetts*, VI, 196.
Coleridge, II, 278; friend, II, 277; translation of Wallenstein, quotation, II, 377; mouthpiece of mind of man, III, 328; immortality will be proved from intellect, III, 539, 540; a churchman, IV, 152, 153; solitary, V, 328; at Andover, VI, 266; influence of, VIII, 558; quoted on Greek women, X, 350.
Colfax, Schuyler, IX, 393.
College, revisited, I, 116; E.'s, V, 203; futile, V, 254; hide-bound, VII, 56.
College anniversaries, VII, 60.
Collins, in the kitchen, VIII, 130; *Ode to Evening*, X, 201.
Columbus, III, 12; at Veragua, VIII, 152, 153; letter of, VIII, 171, 172.
Combinations and inventions of the century, VIII, 344.
Comines, IX, 562.
Commandments, creeds or, II, 419, 420.
Commencement Day, IV, 83.
Commerce, makes love, III, 379; dangers of, V, 285.
Common life, beauty in, classification, IV, 99, 100.
Common mind, trust the, IV, 211.
Common people interest, V, 253.
Common people, VII, 84, 85.
Common sense, IV, 434; VI, 477; X, 136; divinity of, II, 64; against doctrinaires, IV, 112; and vitality, VIII, 506; examples, X, 131.
Commons, the, VII, 407, 408.
Communion with God, IV, 62.
Communism eagerly attacked, VII, 427.
Communist apostles, VII, 186.
Community wages, VII, 274.
Community, experiments in, V, 458.

INDEX

Communities, VI, 292; friendship in, VI, 70.
Companion, fit, X, 244.
Companions of Italian journey, III, 106.
Company, unprofitable, IV, 441, 442; inviting, V, 426; inhumanity and geniality in, VI, 96; undesired, VII, 534; and inspiration, X, 243, 244.
Comparative anatomy, IV, 358, 359.
Comparison, V, 5.
Comparisons, V, 336.
Compass, the, VIII, 556.
Compensation, I, 249; people who sell themselves, II, 72–77; always a price, II, 201; all teaches, II, 389; *Compensation*, origin of poem, II, 432; III, 376; doctrine of, be, not seem, III, 486, 487; confidence in, V, 175; examples in *Faust* and *Edda*, VII, 311. *See especially* Man, Nature and Fate.
Complaisance, mean, IV, 419.
Composer and underparts, VI, 111.
Composition, III, 478; human chemistry, IV, 132; like architecture, IV, 170, 171; justified, IV, 246; joy in, V, 12; necessary, V, 224.
Composure, V, 411; VI, 16.
Compression, V, 213.
Compromise, VII, 18.
Concealment, no, IV, 97; V, 201.
Conceit, IX, 437; of bathing, VII, 527.
Concentration, IX, 547.
Concert, musical, V, 516; IX, 301; oddity and, IX, 498.
Conclusion to wide world, I, 393.
Concord, greeting to, as home, new resolves, III, 361; joy in, III, 430; the Coolidge house in, purchase of, description of place, III, 540–42; life and character in, IV, 352–54; advantages of, VI, 383, 384; magic places of, VII, 249; possible professors of, VIII, 41, 42; celebration of, VIII, 112; worth of, IX, 266; return to, X, 419, 420.
Concord Athenæum, VI, 230.
Concord Fight, VI, 36; veterans' stories of, III, 507; Thaddeus Blood on, III, 516; anniversary of, X, 443, 444.

Concord schools, X, 13, 14.
Condé, VIII, 100.
Condition, virtue and, VI, 473.
Conditions, face, VIII, 55; right, X, 44.
Conduct of life, begin small, II, 476; kingdom of heaven begins, II, 512.
Conduct of Life, IX, 287, 288.
Confessions help, V, 378.
Confidence, feeling of, IV, 119.
Confidences, editorial: ancestry, brothers, II, 40–45.
Confucius, VI, 403; 126; sentences of, IV, 10; on ceremony, VIII, 516; quotations from, IX, 533–35.
Congelation, VIII, 292.
Congeries, man a, of spirits, III, 562.
Congregation, the, IV, 470.
Conscience, II, 368; IV, 97, 98; VI, 107; combats of, II, 126; rights of, II, 157; connects God to man, II, 248; a friend's, IV, 53; must watch intellect, VI, 376; local, or in veins, VI, 440; IX, 84.
Consciousness, private and universal, VII, 431.
Conservatism, best argument of, VI, 522.
Conservative, theorists and, VI, 136; and reformer, VI, 141; X, 28.
Considerateness, VII, 322.
Consolation of Nature, III, 452.
Consolations, slow, V, 206, 207.
Constancy, II, 212; II, 484; V, 565; VI, 26.
Constitution, rugged, VIII, 584.
Constitution, the, union and, V, 328; VII, 27; and Fugitive Slave Law, VIII, 338.
Construction, man's, IV, 129.
Consuelo, as Devil's advocate, VI, 498.
Contemplation, action and, action is not all, II, 239–41.
Contemporaries, IV, 311; V, 85; VII, 150; X, 334; our, VI, 106; E.'s, X, 102.
Content, V, 177.
Continence and abandonment, VI, 203.
Continuity, VII, 195; prayer for, VIII, 463.
Contradictions, VIII, 8.

Contrast, I, 96.
Contritions, VI, 133.
Conventicle Club, song for, I, 7-9.
Convention, the, Stephen Phillips and Garrison, VII, 96, 97.
Convention, servants of, IV, 302.
Conventions, a safeguard, VI, 232; society's, avoid or conquer them, VI, 242.
Conversation, V, 196; value of unspoken part, III, 440; common, III, 457; right, V, 173, 174; living, V, 215; Charles Lane at the, VI, 319, 320; and writing, VI, 348; good and poor, VII, 304, 305; beatitude of, VII, 529, 530; unexpected, eloquence in, IX, 37, 38; Nature's way, VIII, 404.
Conversazione, literary, III, 459.
Conversion, hourly, of life to truth, IV, 227.
Conversion to Church of Rome, IX, 243; 244.
Converting, IV, 426.
Conway, N. H., II, 492.
Coolidge house, in Concord, purchase of the, description of place, III, 540-42.
Copernicus, VIII, 478; IX, 17.
Corinne, III, 254; VII, 292.
Corn, kinds of, VI, 67.
Cornwallis, historic farce of surrender, V, 290.
Corrective wisdom, VI, 199.
Correctness, IX, 398, 399.
Correlation of forces, X, 358.
Cosmogonies, V, 399, 400; ancient, II, 333.
Costume, VII, 175.
Cotton, binds the Union, VII, 201; power of, VII, 242.
Cotton, Sarah, IV, 295.
Counsellor, man's, VII, 43.
Countenance of the first-born, III, 66.
Counterparts, IX, 170.
Counter-revolution is extinguished, VII, 460-62.
Counter-workings, III, 303.
Counting-room, education of, VI, 451.
Country, the, Nature *versus* Art, I, 146; and city, VI, 476.
Country blessings, IV, 187.

Country blood, X, 109.
Country health, VI, 329.
Country life, I, 349-51, 354-56; verses on, II, 367.
Country preacher, the strong, III, 556.
Courage, in daily act, III, 335; equality of opponent, IV, 257; the scholar's, V, 532, 533; VII, 252; indicates love of idea, IX, 246.
Courages, cheap and high, VII, 257, 258.
Courses of lectures, VII, 474, 475; on *Human Culture*, IV, 392, 393; on *The Times*, VI, 131.
Court house shows man, III, 468.
Court session at Concord, VII, 87.
Courtesies, cowardly, II, 452.
Courtesy, III, 445; IV, 181; VIII, 238; VIII, 323; republican, III, 566.
Courts, V, 455.
Cousin, book of, French eclecticism, IV, 404; and Jouffroy, IV, 400.
Cousins, the baby, IV, 235; V, 180.
Coutts, Miss, and street-girls, VII, 435.
Couture, rule of, X, 335.
Cowley and Donne proverbs, IV, 254.
Cows, VI, 424.
"Coxcombs, The," V, 186.
Crabbe, IV, 257.
Cranch and Alexander, moonlight walk with, III, 87.
Crawford, Samanthe, VII, 193.
Crawshay, Mr., trip-hammer of, VII, 387.
Creation, VII, 105; going on, V, 152; IX, 101; higher logic of, VIII, 409; theories of, VIII, 561.
Creative spirit, IX, 11.
Creator, the, latest work of, VI, 59.
Creeds do not satisfy, nor metaphysics, nor ethics, I, 378, 379; dissolving of, after death, II, 211; grow from structure of creature, II, 290; or commandments, II, 419, 420.
Crimes not absolute, VIII, 412.
Criminal statute illegal, VIII, 196.

INDEX 493

Crisis, in Emerson's life, visit to the White Mountains, II, 491–97; of trade, lesson of, IV, 375, 376.
Crises, III, 289; each age has a new, III, 356.
Critics, II, 284; borers, V, 561.
Criticism, VII, 291; obstructive, IV, 464; a woman's, V, 447; must be transcendental, V, 398; written in poetry, VI, 249; first impressions, VII, 39; misleads, VII, 26; whitewashing, IX, 201; on *Conduct of Life*, IX, 307; power of, X, 85; brothers and sisters, X, 133; foreign, X, 133.
Crocker, Alvah, X, 313, 314.
Cromwell, II, 407; VII, 404; *apud* Forster, V, 262, 263.
Crossing stocks, I, 304; VII, 156.
Crossings, VII, 116.
Crowe, Mrs., dinner of, VII, 389.
Cruikshank, VII, 86.
Crump, Mr., IX, 230, 231.
Crystallization, mental, II, 446.
Cudworth, III, 489; IV, 7, 8; VII, 95.
Culmination, VII, 131, 132.
Cultivated class, IX, 554.
Culture, III, 547; V, 111; VIII, 552; German and English, IV, 208; in high sense, IV, 339, 340; its manifold agents, IV, 366, 367; teaches proportion, the methods, IV, 368–70; highest requirement of, IV, 372; and cheer, V, 41; spoiled child of, VII, 516; convenience of, VII, 549; Plato required, VIII, 14; the highest, VIII, 79; man can spare nothing, VIII, 258; common people unconsciously value, VIII, 530; for results, VIII, 539; is a pagan, IX, 187; discarding hobgoblin of the popery, IX, 371; and morals, X, 269; from every social intercourse, X, 335, 336; New England taste for poetry, X, 367.
Curb rein, man is held on, IV, 20.
Curiosity-shop, society's, VII, 211.
Currency, VIII, 265; and personal values, IX, 563.
Current, of thought, X, 287.
Currents, the universal, VII, 195.
Custom, the Circe's cup of, IV, 325; shun, VI, 228; dead, IX, 175.

Dæmons, VI, 528, 529; VII, 17; friend quoted on, VIII, 247.
Daguerre, VI, 418; guess of, VI, 110.
Daguerreotype, VI, 87; sitting for, VI, 100.
Daguesseau, VIII, 411.
Daimonisches, IV, 224.
Damascene writing, IV, 278.
Damascus, woman of, IX, 339.
Dancing test, VIII, 277.
Dandies, VI, 525; of moral sentiment, VI, 45, 116.
Danger, resources in, III, 195.
Daniel, Samuel, extracts from, II, 347.
Dante, V, 265; VI, 244; seat of, III, 115; Flaxman's, IV, 77; his *Vita Nuova*, VI, 418; strength of, VIII, 32–34; transcendent eyes, IX, 206; Parsons's, X, 209–11.
Dark hours, rights of conscience, doubts, II, 156–61.
Darkness, IV, 358.
Dartmouth College, IX, 525, 526.
Dartmouth College Address, V, 10.
D'Auvergne, Pierre, quoted, IX, 249.
Davy, Dr., III, 36.
Day, a winter's, II, 532–34, 536; gifts and demands of a, III, 285; each new, IV, 302; a great man's, IV, 444, 445; glowing with magnificence, VI, 113.
Day, President, X, 41.
Days, how to spend, V, 249.
Days, VIII, 18; dealing with, VIII, 47.
Days, poem, VII, 277; the writing of, VIII, 273, 274.
Deacon, the, II, 296.
Dead-alive, the, IV, 188.
Death, I, 126, 207; II, 444; IV, 335; IX, 272; education after, II, 91; fear of, II, 212; 315–17; 438; verses on, II, 394; coming, II, 413; VII, 174; value of, II, 506; what is? IV, 343, 344; life and, are apparitions, IV, 453, 454; suicide, V, 331, 332; in story, V, 379; elemental, V, 482; poetic, VI, 230; life and, VI, 404; natural and sweet, VI, 520; and judgment, VIII, 445; attitude towards, VIII, 551; and landscape, IX, 59; when unfamiliar, IX, 470.

Debate, v, 78.
Debater, vi, 27.
Debts, pay, ix, 299.
December show, viii, 72.
De Clifford, vi, 69, 70.
Decorum now in demand, iii, 549.
Dedication, i, 111; 132, 133; 176; 205; 231–34; the spirit of America, i, 160–62.
Dedication to *Wide World* (journals), i, 10, 11.
Deed, word and, viii, 15.
Deep natures, vi, 71.
Defeat may be gain, iv, 310.
Defects, natural, i, 365.
Defences, vii, 194.
Deference, vi, 439; excess of, iii, 470; and room, vi, 513.
Definitions, v, 74.
Degeneracy, vii, 34.
De Gérando, ii, 283; on ancient philosophies, ii, 330–34.
Deinon, to, x, 75.
Deist, Nature a, a resource, no fool, v, 57–59.
Deity, inquiry concerning, ii, 237; poor God, x, 146.
Delight, wild, in man, iii, 459.
Deliverances, vii, 138.
De Loy, Aimé, quoted, ix, 558.
Deluge, x, 217.
Demiurgus, the, vi, 400; question of, vi, 318.
Democracy, iv, 95; viii, 140; root of, iii, 369; seamy side of, iii, 405; English view of our, iii, 509; New York, vi, 311; American, vi, 353; *versus* Aristocracy, ix, 460.
Democratic Party, x, 52.
Democrats, the, magnetic, v, 423; and Whigs, vi, 275, 276.
Demoniacal force, the, iv, 96.
Demonology; its traces in Christianity, v, 163, 164.
De Montluc, Maréchal, ix, 486.
Demosthenes, iii, 386, 387.
Denial, strength wasted in, vi, 122.
Dependence on others, v, 486.
Depression, viii, 566.
Depression of E., ii, 117.
De Quincey, anecdotes of him, vii, 388–91; dinner with, at Lasswade, vii, 397; attends lecture, vii, 398.

Derby, vii, 356.
Derry Academy, ii, 426.
Dervish, the, viii, 519.
Descartes, viii, 18.
Descent, our, vi, 497.
Deserted house, the, vi, 162.
Design, ii, 488; ix, 301; above finish, viii, 532.
Despair, ix, 175; time of, viii, 210.
Despondents, their remedy, v, 45, 46.
Destiny, vii, 512; and toleration, vi, 19. *See also* Fate.
Detachment, vii, 509; ix, 309; power of, vii, 518.
Details, viii, 571, 572; principles not, v, 306.
Determination of character in men, iii, 416.
De Tocqueville, vii, 485.
De Tocqueville, Mme., on language, vii, 551.
De Vere, Tennyson and, vii, 404; his care of Tennyson, vii, 447.
Devil's-needle day, iv, 494.
Dew, v, 550; spiritual, iv, 494.
Dewey, Chester, iv, 423; his *Plants in Massachusetts*, vi, 193, 194.
Diagonal in teaching, vii, 83.
Dial, the, new journal's position, v, 386; purposes of, v, 448; attack upon, v, 471; problem, vi, 163, 164; writers, vi, 367.
Diamond, invention of, vi, 370.
Diamond edition, man a, v, 270.
Diamonds, viii, 168.
Diaries and autobiographies, v, 516.
Dickens, iv, 436; his *American Notes*, vi, 312, 313; service of, vii, 186; on Thackeray, x, 7.
Dictionaries, x, 261.
Dictionary, life a, iv, 276.
Diet, sun-spiced, v, 342; trifle of, v, 428.
Diet whims, v, 413.
Differential, the, vii, 175.
Difficulty, brain and, vii, 479.
Digby, Kenelm, quoted, ix, 199.
Dignity and opportunity, man's, v, 356, 357.
Dilettante politics, vii, 533.
Dilettanti of liberty, ix, 243.
Dilettantism may teach, iii, 307.

INDEX

495

Diligence journey to Paris, pleasant companions, III, 147–55.
Dinner-bell, the, VI, 475.
Dinners in England, VII, 417.
Diogenes of Apollonia, II, 339.
Dionysius the elder, X, 242.
Direct speech saves, V, 80–83.
Directions, excess of, V, 483; of the Soul, VI, 80, 81.
Disappointment in art and splendor, III, 100.
Disciples, IV, 461; IX, 189; beware of, III, 280; enslaved, IV, 434.
Discipline, the soul's, IV, 486, 487.
Discourse, unsaid part of, II, 444; architecture of, X, 219.
Discoverers, creative, VII, 316, 317; inspired, VIII, 222.
Discoveries, VIII, 466.
Discussion, reform, X, 216.
Disease, laws of, IV, 455.
Diseases, seeds of, X, 48.
Disguised gods, III, 443.
Disguises, thin, II, 406; the spirit behind, IV, 163.
Disillusioning, life's, VIII, 402.
Disillusionment, III, 69.
Dismal art, VIII, 553.
Dispute, rude, VI, 389.
Disproportion, vice in manners, IX, 341.
Disraeli, VI, 526; VII, 485, 503; O'Connell on, VII, 172.
Dissatisfaction, II, 469.
Dissenter, the, VII, 359.
Distinction, IV, 437.
Districts of thought, VI, 42.
Disunion, IX, 211.
Divine, the, V, 223; in all, III, 321.
Divinity School, Cambridge, the, VI, 104; E. enters, reflections, II, 54; starved at, III, 502.
Divinity School Address, V, 21.
Divinity students, talk to, IV, 420.
Dixon, IX, 4.
Doctors, VI, 402; enthusiasm of, IV, 455, 456.
Doctrines, essential, II, 355.
Doddridge, Dr., Burnap on, II, 237.
Dodging truth, V, 301.
Dodington, Bubb, VIII, 576.
Dog on stage, IX, 146.
Dogmas, religious, pass, II, 120; mischievous, VII, 467.

Doherty, Hugh, VII, 459.
Dollar, the, VII, 288.
Dollars, V, 379.
Domestic manners, and morals, I, 221, 222.
Domestication, VI, 12.
Domo d' Ossola, III, 147.
Donne, VIII, 46; counsel of, II, 291; extracts from, II, 347; verse of, on unity, IV, 252; Cowley, and, proverbs, IV, 254.
Doubts, II, 159.
Drake, Sir Francis, verses on, VII, 365.
Drama, I, 54–57; 106–08; 127; 147–50; 166; 169, 170; 335.
Dramatic fragment (blank verse), I, 254–56.
Dramatic material, VII, 512.
Dramatists, the old, VII, 88.
Dream, a pictorial, IX, 338; of physics and metaphysics, X, 301.
Dreams, II, 448; III, 334; IV, 287; 323; 424; VII, 409; and beasts, II, 453; of idealists, III, 463; and animals, III, 533; landscape not fitting, IV, 388; debate on marriage, V, 499; supply part of education, VI, 178–80; alarming hints from, IX, 120, 121; cannot be recalled, IX, 354; wonder of, X, 174; illusions of, X, 314.
Dress, mood and, VI, 40.
Drifting, study and, III, 460.
Drill, VIII, 165; or creation, IV, 269.
Drones, IX, 186.
Dualism, IV, 248; 435, 436; V, 206; VIII, 211.
Duelling, II, 249.
Dull, the, VIII, 495; freemasonry of the, II, 147.
Dumas, VII, 302.
Dumesnil, A., quoted, X, 110.
Dunbar of Saltoun, III, 537.
Dundee church, VII, 399.
Duomo, III, 104.
Duties, VIII, 76; coming, II, 166; done, III, 519.
Duty, reality of, II, 455; glorious post of, III, 286; is plain, III, 472; a god in disguise, IV, 37; others' opinion of your, IV, 64; first, VIII, 13; our representative, VIII, 469.
Dwight, John S., IV, 456.

INDEX

Each and all, II, 7; III, 298; III, 373; V, 184; treatise on perspective, IV, 21; a day a child, IV, 26; humblest facts serving education, IV, 70; drop a small ocean, IV, 71; and human will, IV, 101; Nature flowering of soul, IV, 282; know all to know one, V, 191; Nature microscopically rich, V, 418; lesson of, VI, 186. *See especially* passages on Nature.

Earning a living, IV, 341, 342.

Earth, illusion of, VIII, 553.

"Earth Song," VII, 127–29.

Earth Spirit, VI, 347.

East and West, VII, 291.

Easter mass in St. Peter's, III, 88.

Eating, man's repulsive, V, 345.

Ecclesiastical councils, VIII, 495.

Ecclesiastical manners, IV, 171.

Echo, the horn's, V, 246.

Eckermann, IV, 199–201.

Eclipse of sun, III, 374.

Economies, individual, VI, 327.

Economy, IX, 162; brave, II, 322; in work agreeable to one's nature, V, 320; real, VI, 513; Nature's, VIII, 232.

Ecstasy and the soul, V, 514.

Edda, VII, 304, 561; Hafiz and, on Fate and Freedom, VII, 269, 270.

Edinburgh, VII, 388; 395.

Edinburgh Review, I, 293.

Education, nowadays, I, 343, 344; good signs in children, II, 246; means of, II, 412; true, coming, III, 350; for adversity, for princes, V, 71; ineffective, Roman rule better, V, 250; raises man above circumstance, V, 441, 442; from Plato, VI, 186; importance of outdoor life and games, IX, 40, 41; at University, X, 38; from intimacy with masters, X, 199; Latin and Greek in, X, 338.

Edwards, *On the Will*, I, 286.

Église Catholique Française, III, 168.

Ego, the solemn, V, 277.

Egotism, V, 431; IX, 519; Nemesis of, V, 384.

Egypt, X, 165; 406–10.

Egyptian temples, IX, 123.

Egyptians, the, I, 321.

Elasticity of a man, IX, 491.

Eleatic school, Xenophanes, Parmenides, Zeno, Heraclitus, Hippocrates, II, 342–45.

Elect, the, V, 375.

Election, V, 78; November, IV, 148; the presidential, VII, 548; of Abraham Lincoln, IX, 286.

Elections, the, III, 358.

Electricity of thought, VI, 328.

Elegance, V, 194.

Elements, all, needed, V, 237; and animals, VI, 407.

Elevation in sorrow, II, 433.

Eliot, John, X, 303.

Elizabethan, the, VIII, 325.

Eloquence, IV, 360; value of simplicity in, I, 73; written or spoken, V, 6; wish for, VI, 493; prodigality, VII, 105; hot or high, VII, 152; enriching, VIII, 147, 148; its difficulties, VIII, 170; war of posts, VIII, 242; test of, VIII, 313. *See also* Conversation, Market, Phillips, W., Pulpit.

Eloquent man, the, V, 48, 49.

Elssler, Fanny, dancing of, VI, 89–91.

Emancipation, IX, 441–43.

Emblems, III, 225, 226; life all, V, 461.

Emerson, Charles Chauncy, IV, 396; remark of, II, 87; letters to, II, 162; letter to, on writing, II, 170–72; departure of, II, 436; on Christianity and the English Church, III, 547, 548; on Carlyle, III, 557; quoted, III, 560; walk and talk with, III, 570–72; talk with, on motives, IV, 14, 15; death of, his life, thought and letters, IV, 39–50; letters about, IV, 63; memories of, IV, 139–41; quoted on love, IV, 409; Edward and, the brothers, V, 545; attraction of, family history, V, 546, 547; Edward Lowell and, VI, 394.

Emerson, Edith, birth of, VI, 130; rejects Heaven, VIII, 256.

Emerson, Edward Bliss, II, 245; IV, 396; letter to, II, 113; return from Europe of, II, 117; letters to, on moments, II, 170; letter to:

INDEX

Dr. Channing and inferior clergy, II, 202; sketch for Sermon by, II, 247; letter in verse to, III, 216; death of, his deliverance, III, 346-48; "Farewell" of, III, 450; epigrammatic answers, III, 565; superiority of, IV, 27; high tone of, V, 545; and Charles, the brothers, V, 545.

Emerson, Ellen T. (daughter), VI, 215; X, 247; birth of, V, 166, 167.

Emerson, Ellen Tucker (wife), II, 218; 293; 406; III, 570; V, 165; VI, 379; engagement to, II, 255, 256; lines to, II, 257; 265, 266; 406; words of, II, 434; death of, II, 356; verses to, II, 384; memories of, III, 258; verses of, VII, 357.

Emerson, George B., IV, 139; botany with, V, 3; on trees, VI, 456.

Emerson, Joseph, of Malden, his diary, VII, 338-41.

Emerson, Mrs. Lidian, III, 446; marriage to, III, 543; on gossip of the hour, V, 70; the wife's counsel, V, 93, 94; on reform-diet, VI, 346.

Emerson, Mary Moody, V, 547; VI, 107; 390; IX, 26, 28, 29; X, 148; her religion, I, 77; on Genius, I, 97; letter to, I, 324-27; letter from: reproof, I, 330-35; letter to, I, 356-59; letter from, I, 370-73; letter to, I, 374-77; letter to, Byron's death, II, 4; reproving letter, "Holy Ghost," II, 27-32; letter to, II, 63-66; 77, 78; 83-85; 90-92; 99-105; 105-10; 111, 112; 121-23; 124; 173-75; letter to, E.'s improving health, House of Pain, its benefit, resignation not easy, II, 178-81; letter to Mrs. Ripley, II, 191-94; letter to, Alexandria, *Bride of Lammermoor*, aspirations for art, letters, and science an argument for immortality, II, 203-05; letter to, dissolving of creed after death, immortality, fear of death, II, 210-12; letter, let preacher give from own store, II, 214; letter to, genius and domesticity of, II, 216; letter to, religious feeling keeps alive; reason in religion, God within, II, 220-25; letter to, prosperity of family, trust against misgiving, II, 258-60; letter to, Human progress, cheering miracle of life, the idea of God, II, 272-74; letter to, Coleridge, conventional or living sermon, II, 276-79; quoted, II, 281; X, 67; 137; 168; letter to, II, 440; penetration of, II, 525; letter to, III, 100-03; on prayer, III, 383; her watcher, IV, 262, 263; on sermons, IV, 445; subtlety of, IV, 480; letters to, ideals and society, V, 95-97; original wild genius of, family quotations, her letter to Charles, Waterford, V, 539-43; letters and influence of, VI, 468; double prayer of, VII, 331; and medicine, VIII, 53; writing of, VIII, 152; on the soul, VIII, 167; blessing of, VIII, 523; amenities of, VIII, 569; and Dr. Johnson, IX, 234; quotations from, IX, 264, 265; 570, 571; death of, IX, 508; speaking of angels, X, 66; read Tasso, X, 202; and good society, X, 302; inspiration of her writing, X, 325; perception of character, X, 383.

Emerson, Ralph, cousin, III, 156.

Emerson, Ruth Haskins, Madam, III, 269; remark of, II, 430; death of, her influence and character, VIII, 427, 428.

Emerson, Waldo, IV, 198; 255; V, 9; 387; 411; birth of, IV, 134; baptism of, IV, 232; and his mother, IV, 432, 433; sayings of, V, 166; prayer of, V, 496; death of, his sayings, VI, 150-54; memory of, VI, 165, 166; anniversary of death, VI, 488.

Emerson, William, E.'s brother, IV, 65; VI, 165; letters to, II, 162; 182; visit of, IV, 235; his probity, IX, 319.

Emerson, William, E.'s grandfather, III, 444; walking proudly, VI, 469; family of, X, 55.

Emigrants, Irish, X, 153.

Endymion, the Capitoline, V, 341.

Engineers and writers, X, 23.

England, III, 171-76; VIII, 343; voyage to, Thoreau left as guardian, VII, 336, 337; landing, VII, 342,

INDEX

343; street sights, VII, 355; climate and manners, VII, 375; birth and manners in, toughness and materialism, VII, 400, 401; the country of the rich, VII, 409; return to, VII, 474; limitations and solidity of, VIII, 73; America's claim on, VIII, 317; her fear of science, her lacks, VIII, 337; measure of, VIII, 349; results of, VIII, 361, 362; wealth and inventions of, VIII, 370; wealth of able men, VIII, 384; spell of, VIII, 388; and France, VIII, 402; flowering of, VIII, 407; is two nations, VIII, 447; Rome of to-day, her solidarity, VIII, 464; the two nations in, VIII, 500; cause of first visit to, VIII, 500; view of, VIII, 522; her epic, IX, 208; no higher worship than Fate, IX, 367; ticketing men, IX, 554; during Civil War, IX, 555; X, 56–58; and America, IX, 571–73.

England, True account of the Island of, VII, 378.

English, childish in Middle Ages, III, 554; impressions of the, VII, 352–55; and American, VIII, 136; and Ambassadors, VIII, 275; a good mixture, VIII, 374; the athletic, VIII, 489; of 16th and 17th centuries, VIII, 544; Defoe quoted, IX, 299.

English acquaintance, VII, 489.

English and American elementary education, VII, 530.

English and French characteristics, VIII, 460.

English aristocracy, X, 16.

English authors, weighed, man and writer must be one, IV, 356, 357; debt to a few, VIII, 494.

English bards, VII, 158.

English blank verse, III, 554.

English book *versus* German book, IX, 182.

English brag, VIII, 326.

English castles, IX, 220.

English Chapel, the, III, 33.

English Church, Christianity and the, Charles Emerson on, III, 547, 548.

English coachmen, VII, 361.

English despair, VIII, 416.

English dinner, the, VII, 487.

English elegies, III, 371.

English finality, VIII, 507.

English finish, VII, 438.

English flowers, III, 175.

English genius, VIII, 360.

English government generous, VIII, 383.

English great men, want of religion in, III, 198.

English language, fine old, VIII, 491.

English limitations, VIII, 302, 303.

English literary history, VI, 481.

English merchants and scholars, VII, 419.

English names, VIII, 325.

English poetry, the splendor of, II, 253.

English poets, old, VIII, 503.

English precedent mischievous in America, IX, 9.

English reformers, no affinity with, VI, 385, 386; and conservatives, VIII, 469.

English religion, VIII, 321.

English reserves, exclusiveness, VIII, 391.

English scholarship, VIII, 11.

English speech, strong, IV, 304.

English statesmen, VIII, 365, 366.

English talent, modern advance, VIII, 381.

English tenacity, VII, 415, 416.

English Traits, IX, 64.

English triumphs in science, art, and letters, VII, 363.

English unchastity, talk on, VII, 440, 441.

English university men, VIII, 353, 354.

English vessels, III, 17.

English visit, result of, VII, 524.

English women, VII, 413.

English worthies, VII, 363, 364.

English writers, individual, III, 508; old and modern, VIII, 550.

Englishman and American, VII, 405; practical, heavy, VII, 419; pocket of, VIII, 545; firm manners of, X, 268.

Englishmen, good, VII, 551.

Ennui, VIII, 405.

INDEX 499

Enthusiasm, I, 211-13; needed, IX, 559.
Enthusiasts, Swedenborgians, Quakers, Methodists, II, 318.
Envy, unreasonable, II, 483.
Enweri; his *Spring*, VIII, 105.
Epaminondas, V, 165.
Epigrams, IX, 13, 14.
Epilogue, to *Wide World*, I, 265.
Epitaph, VIII, 109; of Charlemagne's mother, VIII, 428.
Epochs of life, V, 198.
Equality, VII, 229; of great men, III, 410; mystical in Nature, V, 487.
Equalizations, VIII, 328.
Eras, VII, 68; three, VII, 77, 78; in philosophy, IX, 295; triumphs and, X, 103.
Erigena, Johannes Scotus, quoted, X, 112.
Espinesse, VII, 384.
Essays, matter for, III, 480; the first, V, 506; given to friends, V, 519, 520.
Essence of life, X, 460.
Estabrook farms, VIII, 485; walk to, IX, 274.
Eternal, party of the, IX, 217.
Eternal man, the, VI, 20.
Eternity, V, 209; scholar's assurance of, III, 563.
Ethics, do not satisfy, I, 379; sovereignty of, II, 160; bind Christian and Theist, II, 355; sovereignty of, truth precedes Christianity, II, 516.
Eton, X, 46; visit to, VII, 490.
Eudoxus, II, 342.
Euler, III, 356.
Europe, V, 393; old, III, 16; comes to us in books, III, 202; culture from, VI, 264; England and, VIII, 43; aim in, VIII, 516.
European characteristics, VII, 240, 241.
European influences, VIII, 334.
European mark, VIII, 524.
European writers, IV, 92-95.
Evangelical lady and her uncle, VII, 412.
Eve has no clock, IV, 9.
Evelyn, story of, VIII, 453.
Evening star, X, 135.

Event, tie of person and, VIII, 244.
Events, IX, 188; help, IV, 334; seen freshly, VI, 453, 454.
Everett, Alexander and James Savage, III, 375.
Everett, Edward, Plymouth Oration of, II, 45-47; II, 123; III, 471; IV, 359; IV, 471; VIII, 112; lecture of, I, 21; 207; quoted, I, 67: sermon of, I, 76, 81; Phi Beta Kappa Oration of, II, 100; and slavery, III, 517; account of, VI, 255-57; service of, VI, 403; inauguration of, VII, 166-69; tarnished fame of, VIII, 182; forgets his speeches, VIII, 199; brought us German thought, VIII, 225; pictured terrors of, VIII, 232.
Evidences of heaven, II, 215.
Evil, existence of, I, 115; reason of, II, 120; not normal, IV, 167.
Evil days cry for cure, III, 348.
Evil times also do good, III, 256.
Exact sciences, the, I, 59.
Exaggeration, VI, 65.
Exaltation, VIII, 291.
Example, V, 108; do not worry about, II, 287.
Excellence, VI, 414; justifies, IX, 449.
Exchanges of pulpit, II, 428.
Exclusion, VIII, 582.
Exclusives, VI, 81.
Exhibition Day, I, 67.
Expense for conformity, V, 429.
Experience not valid against soul, V, 519; and idea the twins, VI, 61; promise from, VIII, 257.
Experiment, life is, VI, 302.
Experimental writing, VI, 160.
Experimenting in life, V, 460.
Experiments on living, IV, 194.
Explanation of men, III, 466.
Explorers needed, IV, 388.
Expressing one's self, IV, 418.
Expression, III, 417; Sir James Mackintosh on, II, 477; imitative writing unsound, IV, 34-36; importance of a line, IV, 321; full, rare, VI, 84; good, rare, VI, 92.
Expressors the gods, VIII, 95.
Extempore speaking, IX, 58.
Extravagance, public, VIII, 279.

INDEX

Eye, the, discerning, II, 403; witness of, III, 564; joy of, IV, 358.
Eyes, V, 21; VI, 327; value of, II, 99; and tongue, happy, III, 521; new, IV, 321; of women and men, V, 335; revealing, V, 537; seeing without, VI, 157; asking, VI, 347; and no eyes, VIII, 42.

Fables, a collection, IX, 208.
Face, VI, 40.
Faces, V, 79; V, 269; VIII, 85; IV, 63; two, IV, 291; expression of, V, 126.
Facility, a walking, VIII, 258.
Fact, interpreting of, V, 298.
Faction, V, 64.
Facts, IV, 473; 498; marriage of, II, 288; the great, II, 327; ideas or, III, 519; rank themselves, III, 553; poetry in humblest, IV, 70; the day's gift of, IV, 488; use of, V, 44; detached ugly, V, 54; overvalued, V, 77; settle into place, V, 79; or doctrines, V, 92; hive, V, 418; God gives, find their reason, V, 513; as horses, VI, 157; beautiful, VI, 275; one's own, VII, 465; a superstition to English, VIII, 417; and ideas, IX, 409.
Failures make success, III, 334.
Fairy gifts, VI, 415.
Faith, a telescope, II, 27; when in study, II, 441; sincere, suspected, III, 479; beauty needs, V, 236; increase our, V, 428; poetry of, VIII, 367.
Faiths, curiosity as to other, IV, 101, 102.
Falkland, IV, 320; Clarendon on, IV, 264.
Fall, the soul's, IV, 490.
Falling, V, 163.
False One, The, V, 186.
False, true and, VIII, 223.
Falsehood, X, 338.
Fame, VII, 53; 198; VIII, 140; IX, 214; mankind awards, V, 266; house of, VIII, 205; common, VIII, 528–30; righting itself, X, 145; and fossils, X, 167.
Fame, added verse to poem, II, 210.
Familiarity, IX, 436.
Families, New England, X, 269.

Family types, VIII, 263.
Fanaticism for performance, IX, 203.
Fancies, boy's, VI, 46.
Fancy, V, 121; the Gift of, I, 63, 64; and imagination, III, 525.
Fancy, verses, I, 65, 66.
Faneuil Hall Canons, the, IV, 359, 360.
Faraday, X, 140; Liebig to, on pure science, VIII, 487; on force, IX, 106, 107.
Farewell to St. Augustine, verses, II, 181.
Farie, models of, VII, 450.
Farm, boy on a, IV, 239; the, as school, V, 251; E.'s, VIII, 274.
Farm pests, VI, 388.
Farm work, effect of, VII, 63.
Farmer, the, I, 322; VI, 402; indirect good deeds of, VI, 442.
Farmers, VII, 50; brave, IV, 429, 430; alliance of coming, VI, 193; old-time, VII, 506, 507; respect for, VIII, 72, 73.
Farming, X, 270; follow your calling, V, 390.
Fashion, VI, 96; VII, 130; infernal infantry of, VI, 93.
Fashionist in novels, II, 263.
Fashionists, barometers, V, 319.
Fast-Day Sermon, II, 369–71.
Fate, VI, 225; VII, 553; VIII, 239; IX, 162; time and, fix relations, V, 429; character over, VI, 188, 189; music-box, VI, 317; part of, VII, 559; and freedom, Hafiz and *Edda* on, VII, 269, 270; part of, VII, 559; view of, in society, VIII, 218; competition, VIII, 222; child of, history selects, IX, 114; or circumstance, IX, 115; the necessary and the eternal, IX, 216; and opinions of men, X, 471; souls with and without light, X, 472. *See also* England, Hafiz, India, Instinct, Rectitude.
Fate, verses, II, 80.
Father, mother, and child, IV, 134, 135; good, X, 197.
Fathers, IV, 80.
Favors, conferring, II, 437.
Fear, of criticism, I, 295, 296; of light, V, 149; instructs, V, 202.

INDEX

Fears, transient, III, 353.
Feats, IX, 63; seemingly impossible, VIII, 137.
February thaw, VII, 6.
Federal Government, war-power of, VIII, 28.
Feminine genius of Americans, IV, 87.
Fénelon, II, 387; saying of, II, 285.
Ferney, and Voltaire, III, 152.
Fero, the family of, III, 232.
Ferrara: Tasso, Ariosto, Byron, Jews, III, 127.
Feuerbach, VIII, 77.
Fichte, III, 260; VI, 62.
Fiction, I, 128.
Finalities, none in Nature, VIII, 446.
Financial crisis, the, IV, 209, 210.
Finishers, VIII, 17.
Firdousi, saying of, VIII, 426.
Fire, symbolism, VI, 316, 317; the village, III, 26, 27.
Fireflies, dew and, VI, 212.
First in one's career, VII, 58.
First philosophy, great laws of, III, 489.
First thoughts, and second, II, 436; coincidence of, and third, II, 435; from God, III, 323.
Fisher the Quaker, VIII, 141.
Fitchburg Railroad, X, 313.
Fitness, II, 82.
Flag, the, II, 148; IX, 410.
Flattery in dedications, VIII, 540.
Flaxman, Dante of, IV, 77.
Fletcher, John, V, 185.
Flint's Pond, IX, 110.
Floating ice, VII, 527.
Florence, III, 104; X, 5; 411; leaving, III, 125.
Flower and immortality, V, 425.
Flower-girl, the, Erminia, III, 119.
Flowers, III, 284; VIII, 312; on walk, IX, 43-45; as gifts, X, 160.
Flowing, the, heed the lesson, V, 494, 495.
Fluxions, IX, 361.
Fontenelle, VIII, 348.
Fool of the family, VIII, 348.
"Foolish face of praise," IV, 290.
Fools, wise, IX, 179.
Forbes, John Murray, IX, 377, 378; X, 72-75; 351.

Forbes, Miss Margaret P., letter to, IX, 170.
Force, II, 276; within, II, 472.
Forces, composition of, IV, 305, 306; insufficient, VII, 305; moral, IX, 491; live, IX, 573.
Forefathers, honor to the, II, 371.
Forefathers' Day, verses, II, 33, 34.
Foreignness, loved one's, VIII, 540.
Forerunners, VII, 79.
Foresight, V, 390.
Forest, V, 456; go to the, if poet, V, 444; alluring, VI, 516.
Forest joys, IV, 439.
Foresters, E.'s thoughts are, V, 513.
Forethought and afterthought, II, 94.
Foreworld, the, V, 184.
Forgiveness, II, 254.
Form, pathos of, V, 25.
Forms, shaking off, V, 349.
Forster, John, Carlyle, and Dickens, dinner with, VII, 440, 441.
Fort Hatteras, IX, 337.
Fortune, you carry your own, II, 250.
Fortunate generation, II, 147.
Fortunes, vast, X, 230.
Fossil remains, IX, 343.
Fosters, the, mobbed, VII, 178.
Foundation, our perilous, V, 427.
Four walls, VI, 315.
Fourier, VI, 439; 516; VII, 20; 161.
Fourth of July dinner, III, 158.
Fowler of Tennessee, X, 71.
Fox, Charles James, I, 317-20; VII, 515; VIII, 340; Choate on English and, VIII, 558.
Fox, Captain, clipper voyage of, III, 204.
Fox, George, II, 497-500; III, 493.
Fragments of men, VI, 129.
France, III, 154; VII, 409; VII, 450-74; VIII, 343; 429; and England, VII, 122; notes on, quotations, VIII, 430-33; Montalembert's statement, IX, 63; palace of arithmetic, X, 260.
Francis, Eben, VIII, 227.
Franklin, Benjamin, I, 320; *versus* Homer, I, 376; transcendentalist and, VII, 268; on babies, VIII, 502.

INDEX

Frascati's, III, 169.
Free thinking, I, 238–42; explosive, VI, 470.
Free trade, II, 314; X, 228.
Freedom, V, 119; of man, II, 272; Heaven guards, II, 376; of the wise, II, 388; the terrible, II, 517; and conviction, III, 328; devout, III, 378, 379; the scholar's, V, 31; cherish, V, 220; only way to, VI, 270; of slaveholder, VIII, 382; party of, IX, 49; of the town, IX, 329.
Freed-woman, the Plymouth, IV, 184.
Frémont, vanity of, VII, 206.
Frémont, Mrs., IX, 382, 383.
French, V, 522; rising esteem for the, VII, 468; have street courage, VII, 487; and English, VIII, 37; English and, characteristics, VIII, 460; and metaphysics, IX, 147; the, on English, IX, 200.
French architecture, VII, 452.
French boulevards, VII, 452.
French calculation, VII, 11.
French eclecticism, Cousin's book, IV, 404.
French influence, VII, 465.
French lack of *morale*, VIII, 249.
French language, VIII, 474.
French poetry, VII, 451.
French Revolution, III, 448; VII, 403.
French sentences, VIII, 154.
French traits, VII, 452.
Friction, VII, 153.
Friend, the Possible, I, 28; 80; denied, I, 197; idealizing a, IX, 538; effect of, X, 247.
Friend, The Possible, verses, I, 70.
Friend, To the Possible, poem, I, 61.
Friends, sacred property, II, 242; aid of, III, 268; exacting, V, 451, 452; love of, V, 453; superior, VII, 243; contrasts in, VIII, 293; X, 278; E.'s, X, 357; help of, X, 389; in England, X, 395, 396.
Friendship, I, 314; IX, 273; phantoms, II, 95; longing for, II, 404; an ideal, IV, 464; troubles of, V, 343; reverent, its tides, V, 362; Guy learns, V, 367; true, V, 467, 468; imperfect, VI, 244; paradox of, VI, 505; is truth, VII, 30; and eternal laws, X, 188. *See also* Communities, Mass.
Friendships, two strong natures, IV, 77.
Fringes, the, of life, VI, 419.
Frothingham, Nathaniel Langdon, IV, 272.
Froude, quoted, IX, 215.
Fruit and seed, VIII, 238.
Fruit trees, planters of, VII, 501.
Fruitlands, Alcott describes scheme, VI, 304, 305; visit to, VI, 420, 421; limitations, VI, 452; tragedy and Alcott, VI, 503–05.
Fugitive Slave Law, VIII, 179–82; the old and the new, VIII, 193, 194.
Fugitive Slave Law Speech in New York, VIII, 447, 448.
Fuller, Margaret, IV, 333; VI, 87; 233, 234; visit of, IV, 79; German lessons from, IV, 225; letter to, the period of unrest, IV, 256, 257; portfolio of pictures, IV, 465; letter to, V, 65–67; and F. H. Hedge, V, 248; visit of Alcott and, V, 292; and intervening gulf, V, 324, 325; talk with, VI, 78; unsettled rank of, VI, 97; gypsy talent, VI, 277, 278; riches of thought, generosity, elevation, *Nuovissima Vita*, VI, 363–66; verses of, VI, 369; letter to, in Rome, VII, 283; word from, VII, 368; dies in wreck, her friends, her traits, testimonies of friends, VIII, 115–19; letters of, VIII, 142–44; in society, VIII, 173; *gentilesse* of, VIII, 217; illuminator not writer, VIII, 249, 250.
Fuller, Thomas, his *Worthies of England*, IV, 322.
Furness, William H., X, 442, 443.
Fuseli, on the Greeks, VIII, 560.
Future, living in the, I, 168; E. faces the uncertain, II, 71; the unknown, II, 511; the appeal to the, IV, 328, 329; present and, VII, 332.
Future state, II, 427.

Galen, II, 473.
Galileo, II, 466; homage to, III, 106.

INDEX

Galleries, III, 111.
Gallic cock, VII, 457.
Gambler, VI, 338.
Game, the, VI, 60; the old, VI, 5.
Garden, VII, 293; is honest, VI, 397.
Garden diary, VIII, 47, 48.
Gardening, IV, 271; V, 457.
Gardening medicine, IV, 236.
Gardens, III, 95; VI, 448; and architecture, V, 27, 28.
Gardiner, William, quotations from, IV, 364, 365.
Gardiner, Mr., American Consul in Palermo, VII, 59.
Garrison, William Lloyd, V, 302, 303; VII, 97; IX, 49; X, 18; thunders for peace, VI, 101, 102; honor to, VI, 541; virtue and fault of, VIII, 99; and Phillips, VIII, 433, 434; IX, 455.
Gaston de Foy, V, 452.
Gates and Burgoyne, V, 170.
Gates of thought are found late, VI, 196.
Gauge, everyman's, II, 413.
Gauss, IX, 117.
Gay Lussac, III, 170.
Gay, Martin, I, 238.
Gazetted terms, VIII, 280.
Gems, V, 375.
Genealogy, VIII, 121; of thought, III, 363.
Generals of Civil War, X, 66.
Generation, duty of our, V, 311.
Generation, the, unconscious, VI, 60.
Generalization, IX, 125.
Generalizers are the nobility, VIII, 419, 420.
Generalizing, power of, VIII, 339.
Generic man, acts and emotions in common, IV, 228.
Generous feelings, III, 394.
Geneva, Gibbon's house, III, 151.
Geneva ministers, III, 153.
Genius, *versus* Knowledge, I, 312, 313; is reception, II, 363; is true seeing, IV, 421; anything serves, IV, 252-54; surprises, IV, 284; growth of, IV, 421; anything serves, IV, 436; rare, V, 6; charm, an emanation, V, 144; shirking reform, V, 344, 345; bids work, V, 443; obey even when leading to deserts, V, 530; draws the curtain, V, 553, 554; unsettles all, VI, 23; shafts uniting, VI, 86; all pardoned to, VI, 237; and talent, VI, 370, 371; is tyrannical, VI, 474; the, of the world, VII, 59; unavailable, VII, 120; balance in, VII, 155; charm of, VII, 197; feat of, VII, 295; penalty of, VII, 466; traits of, IX, 312, 313; meets all the conditions, X, 250; devotion of, X, 461; is on great highways, X, 467; works upon inexhaustible part of man, X, 474. *See also* Asiatic, Bonaparte, Carlyle, Emerson, M. M., English, Greek, Health, Influence, Morale, Talent, Temperance, Transfer, Uproar, Virtue, Wonder.
Gentility, real, VI, 71.
Gentleman, a, V, 169; the English, III, 494; and Christian, V, 549; truth and, VII, 75.
Gentlemen, VII, 10; meeting of, VI, 197.
Gentz, *Diary*, quoted, IX, 445.
Genuineness, II, 507.
Geology, sublime, IX, 122.
Geometer, trust the great, VIII, 91.
German, reading, VI, 357.
German, the startled, VI, 79; hidden dreamer, VII, 151.
German criticism of Christian evidences, II, 83.
German culture, X, 53.
Germans, IX, 30, 31; and English, IX, 22.
Germany, VIII, 69; and America, V, 203; elusive, VII, 532.
Giant of Chimborazo, I, 133.
Giants, VIII, 335.
Gibbet at Liverpool, VII, 379.
Gibbet-irons, II, 163.
Gibbon, Edward, I, 290; VII, 100; Hume and, II, 121, 122; house of, Geneva, III, 151.
Gibraltar, Straits of, III, 21, 22.
Gift (ability), to each his, II, 457; apparent to those it helps, VI, 186.
Gift, a wedding, V, 479, 480.
Gifts (abilities), III, 384; sympathy with others', III, 384; of man, the, IV, 120; others', V, 19; varied, IX, 41.
Gifts, IV, 214; 440; X, 160.

INDEX

Giotto, III, 115.
Girl, the high-minded, IV, 379.
Girls, idealizing, IV, 380; golden mean in temperaments of, VIII, 314; boarding-schools for, VIII, 397.
Gladiator, The, and Byron, III, 99.
Glances, IV, 204.
Glasgow, III, 179; VII, 393.
Glasgow University, X, 436.
Gleams, III, 277; from Nature, V, 489.
Gloucester land-purchase, VIII, 170.
Gnothi seauton, II, 395.
God, I, 150–57; 164; within, II, 23; 225; ideas of, II, 289; thought, not experiment, finds, II, 317; substratum of souls, II, 323; neighbor's claim through, II, 353; in all, II, 358; misrepresenting, II, 408; door of, II, 409; the soul, II, 501; clear relation to, III, 274; all works for, III, 282; idea of changes, III, 465; cannot be described, III, 517; in man, individual and universal, IV, 121; in writing always suppose, IV, 270; be not too wise, IV, 417; do not speak of, much, IV, 475; ideas of, V, 73; now, here, face to face, V, 135, 136; the living, neglected, V, 498; your share of, V, 498; the word, VIII, 4. See also Benevolence, Child, Communion, Conscience, Deity, Emerson, M. M., Facts, First, Great, Idea, Idolatries, Invention, Light, Living, Nature, Person, Personality, Pilot, Plotinus, Prayer, Private, Reason, Religion, Renunciation, Resources, Seed, Sermon, Servant, Silsbee, W., Thought, Truth, Universe, Woods, Writing.
God's Message, verses, III, 212.
Godliness, IV, 21.
Gods in ancient art, IX, 136.
Goethe, III, 474; IV, 116; 468; V, 506; VII, 303; extracts from, II, 348–50; vanity of, III, 251; another poor monad, III, 309; and morals, self-culture, III, 313, 314; quotations from, IV, 16, 17; 27; time's verdict on him, IV, 29, 30; judgment of, IV, 212, 213; estimates of, IV, 218; on Seneca and Tycho Brahe, IV, 221, 222; naming of, V, 59, 60; help of, V, 222; service of, V, 395; his *Helena*, VI, 466; breadth and felicity of, VI, 514; strength of, VI, 544, 545; profusion of, VII, 176; quoted, on Napoleon, VII, 280; on Megadhuta, VII, 291, 292; his *Faust*, VIII, 70; his *Winckelmann*, VIII, 91, 92; the pivot, VIII, 249.
Golden mean, the, VI, 22; resources in danger, III, 195.
Golden age, the, V, 401.
Goldoni, III, 8; IV, 343.
Gonzalo, kingdom of, VI, 461.
Good, seen everywhere, II, 11; the unseen, in man, II, 434; normal, evil not, IV, 167; of evil, IX, 304.
Good action, set to grow, II, 442.
Good-bye, Proud World, Poem, I, 347; 368.
Good cause, furtherance of Nature, X, 107.
Good company: fire, water, woods, birds, V, 134.
Good sense, V, 556.
Good writing rare, IX, 345.
Goodies, IV, 443; 491, 492.
Goodness, natural, II, 285; smiles, IV, 112.
Goodwin, Rev. Hersey, sermon of, III, 563.
Goose Pond, IV, 118; V, 161; IX, 91.
Gorgias, VII, 309, 310.
Gospel, at first hand, VIII, 532.
Gospels, and literature, X, 171.
Gothic, cross of Greek and, VIII, 417.
Governing machine, the, VIII, 217.
Government, VI, 527; an obstruction, IX, 51, 52; bad, IX, 267; our, our people and, IX, 369.
Governments, unheroic, IX, 364, 365.
Governor of Malta, III, 35.
Grace, X, 145.
Grace, Robin says, VI, 29.
Grahamite gospel, the, V, 101.
Grandeur, in common folk, VI, 16; time necessary to, VI, 329; from war opportunity, IX, 519.
Grandfather, word of, III, 234; and baby, VI, 203.

INDEX

Grant, General, x, 93.
Gratitude, II, 375.
Grattan, x, 218; quoted, IX, 299.
Gravestones, two, VIII, 20.
Gravitation, VIII, 8.
Gray, Thomas, and Michel Angelo, x, 268.
Great, the way of the, II, 167.
Great Ages, the, v, 565.
Great causes belittled by converts, VI, 120, 121.
Great man, a contradiction to his age, IX, 192; between God and mob, IV, 150.
Great men, limitations of, their value, III, 185, 186; ties of, III, 211; Alfred, Washington, IV, 183, 184; history in a few names, v, 132, 133; uses of, VII, 32.
Greatness, I, 121–23; 200; imperfect, II, 79; elevation of reason, II, 354; we postpone our, III, 272; not cheaply won, III, 476; simple and kindly, IV, 391; Plato and Swedenborg, VIII, 39; from one gift, IX, 114, 115; thoughts rule the world, IX, 175; high steps in character, x, 168; expansion of, x, 238. *See also* Artificial, Riches.
Greaves Library, the, VI, 290, 291.
Greece, I, 158; our debt to, III, 418, 419; art of, IV, 327; fate in India and, VII, 123; games of, IX, 279.
Greek and Gothic, VII, 247; cross of, VIII, 417.
Greek courage and humors, VII, 257.
Greek drama, chorus, IV, 25.
Greek fable, VIII, 410.
Greek genius, the, IV, 144.
Greek language, resolution about, I, 22.
Greek mythology, VIII, 360, 361.
Greek philosophers, II, 336–45.
Greeks, the, I, 388; v, 434; picture of, v, 15; old English study of the, VIII, 499; immortality of, VIII, 525, 526; wrote their metaphysics in names, IX, 559, 560.
Greeley, Horace, VII, 136; IX, 49; energy of, VIII, 229.
Greenfield, I, 280, 281.
Greenough, Horatio, visit of, his philosophy and art, VIII, 318–21; sayings of, VIII, 331, 332; death of, his praise, VIII, 389, 390; on influence of climate, VIII, 552.
Greville, Fulke, VIII, 5.
Grey, Earl, x, 216.
Grief, v, 110; cure of, v, 115; man sheds, VI, 403.
Grimm, Friedrich, quoted, VIII, 425.
Grimm, Herman, quoted, IX, 233; on Vasari, IX, 307; friend not introduced to, x, 142; meeting in Florence, x, 411, 412.
Grove, the, IV, 433.
Growth, IX, 520.
Guest in your own house, be, IV, 189; or friend, VI, 41, 42.
Guide, the, VIII, 206.
Guido, *Aurora* of, v, 217; 341.
Guizot, IX, 87.
Gurney, Ephraim Wales, x, 244.
Gurowski, Adam, IX, 303.
Gustavus Adolphus, v, 315.
Gypsies and apostles, VI, 184.
Gypsy talent, VI, 278.

Habit, I, 136; II, 275; the sermon on, III, 346.
Hafiz, VII, 170; VIII, 328; IX, 145; x, 144; 166; transforms surroundings, v, 562; poem of, VII, 181, 182; 277, 278; and *Edda* on fate and Freedom, VII, 269, 270; spirit of, VII, 278, 279; on thought, VIII, 19; on cheerfulness, VIII, 458; on love, VIII, 487, 488; on the sonnet, VIII, 542.
Hair, x, 357.
Halifax mills, the, VII, 378.
Hallam, VIII, 454; on Swedenborg, VII, 450 : merits and limitations of, VIII, 461.
Hamatreya, VII, 127–29.
Hamilton, Ontario, England in, VIII, 523.
Hamlet, Lear and, v, 124–26; aristocracy in, VII, 320.
Hampden, IV, 320.
Hand, the, IV, 291, 494.
Handel, his *Messiah*, VI, 479.
Handles, right, to thought, IV, 416.
Happiness, defined, II, 111; or serenity, II, 306, 307; unearned, II, 307; E.'s, IV, 398.
Happy temper, VII, 246.

INDEX

Hard times, III, 475; IV, 214; 236; IX, 137; their stern revelations, IV, 241-44.
Hardness, VI, 457.
Harleian Miscellanies, V, 315.
Harlequin, the great, VI, 84.
Harmony, of the world, IV, 111; want of, V, 19.
Harp-shell, IX, 310.
Harrison, President, V, 549.
Harrison campaign, symbols of, V, 425, 426.
Harte, Bret, visit of, X, 362, 363.
Harvard College, III, 543; jubilee, ghosts and boys, IV, 84; education at, IV, 202; and State Street, IX, 215; criticized, X, 258, 259; discipline, X, 288-91; E.'s lecture at, X, 317.
Harvard festivals, VII, 169.
Haskins, Robert, proverb of, II, 442.
Hatem Tai, IX, 539.
Haven, Alfred, V, 142.
Hawthorne, Nathaniel, IV, 479; above his writing, VI, 240; walk with, to Harvard, VI, 258-63; talk with, VI, 414; on Brook Farm, VI, 441; method of, VII, 188; Channing on, VIII, 257; Delia Bacon and, IX, 90; burial of, X, 39.
Hawtry, Dr. S., X, 46.
Haydon, IX, 225; on English navy, VIII, 501, 502.
Hayne avenged, VIII, 197.
Heads, V, 169; the few good, VII, 552.
Health, V, 309; E.'s improving, letter to M. M. E., II, 179; physique of great men, IV, 477; and rules, VI, 267; spread your, VI, 361; genius is, VII, 98; influx and efflux, IX, 294; subjugation of matter, IX, 298; top of, required, X, 42.
Hearing and speaking, III, 559.
Heart of men, speak to, IV, 172.
Heart, the, IV, 340; deep aboriginal region, V, 500; a gate, V, 552, 553; above intellect, VI, 28; bad, VII, 548.
Heat, magic of, IV, 453; V, 421; and imagination in savants, VIII, 177.

Heaven, here, II, 421; the world of reason, III, 488; is sense of power, VIII, 571; and Hell, X, 168.
Heaven-born, results of, VI, 49.
Heavenward view, IV, 288.
Hecker, Isaac T. (Father), IX, 467.
Hedge, Dr. F. H., III, 573; V, 206; visit of, IV, 235; talk with, IV, 250; Margaret Fuller and, V, 248.
Heeren, his *Egypt*, tragedy of the Negro, V, 26, 27.
Hegel, VII, 152; X, 143; 248; 318; Scherb expounds, VIII, 69; quoted, X, 423; and followers, X, 460; and natural science, X, 462.
Heliodorus, founder of novels, VII, 549.
Hell, and Heaven, your attitude, VI, 168.
Help, from diverse men, III, 439; or mind your business, IV, 245.
Helpers in life, IV, 51.
Hemlocks, the, IV, 142.
Henri Quatre, with tricolor, III, 155.
Heraclitus, II, 344, 345; splendid sentences of, IV, 267.
Heralds suffer, VI, 411.
Herbert, George, II, 415; IV, 173; extracts from, II, 348; poems of, V, 5; verses of, VI, 509; his *Man*, VII, 104.
Herbert, Lord, Life of, IX, 519.
Hereafter, unworthily pictured, II, 103.
Heredity, its moral, III, 381.
Hermit, the, IX, 153.
Hero, VIII, 123.
Hero, loyal to beauty, VII, 42.
Herodotus, VII, 512.
Heroes, IV, 451; provided, V, 62; poet's use of, V, 187; of the North, IX, 485; of the war, IX, 577.
Heroic, the, rare, IV, 343.
Heroic characters, II, 372.
Heroic manners, IV, 226.
Heroism means difficulty, V, 427.
Herrick, Robert, III, 483; VIII, 25; the poet's lure, VI, 144; Channing on, VII, 532.
Herschel, III, 197.
Hervey, Lord, X, 16.
Hesiod, quoted, X, 297, 298.
Hesperus, the marble, VI, 325.
Heterogeneity, VIII, 218, 219.

INDEX

Heywood, Dr., and school-boy, IV, 395.
Hierarchy, VI, 417.
Higginson, T. W., VII, 558.
High Church, III, 572.
High reason, low understanding, III, 311.
High sentiments, nourish, II, 391.
High thoughts, IV, 461.
Higher law, VIII, 132; derided, VIII, 110.
Highlands, trip to the, III, 176-79.
Highway, good by the, VI, 273.
Hinckes, preaching of, III, 187.
Hindoo, theology, X, 162.
Hints, of history, II, 97.
Hippocrates, II, 345.
Historians, do not portray man, IV, 164; advocates, VIII, 518.
Historical discourse at Concord, introduction, III, 497-99.
Histories, two, of man, VII, 80, 81.
History, its dark side, meagreness in prosperous times, I, 217-21; its help for ideals, II, 89; study of, II, 127; lessons of, III, 365, 366; we preserve a few anecdotes, facts rank themselves, III, 552, 553; philosophic, IV, 153, 154; true use of, IV, 157, 158; soul in, IV, 165; science and, the service of, IV, 377, 378; writing of, V, 65; all personal, V, 448; is striving thought, VI, 323; teaches principles, VII, 533.
Hoar, Elizabeth, X, 101; the sister, VI, 85; on Campbell's life, VIII, 205; on common sense, VIII, 498.
Hoar, Madam, view of, IV, 407.
Hoar, E. R., Judge, IX, 566, 567; X, 297; genius of, X, 291.
Hoar, Samuel, V, 24; VI, 43; 220; 523; VIII, 93; 180; IX, 542; sober age, III, 526; on just causes, IV, 321; outrage of South Carolina on, VII, 20-23.
Hoar, Samuel (senior), X, 95.
Hoar, Samuel, quatrain, VIII, 330.
Hobbes, Thomas, on books and conversation, VIII, 324; on Democracy, VIII, 462.
Hobbies, good, VII, 324.
Hobby-riding, II, 479.

Hodson, William S. R., *Life of*, IX, 331.
Hogg, James, *Kilmeny*, IX, 346.
Holidays, exhilarating, IV, 442, 443.
Holmes, O. W., VII, 169; IX, 227-29; 404; on lecturing, VIII, 424; convivial talent, IX, 466.
Holmes, Captain O. W., X, 7.
Holy Days, II, 326.
Holy Ghost, II, 27; 359; taming the, VII, 16.
Holy people, X, 341.
Holy River, VIII, 519.
Holyoke, Mount, I, 277.
Home, VII, 230; X, 170; use your eyes at, III, 341; picture of E.'s, IV, 372, 373; the cure, IV, 423; sweet, but sacred, V, 239; in August, IX, 224.
Homer, IV, 439; mouthpiece of mind of man, III, 329; questions for, III, 490; value of, to Americans, VI, 281.
Homerides, V, 331, 332.
Homes, snug and bleak, VIII, 288.
Homology, VIII, 272.
Hooker, General, X, 93.
Hooker, Richard, defines imagination, VIII, 495; and ideal dogmas, VIII, 497, 498.
Hoosac, IX, 577.
Hoosiers, IX, 9.
Hope, III, 18; VI, 543; dupe of, I, 367; a good, II, 213; and trust, V, 119; beginning of, its own fulfilment, V, 251.
Hopes, E.'s, II, 86.
Horace, X, 218.
Horatii, the, VIII, 321.
Horizon feeds us, IV, 288; of brass, English, VIII, 405.
Horoscope, VII, 331; your powers your, II, 513.
Horse-chestnuts, illusion of, VIII, 578.
Horses, of romance, VIII, 404; in Iowa, X, 183.
Hosmer, Edmund, and Henry Thoreau, IV, 395; account of, VI, 180-82; victories of, VI, 201; on Alcott, VI, 240, 241; honesty of, VI, 303; neighbor, VIII, 261; his serenity, IX, 356.
Hospitality, V, 552; law of, IV, 3, 4;

INDEX

problem of, IV, 105, 106; to unbidden guests, IV, 262; to thoughts, V, 138; VI, 128; of minds, VII, 551.

Hospitalities, V, 270.

Host, over-anxious, V, 321, 322.

Hostility, foolish, IV, 460.

Hotel, fire in, IX, 479; and Inspiration, X, 43.

Hotel air, VII, 545.

Hotel rules in Davenport, VIII, 585.

Hotels, VI, 337.

House, E.'s, V, 422; small *versus* large, VII, 47; American, X, 262.

House-hero, II, 454.

Household help, VI, 421.

House-hunting, VIII, 538.

Housekeeping, V, 183; a college, V, 48-50.

Housewife, yield to, IV, 310; the young, IV, 430.

House of Commons, VIII, 583.

Houssaye, stories from, VIII, 347.

Howe, Judge, II, 308.

Howe, Julia Ward, X, 325.

Huddersfield, VII, 381.

Hudson River, X, 200.

Human desires, II, 285.

Human life, lectures on, V, 159, 160.

Human race, and gods, X, 196.

Human relations, II, 476.

Humanity, greater than manners, V, 379; trust your, VIII, 410.

Humble-bee, the, IV, 235.

Humboldt, Alexander von, III, 356; VI, 400; X, 298, 299; his *Cosmos*, VII, 100.

Hume, II, 77; VIII, 426; essay of, I, 292; and Gibbon, II, 121, 122; history of, and modern history, VIII, 322.

Humiliation, VI, 356; in mood of, III, 131.

Humility, II, 476; III, 496; VIII, 14; X, 19; and Pride, II, 300; is a time-saver, III, 516; of great poets, IV, 83; secret of, VII, 286; haughtiness of, X, 231.

Hunger, wolfish, for knowledge, VI, 295.

Hunt, Leigh, his *Abou ben Adhem*, VI, 200.

Hunt, Peter, II, 335.

Hunt, Richard, X, 280, 281.

Hunter, John, IX, 149; X, 265.

Hunterian Museum and Turner's studio, with Owen to, VII, 480-82.

Hurry, V, 519.

Husks, feeding with, III, 273, 274.

Hymn, *There is in all the sons of men*, II, 346.

Hymn-books, VII, 161.

Hypocrisy, II, 509; VIII, 194; sin carries its reward, II, 139, 140; shun, III, 332.

Iamblichus, IX, 88; on Pythagoras, V, 522.

Iceland, VII, 561.

Idea, of God, the, II, 274; the hidden, III, 292; no wall like, III, 565; tyrannous, VII, 106. *See also* Action, Christianity, Courage, Experience, Facts, God, One, Universe.

Ideal, VI, 397; when practised, alarms, V, 312, 313; ideal community, VII, 199-201.

Ideal men, II, 505.

Idealism, III, 486; X, 452, 453; Peter Hunt, II, 335; yearning, III, 395; discomfort shakes, III, 495; books, worship, friends, IV, 12-14; notes on, IV, 25; aristocracy and, V, 276, 277; the Child's, VI, 26; drops of, VIII, 408. *See also* Aristocracy, New England.

Idealism, verses, I, 109.

Idealist, always wanted, VIII, 543; danger of hypocrisy, IX, 6.

Idealists, VI, 323; no pure, in England, VII, 478; rare yet present, VIII, 508; ideas applied, IX, 246; Greeks and Judea, IX, 552.

Idealizing, III, 352; 467.

Ideas, men open themselves to, IV, 26; sovereignty of, IV, 32; successive, working, V, 333; impregnable, IX, 371.

Identity, VII, 54; 89; X, 139; 214; man clings to, II, 101; spiritual man sees, III, 568; perception of, VIII, 46; and centrality, X, 205.

Identities for intellect, VIII, 547.

Idleness, sermon subject, II, 472.

Idols, V, 95; VII, 294.

Idolaters, V, 209.

INDEX

Idolatries or God, II, 269.
Idolatry the backward eye, VI, 190.
Ignorance, shame of, II, 393; the wisdom of, III, 328.
Ill health, II, 68; of E., II, 117.
Illinois, winter in, IX, 7; hard times in, IX, 9.
Illinois settlers, IX, 5.
Illness, E.'s, X, 390-92.
Illumination, II, 381.
Illuminations of science, emblems, III, 225, 226.
Illusion, X, 123; 159; of horse-chestnuts, VIII, 578.
Illusions, IX, 264; are many and pure, IX, 357.
Illustrations, VIII, 280.
Images, inborn, I, 334.
Imagination, evils of, II, 25; its two powers, VII, 160; cultivate, VII, 328; flute of, VIII, 21; heat and, in savants, VIII, 177; we live by, VIII, 504; and memory, IX, 127.
Imbecility of good party, VIII, 212.
Imitators, II, 522.
Immigrants, the drifting, VI, 443; America's sifted, VIII, 226.
Immoral laws scarce in history, VIII, 200.
Immortal, the, VII, 228.
Immortal deeps, VI, 478.
Immortal life, few fit for, IX, 348.
Immortality, II, 211; VIII, 561; X, 203; virtue, and vice, II, 98; aspirations for art, letters and science an argument for, II, 205; high aims assure of, II, 392; felt, not shown, III, 210; at hand, III, 373; falsely taught, the soul affirms, V, 241, 242; best of literature and, V, 340; materialist and, V, 377; real or absurd, V, 497; personal, VII, 176; Goethe on, VII, 522; shooting stars and, X, 96; abstinence from subject of, X, 110; with Tracy and Cass anecdote, X, 121; and intellect, X, 138; viewpoints for, X, 279; and transition, X, 457.
Impersonality, elegance of, IV, 54.
Imperturbability, X, 192.
Impression personal, IV, 79.

Impressions, VI, 6; respect your, V, 144; dulling of, VII, 546.
Improvisation, VIII, 541.
Inaptitude, VI, 69.
Income of scholar, V, 43.
Incomes, large, VII, 460.
Incomprehensible, the, X, 215.
Inconsistencies, on, V, 67, 68.
Independence, II, 301; brave, II, 451; value of, IV, 351; your own, VIII, 482.
India, X, 163; doctrines from, VII, 127; and Greece, fate in, VII, 123; theologic literature of, IX, 197.
Indian, the, VII, 23; the poor, VIII, 9; Oldtown, IX, 111; and rum, X, 53.
Indian ethics, VII, 129, 130.
Indian summer, VI, 281.
Indians, VII, 184; at St. Augustine, II, 169; North American, in Boston, IV, 345.
Indirection, VI, 77; utterance by, V, 189.
Indirections, fatal, VII, 199.
Individual and universal mind, IV, 247-49.
Individualism must remain, VII, 322, 323.
Individuality, Arethusa fountain, IX, 550.
Individuals, riddle of, IV, 14; and communities, VI 314.
Indolent minds, working and, VII, 541.
Induction, VII, 266.
Indulgence, Nature's, V, 308.
Inequality, necessary, VIII, 166.
Inertia, II, 135; VII, 96; man's, II, 376.
Infancy, beauty of, IV, 279, 280.
Infant composure, VI, 197.
Inferno, IV, 216.
Infinite, the foam of the, V, 209.
Infinite Being, justify yourself to, IV, 16.
Influence, V, 510; of genius, III, 351.
Influences, VII, 137; shed, V, 355.
Information, neglected, X, 230.
Ingratitude, II, 165.
Inherited bonds, VII, 156.
Innocence, V, 309; native, VIII, 555.
Insane success, VIII, 348.
Insanity, repose, V, 117.

INDEX

Insanities, humoring, VI, 24, 25.
Insects, VII, 293.
Insight, peace of, V, 150; good will makes, VI, 224; in finishing a chapter, X, 48.
Inspiration, II, 242; X, 46; of Nature, II, 495; fortunate hours, III, 561; "unconscious," explained, V, 384, 385; and depths of thought, VI, 115; and talent, VII, 517; two bids to, VII, 542; Homer and Pindar, IX, 80; newness of subject indifferent, IX, 207; hotel *versus* home, X, 43; task or muse, X, 130; electric machine needed, X, 456.
Instinct, trust, III, 299; retiring, III, 369; and zeal, IV, 301; resistless, VII, 99; fate and, VIII, 391; boy runs to market or wharf, IX, 125.
Instincts, trust your, II, 426; let, write, VIII, 40; guiding war, IX, 363.
Institutions, clothe themselves, III, 370; illusory, V, 175; divinity behind, VI, 269.
Insularity of man, IV, 238.
Insurance, Nature's, V, 62.
Integrity, IV, 341.
Intellect, VII, 432; 516, 517; VIII, 102; powers of, III, 341; character above, IV, 224; its beauty is not partisan, observes, dissolves, reduces, IV, 380-82; love and, V, 431; conversion of, VI, 492; alone a devil, VI, 497; scepticism of, VII, 296; detaches, VII, 325; and love, VIII, 236; celebration of, VIII, 257; the king, VIII, 264; threads from fact to fact, VIII, 504; the sky of, its priest, VIII, 567, 568; dates from itself, IX, 223; flowing, IX, 251; no age to, X, 32, 456; praise of, X, 107; a great cosmical, X, 233; chapter for examples, X, 270. *See also* Beatitude, Being, Character, Coleridge, Conscience, Heart, Identities, Immortality, Interval, Light, Morals, Natural Science, Obedience, Thoreau.
Intellectual powers, X, 300.
Interchange, Nature forces, V, 68.

Internal evidence, II, 325.
Interval, intellect puts an, VI, 242.
Intimations of higher riches, V, 76.
Intoxications, V, 413.
Intuitions, VI, 315.
Invention, V, 121; God's gift, VII, 84.
Inventions, I, 340; X, 359; or moral force, VI, 14, 15.
Inventors, Boyden, Bigelow, VIII, 341.
Invocation of spirits, I, 23.
Inward eye, VI, 489.
Ionian school of philosophers, the: Thales, Anaximander, Anaxagoras, Diogenes of Apollonia, Archelaus, II, 336-39.
Iowa, X, 183.
I Promessi Sposi, III, 122.
Ireland, Alexander, VII, 344.
Irish mother, the, VI, 239.
Irishman, railroad president and, VIII, 460.
Iron, II, 148.
Ironclad, IX, 458.
Irving, VIII, 97.
Isolation, secure through elevation, V, 188; scholar's, VIII, 387.
Italy, visit to, III, 62-147; reflections on, III, 172; Boswellism of travel, III, 340; letter to Margaret Fuller on, VII, 368.
Iteration, V, 218; principles of, IX, 447.
Ivanhoe, opera, III, 119.

Jackson, Abraham, IX, 504.
Jackson, Andrew, II, 408; VI, 351, 352.
Jackson, Dr. Charles T., X, 6; 119, 120; 169; on ordnance and analyzed sound, VII, 556.
Jackson, Dr. James, VI, 206; VII, 267.
Jackson, Lydia. *See* Mrs. Lidian Emerson.
Jacobi, Friedrich Heinrich, quoted, VIII, 418.
Jacoby, IX, 503.
James, Henry, VIII, 109; IX, 278; 190; X, 77; wish of, VIII, 280; on Thackeray, New York and Boston, VIII, 393-95; on governing, IX, 297.

INDEX

James, King, remark of, VIII, 134.
Janus-faced preacher, IV, 462.
Janus reputations, III, 553.
Jardin des Plantes, visit to: strange sympathies in, "striving to be man," III, 161–64.
Jefferson, Thomas, funeral rites of Adams and, II, 113; quoted, IX, 181.
Jeffrey, VII, 388.
Jests, III, 529.
Jew, baptism of, III, 88.
Jews, III, 127.
Job, Book of, I, 264.
Johnson, Dr. Samuel, VII, 285; *Life of*, and his books, reading, IV, 251, 252; never knew nature, IV, 259; step from, to Carlyle, VIII, 463; on Adam Smith, IX, 214; quoted, IX, 231, 232; X, 211, 212; M. M. E. and, IX, 234.
Joinville, quoted, IX, 407.
Joking, odious, VII, 459.
Jonson, Ben, I, 24; II, 234; III, 217; IV, 78; quoted, I, 125; IX, 202; his *Fame*, VI, 466.
Jortin, II, 486.
Jouffroy, III, 170; Cousin and, IV, 400.
Journal, proposal for a, V, 38; discussion of a, VII, 268, 269.
Journal, E.'s, I, 31.
Journal-keeping, E.'s, III, 527.
Journal-writing *versus* mathematics, I, 67.
Journalist, London or New York, X, 33.
Journey abroad, X, 394–99; northward in Italy, III, 103–06.
Jove, the, VIII, 6.
Joy, in thought, II, 195; deep, in Nature, V, 118, 119; not pain, endures, V, 487; or power, VI, 282.
Joys, human, IV, 147; homely, IV, 465.
Judæa, IV, 361.
Judd, Sylvester, VIII, 290.
Judgment, doomed ghosts, IV, 98; good, III, 248.
Judgment Day, VII, 292.
Judgment Days, IV, 110.
Judges, few great, VIII, 468.
July, on the river, VII, 311.
June blood, VII, 287.
Juno, the, VIII, 6.
Juries, Judge Allen on, VI, 433.
Jussieu, III, 164.
Justice, I, 188–91; lasts always, II, 251; seeking absolute good, V, 329.

Kalamazoo, IX, 261–63.
Kane, Dr., quoted, IX, 481.
Kansas, aid for, IX, 51; relief meeting, IX, 62.
Kant, V, 306; VI, 482.
Kaufmann, Peter, IX, 93.
Keats, V, 346.
"Keeping," II, 48.
Kemble, Fanny, Mrs. Siddons and, VI, 337.
Kenilworth, III, 175.
Kentuckian, VIII, 31.
Kepler, VI, 143; robust courage, X, 204.
Kew Gardens, VII, 438, 439.
Keys, VI, 250.
Kindness, elegance of, III, 311; unspoken, IV, 305.
King Laurin, III, 545.
Kings, VI, 367.
King's Chapel, VII, 317.
Kirkland, Dr., and Professor Brazer, VIII, 350, 351.
Kitten, the, VI, 245.
Knight, the, and the Hag, ballad, I, 123–25.
Knowledge, keys of, and progress of, II, 95; all, valuable, II, 229; stored, III, 248; each must arrange his own, III, 545, 546; progress of, V, 510; in use, VII, 106; wisdom and virtue, VII, 114, 115; all gives superiority, IX, 224; only newest is inspiration, IX, 310; is in the world, IX, 348; great unused stock of, X, 70.
Koran, quotations from, X, 135.
Kossuth, VIII, 288; on English and French soldier, VIII, 521.
Kurroglou, VII, 291; the minstrel-bandit, VII, 280–82.

Labor, VI, 229; virtues of, V, 210, 211; calming, V, 218; and letters, V, 517; held in poor repute, VI, 51; writing and, VII, 187.

INDEX

Laborer, manly grace of, VI, 448; and idealist, VII, 327.
Laborers, seek the, VII, 66.
Lafayette, III, 158; X, 98; death of, III, 310; Mirabeau's letter to, VIII, 429, 430.
Laing, VII, 517.
Lake Michigan, IX, 12.
Lamarck, monad to man, IV, 116, 117.
Lamartine, VII, 469.
Lancaster to Manchester, first experience on railway, III, 183, 184.
Landor, V, 23; VI, 32-34; 263; VIII, 526; extracts from, II, 350; quotation, II, 422; 519; at his villa, III, 115; pictures of, talk with him, III, 117; on argument, III, 455; wilfulness, IV, 56; *Pericles and Aspasia* of, V, 194, 202; quoted, X, 185; quoted on Austria, X, 295.
Landscape, the riddle of the, V, 470.
Landscape art, V, 33.
Lane, Charles, and Henry G. Wright, VI, 291; at the conversation, VI, 319, 320; description of, VI, 411, 412; on costume, diet, clergy, animals, VI, 451, 452.
Lanfrey, IX, 51; quoted, IX, 53.
Language, learning a new, III, 390; of thought, III, 491; clothes Nature, IV, 146; only symbols and suggestions, IV, 266; from spoils of all action, V, 213; building of, VIII, 100; anticipating thought, X, 466.
Language-making, VII, 142.
Language-study, VII, 202.
Languages, Charles V quoted, III, 317; as discipline, III, 300; let, lie awhile, VI, 204; passions, IX, 563.
Lantara, VIII, 348.
Laocoön, the, IV, 318.
La Peau d'Ane, VI, 273.
Laplace, IX, 295.
Latent heat, IX, 186.
Latent joy, V, 398.
Latin and Greek, X, 338.
Laughing, V, 98; weeding and, IV, 256.
Lausanne, III, 150.

Law, the, II, 400; why reverenced, II, 321; moral, infinite, II, 417; judge each by his, II, 419; be the channel of, III, 555; of mind, IV, 303; animated, V, 560; and exceptions, VI, 24; working of, VII, 88; confidence in, VII, 101; compensation of, bad, VIII, 242; respect for, VIII, 327; undue reverence for, when immoral, VIII, 479, 480; physical, moral, IX, 490. See also Artist, Higher, Hospitality, Newton.
Laws, maintenance of, V, 303; adorer of the, VII, 542; and will, VII, 547.
Lawyer and abolition, IX, 448.
Leaders, our great, VIII, 216.
Lear and *Hamlet*, V, 124-26.
Learning for the people, VIII, 330.
Leasts, IX, 306; 558; doctrine of, VII, 523; VIII, 145, 146; 236.
Le Blaie, V, 59.
Leclaire the half-breed, VIII, 585.
Lecture, offensive, III, 395; a new organ, V, 234; fault of the, VIII, 167; Philadelphia, IX, 163; E.'s, in Virginia, X, 449.
Lecture topics, V, 17.
Lectures, VI, 362; VII, 82; VIII, 441; E.'s, IX, 177, 178; 259; 293; 321; X, 377, 378; plan of, IV, 118, 119; themes for, IV, 391; on *The Present Age*, disappointment in, V, 372-74.
Lecturing, IV, 189; VIII, 205; X, 129; E.'s, V, 287-89; IX, 75; X, 253; 347.
Lecturing tour, VIII, 109.
Lee, Sarah, her *Life of Cuvier*, extracts from, II, 351, 352.
Lee, Colonel Henry, X, 395.
Leeds, VII, 378.
Legal crime, mischief of, VIII, 187, 188.
Legaré, VII, 243.
Legislators, character in, VI, 507, 508.
Leibnitz, VI, 143.
Leicester, VII, 360.
Lenox, VIII, 392, 393.
Leonardo da Vinci, II, 464; III, 156.
Lessing, X, 196; extracts from, II, 351.

INDEX

Lessons for the wise all around, III, 228.
Les Stériles, VIII, 178.
Lethe, VI, 310; and Beauty, V, 269.
Letter around world, III, 482; value of, II, 172; IX, 252.
Liberia, IV, 162.
Libertine, a dupe, IV, 212.
Liberty, IX, 309; as against mediæval religion, I, 375; history of, VIII, 204; at stake, IX, 396; for America, X, 231.
Libraries, duties of, V, 22.
Library, Carlyle's, X, 44, value of, X, 263; influence of, X, 421.
Licoö, song of the Tonga Islanders, I, 159.
Lie, weakness of a, VIII, 194.
Liebig to Faraday on pure science, VIII, 487.
Life, value of, II, 506; spellbound, III, 239; true, makes every spot a centre, III, 402; tentative, IV, 201; of earth and air and mankind, IV, 355; thought and, interacting, IV, 440, 441; means and ends of, V, 394; and poems, V, 441; talking on, VI, 289; game of, VII, 49; is in thinking, VII, 319; rich, VIII, 155; God communicates, IX, 298; dignity of hard, IX, 439; perception of beauty in, X, 145, 146; short limit of human, X, 444. *See also* Beauty, Child, Cholera, Conduct, Conversion, Country, Death, Dictionary, Disillusioning, Emblems, Emerson, M. M., Epochs, Experiment, Fringes, Helpers, Human, Immortal, Miracle, Natural, Optical Osman, Persons, Poetry, Religion, Romantic, Selection, Sleep, Symbolism, Thoreau, Tides, Wasted, Way, Weather.
Life or Death, verses, II, 130-32.
Light, III, 413; within, the, II, 520-22; always on path, III, 282; for all men, III, 389; God hides in, III, 526; and music, IV, 173; a wandering, IV, 248, 249; tragedy of, that does not guide, V, 103; coming, V, 461-64; the, older than intellect, VI, 377; icy, VII, 110; and shade, VII, 263.

Lights, VII, 155.
Limit, V, 42.
Limitation, V, 12.
Limitations, II, 426; adamantine, VII, 179.
Limits, III, 289.
Lincoln, President, IX, 345; 499; seen in Washington, IX, 375; 387; policy of, IX, 457; criticism and praise of, IX, 556, 557; memorable words of, X, 72; manners of, X, 97.
Lincoln bell, III, 316.
Lind, Jenny, VIII, 129; 247.
Line, no straight, VI, 350.
Lines, to Ellen Tucker, II, 257; on *Death*, II, 383.
Links, in chain of facts dropt, V, 63.
Linnæus, X, 206; and French novels, V, 317.
Lion, small red, VI, 295.
Lions of New York and Philadelphia, the, II, 206.
Listening, activity or, VII, 521.
Literary discussion, reaction from, IV, 457.
Literary justice, VI, 292, 293.
Literary meetings, poor, V, 256.
Literary warfare, VI, 69.
Literary work, unfinished, VI, 98.
Literary world, joy in, VI, 33.
Literature, of a country, III, 555; science and, the old and new, IV, 90-95; on, V, 102; abroad and here, rejection, discontent, slight reformers, V, 528-30; waiting for helpful, VIII, 342.
Liturgy, the English, VII, 257.
Live magnets, VII, 252.
Live people, VIII, 13.
Liverpool, III, 185; sailing from, III, 193, 194; and Manchester, lectures in, VII, 352-55.
Lives, value of, X, 45.
Living, think of, II, 511.
Living God, the, VII, 159.
Living-prayer, verses, II, 97.
Living times, V, 34.
Livy, VII, 135.
Loadstone, VIII, 411; divine in man is, VI, 406.
Locke, III, 501; VIII, 492; Reed quoted on, X, 95.
Locomotive, farmer and, III, 482; the, calls, VI, 322.

514 INDEX

London, VII, 401; 437; X, 413; landing in, III, 171; a magnet, VI, 265; immeasurable, characteristics, VII, 406; and Paris, water, VII, 465; courses of lectures, VII, 474, 475; topics in, VII, 486.
Loneliness, VIII, 260.
Lonely society, V, 457.
Long life implied, VI, 524.
Long Wharf, IV, 377.
Longanimity, V, 355.
Longevity, VII, 217; 266; X, 140.
Longing for persons, for a teacher, III, 100, 101.
Looking-glass, VII, 155.
Looking outward, V, 51.
Looking straight forward, III, 343.
Looking upward or downward, VI, 408, 409.
Lord's Supper, the, V, 160; question of, II, 496-97.
Loss, gain in, IV, 316; V, 207.
Lot, our strange, IV, 215.
Lotus-eaters, V, 212; VI, 43.
Louis Philippe, VII, 411.
Louis XI, IX, 562.
Louvre, the, VII, 455; Leonardo, III, 156.
Love, I, 293-95; true and faint, III, 535; man in, interesting, IV, 331, 332; just and measured, IV, 394; miracles of, V, 216; a reflection, V, 359; transcribing, essay on, V, 411, 412; picturing of, V, 418; be thy art, V, 444; makes us children, V, 451; is of virtue, V, 464; paradox of, VI, 30; the large view of it, VI, 467; initial and celestial, VII, 65, 66; view of, in youth and later, VIII, 162; spring, IX, 178; lover and maiden, X, 131. *See also* Commerce, Friends, Hafiz, Intellect, Persons, Personality, Property, Rest, Woman.
Lovejoy, Elijah, heroic death of, IV, 371, 372.
Lovelace, X, 153.
Lowell, Edward, and Charles Emerson, VI, 394.
Lowell, Francis Cabot, IX, 188; death of, X, 432-35.
Lowell, James Russell, X, 267; *The Biglow Papers*, IX, 359.
Ludgate, VII, 437.

Luigi Monti, mother of, IV, 342.
Luther, III, 377; VII, 515; quoted, III, 354; praise of, III, 366; pious spite of, III, 558; two styles of, VI, 405; his cure for morbid conscience, VII, 304; his effect on thought, VIII, 151.
Luxury, I, 324; VII, 323.
Lyceum, the, III, 409; opportunity of, V, 280, 281; slavery question in, VII, 5, 6.
Lycian marbles, the, VII, 435.
Lycurgus, Solon and, II, 283.
Lyman, Theodore, X, 232.
Lyndhurst, Lord, remark of, VIII, 522.
Lyons, Lord, IX, 379.

Mabinogion, IX, 346.
Macaulay, Thomas B., VII, 485; VIII, 12; 462; story of, VII, 412; strength of, VII, 418; his *History of England*, VIII, 28-30; criticized, VIII, 59; on Bacon, VIII, 483, 484.
Machiavelli, VII, 241.
Machinery, VI, 397; VII, 430.
Mackintosh, Sir James, II, 470; on slave-owners, VIII, 382.
Madrepores, IV, 296.
Magazine, staff for, VII, 38, 39.
Magazines, audiences and, VI, 354.
Magic, IX, 212.
Magnet, II, 213; VIII, 39; IX, 183; X, 409; and Mirror, VIII, 99.
Magnetism, VI, 489; VII, 62; in sexes, VI, 500.
Magnetizers, VII, 91.
Magnetizing of the spirit, VI, 120.
Mahomet, IX, 109; and woman, VI, 353.
Maias of Vishnu, IX, 302.
Maiden, the, V, 374; the magnetic, V, 131.
Mails, the, III, 201.
Maine, visit, X, 392.
Majority, VIII, 101; 429; dupe and victim, VIII, 449.
Majorities, VII, 148; rather uncultured than wicked, VIII, 508.
Makebelieve, city of, VII, 195.
Male words, IX, 198.
Malta, quarantine at, III, 25-30.
Malthus, VIII, 389.

INDEX 515

Man, position of, I, 379; is his own star, II, 250; marriage of spirit and matter, IV, 78; marries all Nature, IV, 136; incalculable, V, 131; is above measures, V, 328; the wise, portrait of, V, 360, 361; before measure, V, 368; O leopard-skinned, V, 375; the receiver, to re-create, V, 524; dimensions of, V, 566; not class, VI, 142; inventory of, VII, 137, 138; representative, VII, 139; not men, VII, 165; a new, VII, 180; fits his place, VIII, 245, 246; all-related, VIII, 264; genius, X, 171, 172; is architectural, X, 192; insight into another, X, 304. *See also* Analogist, Battery, Beast, Body, Books, Bulletin, Capital, Centre, Coal, Congeries, Conscience, Construction, Counsellor, Curb rein, Day, Delight, Dignity, Eating, Education, English, Eternal, Freedom, Gifts, God, Good, Great, Grief, Historians, Histories, Homer, Identity, Inertia, Insularity, Loadstone, Love, Milton, Nature, Natural, Opportunity, Oriental, Poetry, Portrait, Poverty, Prophet, Public, Questions, Range, Religious, Representative, Rich, Riches, Scott, Self, Sermons, Shakespeare, Shrine, Sick, Speculative, Standard, State, Sympathy, Teachers, Temperance, Things, Thoreau, Torpedo, Tree, Unmagnetic, Vegetation, Weeds, Wild, Will, Wise, Woman, Words, Wordsworth, World, Zodiac.

Manchester, VII, 382; Liverpool and, lectures, in VII, 352–58.

Manfred and *Beppo*, IV, 251.

Manhood, rarity of, IX, 150.

Manilius, an early Newton, VIII, 203.

Mann, Horace, V, 250; visit of, IV, 361, 362.

Manners, I, 389–91; demonological, V, 240; have no hurry, V, 244; power of, yet humanity greater, V, 378, 379; require time, VII, 17; one must be rich in, VIII, 521; Charles II, VIII, 562; simplicity in, IX, 265; vast convenience of, X, 50; simplicity and, X, 64; and dress, X, 111, 112; power of superior, X, 131, 132.

Manners, notes for, VIII, 146.

Manse, at the, III, 422.

Mansfield, Lord, decisions of, VIII, 96; in Somersett case, VIII, 132; on investment, VIII, 226.

Mansfield, Mount, X, 253–57.

Manuscript, a fresh, VI, 393.

Man-woman, VI, 210.

Many-sided Man, A, an essay, VIII, 148–50.

Manzoni, VI, 533.

Maple sap, IX, 10.

Marble Lady, the, III, 108.

Marcus Antoninus, VIII, 19.

Mariposa, X, 354.

Market, poetry and eloquence brought to, IV, 82.

Market-wagon procession, the, IV, 203, 204.

Marlboro', to, with Channing, VIII, 130.

Marlboro' Road, the, VIII, 122.

Marriage, VIII, 87; IX, 488; E.'s, II, 266; its gradual unfolding, IV, 104.

Marriage, institution, the, VI, 72, 73.

Mars, Madame, III, 168.

Marsden Lead, IX, 5.

Marseillaise, Rachel sings, VII, 464.

Marshall, John, III, 445; VIII, 584.

Marshfield, VIII, 335.

Marston, his *Patrician's Daughter*, VI, 238.

Martial, X, 218; power of, VIII, 12; on Portia, VIII, 25.

Martineau, preaching of, III, 187.

Martineau, Harriet, Miss, IV, 3; VI, 378; X, 228; visit to, III, 542; book of, IV, 267, 268; her *Deerbrook*, V, 445; trance of, visit to her, VII, 399; quoted, X, 230.

Martyr, don't play the, V, 123.

Martyrdom, I, 136; reserve your, IV, 462.

Martyrs, VI, 367; VIII, 350; cheap, IV, 459, 460.

Marx, Karl, quoted, VIII, 351.

Masked Power, the, VIII, 240.

Mason, Jeremiah, on law-school, VIII, 275.

516 INDEX

Mass, in writing, VI, 155; in friendship, VI, 156.
Mass-meetings, VI, 530.
Massachusetts, VII, 23; VIII, 30; IX, 574; dishonored by Carolina, VII, 13–15; humiliation of, VII, 192, 193; poor in literature, VIII, 339; politics of, IX, 146.
Massachusetts Quarterly, VII, 314.
Masses, property and, VI, 100.
Master, X, 169; be, II, 478; advertising for a, V, 406; discipline of, IX, 304.
Masters, VIII, 34; glory of, V, 148; young poets and the, VIII, 207; in philosophy, X, 455.
Mastery, VIII, 329.
Mastodons of literature, VII, 120.
Materialists, IX, 35.
Mathematics, VII, 513; journal-writing *versus*, I, 67; compulsory, II, 535; college, X, 36–39.
Matlock, III, 174.
Matter, V, 282; VI, 141; and the hereafter, II, 105; respect, stand for the ideal, IV, 32; impregnated with thought, X, 348.
Maud, Empress, verses on, VII, 365.
Maximum and minimum, IX, 115.
Maxwell, Mr., speech of, III, 359.
May, Samuel J., III, 520; and George Thompson, visit of, III, 546.
Maya (illusion), X, 159.
May-Day, X, 201.
May-game, life a, V, 215.
Mayhew School-Committee, II, 431.
McClellan, grand style, IX, 435.
Meaning of texts, inner, II, 508.
Meanings, new, IV, 337.
Meanness and grandeur, II, 173.
Means and ends, II, 322.
Means, strongest are cheapest, VII, 522.
Measure, VI, 22; of men, IX, 103.
Measures, weights and, VIII, 555.
Mechanics' Institutions, VII, 381.
Mediation, VIII, 243.
Medical sceptics, IV, 334.
Mediocre books, X, 263.
Meditation, sad, II, 368.
Meditations, II, 493.

Meeting men, IV, 363.
Meetings, reform, IV, 431.
Melioration, VIII, 86; X, 463; in fruit, VIII, 577, 578.
Melody, strain of, III, 274.
Memorial Hall, X, 332, 333.
Memory, V, 438; VIII, 534; power and peace in, III, 15; delicious, III, 437; books and, III, 506; enchantment of, V, 133, 134; fixes rank, V, 167; not wit, V, 271; knocking in nail overnight, VII, 528; papyrus of, VII, 553; world full of, VIII, 422; little known on, IX, 127; by cause and effect, IX, 171; celestial papyrus, X, 124; some old aunt, X, 286; thought expels, X, 361.
Memories of lost friends, IV, 401, 402.
Men, of God, I, 230; gregarious, VI, 250; rare, VII, 50; are lawful, VII, 78; in Nature, VIII, 35; fit for the day, VIII, 241; our four good and strong, VIII, 320.
Mencius, VI, 459–61.
Mendelssohn's *Phædo*, II, 446.
Merchant, IV, 216, 217; VII, 528; VIII, 151; compared to negro, VI, 66; and hermit, IX, 18, 19.
Merchants, nothing new, VI, 279; praise of, IX, 339.
Merck, IV, 205.
"Mere Morality," III, 424.
Merlin, foresight of, VII, 545.
Mesmerism, VII, 258–60; IX, 61.
Messina, ride to, kindly companions, III, 54–56.
Metamorphosis, VII, 313; VIII, 217; human, II, 271; doctrine of, VIII, 557.
Metaphors, I, 349.
Metaphysician, a true, IX, 126.
Metaphysics, do not satisfy, I, 379; critics, II, 284; passing into history, VII, 284; new, wanted, VIII, 254; practice needed in, VIII, 263; awaits its author, VIII, 507; barren, IX, 147; objection to, X, 336; sympathy and piety correct, X, 455.
Meter, riches a, VI, 82.
Method, E.'s, VIII, 124.
Methodist preaching, II, 178.

INDEX

Methodists, the, III, 284; enthusiasts, II, 318.
Metonomy, VIII, 296.
Metres, humming, VIII, 444.
Metric system, I, 327.
Mexican War, VII, 206; 242.
Mexico, ruins in, V, 523; War with, VII, 219; cannon in, IX, 407.
Michelet, VII, 464.
Michigan railroads, IX, 10.
Midsummer, VII, 553.
Milan, the cathedral and sights, good houses, III, 142–46.
Military band, VI, 211.
Military experience, IX, 42.
Military eye, V, 269.
Millerite, VI, 388.
Milnes, Richard Monckton, VII, 411; and Carlyle, VI, 251; stories concerning, VII, 482–86.
Milton, John, I, 71; II, 236; III, 414; 449; IV, 400; prose of, I, 297; mouthpiece of mind of man, III, 328; association with Edward and Charles, IV, 395, 396; and Young, V, 548; evolution of, VII, 213, 214; on his age, VII, 366; reserve of, VIII, 540; a saint, X, 154; and Swedenborg, X, 191.
Mimicry, V, 325.
Mind, must have material, III, 478, 479; the rich and poor, V, 206; the rule of it, IX, 177; laws of, X, 137; and matter, X, 236; powers of the, X, 453; and Nature, cause and effect, X, 459. *See also* Asylums, Books, Individual, Indolent, Law, Parallax, Plagiarism, Presence, Scott, States, Unity, Universal, Woman-part.
Minds, viviparous and oviparous, VIII, 52; of abnormal and oracular cast, X, 454.
Mines of Truth, the, verses, II, 417.
Minister, revolt against being, II, 448; problems of a, II, 520; must be simple in manners, decorum now in demand, prune the sermon, writing, much self-reliance, III, 548–51; library of young, IV, 324.
Ministers, conduct of, self-denial, do not worry about example, II, 286, 287; Concord, V, 45.

Ministry of the day, sages of old, II, 58–60.
Mino, speaking bird, IX, 219.
Minor key, X, 115.
Minorcans, and Indians, II, 163.
Minority, the, VII, 267; VIII, 456.
Minot, George, IV, 203; 471; X, 93.
Minot House, VIII, 483.
Minute Man, X, 443.
Minutes, use the, II, 215.
Mirabeau, II, 543; letter of, to Lafayette, VIII, 429, 430.
Miracle, IV, 24; of life, cheering, II, 273; of the universe, II, 487; the daily, IV, 354–56; one, V, 370; poet must work a, VI, 118; and stupendous fact, X, 198.
Miracles, II, 289; VII, 44; Christian II, 325; greater knowledge of Nature, II, 414; vulgar view of, IV, 427–39; always spiritual, V, 236.
Miraculous, the, V, 135.
Mirror, a, the sentence, IV, 180; magnet and, VIII, 99.
Mirrors, VI, 9.
Miscellanies, Harleian, V, 315.
Miserere, the, twice heard, III, 85, 86.
Misericordia, the, III, 114.
Misery, wealth, power and, VII, 423.
Mis-estimates among men, III, 406.
Misfortunes, E.'s, of 1855, VIII, 580.
Missionaries, II, 487.
Missionary press, III, 34.
Mississippi, the, VIII, 585; crossing, X, 223.
Mixtures, Nature's, VII, 214.
Mob, Boston, IX, 305; organized, X, 4.
Mobs, insignificant, III, 562.
Model person, the, VII, 512.
Models, artists', VI, 83.
Modern antiques, VI, 400.
Modern facts, poet and, VI, 251.
Molecular interspace, VI, 207.
Moment, the, is all, VI, 44; in writing, VI, 94; in history, VII, 288.
Moments, V, 489; of our Lives, II, 111; letters to Edward and Charles on, II, 170–172; wise, III, 231.
Monadnoc, inspiration of, VII, 41.

INDEX

Monadnoc Camp, x, 149-53.
Monarchs and courts, III, 405.
Money, no-money reform, v, 87; no-money doctrine, v, 235; no-money morality, vi, 62; love of, VIII, 175; power of, IX, 542, 543.
Money matters, III, 371.
Monochord, IX, 28.
Monotones, IV, 491; v, 99.
Monroe, President, II, 395; Adams's eulogy on, II, 411.
Montaigne, II, 440; v, 419, 420; VIII, 97; his rules of rhetoric, III, 272; praise of, III, 538; charities, IV, 406, 407; acquaintance with, VI, 371, 372; his journey to Italy, VI, 453; charm of, IX, 357.
Montesquieu, quoted, IX, 499; x, 315.
Montgomery, and Worsdworth, II, 235.
Montmorenci, hotel, III, 155.
Montreal, VIII, 281-87.
Moods, and weather, v, 479.
Moon, the, IV, 80; and daylight, v, 8; phases of, and the spirit's, v, 488; stars and, v, 559.
Moore, on Campbell, II, 471; his *Sheridan*, IV, 161, 162; memory of, VIII, 570; memoirs of, VIII, 573; quoted, IX, 124.
Moral, at home in the, VI, 348, 349.
Moral beauty, Bancroft, I, 345, 346.
Moral harmony, VII, 188, 189.
Moral law, the, I, 162-64; 186-188.
Moral obligation, I, 250-54.
Moral sense, I, 209-11; native, discoveries in morals, II, 137, 138.
Moral sentiment, must act, IV, 111; and religion, x, 9; courage to affirm, x, 102. *See also* Dandies.
Morale, foundation of genius, x, 331.
Morals, pervading the universe, I, 256-59; discoveries in, II, 138; and intellect, II, 399; the great harmony, III, 207-09; leaving, at home, VI, 10; grim, VI, 480; daily help of, VII, 250; where from, VIII, 558; creating new channels and forms, IX, 501; sufficiency of, in politics, x, 144.
Morbidness, IV, 475.

"More and Less," tragedy of, IV, 497.
Morning, VI, 422; hear what it says, VIII, 167.
Mornings, VI, 322.
Morris, William, x, 246.
Morte d'Arthur, x, 276.
Mortification (personal), I, 139-42.
Moses, the, of Michel Angelo, III, 99.
Most high, go to the, IV, 120.
Mother, and child, IV, 134, 135.
Mother-wit, VIII, 414.
Motives, talk with Charles on, IV, 14, 15.
Mott, Lucretia, VIII, 110.
Mount Auburn, spring day at, III, 270, 271.
Mount Washington, x, 327.
Mountain, The, verse, x, 286.
Mountains, VI, 410; afar, VII, 328.
Mourning, gradual, VI, 271, 272.
Moving universe, the, I, 13.
Muir, John, x, 385.
Müller, Max, IV, 417; 420.
Multiple lives, our, III, 511.
Mundane soul, the, II, 101.
Murat, Achille, II, 155; friendship with, II, 183, 185; account of, and his letter to Emerson, II, 185-91; visit to, II, 161; remembrance of, wild weather at sea, III, 213, 214.
Muse, the, VII, 173; serene, IV, 481; the city of, v, 323; is feminine, VI, 361.
Muses, Pan and the, VIII, 230.
Museum, Natural History, III, 118.
Museums, mortify, VIII, 525.
Music, v, 121; VIII, 154; keeping in, II, 49; inward, III, 20; ringing from the past, III, 442; village, III, 464; nursery, IV, 147; of Nature, IV, 364; masses, v, 189; thoughts during, v, 492; effect of, VI, 91; hearing, VI, 519; heard but once, VII, 66; for sorrow, VII, 265; at York, VII, 375, 376; prior to thought, VIII, 123; universal nature of, IX, 359.
Music-box, of intellect, x, 456.
Musical eyes, v, 138.
Musician, the farmer a, VII, 297.
Musketaquid, IX, 27.
Musts, x, 472.

INDEX

Mystery of poetry, VII, 296.
Mystic, the, VII, 171; in power, VI, 354; materialism does not alarm, VIII, 421.
Mysticism, VII, 20.
Mysticisms, VI, 19.
Mythology, East Indian, I. 304; VII, 121; history in perspective is, VII, 383; serves, VIII, 17.
Mythologies, thread uniting, III, 412.
Myths, beauty of national, VII, 284.

Nahant, VIII, 388; Channing on, VIII, 252.
Napier, Lord, IV, 318.
Names, X, 363; be not overawed by, III, 62; exchanging, V, 93; charm of, VI, 193, 194; valuing, X, 175, 176.
Naming, VI, 330.
Nantasket, VI, 4.
Nantasket Beach, X, 322–24.
Nantucket shore, people and stories, VII, 270–74.
Naples, III, 62–75.
Napoleon III, VIII, 155, 347, 559; England and, VIII, 563.
National will, creating a, VIII, 377, 378.
Nationality, VI, 350; X, 194; war giving us, IX, 552.
Nations, differing rank of, I, 157, 158; estimating, V, 369; culminate, VIII, 345; of one book, VIII, 575.
"Native Americans," VII, 115, 116.
Native force, IX, 128–30.
Natural aristocracy, and spectrum, X, 187.
Natural history, study for resource, III, 297; marry, to life, III, 326; symbolic, VII, 312.
Natural science, V, 120; X, 348; and intellect, X, 204–206; and Hegel's dogma, X, 462.
Naturalist, a village needs, VIII, 131.
Nature, V, 57; simple steps of, III, 287, 288; a book of, uniting botany, etc., and poetry, III, 461; projection of God, IV, 76; working in myriad forms, IV, 122; still undescribed, IV, 145; harmonizes, IV, 331; teaching of, she is all-musical, has no shock, V, 463, 464; message of, derided, yet true, V, 493; continence of, V, 506; song of, ever new, V, 507; questions of, VI, 340; puzzles of, VI, 462; no depth but lateral spaces, VI, 490; never draws the moral, VII, 190; uses all things, VII, 312; oceanic working of, VII, 415; sympathy of, VII, 558; against metaphysics, VIII, 19; great students of, VIII, 51; her dealing with us, VIII, 57, 58; teaching of, VIII, 105; hard to find, VIII, 208; fine instruments of, VIII, 406; helps us to express thought, VIII, 536; shows everything once in the large, VIII, 546; and man, IX, 132; yields each only his own, IX, 440; wealth of, X, 65, 66. See also Analogies, Appeal, Aristocracy, Boy, Bulletin, Channing, W. E., Cipher, Consolation, Country, Deist, Each and All, Economy, Equality, Finalities, Good Cause, Indulgence, Inspiration, Insurance, Interchange, Johnson, Joy, Language, Man, Men, Miracles, Mixtures, Music, Physician, Police, Pope, A., Power, Record, Repetitions, Repose, Resources, Screen, Sight, Significance, Stallo, Sublime, Surprises, Temple, Thermometer, Thoreau, Thought, Truth, Workshop, Worship, Youth.

Nature, E. likes his new book, III, 196; notes for, III, 192, 193; proof-sheets of, IV, 81, 82; new chapter, V, 420, 421.
Nature, Addresses and Lectures published, VIII, 48.
Naturel of each man, IX, 128; X, 315.
Naushon, X, 75; 393, 394.
Nearness, the Soul's, VIII, 22.
Nebraska Bill, the, VIII, 442, 443.
Necessity, II, 165; the beautiful, VI, 185; farms, VI, 202; explorers and, X, 173.
Nectar, drop of, VI, 381.
Nectarius, VIII, 496.
Negatives, IX, 367.

INDEX

Negro, x, 176; tragedy of the, v, 26, 27; advances, vi, 533; heathenizing whites, ix, 421.
Negro soldiers, ix, 484.
Negroes, enlisting, ix, 483.
Neighborhood, a projected, vi, 207; good, viii, 315.
Nemesis, x, 76; levels, viii, 113; appears in slavery question, viii, 201.
Neoplatonists, vi, 376; vii, 93.
Nest of boxes, ii, 523.
New, the old in the, v, 449.
New Bedford, preaching at, iii, 258; Mr. Arnold on, viii, 276.
Newcastle, Eng., vii, 387.
Newcastle, Duke of, ix, 389.
Newcomb, Charles K., vi, 162; x, 209; a religious intellect, vi, 213, 214; and George Bradford, vi, 374; vii, 60, 61; visit of, vii, 321; on Thoreau, vii, 386; a wasted light, viii, 60-62; viii, 121; noble letters of, viii, 395; his rich mind, ix, 199, 200; quoted, on Dante and Goethe, ix, 328, 329.
New England, factories of, iv, 207, 208; proud to serve, iv, 298; old religion of, v, 543-45; 547; idealism of, vi, 300; needs a history, vii, 232, 233; and servant, vii, 315.
New England *morale*, viii, 152.
New England women at Brook Farm, vii, 386.
New Hampshire, vii, 26; hills and lakes, poverty, v, 244-47.
New Hampshire boys, viii, 174.
New Hampshire public men, viii, 299.
New Hampshire statesmen, viii, 180, 181.
New Jerusalem Church, ii, 267.
New lights, ii, 482.
"Newness, The," viii, 579.
Newness, ix, 207; divine, x, 189, 190.
Newport, x, 250; 252, 253.
New questions, iv, 95; v, 458, 459.
Newspaper praise, v, 69.
Newspapers, Bancroft on, iv, 410.
New spirit, inevitableness of, vi, 58.
New thought out of ruins of old, vi, 119.

Newton, Mass., Sunday with mother at, iii, 220.
Newton, Sir Isaac, i, 174, 326; ii, 288, 326, 464; iv, 116; epitaph of, iv, 152; discoverers of law, viii, 102; stark thinker, viii, 382; pippins of, viii, 385; anecdotes of, viii, 545; quoted, ix, 499; particular as universal, x, 205.
Newton, Stewart, sketches of, v, 162.
New truths, use carefully, iv, 449.
New York, viii, 30, 393, 394; the lions of Philadelphia and, ii, 206; landing in, iii, 220; lectures and acquaintances, vi, 163; lecturing in, vi, 335, 336; site of, x, 200.
Nichol, John Pringle, astronomy of, v, 526; in the observatory, vii, 395.
Niebuhr, viii, 524; x, 55; on man and country, viii, 552; on many books, viii, 553.
Niedrig tone, the, iii, 380.
"Nigger," vii, 38.
Night, influences of, iv, 450, 451; four steps, iv, 468, 469; enchants, iv, 499; pageant of, v, 240; enchantment of, v, 557.
Nightingale, The, poem, ii, 313.
Nine Acre Corner, walk to, viii, 297, 298.
Nineteenth century, ii, 71; blessed, ii, 400; events of, viii, 214.
Nitrous oxide, v, 490.
No, say, viii, 261.
Nobility, ii, 354; social, x, 163.
Noddle's Island, ix, 42.
Nomad and pivot, v, 52.
Nomads, v, 51.
Nomenclature in religion, ii, 478.
Nonconformist, vi, 454.
Non-resistance, ii, 418, 419; v, 303.
Nonsense, vii, 260.
Non-voters, vi, 162.
Normanby, Lord, ix, 86, 87.
Norris, John, *Ideal World*, iii, 500.
North, the, strength of, ix, 368.
Northampton, Mass., i, 278-80.
Northampton, Marquis of, soirée of, vii, 423.
North End picturesqueness stirs the painter within, v, 538.

INDEX

Northman, quatrain, VIII, 279.
North wind, IX, 139.
Norton, Andrews, I, 195; V, 34.
Norton, Charles Eliot, IX, 30; 225; X, 229; 395; and Carlyle, X, 397; verse to E., X, 418, 419.
Nose and teeth, V, 310.
Not, land of, I, 173.
Note-books, II, 146.
Nottingham, VII, 358.
Nouvelle Biographie Générale, X, 322.
Novalis, III, 313; extracts from, II, 348.
Novel writing, VI, 226-28.
Novelist, task of, VII, 501.
Novels, I, 116; II, 372-74; V, 514-16; VII, 511; Disraeli, VI, 526.
Noviciate, V, 275.
Now, the living, sought in antiquity, V, 93.
Nowadays, education, I, 343, 344.
Nugent, Lord, justice of, VI, 192.
Numbers do not count, IV, 185, 186.
Nuns taking the veil, III, 99.

Oaths, meaning, III, 560.
Obedience, V, 122; conquers, II, 393; intellect grows by, VI, 212.
Object, the momentary, V, 8.
Observatory, X, 118.
Observer, candid, the, III, 484.
"Occasional Poems," IV, 212.
O'Connell, Daniel, VI, 449; and the slaveholder, V, 107; on Disraeli, VII, 172.
October, IX, 452.
Odium, signs of, V, 30.
Œgger, his *True Messiah*, III, 505; quotations from, III, 512-15.
Œillade, the, III, 436; IV, 280.
Ogden, W. B., IX, 77-79.
Old age, V, 405; X, 47; 382; and grief wrong, V, 550; graceful, VIII, 56, 57; advantages of, IX, 273; insignificance of, a success, IX, 322; and Stone Chapel, IX, 347; death of friends, IX, 360; autumnal haze, IX, 560; its consolation, X, 51.
Old and New, stamp of the, IV, 190.
Old English writers, the, II, 402.
Old religion of New England, V, 543-45; 547.

Old Second Church, closing the, VI, 497, 498.
Old writers, VII, 502.
Oldest thing, the, VII, 244.
Oliphant, quoted, IX, 264.
Oliver Twist, V, 261.
Omens, VIII, 339.
One, glory of the, IV, 250.
One idea, the lie of, IV, 380.
One mind, IV, 60, 61; the generic soul, IV, 52, 53.
Open-mindedness, VII, 80.
Opera, III, 61; in Catania, the, III, 53, 54; prima donna and ballet, III, 112, 113; attractions of Paris, III, 167.
Opera *Ivanhoe*, III, 119.
Opinion, hold your own, III, 124; always helpful, IV, 394.
Opinions, IV, 207.
Opportunity, V, 534; VII, 100; VIII, 274; man's dignity and, V, 356, 357.
Opposition good, V, 351; tonic, VIII, 544; value of, X, 43.
Oppositions in philosophy, VIII, 86.
Optical deceptions, III, 408.
Optical life, VI, 158.
Optimates, IV, 21; 49.
Optimism, I, 205, 206.
Oracles, certain persons utter, IX, 210; of a child, X, 444.
Orator, V, 21; strength of, VIII, 206; and conservative assembly, IX, 275-78.
Oratory, of Barnwell and Upham, I, 68.
Order, aristocratic, X, 216, 217.
Organic remains, modern study of, IV, 129-31.
Organization, V, 276; inward and outward, IX, 21.
Oriental, and Occidental, IX, 116.
Oriental cure, the, VIII, 37.
Oriental man, III, 566.
Oriental scriptures, VII, 241.
Oriental superlative, VII, 280; VIII, 129.
Oriental type of thought, VI, 494.
Orientation, III, 476.
Originalities, VII, 317.
Originality, V, 416; 419; VI, 124; difficult, V, 56; and quoting, IX, 344; new crater, IX, 555; predic-

INDEX

tions, x, 211; of good writer, x, 382.
Orpheus, the right, VIII, 353.
Orphic words, IV, 154.
Osman, VI, 137; VII, 203; 260; his endowment and fortune, V, 431–33; and the fine folk, V, 481; and Schill, simple life, V, 563, 564; and success, VI, 20; goes a-berrying, VI, 49, 48; autobiographical, VI, 49, 50.
Ossian, VIII, 361.
Ossoli. *See* Margaret Fuller.
Otherism, IV, 155; V, 44.
Others, ourselves in, II, 324; endorsement of, VI, 477.
Others, vision of, hope in, VII, 184.
Otis, Harrison Gray, in Faneuil Hall, I, 142; and Judge Spencer, II, 238; on women, VIII, 36.
Out-of-door thoughts, VIII, 532.
Outgrowing, VI, 221.
Overseers of Harvard, X, 245.
Ovid, V, 452; quoted to Tiberius, IX, 556.
Owen, George L., 410.
Owen, Robert, lecture of, VII, 133–35.
Owen, Richard, lectures of, VII, 420, 421; with, to Hunterian Museum and Turner's studio, VII, 480–82.
Oxford, VII, 423; X, 417; grace at, VII, 493.

Pace, IX, 183.
Padua, III, 129.
Pagan, poets are, VII, 123.
Pain, house of, its benefit, II, 180.
Painters, house, IV, 59.
Painters, the old, VIII, 20; 466.
Pairs, IX, 272.
Palermo, E. sails to, sights there, III, 56–60.
Paley, I, 174.
Palfrey, Dr., baptizing, V, 55.
Palm Sunday, Rome, III, 81.
Palmer, Edward, V, 233; VI, 180, 181; no-money reform, his practice, another view, quoting texts, V, 86–89.
Palmerstons, the, VII, 485.
Panic, the, IX, 138, 139.
Pantheism, V, 552; VIII, 329; IX, 45, 46; and atheism, II, 178.

Paper money, IX, 138.
Parable, the urn and the fountain, IV, 58, 59; Jock and Dick, VI, 360.
Parables, force of, III, 510.
Paracelsus, VI, 293.
Paradise Lost, IV, 216.
Parallax, different states of mind, II, 486.
Parallelism, VII, 103.
Paris, X, 93, 413, 414; entrance to, III, 155; news from, VII, 408; seems theatrical, VII, 463; London and, water, VII, 465; life cheap in, VII, 467; merits and attractions of, VII, 470–73; and London to travelers, VII, 486; Renan on, X, 47.
Paris lodgings, shops, VII, 450, 451.
Parker, Theodore, E. and his congregation, IX, 233; death of, IX, 270.
Parkman, Dr. Francis, VII, 233.
Parliament House, VII, 407.
Parmenides, II, 343, 344.
Parnassus, X, 437; your, IV, 52.
Parochial memoranda, II, 437; duties, IV, 455.
Parrot, the, IX, 218, 219.
Parties, political, III, 292.
Parties, evening, V, 23.
Party, drunk with, V, 235; reveals public men, VI, 466; imbecility of good, VIII, 212; Democratic, IX, 84, 85; in and out of power, X, 243.
Party lies, IV, 188.
Party politics, VIII, 265.
Party tactics, thoughtless votes, III, 350, 351.
Pascal, I, 338; X, 29.
Passengers, III, 11; nautical glory of, III, 8.
Passion, VIII, 536.
Passions, IX, 563.
Past, the, V, 302; becoming beautiful, III, 563; lives, IV, 324, 325; leave, IV, 484, 485; ever new, VI, 505.
Pastorate, resignation of, II, 510; resignation of, accepted, II, 525.
Pathetic, the, V, 165.
Patience of Thoreau, IX, 154.
Patmore, Coventry, visit to, with Tennyson, VII, 444, 445.

INDEX

Patriotism, II, 174; Anaxagoras, II, 321; is it a duty? III, 543; the large, VII, 326; from war, X, 79.
Paul, St., extracts from, II, 348.
Paule de Viguier, IV, 206; VIII, 93.
Pauperizing, VII, 184.
Payne, J. T., IX, 355.
Peabody, Miss, letter to, on Swedenborg, III, 530–32.
Peace, X, 216; strength of, IV, 297; lecture on, IV, 409, 410; end of Civil War, X, 93, 94; after Civil War, X, 116.
Peace manifesto, the, V, 91.
Pear tree, VII, 300; 308; VIII, 11; 31; signal of the, VIII, 23, 24.
Pearls, casting, VI, 352.
Pedantry, VI, 42; VIII, 323.
Peel, Sir Robert, VII, 403; VIII, 323, 340.
Peeping, V, 176.
Peevishness, IV, 241.
Penetration, VII, 13.
Penn, William, II, 418.
People, poet should trust the, IV, 199, 200; language of the, VII, 561.
Pepys, VIII, 496.
Perceivers, V, 18.
Perceptions, varied, X, 146.
Percival, VIII, 535.
Pericles and Aspasia, V, 447; VI, 69.
Perkins, Jacob, meeting with, III, 184; on locomotives and steamships, III, 191.
Permanence is nobility of men, VI, 98.
Perpetual flux, IX, 220.
Persecution, silken, V, 42.
Perseverance, II, 274; temperance, II, 319, 320.
Persian scriptures, II, 473.
Person, God not a, IV, 185.
Persons, talk of, IV, 53–55; or thoughts, IV, 424; not things, V, 11; are the age, VI, 19; accept not, VI, 160; and property, love can reconcile, VI, 311; in our life, VI, 407–408; a luxury and convenience, VII, 65, 66.
Personal, ignore the, V, 36.
Personal influence, VIII, 262.
Personality, VII, 150; IX, 191; too little for God, IV, 404; love gives, VII, 334; commands, VIII, 107; is interest of universe, IX, 190, 191.
Perspective, VI, 361; in writing, VIII, 35.
Persuasion, III, 557.
Pertinence, II, 305.
Pestalozzi, II, 475; on effect of surroundings, II, 416; method of, IV, 335.
Petrarch, house and tomb of, III, 129.
Phaedo, VII, 102.
Phædrus, VII, 540.
Phantom men, VII, 336.
Pherecydes, VII, 28.
Phi Beta Kappa, II, 404; cold hurrahs, VI, 230; Sumner at, VII, 228.
Phi Beta Kappa day, V, 30.
Phi Beta Kappa oration, the, in demand, IV, 341.
Phi Beta Kappa poem, the, III, 333.
Phidias, V, 308.
Philadelphia, and New York, the lions of, II, 206; lecturing in, VI, 335, 336.
Philanthropies, respect the, V, 196.
Philanthropy and depravity, X, 5.
Philisterei, IV, 81.
Phillips, Jonathan, on behavior, IV, 224; visit of, IV, 236.
Phillips, Stephen, VII, 97.
Phillips, Wendell, VII, 5; IX, 232; 305; fact-basis for eloquence, VI, 542, 543; Garrison and, VIII, 433, 434; IX, 455; and popular assembly, IX, 250; Cassius M. Clay and, IX, 267, 268; tyranny of talent in, X, 111.
Philosophers, the early, III, 386; visit of the, IV, 278, 279; the old, IV, 472, 473; half-sighted, VI, 361.
Philosophic imagination, Buckminster, I, 323.
Philosophy, IX, 520; true, II, 450; the first, III, 235–39; three degrees, VIII, 37; new, X, 321.
Photometers, men are, V, 188.
Phrases, poetical, I, 7; cant, VI, 525.
Phrenology, IV, 297, 298.
Physical science, strong fancy, III, 538.
Physician, IX, 263; Nature teaches, II, 473; Divine, VIII, 408.
Physicians, V, 85.

INDEX

Physiologie du goût, IX, 97.
Physiology of taste, X, 31, 32.
Picture, poem or, V, 305.
Pictures, III, 93, 94; V, 199, 232; judging, IV, 465, 466; seeing, V, 14–16; how to see, V, 410.
Piety, fragrant, IV, 31; surprise at, IV, 432; sins of, V, 569.
Pigeon Cove, IX, 54.
Pilgrims, X, 340, 341.
Pilot, God the, II, 241.
Pillsbury, Parker, quality of, VII, 201–03; tactics of, VII, 243.
Pindar, splendid sentences of, IV, 267; robust courage, X, 203, 204.
Pines, by house, VI, 396; planting, IX, 96, 97.
Pitt, William, I, 317–20; VIII, 340.
Pivot, nomad and, V, 52.
Places and days, II, 219.
Plagiarism due to common mind, IV, 131.
Plague and fear, VI, 349.
Plain dealing, VI, 11.
Plantain, the, VI, 229.
Plants, future men, VI, 251.
Plato, III, 528; VI, 456; VII, 28; letter to, I, 380–88; splendid sentences of, IV, 267; *Politician* of, V, 369; terrible dialectic of, the *Republic*, his commentators, VII, 54–56; and his interpreters, VII, 92–96; a poet, VII, 119; his title to fame, VIII, 43, 44; power of, VIII, 54; and his followers, VIII, 474; critic of, IX, 119; votaries of, IX, 187.
Platonist region, the, VI, 200.
Play, VI, 229.
Playthings, new, V, 383.
Pledges, III, 267; choice not, III, 385; avoided, V, 252, 253.
Pleiad, lost, IX, 222.
Pliny, quoted, IX, 323.
Plotinus, II, 323; 377; V, 510; VIII, 310; 451, 452; on God, II, 357; on Art, IV, 218–21; quoted, IV, 306; IX, 283; on light, VI, 476; on the dance of the universe, VIII, 518.
Plus man, the, VIII, 141.
Plutarch, III, 567; VII, 92; story from, II, 281; design for a modern, II, 303, 504; his *Apothegms*, III, 544; his *Morals*, passages from, IV, 141, 284–86; elixir of Greece and Rome, IX, 273; quoted, X, 319, 320, 322; 339, 340; moral sentiment of, X, 331.
Plymouth, III, 445; V, 161; ocean, people, flowers, III, 264, 265; visit to, IV, 255; VI, 426–29.
Plymouth beach and boats, VIII, 331.
Plymouth Rock, III, 255.
Plymouth usage, VII, 543.
Po, valley of the, III, 128.
Poem, *Marathon*, I, 143; *The River*, I, 165; *Riches* (*The Caterpillar*), II, 62; *The Nightingale*, II, 313; *Circles*, VII, 212, 213; *Days*, VII, 277; *Freedom*, VIII, 407.
Poem, the effective, VII, 114; of Hafiz, VII, 277, 278; takes care of itself, VIII, 176.
Poem-making, V, 287.
Poems, original, II, 293.
Poet, needs material form, II, 106; must teach citizen, V, 425; cannot spare grief or pain, V, 450; who gives wisdom and faith, V, 483; and poem, the sincere dissembler, V, 520–22; method adding reflection to reflection, V, 47, 48; incorrigible, VI, 243; meals of, VI, 320; blessed lot of, VI, 413; a gambler, VI, 467; duty of the, and his measure, VII, 216; thought of, practical, VIII, 429; goes straight forward to say thought, IX, 312; and religion, IX, 546; and Pleiades, X, 140. *See also* Cæsar, Forest, Heroes, Herrick, Humility, Modern, People, Plato, Politics, Presence, Reflective, Savant, Shelley, Thoreau, Tone, Wind, Wine.
Poetaster, VII, 183.
Poet-crop, the, VII, 53.
Poet-paradox, the, VIII, 209.
Poetry, of, I, 105; notes on: criticism of Wordsworth, Shakspeare, Ben Jonson, Montgomery and Wordsworth, II, 232–36; precedes prose, III, 492; wise, III, 544; true ethical, IV, 425; makes its pertinence, V, 343; crude, V, 417; finest rhymes and cadences yet unfound, VI, 75, 76; miracle of, transit of vast to the particu-

INDEX

lar, vi, 124; all life has, vi, 446; aids of, vii, 64; is truth, it creates, viii, 493; seeks resemblance, viii, 493; which no man wrote, ix, 37; word dragging, ix, 214; power of thought, ix, 460; difference in, x, 275; experimental and real, x, 301; "the Newness," x, 360; in newspapers and private circles, x, 367, 368; magnitude of its suggestion, x, 386; secret of never explained, x, 435. *See also* Beauty, Child, Criticism, English, Facts, French, Mystery, Practical, Prose, Sense, Strength, Tone, Wild.

Poets, strong old, iii, 532; summons to, v, 112; guardians of admiration, v, 140; message of, vi, 190; Tennyson, Burns, Browning, Bailey, vi, 286–88; and stars, vi, 453; old and new, vii, 163, 164; needed, vii, 165; brave, viii, 87; of the middle classes, viii, 294; pretended, ix, 17; single speech, x, 147, 148; some unsightly, x, 369.

Poikilus, Professor, ix, 54.
Point of view, ii, 399.
Poisons, ii, 121.
Polarity, iv, 209; x, 139, 140; American, vi, 346.
Poles, political, vi, 390; of philosophy, vii, 118.
Police, Nature's, vii, 256.
Political economy, sure taxes, iv, 107, 108; and morality, ix, 13; stimulus from, ix, 340.
Political parties, slight differences, viii, 333.
Politicians, tricky, viii, 230.
Politics, v, 77–79; recoils in, iii, 359; measures and popular opinion, v, 330, 331; impure, vii, 253; poet and, vii, 513; our, like European, viii, 277; privileged thieves in, ix, 121, 122; English and American, ix, 157; ours petty, ix, 364; American, x, 144.
Poltroonery, vii, 64.
Pond, be not a, vii, 48.
Poore, Major Ben. Perley, ix, 551.
Pope, Alexander, viii, 98; couplet of, ii, 527; never knew nature, iv, 259.

Pope, the, blesses the palms, iii, 81.
Populace, i, 134.
Population, vii, 514; of Naples, worthless, iii, 67; conditional, vi, 183.
Populations *versus* Locke and Newton, ii, 308.
Porosity, vii, 10.
Porphyry, viii, 451.
Portableness, vi, 24.
Porto Rico, ii, 477.
Portrait, a man, ii, 6, 7; the, of man, iii, 361.
Position, iv, 89; and will, iii, 257.
Positive, great poets use the, iv, 324; and superlative, viii, 520.
Positive degree, x, 167.
Possessions, selfish, ii, 407.
Posterity and ultimate tribunal, viii, 94.
Postponing, iii, 276.
Potato, v, 208.
Potatoes, v, 86.
Potomac water, x, 297.
Poverty, ii, 412; vii, 19; and riches, ii, 463; blessed, ii, 480; the wise man's ornament, iv, 244, 245; honorable, iv, 350; intelligible, vi, 338.
Poverty's praise, ix, 199.
Power, the real, Napoleon, Cromwell, Andrew Jackson, ii, 407, 408; dangerous, ii, 450; iii, 360; Nature's lesson of, iv, 67; unripe, v, 265; exhilarates, v, 417; degrees of, vii, 12; and acting reality, vii, 81; and probity, vii, 430; private, ix, 191; notes on, ix, 489. *See also* Art, Child, Christ, Detachment, Heaven, Joy, Manners, Martial, Masked, Memory, Misery, Money, Mystic, Party, Smallness, Waste, Wealth.
Powers, forms *versus*, x, 109.
Practical poetry, ii, 47.
Practical men yet sleep, iii, 237.
Practical and poetical, vii, 85.
Practicalness, ix, 23, 24.
Praise, i, 338–40; v, 193; a bad omen, v, 320.
Prating, vi, 299.
Prayer, ii, 270; ignorance of influence, i, 79; discussion of, i, 213–

16; public, II, 92-94; letter to M. M. E., II, 175; relation to God, II, 294; entrance into God's mind, II, 431, 432.

Prayers, God makes us answer our, II, 393; particular, IV, 478, 479.

Preach and practice, II, 437.

Preacher, let give from own store, II, 214; opportunity of, III, 475; must be universal, III, 564, 565; secure his acre and independence, X, 171.

Preachers, the coming, III, 331; young, VI, 266; the truckling, VIII, 189; to-day, X, 213.

Preaching, VI, 363; and practice, II, 227, 228; topics in, II, 294; at Waltham, hearers of, IV, 115; down, IV, 143; from memory, IV, 300; and study sickly, home the cure, IV, 423; worthless, IV, 457; foolish, IV, 480, 481; V, 172.

Preachings, Emerson's, on the way home, II, 207.

Precedent, IX, 151.

Prefaces, IV, 486; X, 217.

Preliminaries, spare, III, 368.

Prescott William H., IX, 195.

Presence of mind, poet's power, V, 86.

Present, the, II, 485; VII, 323; past, future, V, 197; knowledge of, V, 304.

Present age, the, V, 353; defense of, I, 374; peculiarities of, II, 164; characterized by gentleman and Christian, V, 549.

Presentiments, great discoveries are, VIII, 127, 128.

Press, the boastful, IV, 458.

Preston, VII, 360; IX, 159.

Price, *On Morals*, I, 78.

Pride, forlorn, affectation, IV, 222, 223; dishonest, IV, 268, 269; of saint, IV, 278; and vanity, VI, 362.

Priest, St. Augustine's, II, 169; must be human, II, 366.

Priestcraft, I, 331-37.

Priests, seeking, VII, 419.

Prima Philosophia, VIII, 533.

Primal powers, great, IX, 332.

Primary men, secondary men and, IX, 184, 185.

Primitive poems, charm of, VI, 441.

Primogeniture, VII, 420.

Princes, education for, V, 71.

Principle, II, 145; male and female, IV, 248.

Principles, hidden in base politics, III, 465; open eyes, III, 517; we are porous to, IV, 271; keep to, IV, 308.

Prison, visit to the, II, 229.

Prisoners, returned, IX, 433.

Private door, God's, III, 557.

Private energy best, VI, 198.

Private theatres, our, VII, 74.

Privileged thieves in politics, IX, 121, 122.

Problem, the, V, 30; of three bodies, IV, 22.

Problems, universal, VIII, 63.

Proclus, VI, 157; VII, 7, 262, 516; VIII, 92; magnificent suggestion, VI, 159; intellect communicable, VI, 199; strong-winged, VI, 205; read for opinion, VI, 376; interprets the oracle on Socrates, VIII, 468.

Profanation, IV, 5.

Profession, choice of, I, 377.

Professions, the new, VIII, 574.

Profile, the, V, 246.

Progress, modern, II, 67; human, II, 272; only in individuals, IV, 85; in individuals, not in race, IV, 158; of species, IV, 306; the mercury of, V, 509.

Prometheus, III, 435; V, 437, 438.

Prompter, the, VI, 17.

Property, owning, position and will, III, 256, 257; a test, IV, 299; talk on, V, 128; question of, V, 459; unimportant, VI, 50; question love only can solve, VI, 128; the web of, VI, 404.

Prophecy, I, 129-31; ideals are, VII, 35.

Prophet, practical man and, V, 430; careless of fulfilment, IX, 409.

Proportion, IV, 335, 336; V, 356; culture teaches, the methods, IV, 368-70.

Propriety, V, 198.

Prose, poetry and, IX, 561.

Prosperity, and arms, II, 40; of family, II, 259; and slavery, IX, 453.

INDEX

Protectors, our disguised, III, 315.
Protest, attitude of, IX, 482.
Protesters, the band of, V, 259, 260.
Proteus, III, 344.
Proverbs, V, 35; 55; IX, 536, 537.
Providence, I, 112–15; II, 26; 288; visits of, VIII, 249.
Providences, IV, 199; petty, II, 291.
Provocation of thought, VI, 138.
Prudence, VIII, 208; reign of, V, 314.
Pseudo-sciences mask truth, VI, 245.
Pseudo-spiritualism, IX, 502.
Puberty, III, 376.
Public concern, or private, II, 527.
Public man, the born, VI, 32.
Public opinion, II, 229.
Public schools, VII, 362.
Publishing, the good of, III, 492; be slow in, V, 402.
Pückler-Muskau, IV, 362; on English dandy, IV, 9.
Pulpit eloquence, I, 14, 15.
Punch, X, 69.
Purist voter, the, VIII, 280.
Puritan movement, the, I, 306–08.
Puritans, the, melioration, I, 351–53; rear-guard of the, VI, 52.
Purity necessary for judgment, III, 504.
Pursuits, IX, 155.
Pusey, Dr. E. B., X, 349.
Push, perpetual, VIII, 248.
Pym, IV, 320.
Pythagoras, II, 340, 341; Iamblichus on, V, 522; incarnation, VIII, 239, 240; just fame of, VIII, 474.
Pythologian Society, records of the, I, 33–51.

Quaker, III, 426.
Quaker conversation, III, 229.
Quaker meetings, III, 265.
Quakers, IX, 15; enthusiasts, II, 318; in France, X, 156.
Qualities, VI, 408.
Quality and amount, VIII, 126, 127.
Quarrels, VI, 25.
Quarterly journal, a, VII, 263, 264.
Quatrain, "Nature in Leasts," VIII, 327; "Samuel Hoar," VIII, 330.
Quebec, VIII, 281.
Quentin Durward, V, 514.
Quest, hold to your, V, 533, 534.

Question, facing the, III, 295.
Questioner, and answers, VII, 125.
Questionings, good seen everywhere, II, 9–13.
Questions, VII, 102; unanswered, II, 467; each man's, IV, 19.
Quetelet statistics, VIII, 478.
Queteletism, VIII, 505.
Queue, soldier's, IV, 291.
Quiddle, II, 114.
Quietude, III, 212.
Quincy, Josiah, VII, 168.
Quincy, Josiah, Jr., IX, 103, 104.
Quotation, III, 503; X, 156; helps conviction, III, 466; coming first, VI, 199; dangers of, VIII, 415; adds value, VIII, 490; rightly used, VIII, 527, 528; difference in rendering, X, 218, 220.
Quotations, II, 439, 440; poetical, II, 57; from Œgger, III, 512–15.
Quoting, nothing new, II, 466.

Rabelais, VI, 278, 279; 281.
Raby castle, VII, 387.
Race, genius, of X, 42.
Races, V, 59.
Rachel, VII, 119; sings *Marseillaise*, VII, 464; person and action of, VII, 468, 469.
Radiation, VIII, 525; of manners, VIII, 585.
Radicals, tracts of English, VI, 221, 222.
Railing, V, 4.
Railroad, V, 380; VII, 297; 504; new, VI, 336; Westerners wanting, X, 184.
Railroad rates and stock, IX, 12.
Railroads, VIII, 4; X, 173; prophecy for, VI, 450.
Railway, first experience on, Lancaster to Manchester, III, 183, 184; visit to new, Mr. Perkins on locomotives and steamships, III, 191.
Railway pictures, VI, 339.
Railway ride, III, 305.
Railway stocks, IX, 122.
Rainy-day treats, III, 536.
Raleigh, Sir Walter, VI, 433; quoted, IX, 397.
Ramble, evening, Florence, III, 109.
Randolph, John, IX, 66.

INDEX

Randolph, Philip, x, 319, 320; x, 349; and E.'s anti-slavery work, VIII, 531.
Range, man's, VIII, 409.
Rantoul, VIII, 113.
Raphael, v, 265, 308, 314; angels of, sibyls, v, 15, 16; Four Sibyls of, v, 340; originality of, VII, 523; Michel Angelo and, VIII, 63; quoted, IX, 205; universal, X, 49.
Rarey, IX, 149; 318.
Rawdon, VII, 7.
Rawson, VII, 382.
Raw material for poems and lectures, VII, 215.
Reaction, x, 77; assailant and defence, x, 123.
Readiness, VI, 425.
Reading, II, 251; III, 519; letter to Elizabeth Tucker advising, II, 458–62; for a task, IV, 132; gives vocabulary for ideas, IV, 256; good, v, 248; pertinent, VII, 257; right, VII, 319; lost passages, x, 204; seems guided, x, 422.
Reading man, a, VI, 206.
Readings, at Chickering Hall, x, 282–85; in Boston, x, 378, 379; E.'s last, x, 475.
Real, the seeming, ideal truth, III, 349.
Realism, VIII, 18.
Realists, Kant and blacksmith, VIII, 210.
Realities, which are? VIII, 240.
Reality, IV, 459; VII, 270; VIII, 272; in writing, VIII, 446; rules destiny, IX, 199.
Reason, and Scripture, I, 167–69; and Science in religion, I, 324–27; in religion, II, 85, 222; trust, II, 409; is the divine essence, III, 235; guidance of, III, 389; perfect, III, 394; illumination, III, 456; hours of, immortal, III, 500; eye of, iron lids of, III, 539; hours of, few, IV, 90; makes art and architecture, IV, 102, 103; above understanding, v, 310, 311; is presence not gift of God, IX, 14. *See also* Architecture, Greatness, Heaven, High, Science, Understanding.
Rebellion of 1820, I, 7–9.
Rebels, IX, 574.

Recipes to occupy time, I, 72.
Recluse, the, VI, 506.
Reconstruction, IX, 463–65.
Record, reading Nature's, IV, 130.
Rectitude, VIII, 14; fate and, VIII, 88.
Reed, Sampson, book of, II, 116; his *Growth of the Mind*, II, 124; and Thomas Worcester, talk with, II, 455; talk with, on Swedenborg, VI, 219.
Reed, Dr., of Bridgewater, IX, 366.
Reference, weak, VI, 373.
Reflection, an age of, IV, 110.
Reflections, II, 144; from senior to school-teacher, mortification, I, 137–42; E.'s, on closing school, II, 36–38; entering Divinity School, II, 55; bowing to necessity, II, 115; religion, not of tradition, but of soul, III, 159, 160.
Reflective poet, the, IV, 18.
Reform, license of, v, 40; dreaded, v, 109; perspective of, v, 212; source of, v, 236; lack of zeal for, v, 252; looks not back, v, 466; value of, appears late, VI, 272; standing committee on, VI, 368; and actual world, VI, 503; insight, in, VII, 57; true, VII, 148; sacred, VII, 158; masks reform, VII, 205.
Reform discussion, x, 216.
Reform ideas, v, 405.
Reformer, path of, IV, 349; the brave, or penitent, VI, 28; the rude, and Boston, VI, 134.
Reformers, v, 403; slight, v, 529; Alcott's English, VI, 294.
Reforming age, v, 215.
Reforms, teach, v, 234; enlisting in, v, 293–97; abortive, VI, 405, 406; crude writing, VI, 475.
Refuge, cities of, VII, 82.
Regiment, Massachusetts Fifth, IX, 324; Massachusetts Eighth, IX, 325.
Rejection, VII, 287.
Relation, VII, 154.
Religion, its history, I, 98–104; each must have his own, II, 77; office of, action and contemplation, action is not all, God the Pilot, II, 239–41; sublimed, II, 289; must not fear science, II, 362;

INDEX 529

narrow, III, 199; pasteboard, III, 331; must come through the heart, IV, 30, 31; changes, IV, 95–98; starving, IV, 420; numerical, V, 117; low, V, 180–82; now looks to life, V, 227–29; cry for, V, 380; flowing, V, 551; gives refinement, VI, 328; Catholic and Protestant, VII, 341, 342; and tyranny, IX, 203; Varnhagen quoted, IX, 495; universality in, X, 234; notes on, X, 379, 380; centuries and hours, X, 469. *See also* Astronomy, English, Moral Sentiment, Nomenclature, Poet, Reason, Reflections, Science, Shakers, Spiritual.

Religions, changing yet save, VI, 306.

Religious enthusiasts, III, 432.

Religious feeling keeps alive, II, 221.

Religious forms, outgrown, X, 213.

Religious man, who is? II, 303.

Renan, Ernest, IX, 451; quoted, IX, 446; his *Vie de Jésus*, IX, 579; X, 18; on Paris, X, 47.

Renunciation, first thoughts from God, III, 323.

Repairs, bodily and spiritual, II, 502.

Repetitions of history, V, 219; in Nature, X, 219, 220.

Repose, Nature invites to, V, 439.

Representative at Congress, frighten your, VIII, 392.

Representative man, VIII, 50.

Representative Men sent to friends, VIII, 70.

Representatives in Congress, timid, VIII, 101.

Republic of letters, IX, 527.

Republican party, V, 62.

Republicans, weak, IX, 403.

Repulsions, IV, 239.

Reputation, II, 411; in universe, VI, 139.

Resemblance, X, 113.

Reserves, VII, 427; X, 49.

Resignation, not easy, II, 180; of pastorate, II, 510; accepted, II, 525.

Resolves, II, 309; III, 422; new, III, 361.

Resources, X, 59; use God's riches, II, 518; knowledge of Nature, IX, 417; of inspiration, X, 244.

Respect, for men, III, 221; for friends, V, 416.

Rest and love, V, 301.

Restaurant, VII, 470.

Result, not artist, counts, VIII, 570.

Resurrection, belief in the, II, 126.

Retzsch, IV, 204.

Revelations, true, V, 353.

Review of closing journey, thankful, III, 185.

Reviews, hostile, V, 75.

Revival, coming, IV, 15.

Revolution, VIII, 37; documents of, III, 320; French, III, 448; VII, 403; sign of, VII, 454; old and new, VII, 464; and anti-revolution, IX, 553; a volcano, IX, 573.

Revolutions, VII, 429, 430; X, 237; in England, silent, III, 494.

Revolutionary clubs, VII, 454, 455.

Revue des Deux Mondes, X, 265.

Rewards, V, 527.

Reynolds, Governor, VIII, 522.

Rhetoric, elevated writing, II, 415; fact or name, IV, 169; charm of, V, 465; takes space, V, 482; culture's, VIII, 449; omit negative propositions, IX, 85; Plutarch and Montaigne for, X, 320.

Rhyme, its privilege of truth, Pindaric, warlike daring, V, 225–27; and rhetoric, VIII, 527.

Rhymes, VIII, 46.

Rich and poor, V, 71; VII, 302; 358; VIII, 73.

Rich man, IV, 408; wise man cannot be, IV, 448; to help, VI, 15.

Rich mind, VII, 457.

Riches, VIII, 25; spiritual, III, 410; of man's nature, III, 438; freedom through, IV, 409; accident of, V, 257; acquired or inherited, V, 478; knowing how to use, VI, 67; greatness not leaning on, VI, 469; the undoing of, VIII, 276, 277.

Riches (The Caterpillar), poem, II, 62.

Richter, III, 473; VI, 283; IX, 496, 497; on women, VI, 253.

Riding school, IX, 229.

Right, determination of, II, 154;

struggle for, VIII, 516; perception, of, X, 166.
Rig Veda Sanhita, VIII, 547–49.
Ripley, Dr. Ezra, V, 20; 143; III, 364, 365; utterances of, III, 391, 392; solid facts of, IV, 234; prayer of, V, 18; death of, VI, 52–55.
Ripley, George, VI, 392, 393.
Ripley, Mrs. George, VI, 392, 393; VI, 386.
Ripley, Samuel, V, 270; real preaching of, IV, 379; and Southern coxcomb, VI, 239.
Ripley, Mrs. Sarah Alden, IV, 433; V, 103; IX, 426; Miss Emerson's letter to, II, 191–94; eager scholarship of, VI, 72; account of, VI, 545–50; on holidays, VII, 47; death of, X, 207–09.
Ripple Pond, IX, 179.
Ritson, verses from, VIII, 542.
Rivalry, V, 8.
Rivarol, on Mirabeau, VIII, 347.
River, The, poem, I, 165.
River, V, 423; immersed in a spiritual, V, 427, 428.
River, the Concord, V, 558; blessed, VI, 401.
Rivers, the two, IX, 27.
Robin Hood, VI, 131.
Robbins, Chandler, VI, 455.
Roederer, on Napoleon, his sayings, VIII, 462, 463.
Rogers, Samuel, breakfast with, his house and his anecdotes, VII, 348–51; and aristocracy, VIII, 278.
Roman Catholic convert, VI, 217.
Romance, I, 302–04; a venture in, I, 108–10; waning, I, 119; E.'s, VIII, 124; imaginative book, IX, 422.
Romance, A, verses, I, 117.
Romance writers, IX, 420.
Romans still masters, V, 382.
Romantic dreams, I, 19.
Romantic power of life, V, 468–70.
Romany Girl, the, VIII, 518.
Rome, III, 75–103; by stage to, III, 74; the gift of, III, 102.
Romeo, story of, VI, 320, 321.
Room-mate in hotel, III, 463.
Rosebugs, VI, 225.
Rotation, VIII, 165.

Rotch, Mary, VI, 280; religion of, her experience, III, 258–60.
Rothschilds, the, VII, 424.
Rousseau, his *Confessions*, VII, 318.
Roussel, on women, VIII, 401.
Rowse, Samuel, IX, 154.
Roxbury, I, 232; and Cambridge, teaching in, II, 70.
Ruggles, in debate, VII, 203.
Rulers, the real, II, 81.
Rules of the gods, VII, 496, 497; established, and sentiment, X, 190.
Rural proverbs, VI, 202.
Ruskin, VII, 367; X, 363, 417.
Russell, John L., walk with, V, 61; Saadi, VI, 537; VIII, 310; IX, 564; quotations from, VI, 463–65; IX, 544, 545; classes of, VII, 245; cheerfulness of, IX, 561.

Sabbath, II, 80; III, 317; V, 172; a new, III, 263; consecrated because other days are not, V, 214; a day outweighs a, VI, 216.
Saccharine principle, V, 465; 481.
Sacred persons, the, VII, 84.
Sacrifice, VII, 121; making none, III, 453.
Safeguards, III, 63; VI, 277.
Safford, Henry Truman, boy mathematician, VII, 274–76.
Sages, of old, II, 58.
Said. *See* Saadi.
Sailors, III, 12.
Saint, X, 233; and scholar, VIII, 92.
St. Augustine, Florida, visit to, II, 149–82.
St. Augustine (Florida), verses, II, 149–51.
Sainte-Beuve, quoted, IX, 525; 530; 544; 556; 575; 578.
St. George's Society, speech to, VIII, 283–86.
Saint Grail, Tennyson's, X, 240.
Saint-Hilaire, Geoffroy, X, 366, 367.
St. Paul's, VII, 434.
St. Peter's, moonlight walk with Cranch and Alexander, III, 87; Easter Mass in, III, 88.
Saint-Simon, *Mémoires* of, V, 526.
Saint-skeptics, VII, 136.
Saints, poets and, VII, 229.
Sâkoontalâ, IX, 105.
Salesman, VII, 526.

INDEX

Saliency, VII, 317.
Salisbury, visit to, VII, 490.
Salt fish, sign, V, 36.
Sameness, I, 299–301.
Sampson, George A., letter to, II, 537.
Sand, George, VI, 533; VII, 500; 559; sincerity of, VII, 503; quoted, X, 133.
Sanity, rare, V, 12.
Santa Croce, III, 118, 123; homage to Galileo and Michel Angelo, III, 105, 106.
San Zenobia, III, 122.
Sartor Resartus, II, 530.
Saturday Club, IX, 320; X, 6; II, 12; 25–27; 78; foreshadowed, VIII, 104; behavior at, X, 296.
Saturn, III, 461.
Saunterings — autobiographical, II, 244–46.
Savage, James, Alexander Everett and, III, 375.
Savagery, return to, VII, 508.
Savant, V, 222; poet and, IV, 117.
Saving instincts, III, 268.
Saxondom, VIII, 345.
Scaffoldings, II, 470.
Scale, VI, 22.
Scandinavian custom, VIII, 566.
Sceptic, service of, VII, 59.
Schelling, X, 317, 318; quotation, II, 422; thought of, its growth through others, VIII, 76, 77; distinction of, VIII, 126.
Scherb, expounds Hegel, VIII, 69; lecture of, VIII, 246.
Schiller, II, 525–27; *Wallenstein* of, quotation from, II, 377; Burke and, believers, VII, 512; on poems, VII, 48; on burial, VIII, 554.
Schleiermacher, III, 393.
Scholar, in company, III, 319; invisible tools, facts his treasure, IV, 6, 7; office of the, IV, 259; 280–83; investment of the, IV, 274, 275; must be fearless, V, 82, 83; must not stop for attacks, V, 100; in fashionable society, V, 145, 146; voice of, heard afar, VI, 166; the story of the, VI, 216; his weapons, relation to society, VII, 71; progress of, VII, 113; creed of, X, 470, 471.

Scholar class, the, VIII, 471–73.
Scholars, should be happy and brave, IV, 56, 57; few, V, 113; slackness of, V, 214; question for, V, 445; subservient, V, 536; timid, VII, 36; untrained, VII, 111; perpetual, sacred, VII, 244; hunger of the, VII, 259; posts his books, VII, 542; surrender of, to the worldly, VIII, 486; and times, IX, 100; and invitations, IX, 530. *See also* Courage, English, Eternity, Freedom, Income, Isolation, Saint, School, Soldier, Treasure.
School, a, I, 308–11.
School Committee, scholar and, VII, 30; philosopher and, VII, 56.
Schooling, winter, VI, 302.
Schoolmaster, III, 307.
Schoolmen, VIII, 49.
School-room, escape from his, I, 75.
School-tax, VIII, 237.
Schools, visiting the, IX, 315; Concord, X, 13, 14.
Schopenhauer, quotations from, X, 33, 34.
Science, IX, 125; reason and, in religion, I, 324–27; and religion, II, 362; ethical, II, 488; kills legend, III, 558; the humanity of, IV, 59, 60; and literature, the old and new, IV, 90–95; in humanity, IV, 113; and history, the service of, IV, 377, 378; new, looks within, V, 94; each can explain universe, VI, 246; as a barrier, VI, 529; symbolic, VII, 52; dull, VIII, 9; not chronological, VIII, 478; must have soul, VIII, 505; inspired or dull, VIII, 525; warped, VIII, 565; not a finality, IX, 278; zymosis of, X, 264.
Sciences, apprentice, VII, 252.
Scientists, poetic, X, 364.
Sciolist, the young, VIII, 426.
Scotland, III, 176; English judges in, VIII, 469.
Scots, V, 413.
Scott, David, VI, 264; VII, 92; VII, 388; paints E.'s portrait, VII, 392.
Scott, Sir Walter, *Abbot*, I, 71; *Bride of Lammermoor*, II, 203; heroic characters in, II, 371, 372;

INDEX

Shakspeare and, III, 327; and Coleridge, III, 328; line of, III, 539; and superstitions, x, 358.
Scottish speech, VII, 394.
Scougal, II, 387.
Screen, Nature too thin, IV, 250.
Scribe, chosen by spirit, x, 99.
Scriptures, of the nations, v, 335; love of the great, v, 500.
Sculpture, the ancient, IV, 98.
Scythe, the, v, 414.
Sea, the, Sunday at, III, 205; Ninevehs and Karnacs at, IX, 55.
Sea-line, the, VII, 386.
Seaports, x, 251.
Search, Edward, I. 11.
Sea-serpent, VIII, 366.
Seashore, VI, 104.
Seashore rhymes, VI, 13.
Seaside abolishes time, VIII, 380.
Sea-skies, III, 450.
Sea voyage *versus* college examination, VII, 457.
Second Advent Hymns, VI, 457.
Second Church, the call to, II, 261–262.
Second essays sent to friends, VI, 536, 537.
Secret doctrines, III, 468.
Secrets, IV, 78.
Sect begets sect, IV, 135.
Sectarian, be not a, II, 385.
Sects, IX, 309; Claude Lorraine III, 377; feed on one another, III, 459; and saints, x, 234.
Sedgwick, Miss, characters of, novels, IV, 458.
Sedgwick, Mrs., IX, 450.
Seed, God a, III, 497; divine, IV, 73.
Seed-thought, II, 97.
Seer, child or, VI, 253.
Selection, IV, 330; VI, 23; life is, VII, 203; in Art, VIII, 253; in good writing, x, 303.
Self, II, 319; IX, 190; the higher, IV, 315, 316; revere, VIII, 517; a surprise, x, 264.
Self-culture, Goethe and, III, 314.
Self-denial, II, 287.
Self-depreciation, E.'s, IX, 355.
Self-esteem, I, 301, 302.
Self-examination, I, 242–44; 360–67; 377–80.

Self-help and social relations, IX, 400.
Selfishness, VII, 37.
Self-justifying, VI, 531.
Self-reliance, II, 249; 309–11; v, 480; VIII, 562; advice, pledges, III, 267.
Self-Reliance, verses, II, 518.
Self-respect, x, 163.
Self-seeker, Nemesis of, VI, 70.
Self-service elegant, v, 491.
Self-subsistent and sneer, IV, 365.
Self-testing, III, 28.
Self-trust, v, 192; 433, 434; of divine man, III, 14.
Seneca, Goethe on, IV, 221.
Sennott, George, IX, 437, 438.
Sensation, and soul, VI, 108.
Sense of beauty, VIII, 251.
Sense under poetry, III, 451.
Sensibility, IX, 487, 537; x, 453; character *plus*, v, 372.
Sentence, maker of, III, 395; good, and book, III, 529; a mirror, IV, 180.
Sentences, IV, 81, 82; from ancient philosophers, VI, 436.
Sentiment, I, 346, 347; IX, 137; human, IX, 277; literature of the, x, 10.
Sentimentalist, IX, 427.
September afternoon, a, III, 342; golden, IV, 288.
Serenity, II, 270.
Sermon, III, 220; fragment for, God within, II, 22, 23; conventional or living, II, 278; subject for a, II, 507; prune the, III, 549.
Sermon subjects, animals, idleness, II, 471, 472.
Sermons, II, 477; subjects: unseen good in man, wisdom and ignorance, first and third thoughts, II, 434–36; living, III, 421; real, IV, 232, 233; beauty shuns, v, 39; re-reading, old, v, 271.
Servant, God the, IV, 57; New England, and, VII, 315.
Servants, domestic, VI, 444. See *also* Domestics.
Service, VI, 34; by what you are, III, 404.
Seward, William H., IX, 377, 378; 383–91.

INDEX

Shackford, Charles Chauncy, IV, 166.
Shadow, VIII, 422.
Shaker folly, VII, 40.
Shakers, the, VII, 15, 16; visit to, VI, 261–63; sacrifice culture, VI, 502; second visit to, their dance and religion, VI, 523, 524.
Shakspeare, William, I, 145; II, 101; 122; 233; III, 414; 453; IV, 269; VIII, 39; X, 249; and Wordsworth contrasted, II, 106; and right words, II, 402; Sonnets of, quotations, II, 422, 423; creations of, II, 481; *Hamlet* quoted, III, 260; Sonnets of, III, 299; and Scott, III, 327; mouthpiece of mind of man, III, 329; not popular in his day, IV, 186; curiosity about, IV, 332; must be realized, V, 104; the wonder of, V, 127; as metaphysician, VI, 79; fault of, VII, 140; fancy of, VIII, 154; height of, VIII, 245; plays of, VIII, 350; English Osiris, VIII, 359, 360; superiority of, IX, 187; E.'s notes for speaking at Saturday Club, X, 27, 28, 29–31, 34; true biography of, X, 290; no parallax, X, 382.
Shakspeare festival, X, 21.
Shakspeare quotations, X, 24.
Sham fight, V, 291.
Shaw, Judge, VIII, 201; 509.
Shawsheen River, VIII, 371.
"Shay, The," VII, 339–41.
She-King, The, quoted, VI, 437.
Shelley, VI, 114; 213; VII, 284; quoted, IV, 198; never true poet, V, 344.
Shells, III, 283; brought home, III, 298.
Shepherd, Dr. T. P., his finding Tennyson in Holland, VII, 448, 449.
Sherlock, I, 174.
Ship, praise of, III, 218; of State, VIII, 236.
Ship life, III, 201.
Ship-worm, IX, 307.
Shipyard, VIII, 374.
Ships, names of, IV, 308.
Short Mantle, The, III, 473.
Shortcomings, IV, 371.
Shout to the Shepherds, A, poem, I, 245.

Shrine, man needs a, III, 503.
Sibylline leaves, VIII, 220.
Sicilian crew, absurd, III, 37, 38.
Sicily, embarks for, III, 37; episode in, III, 481.
Sick man, indulgence of, IV, 362.
Sickness, IV, 251; V, 63; use of, I, 78; heroes of, VI, 116.
Siddons, Mrs., and Fanny Kemble, VI, 337.
Sidney, Sir Philip, on Puglione's praise of horsemen, VIII, 503.
Sierra Nevada, III, 23.
Sifting, X, 51.
Sight, Nature gives, V, 407; wait for, VII, 520, 521.
Significance of Nature, III, 466.
Silence, II, 243, 412; of orator, IX, 152.
Silsbee, W., letter to, ideas of God, V, 73.
Similes, IX, 285.
Simonides, IX, 209.
Simple life, V, 397; 564.
Simplon, the, Napoleon, and, III, 148.
Sims case, VIII, 202.
Sin, II, 467; V, 38; is ignorance, II, 75; carries its reward, II, 140; the unpardoned, V, 570; is trifling, IX, 20.
Sincerity, teaching, III, 374.
Singer, the village, V, 269.
Singers, two, V, 255.
Sins may help, even, III, 352.
Siphar trees, I, 170–73.
Sismondi, VIII, 574.
Sistine Chapel, the, III, 81–83.
Situation, II, 250.
Sixteenth-century poets, VIII, 287.
Skating, writing like, VII, 334.
Skepticism, VI, 116; VII, 112.
Skidbladnir, ship, VII, 314.
Sky, VI, 20; blue, VI, 319; sculpture in clouds, VI, 410; our, VIII, 42; states of the, X, 77.
Slave-auction, the, and the Bible meeting, II, 177.
Slaveholder and cotton manufacturer, honor to Garrison, VI, 538–39.
Slaveholders, short way with, VIII, 386.
Slave-labor products, VII, 38.
Slave-trade, II, 80; IV, 302, 303.

INDEX

Slavery, IV, 200; VII, 84; VIII, 337, 338; vision of, I, 177–86; Christianity and, III, 446, 447; warnings from, IV, 374; arouses conscience, VIII, 164; entering question of, VIII, 316; the Constitution and Fugitive Slave Law, VIII, 337, 338; our fathers' blunders in concessions to, VIII, 475, 476; the resistance to, IX, 241, 242; the destruction of, IX, 434; dangers of, escaped, IX, 566.

Slavery question, X, 113, 114; in Lyceum, VII, 5, 6.

Sleep, IV, 142, 143, 373; unbecoming, IV, 442; graces of, V, 440; of a child, V, 459; life a, VII, 161; pranks of, VII, 458.

Sleep, medicine, IV, 236.

Sleepy Hollow, VIII, 554; autumn in, IV, 326, 327.

Sleet, in woods, V, 512.

Sleigh-ride, boy's, IX, 200.

Smallness, power of, VIII, 220, 221.

Smith, Adam, IX, 340.

Smith, Goldwin, X, 72–75.

Smith, Sydney, opinion of, VIII, 577.

Snubs, of E.'s new book, VIII, 88.

Social Circle, the, X, 312; candidates for, VIII, 168, 179.

Social feelings, I, 118, 125.

Social principle, the, II, 268.

Social tests for all, V, 525, 526.

Socialism, VII, 410; oracle dumb on, VII, 428; question of, VII, 431.

Socialist convention, VI, 480, 481.

Socialist orator, VII, 487.

Society, I, 314; or solitude, II, 19; obligations to, III, 124; and realities, III, 262; fatal machinery of, III, 275; always, but best men alone, III, 321; good, four views of, III, 496; relations in, IV, 279; a test, IV, 358; and solitude, IV, 473; ideal, V, 115; good for those who understand it, V, 349; ends of, V, 429; constricts, V, 475; debt to, VI, 352; a boardinghouse, VII, 60; treating as a child, VII, 335; pallid, VIII, 120; laws of, IX, 531. *See also* Artist, Conventions, Curiosity Shop, Emerson, M. M., Unmaskers.

Society and Solitude, X, 312.

Socrates, I, 5, 6; III, 260; Proclus interprets the oracle on, VIII, 468.

Soirées, V, 111.

Soldier, scholar and, V, 336.

Soldiers, VI, 115; needed for Civil War, IX, 575, 576; our young, X, 105.

Solger, Dr., IX, 113.

Solitary Fancies, verses, I, 196.

Solitary, the, VIII, 55.

Solitude, I, 222; II, 49–53; 215; or society, II, 60–62; the soul in, II, 299; of the soul among friends, II, 403; gain from, III, 222; not alone in, III, 263; devils of, III, 305; independence of, in crowd, III, 401; doom of, III, 501; IV, 229; depressing, IV, 398; search for, VIII, 538.

Solon and Lycurgus, II, 283.

Song, verses, II, 132.

Sonnet in Sickness, II, 217.

Sons of great men, VI, 267.

Soprano, the village, IV, 468.

Sorbonne, The, III, 156.

Sorrow and Age, V, 267, 268.

Sortes Virgilianæ, I, 23.

Soul, the, reserves her word, II, 509; the kingdom of, IV, 330; judges but is not judged, V, 140; affirms, V, 242; renouncing birthright of the madness of Christendom, V, 272, 273; meeting your, V, 569. *See also* Almanac, Assessors, Body, Christendom, Church, Circumstance, Directions, Discipline, Ecstasy, Emerson, M. M., Experience, Fall, God, History, Immortality, Nearness, One Mind, Reflections, Science, Sensation, Solitude, Speech, Tides.

Souls, VIII, 311.

Sound, analyzed, X, 169, 170.

Source of things venerable, III, 433.

South, visit to, II, 133; and North, IV, 275; compensation to, would be cheap, VIII, 202; shooting complexion, IX, 121; insanity of, IX, 211, 212; self-reliance of, IX, 308.

South Carolina, IX, 49; outrage of, on Samuel Hoar, VII, 20–23.

South Wind, The, verses, VI, 321.

INDEX

Southern courtesy, II, 141.
Southern life, VIII, 218.
Southern students, IV, 312, 313.
Southern victories, IX, 456.
Southerner, the, VII, 206; VIII, 100.
Southerners, the, IX, 328; bad cause of, IX, 327.
Southey, *Chronicle of the Cid*, IX, 168.
Space and time, IX, 100.
Spanish proverbs, II, 480.
Spanish paintings, VII, 455, 456.
Spartan, the, IV, 5.
Speaker, not topic, VI, 296; young, VIII, 221.
Speaking, extempore, II, 440; good, III, 485; for courtesy, X, 227.
Spectator, a proposed, II, 15–17.
Spectator, or actor, VI, 133; E. calling himself a, X, 191.
Spectatorship, VI, 275.
Spectrum, X, 187.
Speculations in the future, I, 30.
Speculative man in conversation, IV, 309.
Speculators, Yankee, VII, 299, 300.
Speech, II, 412; native vigor in, II, 449; thought and, II, 522; the soul's, IV, 124; or writing, V, 257; climate of, VII, 553; heat in, VIII, 147.
Spencer, Judge, Mr. Otis and, II, 238.
Spending, wise, V, 27; is gain, VII, 156; of poor and rich, IX, 52.
Spenser, Edmund, VII, 229.
Spheral people, VIII, 230.
Spheres, VI, 480.
Sphinx, III, 525; VIII, 345.
Spinoza, X, 237.
Spirit, the, X, 189; trust, III, 435; essentially vital, endures, IV, 127; heed, V, 289. *See also* Boldness, Creative, Disguises, Magnetizing, Man, Moon, Scribe, Strength, Time.
Spirit-rappings, VIII, 452.
"Spiritual," popular use of the word, IX, 189.
Spiritual religion self-evident, III, 397, 398.
Spiritual laws, III, 423.
Spiritual Laws, verses for, VII, 217.
Spontaneity, IV, 292.

Spontaneous thought, V, 385, 392.
Sprained foot, IX, 223.
Spring, V, 519; IX, 178, 216, 488; return of, I, 19; promise of, VI, 379.
Spring day at Mount Auburn, III, 271, 272.
Stable-men, talk of, IX, 497.
Stage-driver, VI, 528.
Stage passengers, IV, 193.
Stagnation, days of, VII, 210.
Stallo, on Nature, VIII, 77; quoted, X, 423.
Standard man, the, III, 249.
Standing, V, 409.
Stanfield, Mr., VII, 479.
Stanton, Edwin M., IX, 376.
Staples, Sam, neighbor, V, 194, 195; IX, 413.
Star, the unsuspected, VI, 210.
Stars, III, 13; IV, 492; V, 392; real influence from, III, 264; conjunction of, inspiration, fortunate hours, III, 561; falling, IV, 148; antidote of pyrrhonism, IV, 403; seen through telescope, X, 117.
Star-shower of 1834, the, III, 372.
Starving, fear of, VI, 303.
State, man implies the, III, 414; what is the? VII, 18; poor, well meaning, VII, 220–23.
State Department, IX, 379.
States of mind, II, 219; VIII, 274.
Statues help us, VIII, 557.
Stave, origin of, VIII, 566.
Steam-engine, IX, 495.
Steamships, the first ocean, IV, 430.
Steerage, the, III, 214.
Steps, VI, 317; geology shows the, VIII, 524.
Stereopticon, IX, 287.
Sterling, John, IV, 389, 390; V, 313; and Carlyle, V, 352; on sculpture, VI, 248.
Stewart, Dugald, II, 308; extracts from, II, 388.
Stimulation, low, VIII, 560.
Stoicism, IX, 500.
Stoke Pogis, visit to, VII, 490.
Stonehenge, visit to, VII, 490.
Storey, Charles, X, 4.
Stories illustrating the times, VI, 78.
Storm, at sea, III, 203; the winter, III, 422.

536 INDEX

Storm, The, verse, II, 209.
Story, V, 94.
Stove when ill, V, 162.
Stow, Cyrus, VIII, 156; redeems bog, VII, 306.
Strabo, quoted, X, 235.
Stranger, V, 47, 49.
Strawberries, V, 238.
Street sights, III, 157.
Street singers and caffès, III, 96.
Strength, unconscious, III, 345; waste, IV, 368; the true, of the spirit, VI, 309; beauty and, in poetry and art, VIII, 300, 301.
Stubler the Quaker, III, 228.
Study, plan of, II, 21; and drifting, III, 460; preaching and, sickly, home the cure, IV, 423.
Style, II, 96; a test, VIII, 489; notes on, VIII, 491.
Styles, VII, 216.
Subject, indifferent, IX, 23.
Subjective, true and false, V, 347.
Subjectiveness, Bonaparte, X, 468.
Subjects, IV, 263.
Sublime, moral, II, 405.
Sublime law, Nature's, V, 512.
Success, deprivation of, V, 570; is adjustment, VII, 515; a measure of brain, VIII, 505; of George Stephenson, IX, 125; of Columbus, IX, 125; of the North, IX, 428; stimulus of, X, 175.
Successful Americans, VII, 204.
Suggestion for writing, X, 235.
Suicide, III, 231.
Sumner, Charles, VIII, 210; IX, 375, 393, 452; at Phi Beta Kappa meeting, VII, 228; attack upon, IX, 46; and Brooks, IX, 156; tribute to, X, 291–95; death of, X, 429, 430.
Sumner outrage, the, IX, 47.
Sun, to find the, III, 239; and shade, V, 443; equalizes places, VI, 449.
Sunday, IV, 477.
Sunday-School meetings, II, 379.
Sunday Schools, origin of, II, 413.
Sunset, III, 418; VIII, 419; 503; from the hill, V, 46, 47; liquid, V, 558; buying a, VIII, 13.
Sunsets, VI, 235.
Superficiality, profoundness of, VI, 27.

Superiority, a surprise, IV, 391; in persons, VII, 86.
Superiors and inferiors, VII, 527.
Superlative, V, 387; VI, 22; positive sufficient, V, 162, 163; love of, VIII, 74; true and false, VIII, 324.
Superlatives, III, 484; Italian, III, 120; avoid affection's, III, 383.
Supernatural, the, IX, 193.
Superstition of knowledge, IV, 388.
Superstitions, present, VII, 204; of the age, VII, 317, 318.
Supreme Court, United States, IX, 186.
Surface, VII, 191; prevails, VI, 206.
Surface-life, VI, 165.
Surfaces, IX, 116.
Surprises, Nature's, IV, 123; life's daily, VI, 324.
Surroundings, your own, III, 536.
Susceptibility, VI, 56.
Suum cuique, II, 471.
Swamp-flowers, the, VI, 393.
Swan, Margaret, high experience of, VIII, 306.
Swearing, V, 484; VI, 236; innocent, VI, 357.
Swedenborg, IV, 482; V, 145; 477; VII, 515; VIII, 22; X, 198; quoted, IV, 6; position of, IV, 497; force of, V, 350; an interpreter, dangerous teacher, VI, 185; hopeless Hebraism of, gates of thought are found late, VI, 196; talk with Sampson Reed on, VI, 219; fallacy of "The Word," did not see "the Flowing," VII, 116, 117; and sin, VII, 123; and Very, VII, 136; result of, VII, 154; large stature, VIII, 16; does not awaken sentiment of piety, VIII, 72; ideas of, received to-day, VIII, 477; good for his age, VIII, 507; quotations from, X, 326, 480, 481; Milton and, X, 191.
Swedenborgian, V, 142; 76.
Swedenborgian sermon, III, 430.
Swedenborgianism, V, 80; E.'s, III, 266.
Swedenborgians, II, 124; IV, 333; enthusiasts, II, 318.
Swiss landscapes and heroes, IX, 280.
Switzerland, a taste of, Vevay, Lausanne, III, 148–50.

INDEX

Sword, the, use of, IX, 362.
Sylvan, possession of land, VIII, 379.
Symbolism, VI, 317; of life, IV, 245; Nature's, VI, 77; meaning of what I do, VIII, 63.
Symbols, III, 358; cabinet of shells, II, 478; help, instances, III, 528; their use, IV, 240; works as, VI, 191.
Symmetry, VI, 499.
Sympathies, strange, in Jardin des Plantes, III, 162.
Sympathy, IX, 272; 355; with others' gifts (abilities), III, 384; due, IV, 288; for mourner, IV, 345; the might of, V, 19, 20; is missed, V, 41; man thankful for, V, 137; but partial, VI, 471.
"Symposium, The," IV, 250; 289; V, 196; of E.'s friends: Alcott, Hedge, etc., feminine genius of Americans, art proper to the age, IV, 85–89; at Alcott's, IV, 113, 114; meets, V, 168; Alcott desires, VII, 248, 249.
Synesius, VIII, 452.
Syracuse, its sights, III, 38–48.
System, postpone your, IV, 294; love of vitiating, V, 321.
System-grinders, III, 523.
Systems, IX, 326.

Table d'hôte, VII, 456.
Tabooed subjects, IV, 293.
Tacitus, on North Sea, VIII, 369.
Tail, the, VII, 151.
Taine, quoted, IX, 529.
Talent, and character, III, 374; comforts of, VI, 210; genius and, VIII, 581.
Tales, sad, V, 258.
Taliessin, X, 147; 348.
"Talking shop," II, 314.
Talking from memory, II, 441.
Tallahassee, II, 161.
Talleyrand, VII, 9, 24; Hamilton-Burr anecdote, IX, 392.
Tamlane, III, 544.
Tantalus-life, III, 556.
Taormina, III, 56.
Tardy spring, the, IX, 415.
Tariff, VIII, 265.
Tasks, IV, 18; home, V, 257.

Tasso, III, 95, 127; M. M. E. read, X, 202.
Taste, IV, 194; respect your, III, 337.
Tax, none on daybreak, IV, 64; refusing the, VII, 221.
Taxes, sure, IV, 108.
Taylor, Edward (Father), III, 421; VII, 75, 76; IX, 498; sermon of, III, 431; at battle-ground, III, 543; his power and charm instinctive, IV, 155–57; eloquence and happiness of, his similes, IV, 191, 192; his power and charm, V, 404; on insults, VI, 63; in Concord, VII, 70–74; eloquence of, VII, 90–91; quoted, IX, 19.
Taylor, Henry, *Van Artvelde* of, III, 453.
Taylor, Thomas, VIII, 361; X, 185; defines Christianity, VI, 470; novel and solitary path of, VI, 509, 510; on Bacon, VII, 36.
Tea, poetry in chest of, V, 517.
Teacher, true attitude of a, II, 380; longing for, III, 101.
Teachers, must study man, not text, III, 225; the two sorts of, IV, 457, 458; from within and without, V, 143–45; real tests, VII, 224.
Teachers' meeting, IV, 126; 394, 395.
Teamsters, VII, 184.
Tears, IV, 339.
Tecumseh, Colton's, VI, 167.
Tediousness, rustic, IV, 408.
Teeth, V, 56; nose and, V, 310.
Telegraph and human heart, VIII, 459.
Telegraph operators, IX, 8.
Temperament, Emerson's own, cold, II, 123; scale of, VI, 55.
Temperaments, of too much determination, IX, 222.
Temperance, II, 320; 468; V, 333; VII, 246; rigorous for man of letters, IV, 36; false, V, 258; sign of intrinsic worth, V, 299, 300; in love of beauty, VI, 4; elegant, VI, 69; makes genius, VIII, 499.
Temple of Nature, I, 355.
Temple, Solomon's, III, 330.
Temptation, I, 265; II, 415; V, 491.

Ten seditious commandments, VIII, 236.
Tenacities, VII, 162.
Tendency and men, VI, 451.
Tending, VII, 194.
Tennyson, V, 6, 57; VI, 243, 286–88, 465; VIII, 455, 526; new volume of, IV, 411, 412; VI, 218; and De Vere, VII, 404; will not go to France, his habits, De Vere's care of him, his brothers, anecdotes, VII, 446–48; Dr. Shepherd's finding him in Holland, VII, 448, 449; his *In Memoriam*, VIII, 163; verses from, VIII, 450; lines of, VIII, 466; poems of, IX, 152; his *Idylls of the King*, IX, 207; Saint Grail, X, 240–42.
Tests, V, 151; use our own, V, 355; of writer and speaker, VII, 215; suggested for colleges, VIII, 582; for men of letters, IX, 7.
Teutonic granite, VII, 554.
Texas, VII, 26; annexation of, VI, 494, 495; anti-annexation convention, VII, 4.
Texts, quoting, V, 89.
Thackeray, William Makepeace, VIII, 393, 416; his *Vanity Fair*, VIII, 113; story of, VIII, 577; Dickens on, X, 7.
Thales, II, 336.
"Thank you," life in the expression, VI, 86.
Theanor and Amphitryon, a parable, VI, 310.
Théâtre Français, III, 168.
Theism, IV, 55, 403.
Theocracy, character brings, V, 368.
Theogonies, II, 334.
Theologic war, II, 140.
Theology, objective, a discipline, II, 509; pagan, of our churches, IV, 305; new, IX, 521.
Theorists and conservative, VI, 136.
Theory, beware, V, 149.
There is in all the sons of men, hymn, II, 346.
Thermometer, Nature a differential, V, 456.
Thierry, his *History of the Normans*, VIII, 378, 379.
Things, preacher must preach, V, 200; and men, V, 254; the divine language, V, 376; man must conquer, VI, 12.
Thinkers, and livers, VI, 517; not partisans, VIII, 120.
Thinking class in war-time, IX, 366.
Thirty nations, our, VIII, 232, 233.
Thomas à Kempis, III, 528; Fénelon, Scougal and, II, 387.
Thompson, George, III, 548; Samuel J. May and, visit of, III, 546.
Thoreau, Henry D., VI, 74; 371; VII, 241; VIII, 273; IX, 401; Edmund Hosmer and, IV, 395; walk with, his view of college, IV, 397; walk with, IV, 432; IX, 47, 48; 91, 92; 96, 97; 99; 112, 113; 155, 156; talk on property and on writing, V, 128–30; lives now, V, 208; *Sympathy* of, V, 241; on diet, V, 414; as helpful friend, V, 505; as poet and helper, V, 557; saying of, on man, VI, 298; verses of, VI, 304, 305; paradoxes of, VI, 440; his *Inspiration*, VI, 494; VIII, 64; his secret of life, VI, 496; in word and act, VI, 515; on philosophies, VII, 99; on society, VII, 209, 210; in jail, VII, 219; on food and art, VII, 321; left as guardian, VII, 336, 337; Newcomb on, VII, 386; the wood-god, VII, 498; and Alcott, VII, 499; Channing and, on Alcott, VII, 552; and Heaton, VII, 557; walk with, to Acton, VIII, 40, 41; and Concord, VIII, 62; on thought, VIII, 119; a talk with, VIII, 135–38; 260; gifts of, VIII, 227, 228; meets his walking thoughts, VIII, 294; on lightning-rods, VIII, 300; E.'s debt to, VIII, 303; and the preacher, VIII, 305, 306; hope of, VIII, 339; austerity of, VIII, 375; the stoic, VIII, 397; standard of, VIII, 415; and little girl's question, VIII, 425; helpful counsel of, VIII, 450; on California gold-digging, VIII, 467; question of, VIII, 567; on health of intellect, VIII, 569; and coöperation, IX, 15; reporting his observations, IX, 34; as naturalist, IX, 45; August walk with, IX, 59, 60; and Nature, IX, 144; patience, IX,

INDEX

153, 154; on John Brown, IX, 247, 248; when dying, IX, 413; death, IX, 417, 418; his bequest of books, IX, 419, 420; choice of, IX, 425; quotations, IX, 427; 441; 547; X, 20; 470; selections from his Journal, IX, 430–32; and bluebird, IX, 498; and meeting-house bell, IX, 507; Journal of, IX, 522; letter of, X, 14; criticism of, X, 311.

Thoreau, John, Jr., kindness of, IX, 360.

Thoreaus, voyage of the, V, 251.

Thorwaldsen, III, 79; V, 14.

Thought, your, God's gift, II, 282; the stirring of, II, 494; like traveller, III, 532; the common, V, 25; hunger for, its joy, V, 147, 148; visible, eternal, universal, V, 177–79; not absorbed, VII, 78; glittering and turning to dead scale, VIII, 278; for sale, VIII, 365; an invisible horse, VIII, 522; Nature helps us to express, VIII, 536; the thin stream of, VIII, 542; identical, oceanic, VIII, 563; uttered in virile manner, IX, 197, 198; ductile, expansive, X, 165; enriched by vivid, X, 213; expels memory, X, 361; like new bird may not come again, X, 365; its rank stamped on it, X, 465; automatic action of, X, 469. *See also* Acceleration, Action, America, American, Annals, Beauty, Best, Bonaparte, Books, Christ, Current, Districts, Electricity, Everett, E., First, Fuller, Margaret, Gates, Genealogy, God, Hafiz, Handles, High, History, Hospitality, Inspiration, Joy, Language, Life, Luther, Music, Nature, New, Oriental, Persons, Poet, Poetry, Provocation, Speech, Spontaneous, Swedenborg, Thoreau, Tides, Trade, Twilight, Woodman, Work, Writing.

Thoughtfulness of great men, III, 333.

Thought-givers, IV, 307.

Thoughts, that set one aglow, II, 405; waiting for, III, 443; inexorable, IV, 123; few in an age, IV,

389; uncovering, VI, 123; few because elastic, VIII, 575; dealing with, IX, 109.

Thrasimenus, Lake, III, 103.

Three Dimensions, The, VI, 419.

Thrones, IX, 92.

Tiberius, II, 8.

Ticknor, George, lecture, I, 65.

Tide of life, ebb, V, 276.

Tides, IV, 225; VIII, 254; of thought, I, 284, 285; II, 136; of the soul, III, 304.

Tiedemann, IX, 521.

Timæus, the, VI, 213; VII, 74.

Time, IV, 122; X, 288; infancy has fled, I, 208; terrible flight of, I, 234–37; optical, IV, 476; and space illusions, V, 123, 124; and fate fix relations, V, 429; infinite, V, 481; if world would wait, V, 518; inversely as spirit, VI, 117; breast-pocket of, VI, 305; hurtful, IX, 32; space and, IX, 100.

Timeliness, VIII, 208.

Times, express life of your own, IV, 38; stories illustrating, VI, 78; brain and solar system, VIII, 90–92; Parliament on, VIII, 93.

Times, The, course on, VI, 131.

The Times (London), VII, 380; influence of, VII, 360; writers of, VII, 415.

Timing, VII, 118.

Tischbein, IV, 206.

Tissenet and Indians, VIII, 279.

Titmouse, the, IX, 405.

Tivoli and Villa d' Este, expedition to, III, 97, 98.

Tobacco, X, 154.

To-day, VI, 477; its shining remembrance, V, 514; all important, VI, 211; impenetrable folds of, VIII, 453.

To-day, poem, I, 368.

Toilers, respect the, VII, 519.

Token from mountain or tree, VIII, 247.

Tokens, V, 72.

Tombs, IV, 322, 323.

Tone, IV, 364; V, 110; 314; shows advance, V, 141; signifies, VI, 88; poet must strike true, VII, 207, 208; low, VIII, 169; in poetry, X, 277.

Tonga Islanders, the, Licoö song of, I, 159.
Tool-room in the barn, the, IV, 283.
Tools, VI, 425; lesson of, VII, 306; of the age, VIII, 244.
Topics, favorite, VIII, 488; for lectures, X, 329, 330.
Torchlight processions, VII, 458.
Torpedo, man a, to man, VIII, 290.
Torpor, intellectual, III, 485.
Torrey, funeral of, VII, 183; burial of, VII, 192.
Toussenel, his *Passional Zoölogy*, VIII, 403.
Town, unit of Republic, VIII, 420.
Town and Country Club, VIII, 103, 104.
Town crier, X, 203.
Town-meeting, IX, 566.
Towns, use of, X, 53, 54.
Toys, children's, V, 163.
Tracy, Albert H., of Buffalo, VIII, 172, 173; X, 121; talk with, IX, 64–67.
Trade, I, 259–64; IV, 311; VI, 503; triumphs of, VI, 481; thought follows, VII, 8, 9.
Traders and thinkers, VII, 557.
Tradition, loss of the Christian, II, 85; beware, III, 420; in teaching omit, IV, 119.
Traditions of ancestors, IV, 230.
Tragic characters, IX, 50.
Trances for hire, VIII, 298.
Transcendental Movement, the, VI, 98; VI, 521.
Transcendentalism, defined, IV, 114.
Transcendentalist, and Franklin, VII, 768.
Transcendentalists (Rev. T. T. Stone), VI, 52.
Transfer, genius making, VII, 519.
Transfiguration, the, III, 78.
Transformation, rule of, V, 484.
Transit, thinker must furnish, VIII, 529, 530.
Transition, charm and power of, VIII, 501; and immortality, X, 457; ascending effort, X, 462.
Translation, VII, 89.
Translations, VIII, 35; of the classics, VIII, 289.
Transmigration, VI, 419; VII, 93, 94; 120, 121; tropes and, VI, 40.

Transparency, theory of, VII, 546.
Transubstantiation, IX, 546.
Travel, VI, 382; VII, 141; overestimated, II, 453, 454; Boswellism of, III, 340; your native spot, IV, 296; real, VI, II; without a call, VI, 265; humiliates, VI, 329; help of, VII, 69.
"Traveller, The," V, 140.
Travelling, V, 106.
Treasure everywhere for scholar, III, 247.
Trebellius on the Gauls, VIII, 582.
Tree, nourishment of, IV, 308; and man, V, 561.
Trees, V, 9; the gift of, IV, 225; my, IV, 228; teach the planter, V, 567, 568; and cultivation, VIII, 23.
Tremont House, landlord of, IV, 399.
Trent Affair, IX, 387.
Trial by war, IX, 459.
Tribal bias, VIII, 564.
Tribulations, IX, 230.
Tribunal, posterity and ultimate, VIII, 94.
Trick in conversation, VI, 257.
Trifles, eat the hours, III, 562; age of, IV, 479, 480; manners in, VIII, 299.
Trismegisti, IV, 498; V, 112.
Triumphs and eras, X, 103.
Troilus and Cressida, VIII, 367.
Tropes, VI, 18; VII, 177; and transmigration, VI, 40.
True men, III, 477.
True Thomas, verse, VII, 251.
Truro, Channing on, VIII, 252.
Trust, ideal doctrine of, gratitude, II, 375; joyful, III, 454.
Truth, simple, II, 311; every one's concern, II, 324; to self, II, 379; abysmal our ignorance, II, 481; immortal, II, 501; seek, II, 513–15; many-sided, II, 523; demands your defence, III, 269; ideal, III, 349; Luther's creed will need little adjustment, III, 382; sacrificing, III, 412; or appearance, III, 488; speaking, IV, 4; people hungry for, IV, 391; all nature helps him who speaks, IV, 484; the starlit deserts of, IV, 493; rich if we could speak, V, 455; against what

ns called God, VI, 161; serve, VII, 141; and not citing authority, X, 193; and phenomenon, X, 468. *See also* Advance, Beauty, Child, Christianity, Conversion, Dodging, Friendship, Gentleman, Poetry, Pseudo-sciences, Real, Rhyme.

Tucker, Ellen. *See* Ellen Tucker Emerson.

Tucker, Elizabeth, letter to, advising reading, II, 458–62.

Tucker, Margaret, death of, II, 530, 531; notice of, II, 538, 539.

Tucker, Mrs. (Ellen's mother), death of, III, 110.

Tuckerman, F. G., *Rhotruda*, IX, 318.

Tulips and corn, VIII, 213.

Turbine, IX, 145.

Turk, the, X, 154.

Turn, your, V, 60, 61.

Turner, studio of, with Owen to, VII, 480–82.

Turner, J. M. W., pictures of, VII, 479; VIII, 164.

Turner, Sharon, systematizing of, III, 567.

Turnpikes, I, 269.

Turns, IV, 362, 363; V, 79.

Tuscany, III, 103.

Twilight, thought's, V, 484.

Tycho Brahe, IV, 221, 222.

Tyler, G. W., his prowess, VI, 68, 69.

Tyrants, disguised, VIII, 243.

Uffizzi, the, the Marble Lady, III, 108.

Umbrian towns, III, 103, 104.

Uncle Tom's Cabin, VIII, 346.

Unconscious writing, V, 342.

Underlings, our public men, VI, 446.

Understanding, IX, 206; of friends, II, 482; and reason, IV, 74; V, 13; the apostle of, IV, 379; reason above, V, 310, 311.

Uneasiness in society, IV, 65.

Union, imperfect, with friends, IV, 238; and independence, VI, 297, 298; in individualism, VI, 316; moral and intellectual, VIII, 260; of ideas, IX, 249.

Union, the, X, 82–84; and Constitution, V, 328; made odious, VIII, 187; infirm, IX, 148.

Unitarian, when transformed Calvinist, IX, 408.

Unitarian preacher, and orthodox hearer, III, 426.

Unitarian weakness, V, 243.

Unitarianism, Calvinism and, II, 424; weak, Calvinism's strength and, III, 199, 200.

United States, Napoleon quoted on, X, 62.

United States Commissioner, VIII, 235.

Units and laws, III, 291; IV, 436; VI, 25; X, 236; the mind seeks, IV, 115–17; and variety, IX, 168.

Universal beauty, III, 372.

Universal forces, IX, 490.

Universal language, III, 495.

Universal laws, IV, 107.

Universal mind, II, 217; VII, 436.

Universalists, be, V, 499.

Universe, God's orderly, II, 437; miracle of the, II, 487; the hospitable, III, 6; from an idea, VII, 172; tilled with light, X, 463.

Universe, The, a quotation-book, I, 86–91.

Universities, help of, VII, 536; retrospective, VIII, 412; accomplish something, VIII, 580.

University, VII, 470; scholar secured, X, 134.

University reform, X, 197.

University system, VII, 362.

Unmagnetic man, the, VII, 247.

Unmaskers, society hates, VI, 103.

Unsaid, the, IV, 495.

Upanishad, quoted, IX, 56; 303.

Upham, Charles W., IV, 5; **Barnwell** and, oratory of, I, 68.

Uprising, causes of, VII, 462.

Uproar, or Genius? VII, 31.

Urn, the, and the fountain, parable, IV, 58, 59.

Usage hardens, VI, 31, 32.

Usefulness honorable, V, 264.

Utilitarianism, II, 455.

Vain world, I, 134.

Valetta, St. John's at, III, 31.

Valuations of cities, VIII, 166.

Value, intrinsic, IX, 116.

INDEX

Van Buren, letter to, IV, 430.
Van Burenism, V, 76.
Van Helmont, VIII, 76; 121.
Vanity, V, 172.
Van Mons, nurseries of, VII, 290, 291.
Variety, V, 567.
Varnhagen, IX, 459; quoted, IX, 398; 495; 505; 450; X, 315, 316; 445.
Varuna, VIII, 549.
Vasari, anecdotes of, VIII, 211; Grimm quoted on, IX, 307.
Vase, Etruscan, IV, 491.
Vast, the, V, 48.
Vatican galleries, the, III, 77.
Vatican splendors, the, III, 91–94.
Vauvenargues, X, 98.
Veda, quoted, X, 159.
Vedanta, VII, 110.
Vegetation, the, in man, VII, 135.
Veneration, IV, 495; incarnated, IV, 446.
Venetian pictures, churches, III, 132, 133.
Venice, III, 130–37.
Veracity, VI, 386.
Vermont, X, 253; visit to, II, 384.
Verona, III, 139.
Versatility, II, 133.
Verse: *At the Old Manse, The Storm,* added verse to poem *Fame,* II, 208–10; to Ocean, X, 79.
Verses, I, 291; 321; 75; III, 10, 11; 64; *A Romance,* I, 117; *Solitary Fancies,* I, 196; *Shakspeare,* I, 297; *Thought,* I, 305; *Forefathers' Day,* II, 33, 34; *Leaving the old life,* II, 38–40; *Fate,* II, 80; *Livingprayer,* II, 97; *Life or Death; Song,* II, 131, 132; *St. Augustine,* II, 149–51; *in exile,* II, 179; *Farewell to St. Augustine,* II, 181; *on spontaneous utterance,* II, 196; *autobiographic,* II, 197–201; *on the independent life,* II, 264; *on country life,* II, 367; *The days pass over me,* II, 388; *On Death,* II, 394; *The Mines of Truth,* II, 417; *SelfReliance,* II, 518; *on the travelling American,* III, 206; *God's message,* III, 212; *Compensation,* III, 376; *The South Wind,* VI, 321; *The Poet,* VI, 187, 188; *Eternity, Time, the Poet,* VIII, 66–68; *trial, Song of Nature,* and *Waldeinsamkeit,* IX, 130–32; E.'s trial, IX, 314; for *May-Day,* IX, 505, 506; for *Spiritual Laws,* VII, 217.
Very, Jones, IV, 423; V, 110, 111; 141; 221; VI, 51; 290; VII, 120; visit of, V, 98; his attitude of protest, spiritual state, manners, V, 104–06; walk in autumn woods with, V, 381, 382; admissions and objections of, VI, 131, 132; quoted, X, 1–8.
Vesicle, the, VIII, 244.
Vestiges of Creation, VI, 51, 52.
Vevay, III, 150.
Vice, V, 71.
Vicenza, III, 137.
Victims, Alcott's, VI, 284.
Vigor, VI, 530; VIII, 422; wild, II, 441.
Vikings, code of, X, 138.
Villa d' Este, expedition to Tivoli and, III, 97, 98.
Village, explains world, VI, 110; all characters in your, VIII, 488.
Village manners of politicians, IV, 112.
Villagers, the reverend, IV, 444.
Vine, the, VIII, 34.
Violets, boy and, VI, 157.
Virgil, tomb of, III, 67.
Virgin, the, VIII, 467.
Virginia, IX, 248.
Virility, VIII, 340.
Virtue, and genius, II, 165; enterprising, II, 311; temperamental, II, 313; purges the eye, III, 211; elegance of, III, 427; sure of its due, III, 520; adherence to nature of things, IV, 97; genuine, prevailing, IV, 183; obscure, IX, 237.
Virtues, the circle of the, I, 110; severe and restrictive, III, 321.
Vishnu Purana, VII, 124; 127; 258.
Vishnu, three steps of, VIII, 549.
Vision, a, I, 119, 120; of retribution, V, 485; when it comes, V, 511.
Visions, perception of, VI, 113.
Visit, short, V, 445.
Visit, The, poem, VI, 442, 443.
Visitor, IV, 474.
Visitors, IX, 108; serious, V, 193; tedious, VI, 280; exacting, VI, 392.

INDEX

Visits to sick and dying, II, 438.
Vitality, V, 535, 536.
Vivian Grey, Disraeli's, IV, 216; VI, 228.
Vocabularies, V, 99.
Vocabulary treacherous, V, 135.
Vocation must express itself, IV, 418.
Voice in choir, V, 167.
Voices, effect of, IX, 406.
Voltaire, Ferney and, III, 152; quoted, IX, 507.
Volunteer army, IX, 446.
Von Hammer, IX, 539.
Votes, thoughtless, III, 351.
Voters, IX, 454.
Voyage, southward, II, 133; to England, Thoreau left as guardian, VII, 336, 337; homeward, VII, 493.
Vulgarity, excuse of, IV, 489.

Waiting, II, 427; III, 273; 403; IV, 498; V, 469; VI, 397.
Walden Pond, IX, 415; frozen, IV, 166; afternoon by, IV, 265, 266; visitors of, VI, 66.
Walk, to the Connecticut, I, 268–84; to Fairhaven Hill, V, 266; in autumn woods with Jones Very, V, 381, 382.
Walking, IX, 33, 34.
Walking-journey, I, 144.
Walks, twilight and morning, III, 120, 121; with Channing, VII, 506, 510, 531, 536; VIII, 65, 294, 297, 352, 485; IX, 110; with Thoreau, IX, 43, 59, 91, 112, 155.
Wall, William, sayings of, VIII, 453.
Walpole, Horace, V, 281.
Waltham, preaching at, III, 302; hearers of preaching, IV, 115.
Wanderings, first, III, 76.
Want and have, IV, 99.
Wants, three, VI, 112.
War, II, 529; letter to Henry Ware on the abolition of, III, 574; foolish, IV, 275, 276; iron lobsters of, IV, 325; the state of, IV, 351; polite, V, 531; a teacher, VIII, 481, 482, 335; clears the air, IX, 325; educating us, IX, 330; misfortune of, IX, 330; a new glass, IX, 358; the searcher of character, dynamometer, IX, 411, 412; North and South, IX, 443; European opinion of Civil, IX, 444; service of, IX, 461–63; uses of the, IX, 492–94; northern elements of success, IX, 541; men needed, IX, 576; benefits of, X, 105, 106; opens new doors, X, 141.
War, verse, IX, 246.
Warblers, IX, 204.
Ward, Samuel G., V, 530; VII, 242, 243; IX, 500, 501; letter to, V, 305; marriage of, V, 468; on women, VI, 240; view of, VIII, 234.
Ward, Thomas Wren, view of, VIII, 233.
Ware, Charles P., X, 309.
Ware, Henry, VI, 455, 456; letter to, on abolition of war, III, 574.
Ware, William Robert, X, 266.
Warnings, IV, 186.
Warren, Charles Henry, toast of, IV, 294.
Washington, city of, VI, 389; VII, 253; IX, 333; lecturing in, VI, 335, 336; visit to, IX, 372–96.
Washington, George, noble face of, VIII, 300; and Chateaubriand, X, 350.
Waste power, V, 563.
Wasted life, II, 528.
Watchers, scholars are, III, 407.
Water, V, 257; the age of, VII, 198.
Water, verse, VI, 92.
Waterford, X, 327, 328.
Watts, Dr. Burnap on, II, 236.
Wave, teaching of the, III, 291.
Way of life, E.'s own, V, 114.
Wayne, General, X, 302.
Wayside Inn, VII, 555.
Wealth, VII, 359; quiet strength of, VI, 444; real, VII, 117; is reverence for superiority, VII, 320; is power not a toy, VIII, 219; and Labor, VIII, 328; vulgarity of, VIII, 449; a commanding position as regards ends, IX, 162; for emergencies, X, 173; advantages of, X, 199.
Weans and wife, V, 112.
Weather, V, 287; at sea, wild, remembrance of Achille Murat, III, 213, 214; life's, VII, 13.

INDEX

Weathers of life, March, VII, 289.
Webster, Daniel, I, 174; III, 308; 455; 471; 565; IV, 172; 359; VI, 455; VII, 219; 234; description of by Mr. K., I, 16, 17; reply of, to Hayne, II, 295; oratory of, III, 255; Carlyle sees, V, 243; editors and, VI, 79; changed, VI, 91; estimate of, VI, 341–46; ambition of, VI, 381; oration of, VI, 416; at Concord, VI, 429; and Choate, VI, 432; VII, 87; his force and standing, VI, 433–35; Adams compared with, VI, 508; coming of, to Everett's inauguration, VII, 167; method of, VII, 223; secondary, VII, 543; wanted courage, VIII, 45, 46; desertion of, VIII, 111; in the Senate, VIII, 174; and liberty, VIII, 180–82; fall of, VIII, 180–89; and materialism, VIII, 216; treachery of, VIII, 231; fate of, overtakes him, VIII, 301, 302; dying, praise and blame, VIII, 335, 336; and the judge, VIII, 537, 538; and young patriots, X, 114.
Weeding and laughing, IV, 256.
Weeds, man and, IV, 467; V, 550; Thoreau praises the, VIII, 307; suggestion from, VIII, 571.
Weiss, John, VI, 214; X, 245.
Wellington, superiority of, VIII, 368.
Welsh Triad, VIII, 367.
West, the unpoetic, III, 308; the advancing, V, 531; journey to, VIII, 114.
Western banker, IX, 11.
Western journey, X, 351, 352.
Western lecturing, IX, 3; X, 92; 181; 222.
Western railroad trip, IX, 260–63.
Western trip, VIII, 161.
Westminster, III, 173.
Westminster Abbey, IX, 221.
West Point, visit to, IX, 511–18.
Whalers, stories of the, III, 261.
What and *How*, IV, 211.
Whewell, VII, 439.
Whig and spiritualist, VI, 10.
Whig depression, VII, 12.
Whig doctrine, VIII, 310, 311.
Whig party, VII, 54.

Whigs, V, 466; VII, 179; and Tories, underlying merits, III, 356–58; school to teach, idealism, VI, 57; admit a sick world, VI, 65; Democrats and, VI, 275, 276; sages, poets, women and, VII, 122.
Whiggery timid, VI, 88.
Whiggism, VII, 99.
Whip, needed, VII, 268; for top, VII, 313.
Whipple, IX, 187.
Whisper, wonderful, X, 187.
White House, the, IV, 320.
White lies, VI, 254.
White Mountains, visit to, II, 492.
White Pond, VII, 536; with Channing, IX, 523.
Whitefield, Chauncy and, I, 330; on his wife, VII, 233.
Whitewashing, VI, 35.
Whitgift, Archbishop, VIII, 132.
Whitman, Walt, IX, 401; 540; X, 147.
Whole and parts, V, 84.
Wholes, IX, 422.
Wild fire, the, of eloquence, VII, 185.
Wild geese, IV, 415.
Wild man, tame men, IV, 331.
Wild poetry, V, 476.
Wild stock in nations, VI, 67.
Wild type of man, VI, 45.
Wilds, Mr., IX, 301, 302.
Wilhelm Meister, III, 309; V, 515.
Wilkinson, J. J. G., VIII, 224; VII, 319; X, 92; on Swedenborg, VIII, 21; quoted, IX, 124.
Will, the, education of, III, 249, 250; harmony of, III, 345; the man of, V, 130; keep the true, V, 139; breath of, in universe, IX, 217; acts of, are rare, IX, 345.
William of Wykeham, VII, 550.
Williams, I. T., X, 120.
Williamstown, X, 116.
Williamstown Address, The, VIII, 470.
Willson, Forceythe, X, 110.
Wilson, John, VII, 388; lecture of, VII, 395.
Wilson, Sir Robert, quoted, IX, 334, 335.
Winckelmann, X, 185; defines beauty, III, 451.

INDEX 545

Wind, a poet, II, 82; and calm, III, 7; of time, IV, 498.
Wind-harp, IX, 334.
Windsor, visit to, VII, 491, 492.
Wine, poet's, VI, 375, 376; wealth and, IX, 232.
Wings or boots? VI, 475.
Winter, IV, 136; mild, IV, 387; a general, with E., V, 516.
Winter drive in West, IX, 263.
Winter ride, thoughts in, III, 392.
Winthrop, Robert, his oration of despair, VIII, 307–10.
Wisconsin, VII, 443.
Wisdom, VII, 130; and virtue bound together, II, 299; and goodness one, II, 361; the unteachable, II, 387; and ignorance, II, 434; manifold, IV, 37; not personal, VII, 357; in reform, VII, 425.
Wise man's matter, II, 463.
Wise man sides with assailants, IV, 370.
Wise word, one, V, 138.
Wise, Governor, and John Brown, IX, 245.
Wit, elastic, III, 504; history of human, III, 523; troublesome, IV, 188, 189; ready, VI, 247; in trade, VII, 543.
Witch-laws, VII, 198.
Withington, William, I, 286; letter to, on studies and reading, I, 288.
Wits, anomalous, III, 493.
Woes, do not waste time on, IV, 29; the time's, V, 278.
Wolf unreformed, VIII, 183.
Wollaton Hall, VII, 357.
Wolsey, VIII, 102.
Woman, Burns's remark, II, 479; natural trait, III, 301; limitations of, yet trust, IV, 337, 338; the new, IV, 338, 339; the fine, IV, 423; tragedy of, V, 16, 17; attraction of, V, 361; unsphered, VI, 63; ideal place of, VI, 73; our help from, VI, 134; our conscience, VI, 299; real state of, VI, 369; the soul hermaphrodite, VI, 378; position of normal, VI, 405; and marriage, VI, 514; musical character of, her pathos, VI, 519; love must right, VII, 534; internal neatness, VIII, 253; *tours de force* of, VIII, 305; looking to man as guardian, IX, 23; sarcasm and attraction, IX, 210; man, genius and, X, 171, 172.
Woman, from Calidasa, IV, 316, 317.
Woman-part in mind, VI, 192.
Woman's convention, VIII, 258–60.
Women, fine, III, 311; VI, 356; minds of, IV, 81; love appearances, IV, 299, 300; pathos of, V, 26; in England, VI, 298; critical eyes of, VI, 390; devoted, VII, 498; sail, not steer, VIII, 175; side-issues of, VIII, 414; teach us, VIII, 425; rights and interests of, VIII, 559.
Wonder, II, 479; X, 454; attitude of, II, 304; before genius, VI, 121.
Wood, Antony à, VII, 534.
Wood, price of, IV, 145, 146.
Wood-god, the American, IV, 289.
Wood-god, Thoreau the, VII, 498.
Wood-gods, I, 146.
Woodlot, X, 261.
Woodman, the, real thought of, V, 436.
Wood-thrush, V, 237.
Woods, going into, III, 222; blessed are, III, 378; oracular, IV, 66; the May, IV, 459; live with God, IV, 466; waiting, V, 32; a prose sonnet, V, 263, 264; a temple, V, 339; not taxed for use of, V, 422; the Sabbath of the, V, 549.
Worcester Cathedral, VII, 361.
Worcester, Thomas, talk with Sampson Reed and, II, 455.
Word, the right, II, 401; a million-faced, VI, 139; one, in a book, "arrested development," VII, 69; the solving, VII, 91; men existing to say a, VIII, 422.
Words, preaching, IV, 277; age of, V, 254; man returns to old, VI, 127; mere suggestions, VI, 274; classifying, VI, 514; new use of, VII, 359; old, wise, VIII, 17; slang, VIII, 20; great, VIII, 271; Saxon and Latin, VIII, 421; *versus* experience in writing, X, 95.
Wordsworth, IV, 55; 246; VI, 244; 264; IX, 53; Shakspeare and, contrasted, II, 106; selections from, II, 230, 231; criticism of, II, 232; Montgomery and, II, 235; extracts from, II, 388; and right

words, II, 402; praise and criticism, II, 429, 430; chagrin at reading, II, 534; anecdote of, III, 174; visit to, he repeats his verses, speaks of Dr. Channing, III, 182, 183; and Carlyle, reports about, III, 188; mouthpiece of mind of man, III, 329; *Ode to Duty*, III, 532; limitations of, III, 535; security in, III, 560; platitudes of, III, 561; image of, from skating, IV, 398; makes sane, V, 393; call on, VII, 400; his *Royal Osmunda*, VIII, 558; his *Prelude*, IX, 151; preëminence gradually acknowledged, x, 68; is manly, x, 267.

Work, ephemeral or lasting, IV, 180; gives thought, VIII, 74.

Work-cure, VIII, 171.

"Work on," VI, 398.

Working, necessity of, IV, 447.

Works, find their level, III, 300; proper, VII, 140.

Workshop, Nature's, IV, 131.

World, our teacher, II, 87; man creates his, IV, 64; scriptures of, IV, 415; your, is new, IV, 475; the rich, IV, 481; propping the, V, 230, 231; eaten as apple, V, 485; and opinions, VI, 64; many baits of, VI, 324; self-sufficient, VI, 355; odd, VI, 356; the opaline, VI, 401; wears well, VIII, 140.

World-flower, VIII, 69.

World Secret, the, VI, 494.

World-temple, the, VIII, 52.

Worship, VII, 68; formal and polemic, II, 424; misplaced, III, 324; reason of need of, III, 330; Nature prompts, IV, 36; saint's dangerous, V, 555; and invulnerability, IX, 211.

Worth, in the worthless, II, 382.

Wreaths, IX, 92.

Wren, Christopher, VIII, 455.

Wright, Henry G., Charles Lane and, VI, 291.

Writer, who has message, IX, 423; and real facts, X, 382.

Writers, unmagnetic, V, 403; suggestive, VI, 291, 292; unpopularity of, VII, 502.

Writing, for Americans, II, 14; joy in, II, 71; test of good, poems, II, 401; silence on subject of, III, 273; mischief in art of, III, 332; much self-reliance, III, 550, 551; architecture of, IV, 336; do not save thought in, IV, 347; art of, IV, 483; faithful, V, 21, 22; talk on, V, 128, 129; no age in good, V, 286; comes by grace of God, VI, 21; reading and, VI, 41; autobiographical, VI, 73, 74; by God's grace, VI, 132; impossibility until done, VI, 506; at odd times, VII, 186, 187; manner necessitated, VII, 319; omit all that can be spared, IX, 436. *See also* American, Conversation, Damascene, Experimental, Experimenting, Expression, God, Labor, Mass, Moment, Perspective, Reality, Reforms, Rhetoric, Skating, Speech, Selection, Suggestion, Unconscious, Words.

"Writing down," II, 243.

Writings, town and field, II, 307; endure, III, 411.

Wyer, Robert, on women, III, 538.

Wykeham, VIII, 349.

Wyman case, VI, 429.

Xenophanes, II, 342, 343.
Xenophon, IV, 147.

Yankee, the, fatal grip of, VI, 326.
Yankeedom, VII, 211.
Yates, preaching of, III, 187.
Yea, X, 326; and Nay, X, 250.
Year, the, II, 299; the closing, II, 441.
Year-flower, the, VIII, 557.
Yearnings, V, 567.
York minster, VII, 375.
Young, Milton and, V, 548.
Young, Brigham, IX, 540.
Yourself, true to, III, 205.
Youth, IX, 322; do not lose, V, 307; of Nature, VI, 112; joy of, IX, 311.

Zanoni, Bulwer's, VI, 226, 227.
Zenith, VI, 394.
Zeno, II, 344.
Zodiac, man's, VII, 120.
Zohak and Eblis, VII, 323.
Zoroaster, II, 475; X, 139.
Zymoses, X, 215.

DISCARDED